Student-Centered
Classroom Assessment

Student-Centered Classroom Assessment

Richard J. Stiggins
Assessment Training Institute

Merrill,
an imprint of Prentice Hall

Upper Saddle River, New Jersey   Columbus, Ohio

Library of Congress Cataloging-in-Publication Data

Stiggins, Richard J.
    Student-centered classroom assessment / Richard J. Stiggins.
        p.   cm.
    Includes bibliographic references and index.
    ISBN 0-02-417350-9
    1. Educational tests and measurements—United States.
I. Title.
LB3051.S8534   1994   93-29232
371.2'6—dc20   CIP

Cover art: Karen Guzak
Editor: Kevin M. Davis
Developmental Editor: Linda Kauffman Peterson
Production Editor: Laura Messerly
Text Design Coordinator: Jill E. Bonar
Cover Designer: Patti Okuno
Production Buyer: Patricia A. Tonneman

This book was set in Garamond by The Clarinda Company, Inc.

 ©1994 by Prentice-Hall, Inc.
A Simon & Schuster Company
Upper Saddle River, New Jersey 07458

Printed in the United States of America
10 9 8 7 6 5 4 3

ISBN   0-02-417350-9

Prentice-Hall International (UK) Limited, *London*
Prentice-Hall of Australia Pty. Limited, *Sydney*
Prentice-Hall Canada Inc., *Toronto*
Prentice-Hall Hispanoamericana, S.A., *Mexico*
Prentice-Hall of India Private Limited, *New Delhi*
Prentice-Hall of Japan, Inc., *Tokyo*
Prentice-Hall of Southeast Asia Pte. Ltd., *Singapore*
Editora Prentice-Hall do Brasil, Ltda., *Rio de Janeiro*

This Book Is Dedicated to My Mother and Father

A Critical Message to the Reader

G reetings to you and welcome! We are about to take a very special journey together—a journey through the diverse and critically important world of educational assessment. Indeed, your success as a professional educator, whether as a classroom teacher or an administrator, will depend on your understanding of this world and your ability to work effectively within it. As you shall see, both student achievement and academic self-concept are determined, by and large, on the basis of students' perceptions of their own success in the classroom. Those students rely almost completely on the day-to-day, week-to-week, and term-to-term assessments of that achievement conducted by their teachers to judge their current success and their hope of future success.

For this reason, students count on us, their teachers, to know what we're doing when it comes to assessing achievement. If we do, in fact, know how to assess well, and if we gather sound information about student achievement, we have the opportunity to contribute immensely to their success in school. But if we do not understand the principles of sound assessment and therefore systematically mismeasure actual academic achievement, we are likely to do great harm to our students, both in terms of their actual achievement and their academic self-concept. For this reason, our journey through the world of classroom assessment is an important one indeed.

A SPECIAL PHILOSOPHY

The chapters that follow present a special philosophy about classroom assessment—a philosophy that places students at the center of the assessment equation.

To assist you in understanding this philosophy and in interpreting the assessment advice offered herein, let me spell out some of the values on which it is based.

Without question, the single most important value any teacher must bring to the classroom assessment process is a very strong sense of caring about student well-being in school. As teachers, we must not just believe that all students can learn, but must really want each and every student to feel the exhilaration of success in school and beyond. Our goal must be to have each student feel free from academic and personal harm in school. For this reason, we must all become fanatics about the thoughtful, sensitive use of assessment within the instructional environment. There are five principal reasons sound assessment is such a crucial part of the instructional process.

First, our classroom assessments define for students the outcomes we value—they define the truly important achievement targets. Second, classroom assessments provide the basis of information for student, parent, teacher, principal, and community decision making. Third, they motivate students to try—or not to. Fourth, they screen students in or out of programs, giving them access to the special services they may need. And fifth, classroom assessments provide at least part of the basis for teacher and principal evaluation.

Because of all the roles they play, classroom assessments make major contributions to the effectiveness of schools and classrooms. For all of these reasons, these day-to-day assessments can help students prosper.

Over the past fifteen years, I have endeavored to understand how assessment can fit productively into the day-to-day instructional process. In addition, I have learned valuable lessons about the meaning and impact of classroom assessment as a parent watching a youngster experience all the good and bad of classroom assessment during her years in school. These simultaneous learning experiences as a researcher and a parent have helped me understand that it is the day-to-day classroom assessment processes that drive the teaching and learning processes in schools.

We all know that classroom assessments are not the tests that command all of the public and political attention—that eat up the assessment budget each year. It is not our classroom assessments that draw all of the news coverage and editorial comment. Nevertheless, anyone who has taught knows that it is classroom assessments—not standardized tests—that provide the energy that fuels classroom practice. For this reason, those classroom assessments absolutely must be of high quality.

A COLLABORATIVE EFFORT

We can achieve this goal together by collaborating in the process of understanding and applying a common-sense meaning of assessment quality. As my part of the collaboration, in the chapters that follow, I offer practical assessment ideas communicated in everyday language with understandable classroom examples. You can fulfill your part of our bargain by studying these ideas, reflecting upon them and/or discussing them with fellow students or colleagues, trying them out in your instructional context, and adapting these ideas to meet the needs of your students.

The success of our joint efforts on behalf of sound classroom assessment will hinge on the extent to which you actively strive to make your own personal meaning of the material presented herein. For this reason, I have inserted "Times for Reflection" throughout the text. If you will take time to think about the issues at the time they are raised in the text, you will have a much easier time connecting the assessment ideas presented to your prior knowledge and experience.

Further, as we journey together, read critically. Ask tough questions about what you read here and test the assessment strategies suggested against your own good judgment. In these ways, you will become a critical consumer of assessments and the information they provide.

A TOUGH CHALLENGE

Be advised from the outset that the following chapters contain some rather complex material. You will also find that there is much to learn about the assessment process. This goes with the territory. Nowhere in this text will you hear me say that the assessment task is easy—only that is is critically important.

Don't be put off by complexity or scope of assessment. Dig in and master it! If you do, both you and your students will benefit greatly. Assessment has a reputation for being quantitative, complicated, dry, and boring. This need not be the case, however. Rather, assessment can be both challenging and empowering! Over the decades, many educators have faced assessment training with some trepidation. Even today, most see assessment as the process of quantifying student achievement. Typically, that leads to inferences about the mathematical nature of assessment, math anxiety sets in, and panic follows close on its heels. Please try to let that fear go right now, if you can. There is no need for math anxiety here. Assessment is *not* a mathematical challenge. Assessment is a challenge in clear thinking and effective communication.

A ROADMAP OF OUR JOURNEY TOGETHER

Our journey will unfold in four parts: Understanding the Classroom Assessment Context, Understanding Assessment Methods, Classroom Applications of Assessment, and Communicating about Student Achievement. Each part offers unique perspectives on the classroom assessment process, yet the four parts present a unified overall picture of the assessment process and its place in day-to-day instruction.

Overview of Part 1.   Our journey begins by defining assessment roles and responsibilities and by describing the essential elements in the classroom assessment process. As Part 1 unfolds, you will see what it means to be a responsible, well-prepared classroom assessment professional, as we talk about what it really means to be assessment literate. What is a quality assessment, anyway? How does a sound assessment differ from an unsound one? What competencies must one master to assure sound assessment from the classroom to the boardroom?

We also will explore critically important changes taking place in our perceptions of the role of schools in our society. The very function of schools is changing in deep-seated and fundamental ways. These changes make it essential that each and every educator, and indeed everyone involved in the setting and implementation of educational policy and practice, attain a certain level of assessment literacy—a fundamental understanding of the basic principles of sound assessment.

We will march right inside the world of assessment in schools by exploring all of the different levels of users and uses of assessment. Three different levels of assessment use will be explored: instructional uses, instructional leadership uses, and uses in setting policy. Through this discussion of the meaning of quality and various assessment roles and responsibilities, I will make it perfectly clear why the teacher lies at the heart of the assessment matter in school.

We will explore the two key elements in the classroom assessment quality-control equation: (1) knowing what is to be assessed and (2) knowing how to assess it. With respect to the *what* of the assessment equation, the critical question will become: Do you know what it means to succeed in your classroom or school? If you do not know the meaning and limits of this target, and cannot convey them in meaningful terms to your students, you doom them to fail.

With respect to the *how* of the classroom assessment equation, you will learn about the four different modes of assessment available for classroom use. And most importantly, you will see how these various methods can be aligned with the various kinds of outcomes we value to produce assessments that make sense to students, teachers, parents, and all involved in the educational process.

Overview of Part 2.   Once the stage is completely set in Part 1, we will begin an in-depth study of the assessment methods we have available for classroom use. Part 2 is divided into four chapters, one each on the design and development of selected response tests (multiple-choice, true/false, and the like), essay tests, performance assessments (assessments based on observation and judgment), and assessments that rely on direct personal communication with students, such as questioning during instruction, interviews, and conferences.

Each of these chapters presents its assessment alternative in a manner calculated to help you understand how its potential contributions lead to effective instruction. First, we discuss the kinds of achievement targets with which the method aligns. Then, we outline keys to effective development. We conclude each chapter by discussing productive ways to bring students into the assessment process as full partners—ways to use assessment as a very effective teaching tool.

Over the decades, each of these four basic assessment methods has experienced its time of prominence and of disfavor. As a school culture reflective of the larger society, our views and attitudes about the various ways of assessing seem to ebb and flow. Right now we are in the midst of a time that favors performance assessment. We used to place more emphasis on selected response tests. Times change. However, in this book we will strive to present a balanced view of sound assessment practice, including many methods as viable options.

The bottom line is that we face a huge classroom assessment challenge as we move into the twenty-first century. We have many different kinds of increasingly complex outcomes to assess. As a result, we have no business discarding any of the tools we have at our disposal. For this reason, each chapter in Part 2 is written from a decidedly positive point of view about the potential of the assessment method being discussed. This positive bent is tempered, however, by the resolute position that each method can and will reach its potential only if its developer and user adheres to accepted rules of evidence for using it well. Those rules, too, are spelled out in Part 2.

Overview of Part 3.   With a solid foundation of basic assessment methodology in hand, we will turn our attention to classroom applications. This part of the book is divided into four chapters that deal with the assessment of different kinds of achievement targets. We will explore the assessment of student reasoning and problem solving in all of its many forms, proficiency in demonstrating important skills and in creating products that meet standards of quality, and attainment of important affective outcomes. In addition, we will explore the role of large-scale standardized testing in the classroom.

Each of these chapters will examine the potential match between the kind of target being addressed and the four kinds of assessment methods studied in Part 2. In addition, you will find many examples in the union of method and target that reveal creative ways to use effective classroom assessment to generate accurate information about student achievement and to use assessment as a teaching strategy.

The goal in Part 3 is to make classroom assessment live in your mind, not as a set of abstractions, but as a real, potentially useful set of concepts, tools, and strategies that can bring students into the teaching and learning process in new and creative ways.

Overview of Part 4.   This concluding section is divided into three chapters that deal with communication about student achievement from various perspectives and a chapter that summarizes our entire journey together.

We begin with a discussion of report cards and grades in the context of performance-based schools and educational programs. We will explore what it is we need to communicate via grades and how we can go about gathering and summarizing that information through report cards and grades most effectively in the future.

The discussion of communication options doesn't stop there, however. We will use report cards as a point of departure for exploring many other possibilities. Among these are more detailed checklist and narrative reports, student-teacher conferences, student-led parent-teacher conferences, and portfolios. These are presented as communication alternatives that show great promise in the information age.

In Part 4, we also address communication about the meaning of quality assessment across levels of responsibility in the educational process. The potential contributors to the creation of a positive, constructive assessment environment in schools includes legislators, state department of education personnel, local school boards, district staff, principals, teachers, parents, and students. We will detail the specific nature of the contribution of each and the critical need for effective communication among contributors.

Throughout our journey two themes will permeate. First, we must know how to develop and use sound assessments and how to use them well in each and every classroom. Second, students can and should be full partners in the assessment process. Our challenge is to find creative ways to use student self-assessment as a teaching strategy. This book is devoted to meeting both of these challenges.

ONE FINAL THOUGHT

Let this book represent the beginning of a career-long exploration of discovery on your part. It is not possible to cover all critical elements of educational assessment in one introductory volume. For this reason, it is important that you regard our journey as a first excursion into the realm of assessment, to be followed by others as you move on to more advanced topics. I will give you a list of additional readings at the end of our trip. Now and always, you must endeavor to seek new understandings of assessment.

If you are ready, then, let our journey begin.

Rick Stiggins
Portland, Oregon

Acknowledgments

S tudent-Centered Classroom Assessment represents the results of twenty years
of preparation under the tutelage of many outstanding primary, elementary,
junior high, and high school classroom teachers. In a very real sense, this book
conveys the collective wisdom of those many teachers, who shared openly of their
assessment ideas, uncertainties, and frustrations. First, let me express deep appreciation to them for sharing their students and learning environments, and for communicating about assessment issues in such a frank and honest manner. They wel-
comed me into their world, and helped me to understand it.

Special thanks also to my wife, Nancy Bridgeford, and Sharon Lippert of the
Assessment Training Institute team. Nancy possesses that uncanny ability to ferret
out writing that fails to convey clear meaning. Nowhere is effective communication
more important or more challenging than in a book like this. Nancy made effective
communication possible here. Sharon not only prepared all versions of the book
manuscript, but she also has prepared most of the previous versions of these ideas
as we have accumulated them over the past two decades. Her patience and sense
of presentation contributed immensely to this final product.

Several members of the staff of the Northwest Regional Educational Laboratory,
Portland, Oregon, contributed to the completion of this volume, both as reviewers
of drafts of the final product and as partners in the classroom assessment research
that culminates here. Special thanks to Judy Arter, Ruth Culham, Vicki Spandel, and
Bob Rath—outstanding teachers all—and to Maggie Rogers, for a wealth of information. A special remembrance also to Nancy Faires Conklin, who continues to in-
spire.

Others contributed by providing assessment strategies and/or by reviewing and
making constructive suggestions about various chapters. These contributors include

Eric Bigler, Cindy Clingman, Dan Duke, Edys Quellmalz, Doris Sperling, and Tia Wulff.

Special thanks to the Macmillan team of editors Kevin Davis, Linda Peterson, and Laura Messerly, and freelance copyeditor Robert Marcum—a truly skilled word crafter. In this context, let me also acknowledge the contributions of the following reviewers during the preparation of the manuscript: Susan M. Brookhart, Duquesne University; Leland K. Doebler, University of Montevallo; Betty E. Gridley, Ball State University; Thomas Haladyna, Arizona State University West; Robert W. Lissitz, University of Maryland; Ronald N. Marso, Bowling Green State University; Michael A. Miller, Mankato State University; and Kinnard White, University of North Carolina, Chapel Hill. They shared openly of their wisdom and criticism, and they will find the fruits of their labor in the final product.

We know far more as a community of learners than any of us does alone. The insights shared herein arise from many classrooms, representing the collective wisdom of many who care first and foremost about student well-being in the context of educational assessment.

Rick Stiggins
Portland, OR

Brief Contents

Table of Contents

PART THREE

Classroom Applications   **231**

PART FOUR

Communicating About Student Achievement   361

PART ONE

Understanding the Classroom Assessment Context

If measurement is to continue to play an increasingly important role in education, measurement workers must be much more than technicians. Unless their efforts are directed by a sound educational philosophy, unless they accept and welcome a greater share of responsibility for the selection and clarification of educational objectives, unless they show much more concern with what they measure as well as with how they measure it, much of their work will prove futile and ineffective.

E.F. Lindquist (1901–1978)

CHAPTER 1

A Principled View of Classroom Assessment

Chapter Objectives

Important Note: As we study the principles of sound classroom assessment together, we will refer consistently to the need for each teacher to be able to define and assess five different kinds of learning outcomes. To assist you in understanding and applying these kinds of achievement targets in your classroom, I have categorized the objectives of each chapter of this book in those terms. Thus, as you study, you will be striving to attain

- *Knowledge outcomes*—material to be mastered either through memorization or via reference
- *Reasoning outcomes*—ways to use knowledge outcomes to meet specific problem-solving challenges
- *Skill outcomes*—things students should be able to do as a result of mastering the material presented
- *Product outcomes*—things students should be able to create as a result of mastering material presented
- *Affective outcomes*—feelings students might experience as a result of study and application of material presented

Each chapter will begin with objectives classified in these terms as appropriate and will conclude with a list of exercises intended to advance your attainment of those objectives.

As a result of studying the material presented in Chapter 1, reflecting upon that material, and completing the learning exercises presented at the end of the chapter, you will

1. Master content knowledge:
    a. Know seven key principles of sound classroom assessment.
    b. Know five key attributes of sound assessment.
2. Be able to use that knowledge to reason as follows:
    a. Translate the seven principles into terms that have personal meaning for you.
    b. Think of personal examples of assessments that met and failed to meet the five attributes of sound assessment.
3. Attain the following affective outcomes:
    a. See many different modes of assessment as useful.
    b. See classroom assessment as the most important level of assessment for student well-being.
    c. See students as the most important users of assessment results.
    d. Value quality assessment under all circumstances.

Note: The objectives of this chapter do not include the mastery of any process skills or the creation of any products.

V isualize yourself at a particularly important meeting of the school board in the district where you teach. The crowd is unusually large, the news media are present, and anticipation runs high. This is the once-a-year meeting at which the district presents the annual report of standardized test scores. Everyone wonders whether scores will be up or down this year. How will your school compare with all the others? How will your district compare to others in the area?

What most of those present don't realize as the meeting begins is that, this year, they are in for a big surprise—with respect to both the achievement information to be presented and the manner of the presentation. To make the presentation, the chair of the school board introduces the assistant superintendent in charge of assessment.

The assistant superintendent begins by reminding the board and the members of the community that the standardized tests used in the district sample broad domains of achievement with very few test items. Thus, they provide only the most general picture of student achievement. She points out that the only assessment format used is the multiple-choice test item—a format capable of reflecting only a small, but important, part of the total array of outcomes valued in this district. Much that we value, she points out, must be assessed by other means. She promises to provide an example later in the presentation.

Further, the presenter reminds the board that last year they approved an assessment policy changing district practice from a testing plan of administering the test battery to every pupil at every grade to a plan relying on random sampling of students at each grade level. The board had understood that the number of students tested would be greatly reduced. Thus, the cost of testing could be greatly reduced without sacrificing quality in the average test scores they wanted, both for individual school buildings and districtwide.

In this context, the presenter informs the board that the cost savings were used to develop and implement assessments that provide greater detail on student achievement in performance arenas not testable by means of multiple-choice tests. Again, she promises examples later in the presentation.

Having set the stage, she turns to carefully prepared charts depicting average student performance in each important achievement category by grade and building, concluding with a clear description of how district results had changed from the year before and from previous years. As she proceeds, board members ask questions and receive clarification. This is a routine presentation that proceeds as expected.

Then comes the break from routine. Having completed the first part of the presentation, the assistant superintendent explains how the district has used some of the assessment monies saved through reduced standardized testing. As the board knows, she points out, the district has implemented a new writing program in the high school to counter low levels of writing proficiency among graduates. As part of their preparation for this program, the English faculty attended a summer institute on the assessment of writing proficiency and the integration of such assessments into the teaching and learning process.

As the second half of the evening's assessment presentation, the district's English department faculty will share the results of their evaluation of the new writing program.

As the very first step in this presentation, the English chair distributes copies of a writing sample to the board members, asking them to read and evaluate it. They do so, expressing their dismay aloud as they go. They are indignant in their commentary on this sample of student work. One board member reports in exasperation that, if this is a sample of the results of that new writing program, the community has been had. The board member is right. It is, in fact, a pretty bad piece of work!

But the chair urges patience and asks the board members to be very specific about what they did not like about this work. As the board registers its complaints, the faculty records the specifics as they are presented. The list is long.

Next, the faculty distributes a second sample of student writing, asking the board to read and evaluate it. Ah, this, they report, is more like it! This work is much better! But be specific, the chair demands. What do you like about this work? Positive aspects are listed: good choice of words, sound sentence structure, clever ideas, and so on.

Then, having set the school board up, the faculty springs the trap: The two pieces of writing were produced by the same writer, one at the beginning and the other at the end of the school year! This, the chair reports, is evidence of the kind of impact the new writing program is having on student writing proficiency.

Needless to say, all are impressed. However, one board member asks, how typical is this kind of improvement among all students? Having anticipated the question, the faculty produces carefully prepared charts depicting dramatic changes in student performance over time on rating scales for each of six clearly articulated dimensions of good writing. They accompany their description of student performance on each scale with actual samples of student work illustrating various levels of proficiency.

Further, after this phase of the presentation, the chair informs the board that the student whose improvement had been so dramatically illustrated is present, along with her teacher. They are both willing to talk with the board about the nature of her learning experience.

Interest among the board members runs high. The student talks about how she has come to understand the truly important differences between good and bad writing, how she has learned to assess her own writing and to fix it when it doesn't "work well," and how she and her classmates have learned to talk with her teacher and each other about what it means to write well. Her teacher talks about the improved focus of writing instruction, increases in student motivation, and important positive changes in the very nature of the student-teacher relationship.

A board member asks the student if she likes to write. She reports, "I do now!"

This teacher, student, and classroom-centered part of the assessment presentation overshadows the test score presentation in the minds of participants. There is a good feeling in the air. Clearly, both the writing assessment training and the new writing program are working to improve an important facet of student achievement.

Obviously, this story has a happy ending. Can't you almost visualize yourself walking out of the boardroom at the end of the evening, still hearing participants comment on how they wished they had had such an experience in high school? I sure can. Can't you just anticipate the wording of the memo the superintendent will soon write to the English department? How about the story that will appear in the newspaper tomorrow? Everyone involved here—from student to parent to teacher to assessment director to (at the end) school board members—knew what they were doing from an assessment point of view. They knew the meaning of quality assessment. This is an environment governed by an atmosphere of assessment literacy.

ASSESSMENT LITERACY IS THE KEY

Because the staff and faculty in this particular district knew and understood the principles of sound assessment, and because they knew how to translate those principles into sound assessments, quality information about students, and effective instruction, a wide range of benefits accrued to all involved. Several examples follow.

The Positive Results

To begin with, the students not only became more proficient as writers, but they also knew precisely when and why that happened. They were empowered by their teachers to use the assessment tools that allowed them to take responsibility for their own achievement. The mystery surrounding the definition of good writing was removed. Clearly, this openness paid off.

Similarly, the English faculty was empowered to evaluate their own program. They were entrusted with the responsibility and were provided with the training and writing assessment tools needed to do that job. Not only did they use these new tools to fulfill their program evaluation responsibility, but they turned them into teaching tools, too.

Further, they didn't retain the meaning of academic success as if it were some mystical treasure to be divined somehow by their students. Rather, they shared their vision of success openly. As a result, students learned.

Other positive things happened, too. From an assessment point of view, limited district assessment resources were divided productively between those assessments that are likely to serve policy makers (districtwide assessment) and those that are likely to serve teachers and students in the classroom. The assessment environment is in balance.

Also from an assessment perspective, both during instruction and during the school board presentation, meaningful words and examples rather than just scores and grades were used as the basis for communicating about student achievement. And the resulting richness of mutual understanding of the real meaning of student success was compelling. Assessment is more than a set of numbers here. Things are in balance.

Still under the assessment heading, assessments that relied on observation and professional judgment (i.e., subjective assessments) are acknowledged to be of value in this context. You can bet that if our skillful assistant superintendent in charge of assessment had concluded the meeting by asking the school board if they would like to see more evidence of student achievement depicted in the form of performance assessments, she would have received a resounding *yes!* The assessment methods in use in this district are sensitive to the important outcomes.

And, one final positive aspect of this story is that a good part of the evidence that held sway with the policy makers was both generated by teachers in their classrooms and presented in a public forum in a way that established teachers' credibility as dependable sources of information on student achievement.

In one sense, their presentation revealed what good teachers they really are. I don't mean to say that it showed them to be good teachers because writing proficiency improved dramatically—although that was an important outcome. Rather, I mean to point out that they were revealed to be good teachers of the school board, using hands-on applications of their newly acquired assessment methods to expand the horizons of the school board with respect to what represents sound assessment of student achievement. Common sense and a balance of perspectives on assessment ruled the day.

The Things that Can Go Wrong

But for every such positive story in which sound assessment feeds into productive instruction and important learning, there may be another with a far less constructive—perhaps even painful—ending. For instance, some unfortunate students may be mired in classrooms in which they are forced to try to guess at the meaning of academic success, because their teacher either lacks a vision of that meaning or chooses to keep it a mystery as a means of retaining power and control. When these students guess wrong and fail the assessment, not for a lack of motivation but for a lack of insight as to what they were supposed to achieve, permanent damage can be done to emerging academic self-concepts.

Then there are those students who prepare well, master the required material, and fail anyway, because the teacher prepared a test of poor quality, thus mismeasuring achievement. And, there are students whose achievement is mismeasured because the teacher placed blind faith in the quality of the tests that came with the textbook, when in fact that confidence was misplaced. Still further, some students fail not because of low achievement, but because their teachers' performance assessment judgments are riddled with the effects of gender or ethnic bias.

This list of dangers could go on and on: school boards might make poor policy decisions because they fail to understand the limitations of standardized tests or the meaning of the scores these tests produce. Further, these policy makers may have had nowhere to turn for guidance in such assessment matters because of a lack of assessment literacy on the part of administrators who advise them.

When these and other such problems arise, an environment of assessment illiteracy dominates and students will be hurt.

Our Common Mission

Our joint challenge in this book is to begin the professional development needed to assure high-quality assessment in your classroom. We must strive together to develop assessment literacy among all concerned about the quality of our schools and the well-being of students.

Assessment literates are those who understand the basic principles of sound assessment. But just understanding the meaning of sound assessment will not suffice. We must demand adherence to high standards by acting purposely to meet those standards in all assessment contexts and by pointing out to others when their assessments fail to measure up. As we implement assessments in the classroom or the boardroom, we must know how sound assessment relates to quality instruction and strive to maintain a balanced use of assessment alternatives.

In the future of our educational system, there will continue to be both standardized testing *and* classroom assessment. We must appreciate the differences between the two, so as to be able to assure the quality of each.

In the future these assessments will continue to serve both as providers of information for decision making *and* as teaching tools. We must understand the differences between these two uses if we wish to take full advantage of the power of assessment to promote learning.

In the future there will continue to be paper and pencil *and* performance assessments. Each carries with it a different set of rules of evidence for obtaining quality results. Know and follow them and you can assist students. Violate them and students will suffer. Our task is to study those rules together.

Those who are assessment literate know the meaning of assessment quality with all of its nuances and know that we are never justified in settling for unsound assessments. That literacy is our goal as we visit the world of classroom assessment together.

A SET OF GUIDING PRINCIPLES

In the chapters that follow, I will share a vast array of assessment tools, strategies, admonitions, and examples—all aimed at making the many meanings of sound assessment clear to you. As we proceed, you will find certain themes occurring repeatedly. These are graphically portrayed in Figure 1–1, and are addressed in greater detail in the remainder of the chapter. They represent both important assessment realities teachers face in classrooms and important values that I personally have come to hold about classroom assessment. I share them with you here at the outset as a set of seven interrelated principles of sound assessment that map the path to quality. The order in which they are presented is unimportant. All are profoundly important—together, they represent the foundation of your preparation to assess well in the classroom.

As you read about these principles, reflect back on the account of the school board meeting presented above and you will see why I started our journey together in that particular fashion.

Principle 1: Clear Thinking and Effective Communication

Mention assessment and the first thoughts that come to mind are those of scores, numbers, and quantified indexes of how much was learned. However, in our account of the school board meeting, the English faculty communicated effectively with their students (whether as real students or as school board members!) through the thoughtful use of examples of student performance. Sound assessment requires clear thinking and effective communication—not just the quantification of achievement.

While many assessments do translate levels of achievement into scores, we are coming to understand two important realities more and more clearly. First, numbers are not the only way to communicate about achievement. We can use words, pictures, illustrations, examples, and many other means to convey meaning about student achievement. And second, the symbols used as the basis of our communication about student achievement are only as meaningful and useful as the definitions of achievement that underpin them and the quality of the assessments used to produce them.

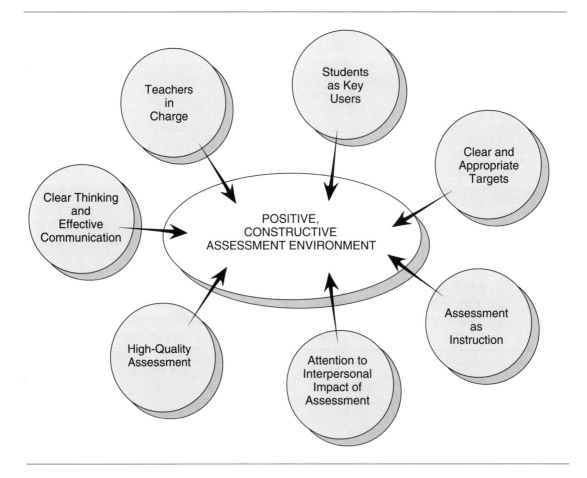

Figure 1-1.
The Principles of Sound Assessment: A Critical Blend

Time for Reflection

Can you think of a time in your life when information about your achievement was summarized and presented in some form other than a number, score, or grade? What medium of communication was used? How effective was the communication?

Principle 2: Teachers in Charge

Teachers direct the assessments that determine what students learn and how they feel about it. In our opening account, the assessments that contributed to a stronger writing program were not the districtwide tests reported at the opening of the board presentation. Rather, the critical assessments were those carried out by the English faculty.

In most educational contexts, it is the standardized district, state, or national assessment results that command all of the resources, news coverage, and political power—as though they were the only assessments that count. Nothing could be further from the truth. These highly visible assessments are not even in the same league as teachers' classroom assessments in terms of their impact on student well-being.

Nearly all of the assessment events that take place in students' lives happen at the behest of their teachers. The typical teacher can spend as much as a third to half of his or her professional time involved in assessment-related activities (Stiggins & Conklin, 1992). Teachers make decisions about how to interact with their students on average at the rate of one every two to three minutes—and most of those have antecedents in an assessment of student achievement—asking questions and interpreting answers, watching students perform, examining homework assignments, and using tests and quizzes, among other means (Shavelson & Stern, 1981). Assessment is almost continuous in many classrooms.

Clearly, classroom assessments are the assessments that are most available to teachers. They also are most closely aligned with day-to-day instruction and are most influential in terms of their contribution to student, teacher, and parent decision making (see Principle 3). Without question, teachers are the drivers of the assessment systems that determine the effectiveness of schools.

Time for Reflection

In research completed at Stanford University (Haertel et al., 1984), high school students were asked how much importance they attached to their teachers' classroom assessments versus the district's standardized tests. What do you think they said and why?

Principle 3: Students as Key Users

Students are the most important users of assessment results. In our account of the school board meeting, students learned to improve because they were shown the differences between their performance and understandable standards of quality performance. They learned these things from their teachers, based on practice through classroom assessments.

There are other assessment users throughout the educational process, and they are also important people. We will analyze these other assessment users and their information needs in detail in chapter 3. However, no one but students use the results of their teachers' classroom assessments to set expectations of themselves. Students decide how high to aim based on their sense of the probability that they will succeed. They estimate the probability of success based on performance on previous classroom assessment experience. No single decision or combination of decisions made by any other party exerts greater influence on student success.

Time for Reflection

What do you think are the other most important decisions students make based on classroom assessments of their achievement? Why do you think are these the most important?

Principle 4: Clear and Appropriate Targets

The quality of any assessment depends first and foremost on the clarity and appropriateness of our definition of the achievement target to be assessed. In the opening account, a breakthrough in student writing achievement occurred because the English faculty returned from that summer institute with a shared vision of writing proficiency. They built their program, and thus the competence of their students, around that vision.

We cannot assess any educational outcome effectively if we do not know and understand what that valued outcome is. There are many different kinds of valued outcomes of our educational system, from mastering content knowledge to complex problem solving, from playing a flute to speaking Spanish to building a strong cooperative problem-solving team. All are important. But to assess them well, we must ask ourselves: Do we know what it means to do it well? Precisely what does it mean to succeed academically?

We are ready to assess when we can answer these questions with clarity and confidence.

Time for Reflection

List two of the achievement targets you expect your students to hit. Try to define each in specific terms, in writing. Do you find this task easy or difficult?

Principle 5: High-quality Assessment

High-quality assessment is an absolute must in all assessment contexts. Sound assessments satisfy five specific quality standards. All assessments must meet all standards. No exceptions can be justified. These five standards, described below, are illustrated in Figure 1–2. This is the first of many discussions and illustrations of these quality standards that permeate this book. On this first pass, I intend only to give you a sense of the meaning of *quality*.

First, sound assessments arise from clear achievement targets. You can ask this question about any assessment: Can the developer and user of this assessment provide a clear and appropriate description of the specific educational outcome it is designed to reflect? If the answer is yes, proceed to the next standard. If the answer is no, realize that there is a very real danger of misassessment.

Standard number two asks that we consider the purpose for an assessment as we design it. It is impossible to develop a quality assessment unless and until we know how the results it produces are to be used. So again, about any assessment you can ask: Does the developer understand the intended uses and has the

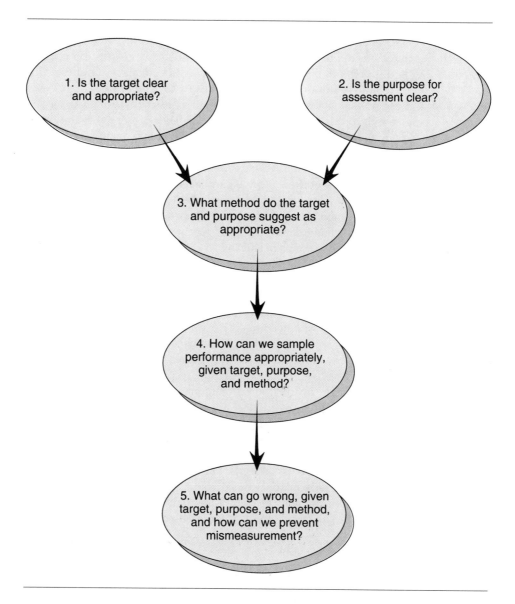

Figure 1–2
Keys to Sound Assessment

developer taken user needs into account in developing and implementing the assessment?

Quality standard number three holds that a sound assessment depicts achievement through the use of an assessment method that is, in fact, capable of reflecting the valued target. To test mastery of scientific knowledge, we might use a multiple-choice test. But when our challenge is to assess the ability to speak Spanish, we must turn to another method altogether. Thus, you can ask this question about any assessment: Is the method used here capable of accurately reflecting the kinds of outcomes the user wishes to assess? If the answer is yes, proceed to the next standard. If it is no, be aware that student achievement is about to be misassessed.

Standard number four admonishes us to sample student achievement appropriately, so we may have confidence in our assessment results. Any assessment includes a sample of all the exercises we could have presented if time were unlimited. A sound assessment gathers a representative sample that is large enough to yield confident inferences about how the respondent would have done on an infinitely large assessment. So about any assessment, you can ask: Has sound sampling methodology been followed here, so we can have confidence in the results? If the answer is yes, proceed. If it is no, critical consumers of assessment information should begin to be concerned about student well-being.

Finally, standard number five demands that we design, develop, and use assessments in ways that permit us to control for all sources of extraneous interference that can cause us to mismeasure achievement—all sources of bias that can rob assessment results of clear and appropriate meaning. There are far too many to list here, but we will cover them in the remaining chapters of this book. They all are critically important. So about any assessment, you can ask: Have the important sources of bias been accounted for during development and use? If the answer is no, you must urge action to address unaccounted-for sources of error.

Violate any of these criteria and you place students at risk. Unsound assessments can lead to misdiagnosed needs, failure to provide needed instructional support, use of inappropriate instructional treatments, counterproductive grouping of students, and misinformation provided to student and parent decision makers, among an even wider variety of instructional difficulties.

But over and above these potential problems, when assessments are developed over time and are used repeatedly by those who fail to understand the valued outcome, fail to identify user needs, fail to select a proper assessment method, sample achievement inadequately, and/or fail to avoid bias, and who thus systematically misassess the achievement of their students, even deeper problems can arise. This leads to the sixth principle of sound assessment.

Time for Reflection

Think of one time in your life as a student when you were given an assessment to complete that failed to meet one or more of the five quality control standards listed above. Which standard was missed and what effect did that lack of quality have on you as a learner?

Principle 6: Attention to Interpersonal Impact

Assessment is a very complex interpersonal activity that is virtually always accompanied by personal antecedents and personal consequences. Classroom assessments are never the dispassionate scientific act some make them out to be. When we allow our students to be assessed, we expose them to the possibility of academic and personal benefit and harm. In the face of assessment, we all become vulnerable at some level. Our assessments link our students to their constantly emerging academic and personal self-concepts. They provide students with the link to their sense of control over their own well-being in school. Students are more likely to feel in control when they know how to succeed, and feel they can influence their own destiny (Messick, 1989). They lose control when they either don't understand the meaning of success or feel doomed to fail. Sound assessments can keep them feeling in control.

That means we must always strive for the highest-quality assessment, communicate results in a sensitive and private manner, and anticipate results so as to be prepared to offer specific support to students whose achievement is low. The younger the student, the more critical these guidelines become.

Time for Reflection

Think of a time in your life as a student when an assessment of your achievement made you feel good about yourself as a learner. What was it about that particular experience that left you feeling so good? Think of a time when an assessment left you with a negative academic self-concept. What was it about that experience that was so negative?

Principle 7: Assessment as Instruction

Assessments and teaching can be one and the same. They do not have to be one and the same—but they can be when we want them to be. Sometimes, it's all right to conduct an assessment merely as a status check not linked to an immediate instructional use. But it's also all right to regard assessment as a powerful instructional tool.

Perhaps the greatest potential value of classroom assessment is its ability to make students full partners in the assessment process. I do not just mean by having them trade papers or homework assignments so they can grade each other's work. This concept of full partnership goes far deeper.

Students who internalize valued achievement targets so thoroughly as to be able to confidently and competently evaluate their own and each other's work almost automatically become better performers in their own right. Specific suggestions for melding assessment and instruction in this way occur throughout the chapters that follow.

Time for Reflection

What do you think might be some keys to turning assessment experiences into learning experiences, too? Brainstorm some ideas and save your list for later reference.

CHAPTER SUMMARY: THE MATTER OF ASSESSMENT COMPETENCE

Considered together, the seven principles discussed in this chapter form the foundation of the assessment wisdom all educators must master in order to manage classroom assessment environments effectively. Thus, in a sense, they form the foundation of classroom assessment competence.

Those teachers who are prepared to meet the challenges of classroom assessment understand the need to do their homework by thinking clearly and communicating effectively. They know why it is critical to be able to communicate their expectations to their students and their families and why it is essential that assessments be done well and also communicated effectively.

Well-prepared teachers realize that they lie at the heart of the assessment process in schools and they take that responsibility very seriously. Unfortunately, as you shall see in the next chapter, as a society and as a community of professional educators, we have not supported teachers over the decades in their preparation to fulfill this responsibility. But that must change—professional development in assessment must become a very high educational priority.

Competent teachers understand the complexities of aligning a range of valued achievement targets with appropriate assessment methods so as to produce information on student achievement that both they and their students can count on to be accurate. They understand the meaning of sound assessment and they know how to use all of the assessment tools at their disposal to produce that accurate information.

Effective classroom assessor/teachers understand the interpersonal dynamics of classroom assessment and know how to set students up for success in part through using the appropriate assessment as a teaching tool. They know how to make students full partners in the processes of defining the valued outcomes of instruction and transforming those definitions into quality assessments.

As teachers bring students into the assessment equation, thus demystifying the meaning of success in the classroom, they acknowledge that students use assessment results to make the decisions that ultimately will determine if school does or does not work for them. Our collective classroom assessment challenge is to be sure students have the information they need, in a form they understand, and in time to use it effectively.

EXERCISES TO ADVANCE YOUR LEARNING

Knowledge Outcomes

1. Memorize the seven principles of sound classroom assessment. Keep them in the front of your thoughts throughout our journey.

2. Memorize the five key attributes of a sound assessment. Prepare to use them as the threads that bind the following chapters together.

Reasoning Outcomes

1. Translate the seven principles into your own words and write a brief paragraph conveying your interpretation of each.

2. Translate the five key attributes of a sound assessment into your own words and write a brief paragraph conveying your interpretation of each.

Affective Outcomes

1. Some contend that it has been a mistake to rely so completely on multiple-choice tests over the years as indicators of school achievement. They feel that we should turn to total reliance on performance assessments. How do you feel about this issue?

2. Principle 2 stipulates that classroom assessment is far more important than standardized tests to student well-being. Do you agree? Why?

3. Principle 3 stipulates that students are the most important users of classroom assessment results. Do you agree? Why?

4. Quality assessment is presented as essential in this chapter, yet sometimes this value comes into direct conflict with the resources available to achieve such quality. Sometimes we just cannot afford it. In your opinion, is it ever acceptable to risk mismeasuring student achievement due to the lack of resources to do it right?

Changing Assessment Times Bring New Assessment Responsibilities

---

Chapter Objectives

As a result of studying the material presented in Chapter 2, reflecting upon that material, and completing the learning exercises presented at the end of the chapter, you will

1. Master content knowledge:
   a. Know a brief history of achievement testing in the United States.
   b. Understand forces for change in assessment in schools in the 1930s and 1990s.
   c. Know the reasons for the insufficiency of centralized, standardized testing as a basis for school improvement.
   d. See the differences between a declining old era of assessment and an emerging new era.

2. Be able to use that knowledge to reason as follows:
   a. Understand the rationale for the rapid expansion in the array of assessment methods being used in schools today.
   b. Differentiate roles and responsibilities of all participants in the educational process.
   c. Understand the evolving mission of schools in the United States.

3. Attain the following affective outcomes:
   a. See the performance-driven mission of school as productive.
   b. See change in the nature and complexity of achievement targets as inevitable.
   c. Value the full array of assessment methods available for our use in schools.

     d. Appreciate the critical role of assessment in the classroom.

     e. See quality assessment as critical to student well-being.

Note: The objectives of this chapter do not include the mastery of any process skills or the creation of any products.

The assessment roles and responsibilities of all involved in the educational process have begun to change rapidly. These assessment changes mirror other positive and productive transformations occurring throughout the American educational system. In fact, many believe that schools as we have know them are being transformed into an entirely new kind of social institution. Society has begun to demand that schools deliver students who have learned—schools are becoming performance-driven institutions. This means educators will be held accountable for more than just providing opportunities for learning. Rather, we will be held accountable for the actual achievement of our students.

The implications of this redefinition of the mission of schools are profound—and nowhere more than in the realm of assessment. I believe we are witnessing the end of a sixty-year-long era of assessment and the beginning of a whole new era.

In the passing era, assessment was defined as the quantification of student achievement, so scores could be used to sort and rank students from the highest to the lowest achiever. Schools were deemed effective if they produced a dependable rank order of students at the end of the schooling experience. In the emerging era, assessment is defined in broader terms than just scores and schools are deemed effective only when and if they produce students who can demonstrate certain specified competencies. Assessments in this case serve to document student attainment of those valued outcomes.

Our goals in this chapter are to understand the nature of these changes in the role of assessment in schooling and to see the implications of those changes for the classroom teacher.

CHAPTER ROADMAP

In this chapter, we will reach these objectives by analyzing the forces for change and by examining the active ingredients in the change process, as depicted in Figure 2–1. More specifically, we will do the following:

- Provide a brief historical perspective from which to understand the nature and extent of the changes in assessment.
- Clarify the forces promoting these changes.
- Describe how the assessment community is responding to these forces for change.
- Examine the implications of these changes for all concerned with school quality.

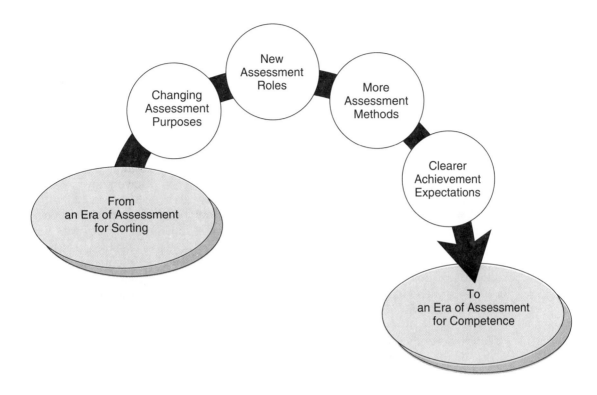

Figure 2-1
A Time of Assessment Transition

A BRIEF HISTORY LESSON

To set the stage for our examination of the rapid evolution of education and to better understand the role of assessment in the educational process, let's travel back
several decades to the last time we underwent such a fundamental reexamination of
our assessment priorities. The assessment era that we see coming to an end in the
1990s had its origins in the 1920s and 1930s. By examining the contemporary social
and educational forces at work, we can gain important insights into the emerging
nature of educational assessment at that time.

Formal Education Optional

For example, in those days, the United States was built on an agricultural economy,
with some heavy industry emerging in the northeast. As a result, Americans could
secure economic well-being without a great deal of formal education. For this reason, school dropout rates in those days were three times those of today. However,
those leaving the educational system were not labeled "at-risk youth" as they are
today, because our social and economic structure offered opportunities for them to
contribute and to succeed.

Ethnic Diversity

Also during the 1920s and 1930s, America's post–World War I ethnic population was becoming increasingly diverse, with immigrants from the world's cultures arriving at all borders in huge numbers. We began to conceive of America as the great melting pot. We aspired to a common language, culture, national experience, and heritage. To achieve this end, we sought a homogenizing experience, and decided that schools could provide that common ground. So we conceived of the standard curriculum for all students, and we sent out word via compulsory attendance laws that everyone would have to come to school and be educated.

School Serves Social Function

And so, to school they came—in unprecedented numbers, thus presenting educators of those times with the immense challenge of schooling the masses with very limited resources. To meet this challenge, educational leaders conceived of "assembly line schools," schools in which young children entered the system and stopped at the first point on the assembly line. They allowed a fixed amount of time—one year—for them to master the required standard curriculum. In that kind of system, there would be variation in the amount learned by any individual by the end of first grade.

Students then moved on to stop two. Those who mastered a great deal at stop one on the assembly line would learn much more. Those who learned little at stop one would learn little more at stop two. The amount of variation in achievement among students increased. And so it would go through several years of public school education. The variation in student achievement would continue to expand.

This, educators decided, would be an important social function of schools. By creating a continuum of achievement, schools could facilitate the channeling of students into the various segments of our economic and social structure. In effect, this sorting function formed the foundation for the era of assessment that was about to begin because, in the midst of this evolution of schools in the 1930s, there appeared on the scene a new kind of achievement test—a format that appeared to fill several critical needs.

Time for Reflection

Think about your own educational experience. To what extent have the opportunities you found open to you been a function of your place in the rank order of students? College admissions certainly is an obvious example. Can you think of other instances? What was the basis of the ranking used? What was the experience like for you?

A "New" Kind of Test

This new kind of test was referred to in the professional literature as "scientific" (Scates, 1943) in that it was capable of controlling for inherent biases and idiosyncrasies of teacher subjective judgment, which prior to this time had formed the basis for assessment in schools. Also, as advocates pointed out, this new kind of test could be mass produced, mass administered, and mass scored very efficiently—and efficiency was seen as essential in those times of rapid growth in education and limited resources to accomplish it.

This test also brought with it an even more important advantage: It was able to produce the quintessential sorting criterion—a score had exactly the same meaning for every student who took the same test. It offered concrete, apparently "scientific" support for the sorting function of schools.

This new entry in the assessment arena was, as you may have deduced, the objectively scored paper and pencil test. Because of its great efficiency and the comparability of its scores, this assessment option became so popular that it dominated our conception of educational assessment for sixty years.

AN ERA OF DISCONNECTED EFFORTS

The era of assessment that began in the late 1920s and stretched to the late 1980s can be characterized in terms of three very important patterns of professional practice, one involving teachers, another involving assessment personnel, and a third involving administrators and policy makers.

Differentiated Functions

First, very early in this era, educators separated two critical functions. On one hand, teachers would have responsibility for teaching. Their challenge would be to master and apply the technology of instruction. And on the other hand, assessors would assess. Their professional challenge and role would be to master and apply the rapidly emerging technology of testing.

In effect, local teachers and administrators abdicated responsibility for high-stakes assessment and entrusted that responsibility to the measurement community, purposely separating assessment and instruction and assigning them to different parties. This amounted to saying, Teachers, you teach and you don't need to know anything about assessment. And assessors, you test and you need not know anything about teaching. Training programs, certification requirements, and job responsibilities were defined for all according to this functional differentiation.

Psychometric Development

This led to the second important pattern of professional practice that characterized this era. Once in charge, the assessment community launched a sixty-year-long program of psychometric research and development that had some very important characteristics. Assessors began to define *assessment* as the quantification of student achievement. This permitted the introduction of sophisticated mathematical models for the description of student achievement to the summary of achievement information. As a result, the world of testing quickly became quantitatively complex and highly technical in its vocabulary. This technical assessment vocabulary served to facilitate efficient and effective communication among assessment specialists. However, few outside the field could understand it. As a result, assessment experts could communicate very well among themselves, but outsiders (teachers, administrators, and policy makers, in this case) were left out of the assessment process. In effect, an impenetrable wall was constructed between assessment and instruction due to a lack of common understanding, and that wall grew very high very quickly.

The March Toward Layers of Standardized Testing

Once school officials began to understand the great efficiency of these new objectively scored paper and pencil tests, they took the first steps in what also turned out to be a sixty-year march, toward ever more centralized assessment of student achievement, adding layer upon layer of standardized testing programs.

Scholarship Testing.   This march began modestly in the 1930s with a few local scholarship testing programs, which relied on the emerging objective testing technology to serve their sorting and selecting needs. Thus, right from the outset, quality tests were those that maximized individual differences in student achievement. These differences would serve to rank examinees for the award of scholarships.

College Admissions Testing.   These local applications were so effective that by the late 1940s we had begun the same kind of assessment program at the national level with our first national college admissions testing programs, the College Boards. These applications of the new testing technology as a sorting criterion aligned very well with the perceived mission of schools. Both were to rank students.

Published Test Batteries.   The technology continued to evolve as a sorting and selecting tool. By the 1950s, test publishers were selling standardized versions of objective paper and pencil tests for use at all grade levels. The test user guides were careful to point out that scores on these tests were intended to serve as one additional piece of information to be used by teachers to supplement their classroom assessments and help sort students into proper instructional treatments. Remember this purpose; it is a critical issue in the whole historical picture.

In the 1960s, society began to raise serious questions about the effectiveness of schools. With Russia first into space, for example, our society began to question the quality of math and science education in schools. In addition, the upheavals surrounding the Vietnam War, the Civil Rights movement, student protests, and the like gave rise to and fueled an environment of questioning and challenging. Many social institutions came under scrutiny—including schools. This general reexamination of our social priorities and institutions gave birth to the sense that schools (and the educators who run them) might need to be held accountable for more than just providing quality opportunities to learn—for more than just sorting students according to achievement. Rather, they might be held responsible for producing real student learning, for assuring that all students attain certain specified outcomes.

Testing for Accountability.   In response to the 1960s challenge that schools might not be "working," administrators in those days, to evaluate their programs, were forced to turn to their only source of relatively believable student achievement data: scores from commercially available standardized objective paper and pencil achievement tests.

This represented a profoundly important shift in our perceptions of these tests. They changed from being seen as just one additional piece of information for teachers, to being seen as standards of educational excellence. The underlying testing technology did not change. These were still tests designed to maximize individual differences among students based on assessments of very broad domains of content. All that changed was our perceptions of the tests and the meaning of their scores. They came to be seen as the guardians of our highest academic expectations—a use for which they were never intended by their original developers.

Remember that these changes in the manner in which these tests were viewed and used were motivated by the laudable desire for school improvement. Besides, these changes occurred in the midst of an assessment era that had differentiated the teaching and assessing functions. Neither teachers nor administrators were trained in or expected to understand the basic principles of sound assessment. They could not have been expected to understand how inappropriate these changes actually were.

However, throughout the 1960s, as testing for accountability grew in popularity, we saw little change in the nature of our schooling experience or its results. So we asked, if local district testing programs do not promote school improvement, why not try statewide testing programs? Surely, we said, if we have a statewide criterion of excellence, schools will improve.

Statewide Testing.   So, during the 1970s, statewide testing programs spread across the land. And significantly, many states opted to develop their own tests to be sure they focused on important educational outcomes in that state. They tended to move away from tests designed to sort. Nevertheless, there was not marked change in the nature or quality of schools.

National and International Assessment.   So, as a society, we said, if local or state testing doesn't lead to school improvement, perhaps we should try national assessments of student achievement. Surely, if we conduct a national testing program and rank states according to performance, schools will be forced to improve. Thus, in the 1970s and 1980s, we added the National Assessment of Educational Progress, along with international testing programs, in the hope that testing achievement at ever more centralized levels would somehow lead to school improvement. But alas, little evidence of school improvement was forthcoming.

You can see the pattern of practice that emerged over these decades. Our collective view of the path to school improvement seemed to be that, if we just test achievement, schools will improve as if by magic and everything will be fine. Further, there is evidence that this perspective continues to influence practice today.

National Every Pupil Test. To illustrate, as we moved into the 1990s—as concerned as ever about the quality of schools—we were poised to repeat the same behavior, as we faced the prospect of the mother of all centralized, standardized tests: the national every pupil examination. Once again, advocates of a complex national testing program repeated the same hollow admonition: Just test it and schools will get better, as though the addition of yet another level of testing would somehow succeed where others have not. Fortunately, at the time of this writing (mid 1993), it appears that the political winds have changed and a national every pupil examination program will not be launched.

Each step in the above progression (outlined in Figure 2–2) has been carried out in the service of school improvement. The national price tag for these programs totals hundreds of millions of dollars (U.S. Congress, Office of Technology Assessment, 1992). Yet schools seem to have changed very little.

Time for Reflection

Before you read on, please reflect: Why do you think these various layers of multimillion-dollar standardized testing programs have had so little discernible impact on schools and student learning? In your opinion, what has kept these assessments from being viable forces for school improvement? List some reasons and discuss them with colleagues.

Reasons for Minimal Impact

I can think of at least three distinct reasons why large-scale standardized assessment has promoted little by way of school improvement.

No Link to Instruction. First, simply administering tests without establishing links between and among the assessments and teacher development or instructional strategies is too superficial a change strategy to have any discernible impact on schools.

Figure 2–2
The March Toward Centralized Testing

1930s	Scholarships
1940s	College admissions
1950s	Assessment in classrooms using published test batteries
1960s	Districtwide testing for accountability
1970s	Statewide testing
1980s	National assessment International assessment
1990s	National Every Pupil Test

The act of assessing something generally does not make it change. Additional action is needed along with the assessment.

Narrow Coverage of Assessments.   Second, because of the mass nature of the test programs, often requiring the testing of tens of thousands of students at one time, examiners were forced to rely on efficient objective testing strategies—tests incapable of producing a sufficiently high-resolution portrait of student achievement to inform meaningful improvement.

Invalid Assumptions about the Origins of Improvement.   Third, and perhaps most important, all of the centralized testing programs described above operate on the assumption that the decisions that exert the greatest influence on school quality are made at school management and policy levels; that is, somewhere outside the classroom. They assume, for example, if we just provide the right information to the right people in Washington, DC, the state capital, or the district office, they will make the right decisions and schools will improve.

This view of the origin of school improvement is naive and obviously counterproductive. The halls of political power are not where school improvement originates. There are three groups of decision makers who determine the quality and therefore the impact of American schools. In order of importance, they are students themselves, their teachers, and their parents. All three are informed in their decision making by the same source of information on student achievement and that source is *not* national, state, or local standardized testing. They all rely on teachers' day-to-day classroom assessments of student achievement.

For this reason, the path to school improvement lies not through more standardized testing, but through the development and use of the best quality *classroom assessment* we can generate!

Time for Reflection

Reflect on your life as a student and, if appropriate, as a teacher and/or parent. First, list some of the decisions you have made as a student over the years based on performance feedback that came from your teachers' classroom assessments of your achievement. Second, list some of the instructional decisions you make or might make as a teacher based on your day-to-day classroom assessments of the achievement of your students. Third, list some of the decisions you make or might make as a parent based on information you receive from your child's teacher—information derived from that teacher's classroom assessments. And finally, list some of the decisions you make or might make as a student, teacher, and parent based on standardized test scores. Having listed these decisions, rank the four lists from highest to lowest in terms of their likely impact on academic well-being. Which is highest in impact? Which lowest? What factors contribute to these differences in impact? Save your lists. You will want to refer to them while reading the next chapter.

Summary of the Old Era

To review briefly, in the past assessment era, as a school culture, we separated assessment from instruction and placed responsibility for each in different hands. We took the testing technology to high levels of psychometric complexity very quickly, making it difficult for those who most directly influence student achievement to understand it. And we layered testing programs one on top of another in a vain attempt to enhance the quality of schooling.

Upon reflection, however, some might ask, How can you possibly believe this era is coming to an end? These patterns of professional practice seem to be continuing today unabated. In the 1990s, both teacher and administrator training programs remain devoid of relevant assessment training (Schafer & Lissitz, 1987). This has the effect of leaving the practice of assessment solidly in the hands of measurement experts. The assessment and instruction functions appear to remain separated. Further, psychometricians continue their ever more sophisticated applications of technical test development theories and complex test score scaling models. And still further, as indicated above, the march toward ever more centralized testing continues. How, then, could I argue that these patterns of behavior are characteristic of a bygone era?!

The answer lies in understanding the changing nature of American education.

THE FORCES FOR ASSESSMENT CHANGE

Toward the end of the 1980s, several powerful new forces came into alignment, leading to the decline of the old era and heralding the new. As I describe these forces, understand that the point is not that the old era is dead and gone. It continues to exert influence, but the forces that fueled it in the 1940s, 1950s, 1960s, 1970s, and early 1980s are gone. New and vastly different forces are now fueling the emergence of a new era of assessment.

The Demand for Accountability

The first force in the new order is the accountability movement. This is the movement, born in the 1960s, that contends that schools must become performance-driven institutions, that educators must be held accountable for student attainment of specific academic outcomes.

This sense of mission for schools has gone through several incarnations over the past thirty years. The first version had us speaking of "mastery learning models and criterion-referenced testing" in the late 1960s. Next, we were confronted in the 1970s with the "behavioral objectives movement," followed by an emphasis on "minimum competencies" in the early 1980s. And finally, as we ended the 1980s and entered the 1990s, we heard reference to the currently popular label "outcomes-based education." All of these share the same underlying philosophy: schools are working effectively only when they articulate clear and specific achievement targets for their students and build instruction around the principle that all students attain those standards (i.e., they become performance-driven institutions).

The first three incarnations of this idea—mastery learning, behavioral objectives, and minimum competencies—came to represent only fads in education. They failed to take hold, in my opinion, because they were good ideas that appeared on the education scene ahead of their time. Outcomes-based education (the most current version), on the other hand, is consistent with the tenor of current social and economic times and is therefore commanding immense attention in districts, schools, and classrooms across the land.

What changed in our perceptions of school and society to make it possible for this particular form of the outcomes-based education idea to take hold when the others did not? I submit that it was a profound change in our social and economic reality and a corresponding change in our view of the role we want schools to play in our society.

The Forces for Change

For sixty years, we wanted schools to sort students along a continuum of achievement so they could be channeled into the various segments of our economic structure. As long as schools sorted well, we were satisfied. It didn't even matter what they sorted on, as long as the ranking *appeared* credible. Essentially, this sorting system was blind. While this may sound extreme, consider the evidence. The primary evidence of lack of concern for the basis for sorting is the fact that there are very few teachers or administrators in the United States today who really know what is tested on the commonly used college admissions tests, nor do they know how material covered on those tests aligns with the high school curriculum. How can we label such a system as other than blind, when it is based on a test that is a mystery to almost everyone involved? If we had cared what we sorted on, we would have made sure curriculum and test were aligned and that students were systematically prepared to perform as best they could. We have consistently failed to do so for decades.

For more evidence of blind sorting, we need only regard our report card grading system. For decades, it has been acceptable for two teachers teaching the same course in the same high school to hold completely different expectations of their students, rely on completely different assessments (which may both have been of inferior quality), and have an A in one class mean something fundamentally different from an A in the other. No one cared! Why? Because, regardless of the underlying meaning of any grade, each teacher contributed a grade that could be combined with all other grades to generate a grade-point average, which in turn permitted the determination of a rank in a class, which sufficed for sorting. The underlying basis of the sorting did not matter.

Sorting Insufficient for At-risk Youth.   Cracks began to appear in this system in the mid 1980s, when we began to understand that, if all schools do is rank students, those in the bottom third of the distribution have no way to contribute in our economic structure. This is precisely why we began to label them as being "at risk." They were at risk of leaving school, and they were at risk of being left out of our social and economic system. As a result, the attainment of competence began to replace ranking as school's mission for these students.

Sorting Insufficient for Employers.   Further, our system of using schools merely to produce a rank order of students began to fray around the edges in the late 1980s when employers began to tell us that transcripts, grade-point averages, and rank in class failed to assure them that their newly hired employees could read, write, work on a team, solve complex problems, and bring a strong work ethic to the work place. As a result, the attainment of competence began to replace ranking as school's mission for these students, too.

Sorting Insufficient for College Admissions.   Finally, the institutionalized sorting process began to show serious cracks in its armor in the early 1990s when the very heart of that process, the college admissions system, began to confront the demographics of a rapidly declining pool of available eighteen-year-olds. It became clear that colleges would face increasing competition for fewer students and that recruitment, placement, and retention would be as important as ranking and selection in colleges' efforts to obtain good students. Colleges, wanting to provide programs designed to meet specific student needs, have begun to request more than just rank in class. They now seek information on specific needs, so they can plan programs to meet those needs so students will stay in college.

All of these forces have brought educators to the realization that the schools of the twenty-first century will be more than sorting institutions. They need to assure student attainment of those competencies that will permit them to survive and prosper after school—they need to be performance- or achievement-driven institutions.

Understand that this does *not* mean that we will stop being a competitive or sorting society. Some colleges will continue to be selective and employers will seek ways to identify the best candidate for each job. Note, however, that it is they who will do the sorting and selecting—not public schools. The mission of schools is to assure that each student achieves maximum competence, given each student's capabilities. The sorting comes *after* schools have done their job.

Time for Reflection

Think of three groups of students: those traditionally low in the rank order of achievement, those in the middle of the distribution, and those at the high end. For each group, identify one advantage and one disadvantage of our change from schools that sort to schools that strive for competence. What conclusions do you draw from this analysis?

The Search for Clear and Appropriate Achievement Targets

The realization that we will be held accountable for student attainment of outcomes has caused educators to attend to what those outcomes should be. During the 1980s, vast resources were devoted to a comprehensive, multifaceted reexamination of the valued outcomes of education.

Virtually every state assembled commissions of teachers in the 1980s to evaluate the curriculum and articulate valued achievement targets in the state. Many of the national professional associations of teachers assembled national commissions to spell out valued outcomes in their special field of study. The major research universities turned high-resolution research microscopes on such valued outcomes as the ability to read, write, do math, and understand and use science. And finally, the business community, who could not have cared less about the nature and quality of schools in the 1930s, began to tune in to the importance of education for their business well-being in the 1980s. They began to play a role in reexamining work-related outcomes.

The investment of all these institutions in the infrastructure of education during the 1980s continues in the 1990s. The effort is proving productive in two important ways. First, these outstanding efforts yielded refined visions of competence heretofore unavailable to the educational community. We acquired a more complete understanding, for example, of the cognitive operations involved in reading (Valencia & Pearson, 1987). We also attained a more refined picture of the attributes of sound writing (Graves, 1986), and of reasoning and problem solving (Marzano, 1991). These represent just three of many such refined visions generated over the past decade that hold the potential of allowing us to produce better achievers faster than ever before.

Paradoxically, however, as these visions came into focus, all of us in the education field, teachers, assessors, and administrators, were startled to find that the important outcomes of education are far more complex than previously realized. For example, we began to realize that even an outcome as fundamental as student mastery of subject matter knowledge—the cornerstone of American education—needed to be redefined. Since the amount of new knowledge is doubling every few years, we now understand no one can memorize it all or even hope to remain current through memorization. Further, we understand that knowledge today may well be different tomorrow, as the already rapid pace of scientific and social discovery accelerates.

As a result of these factors, we now understand that by the year 2000 we will need far more than information memorizers. We will need information managers: people who can access information when they need it, use it to solve problems, and then let it go—a much more complex outcome than memorizing soliloquies and vocabulary lists!

As we came to the end of the 1980s, we became painfully aware of a serious dilemma arising out of these sharper images of increasingly complex targets: we began to realize how few of these outcomes can be translated into multiple-choice test items. Such tests do not lack value. They will continue to provide useful information about student attainment of highly valued outcomes. But what transpired at the end of the last decade was a maturing of the educational community that, in effect, permanently sensitized them to the insufficiency of the objective test format.

Time for Reflection

Can you think of some highly valued educational outcomes that cannot be assessed using multiple-choice test items? Can you think of some that can? Make a list of each. What differences do you notice between your two lists?

The Search for More Complete Assessments

Faced in the late 1980s with the inevitability of being held accountable for outcomes far more complex than previously realized, and for which traditional modes of assessment would be insufficient, we in education began to cast about for assessment alternatives. What we found and set our hearts upon having was not new, but it seemed to hold the promise of providing the richer kind of information about student achievement that we wanted and needed. We discovered the many faces of performance assessment methodology: direct writing assessments, portfolios, exhibitions, demonstrations, and so on.

Essentially, what we discovered was a methodology that held the promise of reflecting the very outcomes that could not be translated into objective test items, such as the ability to write, speak (in English and other languages), read aloud, demonstrate complex achievement-related behaviors, and create complex achievement-related products. We discovered a set of assessment methods that have one important feature in common: they all rely on teacher observation and professional judgment as the basis for evaluating student achievement. Subjective assessment, a method previously judged dangerous at best and unacceptable at worst because it was so fraught with the dangers of bias, came to be seen not only as a viable option, but for many highly valued outcomes, as the *only* acceptable way to assess.

The inevitable result of this discovery has been to bring two eras of educational assessment into direct conflict with one another, yielding an identity crisis in assessment in American education.

Time for Reflection

Performance assessment requires that teachers observe student achievement and make judgments as to whether standards have been met. However, there are circumstances that might make these subjective judgments incorrect. What do you perceive to be potential problems with subjective assessment? What can cause us to misjudge student achievement?

CLASSROOM ASSESSMENT IN TRANSITION

Changing Roles

One dimension of the identity crisis in assessment has been confusion about assessment roles and responsibilities. Without doubt, the most important role changes are occurring for those not traditionally thought of as assessment experts—classroom teachers.

For example, in the old era, teachers were not seen as needing to know a great deal about assessment. (Remember, educators had devised the objective paper and pencil test to counter the perceived inadequacy of classroom assessments.) In the new era, however, our perceptions of teachers as assessors are changing. Teachers are playing an ever-increasing role in defining the valued outcomes of education through their professional associations and their work in defining curricula. Those who spell out the achievement targets define what is to be assessed. This is why, as a teacher, you must be crystal clear about your expectations of students.

Further, we are just now coming to appreciate teachers for the critical role they have always played. Teachers are, in fact, the "hidden assessors" in our schools, conducting nearly all of the assessments carried out in American education. And those assessments inform virtually all of the instructionally relevant decisions made by students, teachers, and parents. This is why, as a teacher, you must be a competent, confident assessor of student achievement.

But there is yet another, even more important, reason you must become a master assessor of student achievement: You must teach students to be self-assessors—a skill that will form the basis for the future success of outcomes-based education in America. Teachers who possess a clear vision of the meaning of academic success must share that vision with their students for those students to become competent performers. That goal has been reached only when students can recognize deficiencies in their work and know how to fix them. Your assessment role is one of unraveling the assessment mystery for your students.

This brings us to a new task: we must begin to reexamine the student's role in assessment in American education, too. Our comprehensive reexamination of achievement targets over the past decade has revealed that student self-assessment is not just an engaging activity. Rather, it turns out to be the very heart of academic competence.

Let me illustrate. Researchers who have studied the reading process have shown us that individuals, whether children or adults, who cannot monitor their own reading comprehension and adjust reading strategies when they sense that they are not "getting it," cannot become competent readers. Those who cannot self-assess cannot read (Valencia & Pearson, 1987). On another front, we now know that writers who cannot monitor the quality and effectiveness of their own written communication, and know how to fix it when it isn't "working" cannot become competent writers. Self-assessment is the very heart of the writing process (Hillocks, 1986).

Stated generally, any students who must wait for their teacher to tell them that they have done well in order to know that have not yet learned to hit the target, because they cannot recognize quality performance when it has been exhibited. For this reason, effective outcomes-based education requires competent student assessors.

Similarly, we cannot pass completely into the new era of assessment until the assessment role of the principal changes. The ability to interpret and use building-level achievement test data is no longer enough. If principals are to support teachers in productive ways, they must be capable of leading in classroom assessment, too—a part of instruction that we have said can command as much as one-third to one-half of a teacher's professional time. This means principals must be sufficiently versed in the meaning and application of the basic principles of sound assessment to make that arena of professional practice a prominent part of their supervision of teachers. That means being able to evaluate and promote sound assessments in those teachers' classrooms.

Time for Reflection

Have you ever been called upon to assess your own achievement in school? What was that experience like for you? What form of achievement did you self-assess? Were you accurate in your assessment? Did you know how to carry out such an assessment? What help did you receive from your teacher? What effect did that assessment have on you, as compared to when you were assessed by others?

Changing the Practices

Changes in assessment roles and responsibilities will not be enough, however. We must also change the manner in which we define and conduct the assessment process itself. Four specific and interrelated changes are needed. They are listed in Figure 2–3 and addressed in detail below.

First, we must start thinking of assessment purposes as extending far beyond just accountability. The assessment process can serve both as an instructional tool

- Assessment serves both instructional and accountability functions.
- Valuable assessment information filters down from large-scale assessment contexts and up from the classroom.
- Assessment works best when students understand the achievement to be assessed well before assessment.
- Assessments can rely on a wide variety of methods, not just multiple-choice tests.

Figure 2-3
Important Changes in Our View of Assessment

and as the basis for determining the effectiveness of schools. Both are important uses! However, they are different. They serve different users with different information for different reasons. As a result, they are planned by different assessors, administered under different conditions, and used in fundamentally different ways. Further, they require different preparation to develop and carry out, and different definitions of the meaning of quality assessment. These differences must be honored and limited assessment resources must be divided equally between them so as to assure the quality of each.

Second, we must start thinking of assessment as being far more than just a large-scale testing enterprise in which data are gathered in a centralized manner and then filtered down to other levels of decision making. Rather, we must expand our visions of assessment to consider the potential of assessment systems in which data are gathered at the classroom level and are aggregated upward for decision making at other levels. Such systems could be designed to produce information on student achievement that is at least as sound as that resulting from currently popular top-down systems and would have the decided advantage of offering teachers much-needed training in assessment processes they could then use on an ongoing basis.

Third, we must stop thinking of assessment as being fair or rigorous only if the achievement target is a mystery to the student. For instance, as mentioned earlier, when I ask teachers how many can tell me what is tested on the Scholastic Aptitude Test (SAT, also called the College Boards), very few have any idea. In fact, if they knew what was tested, they would teach students by concentrating on those things and everyone might score higher, thus reducing the variation in student achievement. But if we reduce variation, sorting would become much more difficult. So we keep the target of the assessment a mystery, allowing two sources of variation in student performance to contribute to the spread of student scores: variation due to the student's ability to figure out the target and variation due to the student's ability to deliver.

This represents an example of a sorting-era application of assessment. However, our mission is no longer to conduct a sorting exercise; rather, it is to ensure competence. This requires that the target be made clear to examinees, so they can zero in on it and work away until they hit it. For this reason, we must begin to think of assessments not as mysterious events, but rather as events where all involved do everything possible within the constraints of ethical standards and the principles of sound instruction and assessment to maximize student performance.

In short, we have reached an era in American education where attainment of outcomes is the primary purpose of schools and only assessments that focus clearly on specified educational outcomes can serve to measure success in such a context.

Time for Reflection

During your life as a student, have you ever worked with a teacher who was difficult to "read" when it came to exams—a teacher who never seemed to help you anticipate what was coming on upcoming test? What effect did that have on your learning in that class?

Table 2-1

Changing Assessment Roles and Practices

Changing Roles	Former	Current
Teacher	Teach	Define outcomes
		Teach
		Conduct the primary assessments
Student	Be assessed	Assess self and peers
Principal	Interpret standardized test results	Interpret results and provide support in classroom assessment
Changing Practices	**Former**	**Current**
Purposes	Accountability	Accountability
		Instruction
Uses	Test results filter from top down	Results filter top down and from classroom up
Targets	General in nature	Highly focused
	Not openly shared	Openly shared with all
Method	Primarily selected response	Primarily essay and performance assessment with some selected response

Fourth, we must start thinking of assessment as far more than just a collection of multiple-choice test items, or as objective tests only. Objective tests can be immensely efficient, and should continue to be used in contexts where the achievement target and practical circumstances allow them to be used well. But when targets require a different mode of assessment, a different mode must be used. For instance, in assessing communication skills, such as writing, speaking, or reading, performance assessments are not just an acceptable option, they are a necessity. Or, when assessing complex problem-solving proficiencies, such as in mathematics or science, it may be necessary to rely on direct personal communication with the student, perhaps via the interview. Sound assessment in the new era will require that we (a) specify clear outcomes, (b) understand the broad array of assessment tools we have at our disposal, and (c) know how to marry the two in ways that make sense. And we must understand that no single mode of assessment can meet all of our needs.

These changing classroom assessment times are summarized in Table 2–1.

CHAPTER SUMMARY: A TIME OF TRANSITION

The world of public school education in America is undergoing revolutionary change. The very role of schools in American society is being redefined. We used to regard students as having been well served when they had been reliably ranked in terms of achievement. No more. In the future, we will regard students, professional educators, and schools as successful only when our students can be judged competent. Thus schools that used to be held accountable for providing quality opportunities will be evaluated in terms of the student outcomes they produce.

Those outcomes used to be defined in terms of a small number of simple achievement targets that remained quite stable over time. In the future, the targets will increase in number and complexity and accelerate in their rate of change. As a result, simple objective tests of the past must be supplemented (not replaced) by a broader array of performance assessment–based methods. Further, the assessment processes that heretofore resided only in the hands of the assessment experts must be placed in the hands of practicing teachers and administrators.

That means those practitioners—you, the teacher and/or supporter of the instructional process—must be capable of ensuring the quality of the assessments used in classrooms and school buildings. Thus the rules of evidence for assuring the quality of an assessment that were the special province of assessment experts must be shared in an understandable and usable form with all concerned with the quality of schools.

These changes reflect our transition into a new era of education and of educational assessment. This transition will bring new roles and responsibilities to all concerned. Policy makers must devise and put in place educational policies that go beyond simply ensuring proper treatment of students to ensuring student competence. Principals must go beyond being school managers to being instructional leaders capable of leading in assessment as well. Teachers must go beyond being givers of information to serving as coaches capable of detecting student needs and ensuring student success through sound classroom assessment integrated into the teaching and learning process. And assessment experts must move beyond serving as sources of data for decision makers to being both sources of data and sources of wisdom about sound assessment and its relationship to instruction.

These are times of rapid and profound change in American education. Nowhere are those changes more apparent than in the field of educational assessment. Your professional challenge is to prepare carefully for the future.

EXERCISES TO ADVANCE YOUR LEARNING

Knowledge Outcomes

1. Briefly outline the history of achievement testing in the United States.
2. List the social forces of the 1920s and 1930s that spawned old-era assessment processes.
3. List the forces that brought an end to the old era and that support the era of performance based assessment.

4. Describe why large-scale, districtwide, statewide, or national standardized tests are insufficient assessment for purposes of local school improvement.

5. Make a comparison chart that relates the old era of assessment to the new, showing similarities and differences.

Reasoning Outcomes

1. Why do we need many different forms of assessment in the classroom? What are the differences in the roles to be played in the classroom by paper and pencil tests and performance assessments, for example?

2. Compare the assessment roles and responsibilities of teachers, students, and principals. How are they alike? How are they different?

Affective Outcomes

1. In your opinion, do you think the changes in the mission of schools from ranking students to ensuring competent students will be positive and productive? Why?

2. In this chapter, we contended that our outcomes will continue to increase in number and complexity. Do you agree? Why?

3. I have argued in the chapter that it is critical for all teachers, administrators, policy makers, and the community to value the full array of assessments we have at our disposal. Do you agree? Why?

4. Do you think we can and should place higher value as a society on the assessment roles teachers, students, and principals play in the future than we have in the past? Why?

5. In your opinion, which of the following is the more important reason for quality classroom assessment? (a) We need quality information for making key decisions. (b) The assessment process can serve as a productive learning experience for students. Why do you feel as you do?

CHAPTER 3

Understanding the Critical Roles
of Assessment

Chapter Objectives

As a result of studying the material presented in Chapter 3, reflecting on that material, and completing the learning exercises at the end of the chapter, you will

1. Master content knowledge:
   a. Identify key differences between large-scale assessment using standardized tests and classroom assessment.
   b. Identify important uses and users of both large-scale and classroom assessment.
2. Be able to use that knowledge to reason as follows:
   a. Understand rationale for the assessment traditions that have characterized education in the United States.
   b. Analyze tests used at all levels to understand their roles in instruction.
   c. Understand the potential negative impacts of poor-quality assessment.
   d. Infer how students might become partners in classroom assessment and why that involvement will be beneficial.
3. Attain the following affective outcomes:
   a. See the value of quality assessment.
   b. Appreciate the roles of assessment users at all educational levels and be predisposed to act on behalf of all quality assessment.
   c. Value student involvement in the classroom assessment process.

Note: The objectives of this chapter do not include the mastery of any process skills or the creation of any products.

To understand the roles of classroom assessment in the teaching and learning process, we must begin by placing this level of assessment in the broader context of all uses for assessment throughout education. We will accomplish this through analyzing two general categories of use: assessment to provide information that informs instructionally relevant decisions, and assessment as a teaching strategy. Both are important. Each set of uses, mastered thoroughly and implemented thoughtfully, can have a profound impact on the nature and quality of instruction. In this chapter, we examine what this means.

We will explore the many levels and kinds of decisions that permeate the school management and instructional processes, and the role of assessment in each. We will see how and when both classroom assessment and centralized, standardized testing come into play. While the spotlight is on classroom assessment in this book, we can come to understand the critical importance of sound assessment at the classroom level only when we see how it relates to its bigger and much more visible relative.

As we discuss assessment as a teaching strategy, we will explore productive ways to bring students into the classroom teaching and learning process in the role of assessors of their own and each other's achievement. As you study and reflect on this facet of the chapter, it will become clear why sound assessment is the key to both sound instruction and student well-being.

CHAPTER ROADMAP

The itinerary for this part of our journey begins with an analysis of the differences between classroom assessment and large-scale standardized testing. We will compare and contrast them in terms of the following:

- the foundational assumptions from which they arise
- their respective definitions of assessment quality
- the assessment methodologies used in each context

With these differences clearly in mind, we will be ready to explore how each can be used in support of student achievement. We will examine three levels of use: instruction, instructional support, and policy. As illustrated in Figure 3–1, sound assessment at these levels is what provides the firm foundation for maximum student achievement. For each level, we will do the following:

- identify the important users of assessment results
- sample the most important uses of assessment
- list some of the key questions each user must answer with assessment results
- specify the kind(s) of assessment information each user needs to make particular decisions

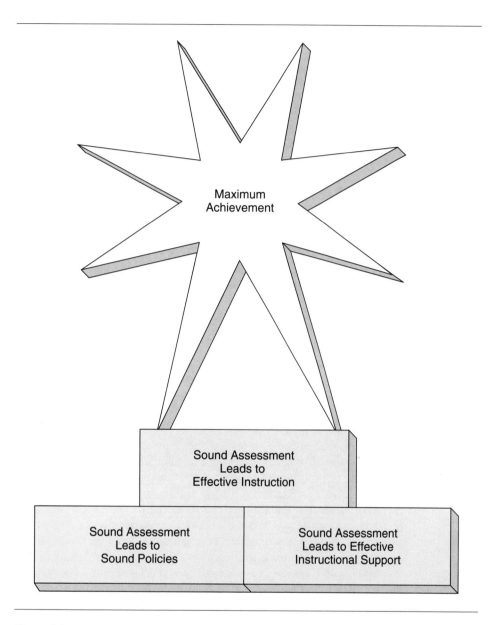

Figure 3-1.
A Concrete Foundation for Maximum Learning

As you shall see, this analysis of users and uses offers a balanced perspective regarding the need for quality at all levels. Both classroom and large-scale assessment serve important purposes. Both make contributions. My purposes are to make clear why standardized testing and classroom assessment are different and to promote clearer understanding of the implications of those differences.

CONTRASTING CLASSROOM AND LARGE-SCALE STANDARDIZED ASSESSMENT

Classroom assessment and standardized testing are different disciplines within the educational assessment field. They arise out of different assumptions about the assessment process, define quality assessment in different ways, and rely on fundamentally different assessment methods.

To explain some of the key differences, let's begin by reflecting on a message from the past. Over fifty years ago, Professor Robert Scates of Duke University wrote eloquently of the differences between the science of objective testing as it emerged in the late 1920s and the art of classroom assessment as carried out by teachers. The lessons he left for us are worth learning today.

A View from the Past

Scates (1943) begins his analysis by pointing out critical differences in background and training between those psychometricians who apply the science of assessment and classroom teachers.[1] Assessment specialists typically are trained in math and science, while teachers are trained in disciplines having to do with interpersonal action.

Differences in Focus.   According to Scates, this difference in training prepares them to attend to and to do different things. For example, their purposes for measuring differ: the scientist seeks to describe, while the teacher seeks to control. The scientist seeks to extract single elements from complex reality, to assess parts, to isolate traits common to all subjects. The teacher, on the other hand, must both understand and describe the complex reality of the individual child, attending to what is unique and changeful. The scientist seeks data to classify, while the teacher seeks information to use in guiding the person to more learning.

Different Methods.   In addition, Scates writes, measurement methods differ. The scientist most commonly relies on one-time observation conducted uniformly across subjects. Comparability of results is paramount so that generalizations can be drawn across subjects. Feedback to the subject is often less important.

The teacher, on the other hand, relies on continuous observation to both assess and evaluate what is unique to the individual. Comparability of data is less important to teachers, and immediate feedback to the student is central to teaching and learning.

Different Assumptions.   Scates asserts that the assumptions upon which measurement rests differ, too. The scientist assumes the underlying meaning of a trait is uniform throughout its range and all that changes over time or across students is the

---

[1]Adapted from "Differences Between Measurement Criteria of Pure Scientists and of Classroom Teachers" by D. E. Scates, from *Journal of Educational Research* (September 1943). Copyright 1943 by Journal of Educational Research.

amount of it any student possesses. Writing proficiency, for example, is always writing proficiency. Over time, students simply learn to write in more contexts.

Teachers, on the other hand, deal with traits that change in their very nature as stages of development unfold within the child. Early childhood writing skills that involve recognizing and making letters and words differ in kind from the skills of composition that characterize the high school English curriculum.

The scientist attends to outcomes that relate only to the discipline being studied, while the teacher attends to outcomes that relate to the realities of the student's life beyond school. The scientist is concerned about how well the subject will do on exercises. The teacher, in contrast, worries about how all the parts come together. As Scates writes:

> The teacher's task is that of the artist—to produce as well as his vision will permit him to see what ought to be produced and as well as his techniques and materials will permit him to follow what his vision pictures. In this process he can find some use for scientific measuring instruments, but they serve only a small portion of his needs, and they are likely to upset his perspective. They will serve, on occasion, as a check on certain limited aspects of what he is trying to do, but he dare not let them shift his attention from the whole picture to the elements that the tests are likely to cover. For he is an integrator, not a scientist. (p. 13)

A Connection to Today.   One need not read Scates too deeply to understand that he was concerned about the centralized, standardized testing programs emerging in schools in the 1930s and 1940s. His was the perspective of the humanist concerned about the child and about the harm testing could do to the well-being of children and teachers. Today, five decades later, many also urge caution when using standardized tests because of their unintended consequences for schools and student well-being (Neil & Medina, 1991; Smith & Rottenberg, 1991).

My intent is not to enter into that argument, as I think debates about which assessment method is best or worst are counterproductive. As you will see, a long list of assessment users need many different kinds of information to meet their various needs. We have a wide range of complex achievement targets to assess. We will need all the tools we have at our disposal to do this job. We cannot afford to throw any—including standardized tests—away. Our challenge is to find ways to use all of these tools well and to use them in balance, as in the school board meeting vignette in Chapter 1.

Because our educational paradigm is evolving rapidly, it is essential that we regard assessment of educational outcomes at all levels with a new and ever more critical eye. I believe that it is critical to follow the trail marked by Scates some fifty years ago, pushing the comparison even further and highlighting additional differences. Only through this kind of analysis can we maintain the balance in assessment perspectives and values that are crucial to student well-being.

More Differences in Assumptions

The underlying assumptions that guide the two types of assessment contain more differences than were noted by Scates. For instance, the role assessment is assumed to play in education differs. Large-scale assessments are seen as the guardians of our educational standards. We use them as hallmarks, as we strive to keep those standards high. That is, we set as our public goal the desire to attain the highest possible test scores.

The role of assessment in the classroom, on the other hand, is to serve as an instructional tool helping teachers meet student needs. Teachers need *accurate* scores for each student, not necessarily the highest possible scores.

Different Goals and Roles.   This leads to profound differences in both the goal and role of the assessor. Often, the covert political goal in the large-scale context, as defined by those in authority, is to attain scores that represent the school program, building, and system in the most positive light. The assessor's challenge often is to obtain the most *positive* data for the assessment resources invested.

The teacher's goal, on the other hand, is to make decisions that benefit students. The challenge in this case is to obtain the most *usable* data for the assessment resource invested.

Very often, the assessment specialist charged with conducting standardized tests acts as the servant of the decision makers, providing the results and then stepping aside. In essence, the data speak for themselves. The teacher, on the other hand, plays all roles, including those of assessor, interpreter, and user of the results. The teacher not only has a vested interest in the results, but the truly effective teacher is a collaborator with the student and parent to attain the highest level of performance possible from each student. In this case, the data speak only when understood in the context of the student whose achievement is reflected therein.

Differences in the Meaning of Quality.   This leads us to another difference: the definition of *sound assessment*. The underlying basis of wisdom that defines the meaning of a quality assessment differs between the two contexts. In the large-scale assessment case, that wisdom is described in the literature of the psychometrician. A good test is one that satisfies clearly articulated validity, reliability, and efficiency standards.

In the classroom, however, the literature that defines a sound assessment is that which describes our understanding of the teaching and learning process. Sound assessments promote learning on the part of the student. This is not to say validity, reliability, and efficiency are unimportant. Certainly, they are critical. But teachers virtually never estimate the technical quality of their assessments as psychometricians do. Teachers often will say an assessment "worked" if that assessment promoted or provided evidence of growth.

To amplify just a bit, for the test technician, the quality of an assessment is a technical matter. The focus of the investigation of quality is on the test. There is the threat of negative sanctions from the measurement community (American Psychological Association, 1985) for those who fail to adhere to published professional standards of test quality.

But for the teacher, quality is not primarily a technical matter. Typically, for teachers it is a people matter. The focus of the investigation of quality is on its impact on students. Assessment works effectively, in the teacher's eye, when it reveals strengths and weaknesses in student performance—when it suggests concrete action on the part of teacher and/or student.

There is virtually never an external review of assessment quality in the classroom, because the sanctity of that classroom has generally been considered inviolate. The only standards normally involved are the teacher's own ethical ones and whatever standards of assessment quality the teacher acquired as a result of professional preparation to teach.

Please understand that this does not mean that teachers should not care about the technical quality of their assessments. They definitely should. The entire point of this book is that, given proper training and support resources, teachers can design and develop sound assessments. But for teachers, the meaning of quality often goes beyond technicalities to issues of student well-being.

More Differences in Methodology

Because classroom and large-scale assessment serve different purposes, they provide different forms of information and must, therefore, rely on different forms of assessment to deliver that information. Let's compare these methods just a bit more.

Differences in Format.   Large-scale assessments tend to rely on the objective paper and pencil test format to produce acceptable data at minimal cost. Huge numbers of tests can be machine-scored very quickly, and computers can generate interpretable score reports with relative ease. It is often the case, out of necessity, that the fidelity of large-scale assessment results be sacrificed somewhat for the sake of economy.

Because of the broad scope and considerable cost of these assessments, they tend to occur infrequently, often no more than once a year. Also, the time allotted for completing them is quite limited, often allowing only minutes per subject matter area tested.

For this reason, very broad achievement targets are defined—often covering two or three grade levels of content with relatively few selected response items. Thus, the content coverage is very shallow. From these samples, then, extrapolations are drawn to broad achievement domains. These tests typically are not high-resolution microscopes.

There are only two kinds of achievement targets that can be assessed in this way. One can assess student mastery of substantive subject matter knowledge and mastery of some important higher-order thinking skills. Since these kinds of targets are valued at almost all grade levels and in almost all subject matter arenas, large-scale assessments can be used to measure important and highly valued educational outcomes. But skill and product targets remain out of reach.

Classroom assessment methods are different. In the classroom, assessment in one form or another is almost continuous. The amount of time allocated for classroom assessment is considerable, often rivaling direct instruction as the most time-consuming activity of the classroom (Stiggins & Conklin, 1992).

Teachers use paper and pencil instruments as soon as students are able to read and respond to them. These include teacher-developed and text-embedded tests and quizzes, homework and seatwork assignments, and even questionnaires. Teachers also rely extensively on observation of and professional judgments about achievement-related products and behaviors, as well as personal communication with students. Examples of the latter include instructional questions, interviews, informal one-on-one discussions, and conversations with others about students. The methods of classroom assessment are far more varied than are those of large-scale assessment, as they are used by teachers more frequently to gather more varied kinds of information.

For this reason, the achievement domains assessed by teachers are much more numerous and precisely defined than are those of the large-scale test developer. Compared to large-scale assessments, many classroom assessments may be regarded as high-resolution microscopes. Still, however, even classroom assessments represent samples of all of the exercises the teacher could have posed given more time. So once again, the teacher must extrapolate to the broader domain. The key difference is that, in the case of classroom assessment, the domain is far narrower.

Because teachers can rely on many methods for data collection, they can assess a broad array of achievement targets. Like the large-scale assessor, they can measure mastery of knowledge and thinking skills using traditional modes of assessment. Unlike large-scale assessors, teachers also rely on direct personal communication with the student and on observations and professional judgments to measure such targets as skills to be exhibited by the student and products to be created by the student that possess certain attributes. Also, unlike the large-scale assessor, the teacher can rely on various kinds of assessment to evaluate affective outcomes: student feelings and dispositions.

Differences in Administration.   Beyond these considerable differences, the conditions of test administration often differ between large-scale and classroom contexts. In large-scale assessment, conditions of administration are standardized to assure comparability of results. Tests often are *speeded,* that is, all students may not finish all exercises. The pace at which students can answer test items is regarded as valuable information for indexing the student's achievement level relative to that of other students.

Classroom assessments, on the other hand, might be standardized for all within the classroom or might be individualized. They might be speeded or the teacher might regard assessments as *power* tests, allotting enough time for each student to attempt each exercise. For the teacher, comparability often gives way to maximizing the student's demonstrated level of achievement. Empathetic teachers often strive to give students the opportunity to succeed—to give them the benefit of the doubt—so as to maximize each student's motivation to continue. The result is a different assessment environment from that of the standardized test.

Differences in Reporting Results.   Further, methods of reporting differ between large-scale and classroom assessments. To begin with, they produce different kinds of results. Large-scale assessments virtually always produce data in the form of a score or profile of scores. All scores are comparable, assuming the test administrator adhered to the standardized procedures. As a result, data can be aggregated from the individual student to the classroom, building, district, state, region, and the nation as a whole. Large-scale assessments report summary scores, often with interpretive aids that permit comparisons of student scores. Since assessments are infrequent, reports of performance on those assessments are infrequent also. Finally, reports often occur well after the assessment has been conducted.

Classroom assessments, on the other hand, may not translate into scores, although they frequently do. They can produce symbols other than numbers that do not lend themselves to summary via mathematical operations. Further, they might result in judgments, insights, and immediate actions on the part of teachers. Not only might they not be comparable for each student, but some assessments might only involve one or a few students, depending on the context. Assessments often have immediate instructional applications. There is rarely a delay of more than a day or two between the assessment and the return of results. Often feedback on results is immediate.

Clearly, classroom and large-scale assessment methods are quite different. These differences are summarized in Table 3–1. Bear them clearly in mind, now, as we review the many users and uses of assessment throughout the educational process.

Table 3–1

Comparing Large-Scale Standardized Assessment and Classroom Assessment

Point of difference	Large-scale	Classroom
Goal	Understand and classify, maintain highest standards	Control and guide
	Obtain highest score	Obtain most accurate score
Focus	Isolated traits common to students tested	Blend of traits withinin each student
	Achievement within disciplines	Skills related to life beyond school
	Traits stable over time	Traits that change over time
Role of Assessor	Uninvolved data collector	Data collector, interpreter, and user
Method of Assessment	One time, infrequent	Continuous
	Tend to be objectively scored	Objective and subjective
	Comparability critical across classrooms	Comparability less important
	A few very efficient modes	Greater variety, less efficient
Administration	Standard for all	May or may not be standard for all in classroom
	Tend to be speeded	Tend toward power
Results	Scores	Scores, descriptions, judgments, profiles, etc.
	Feedback delayed, if offered at all	Feedback immediate
Meaning of quality	Psychometric standards of validity and reliability	Positive impact on student learning
	Defined by assessment field	Defined by each teacher

Time for Reflection

Think of a time in your life as a student when you took an important classroom test prepared and administered by your teacher. Now think of a time when you took an annual standardized test. Describe the differences between these two experiences. How did you prepare for each? How did you feel going into the assessment—confident, anxious, informed about why you were being assessed? What were the differences in how you were informed of results and in how the results were used?

ASSESSMENTS THAT INFORM INSTRUCTIONALLY RELEVANT DECISIONS

If we are to plan instruction to meet student needs, we must ascertain what those needs are. If we seek to find the most effective instructional strategies, we must decide which have the most positive impact on achievement. To make these and other instructionally relevant decisions, we need accurate information on student achievement. Obviously, we obtain that information through both large-scale and classroom assessment. This section provides an overview of these decision-oriented uses of assessment results.

The varied ways that assessment results inform decisions are spelled out in Tables 3–2, 3–3, and 3–4. Taken together, these tables depict the big assessment picture and are intended to promote understanding how each assessment user's roles and responsibilities fit within that picture. They convey a fairly complete list of assessment users and provide a glimpse into the incredible array of important uses of assessment in support of effective schools.

These tables depict three levels at which assessment results can come into play in the instructional process. One level is that of *instruction*. Students, teachers, and parents gather and use the results of student achievement assessment to inform a variety of decisions that influence the outcomes of instruction.

Another level is that of *instructional support*. Decision makers at this level back the teacher up with whatever help may be needed in the form of curricular, professional development, and/or resource support to do the teaching job. Backup may come from the department, building, or district level, or beyond.

The final level of assessment use is the *policy* level. This is where the standards are put in place that govern practice in the school building and in the classroom. Policy influencers, policy makers, and those who enforce policy include the superintendent, the school board, public officials (appointed and elected), and citizens of the community.

Taken together, assessment users in these three categories make the decisions that determine whether schools work. While I obviously have clear opinions about whose decisions are most important, please understand that those values are relative, not absolute. In an absolute sense, all parties listed in Tables 3–2 to 3–4 make important contributions, and their assessment needs all deserve careful attention.

Column one of each table lists the various decision makers whose decisions are (or can be) informed by assessment results. Column two lists samples of the kinds of decisions they make based at least in part on assessment results of some kind. These are not intended to be exhaustive. In column three, I translate each use into a sample question that the user might face in that decision-making context. Ideally, the answer will suggest which course of action to take—the ultimate decision.

To answer each question, the user needs certain kinds of information about students, information reflective of their achievement or feelings. Those information needs are identified in the fourth column. We will explore key dimensions of those information needs after you have an opportunity to examine the tables.

Before continuing, study Table 3–2 carefully. What conclusions or generalizations can you draw from its contents?

We may draw the following generalizations on the basis of Table 3–2:

- All three assessment users make decisions that bear directly on whether instruction produces the desired outcomes.

- At this level, assessment is by and large continuous. This is precisely why classroom assessment events are so much more common than any other kind of assessment.

- At this level, assessment virtually always focuses on the individual student's mastery of specified material. This is why classroom assessment is such a critical ingredient in the outcomes-based education context.

Now turn to Table 3–3 and explore uses of assessment at the level of the instructional leader. See if you see any patterns. Do this before you read further.

We may observe the following patterns in the information presented in Table 3–3:

- In almost every case the focus of the decisions to be made is the instructional program or the teacher, not the individual student.

- Assessment need only be periodic—not continuous.

- Attention at this level is given to assessments of student performance summarized over groups.

- At this level, heavy reliance is placed on the use of assessment results in which assessment instruments or procedures are held constant across classrooms. In other words, some standardization is required if sound decisions are to result.

Before you continue reading, examine Table 3–4, again seeking patterns and generalizations.

We may make the following generalizations on the basis of the information in Table 3–4:

- The focus is on broad domains of achievement, not specific objectives of instruction.

- As with the instructional support level, periodic assessment seems to suffice.

Table 3-2
Users and Uses of Assessment Results—Instructional Level

Users	Sample Uses	Key Question(s) to be Answered	Information Needed
Student	Track own success	Am I meeting the teacher's standards?	Ongoing assessment of mastery of required material
	Identify own needs	What help do I need to succeed?	Sequential assessment of building blocks of competence
	Connect effort to results	Does my work pay off?	Continuous assessment of mastery of material student is trying to learn
	Plan for educational and vocational needs	What will be the next steps in my learning?	Assessment of outcomes that are prerequisites for later possibilities
Teacher	Identify needs of individuals	What does this student need help with?	Continuous assessment of individual mastery
	Identify needs of class or group	What do these students need help with?	Continuous assessment summarized over group
	Group students	Who among my students should work together?	Periodic assessment of individual mastery (if grouped by achievement)
	Grade	What grade should appear in the report card?	Summary of individual mastery of required material
	Evaluate instruction	Did my teaching strategies work?	Continuous assessment of group performance
	Evaluate self	How do I need to develop to be a better teacher?	Continuous assessment of group performance
Parent	Track child's success	Is my child succeeding in school?	Continuous feedback on student's mastery of material
	Identify needs	What does my child need in order to succeed?	Continuous feedback on student's mastery of material
	Evaluate teacher	Is my child's teacher(s) doing the job?	Continuous feedback on student's mastery of material
	Evaluate school	Is this school (district) working for my family?	Periodic comparison of school performance with other schools

Table 3-3
Users and Uses of Assessment Results—Instructional Leadership/Support Level

Users	Sample Uses	Key Question(s) to be Answered	Information Needed
Principal/Vice Principal	Evaluate instructional program	Is instruction in particular areas producing results?	Periodic assessment of group achievement
	Evaluate teachers	Is the teacher producing results?	Periodic assessment of group achievement
		Does the teacher meet minimal performance standards?	
		What kinds of professional development would help this teacher?	
	Allocate resources	How shall we spend building resources in support of instruction?	Periodic assessment of group achievement
Support Teacher (mentor, lead teacher, department chair)	Assist new teachers	What does this teacher need to assure competence?	Continuous assessment of group achievement
	Support instructional program	Which teacher(s) need what help to do the job?	Periodic assessment of group achievement
Counselor/ Psychologist	Identify students with special needs	Who needs (can have access to) special support services such as remedial programs?	Periodic assessment of group achievement
	Match student to program	What student should be assigned to which teachers to optimize results?	Periodic assessment of individual achievement
Curriculum Director	Evaluate program quality	Is the program in a particular area of instruction working?	Periodic assessment of group achievement

Table 3-4
Uses and Users of Assessment Results—Policy Level

Users	Sample Uses	Question(s) to be Answered	Information Needed
Superintendent	Evaluate program	Are programs producing student learning?	Periodic assessment of group achievement of district curriculum
	Evaluate principals	Is the building principal producing results?	Periodic assessment of group achievement of district/building outcomes
	Allocate resources	Which schools need/deserve more or fewer resources?	Periodic assessment of group achievement of district curriculum
School board	Evaluate program	Are students in the district learning?	Periodic assessment of group achievement
	Evaluate superintendent	Is the superintendent producing results?	Periodic assessment of group achievement
State department of education	Evaluate program	Are programs across the state producing results?	Periodic assessment of group achievement of state curriculum
Citizen/Legislator (state or national)	Evaluate program	Are students in our schools attaining outcomes that will allow them to be effective citizens?	Periodic assessment of group achievement of valued outcomes

- Also as with the support level, results summarized across students fill the need.
- And finally, at this level too, assessment procedures must be standardized to some degree across contexts and over time. The decisions to be made require it.

Having seen and reflected upon these three tables, do any general conclusions come to mind regarding the role of assessment in determining and enhancing the effectiveness of schools? Try these and see if you agree:

- Obviously, the assessment process is intricately woven into school functioning. Often the degree of complexity of this portrait of assessment is surprising to educators. Nevertheless, as teachers and instructional leaders, we must all face the complexity and come to terms with it.
- Students count on many people to use sound assessment results in productive ways. All of the questions listed in column three are critical to student well-being. This is why we must continually strive to achieve high-quality assessment.
- Considering the tables together, it is clear that both information gathered continuously on individual student mastery of specified material *and* information gathered periodically for the purpose of comparing students have vital roles, and that both must reflect sensitivity to the principles of sound assessment.

Given this summary of all of the decision-oriented users and uses of assessment, it becomes clear that any assessment policy, any educator, or any educational assessment practice that fails to acknowledge the valuable role of classroom and centralized assessment places students *directly* in harm's way.

USING ASSESSMENT AS A TEACHING TOOL

Assessment helps to make instruction most effective when it produces sound information for sound decision making, as specified above. But Tables 3–2 to 3–4 don't provide the complete picture of the ways assessment can enhance learning in the classroom. Indeed, the very process of assessing—over and above the results it produces—can provide great motivation for students to learn and can promote that learning in many concrete and specific ways.

Methods That Have Stood the Test of Time

Some of the most useful ways of using assessment in instruction have been standard operating procedure for teachers for decades. In addition, we have recently seen a blossoming of exciting new ways of bringing students into the assessment process.

One of the most common and accepted ways to use assessment to promote learning is to use it as a source of motivation arising from the promise or threat of an examination in the future. For students who care to perform well, exam time is heavy-duty study time—time to cram, time for "all nighters." Clearly, we use assessments to motivate.

Another way to mix assessment and instruction is through the use of practice tests, which give students the opportunity to analyze their achievement and prepare one final study push before the "real" test.

Yet another simple way to use the assessment process to enhance learning is by reviewing tests. By carefully going over exams with students after returning them, we hope to reinforce important concepts, address misunderstandings, and thus continue their learning.

Two more ways in which we use assessment events as teaching and learning tools are open-book exams (where new material is learned during the process of preparing responses) and take-home exams (which prolong the learning process, in effect, and urge students to tap resources found outside the classroom).

These strategies integrate assessment and instruction. In a sense, they make the two indistinguishable. However, none of them promote student learning as effectively as does making students full partners in the process of assessing their own learning.

New Methods for Changing Times

We set students up for success when we make sure they know and understand what it means to succeed. We set them up for success when we show them the target, provide practice in shooting at it, and provide an assessment forum for them to demonstrate proficiency. By the same token, we reduce their chances of hitting the target when we keep them from understanding what it looks like.

Time for Reflection

Can you think of a time in your school years when you were left in the dark about an achievement target you were supposed to hit? What was the effect of this lack of vision on your preparation and/or success on subsequent assessment?

Those concerned with student attainment of specific outcomes can take advantage of such open channels of communication by building a special kind of teacher-student working relationship, in which we supplant a power relationship with one of collaboration. The relationship in which the teacher is the possessor of mysterious wisdom and the student's job is to solve the mystery is replaced by one in which student and teacher work together to find a common meaning of successful achievement and to help the student attain that goal. The teacher holding and manipulating all the power cards gives way to shared power and, as a result, the total amount of learning power brought to bear in the service of student achievement is greatly increased for both teacher and student.

This means that, when I teach my assessment course, I cannot succeed until I possess a clear vision of what my students must know and be able to do to become competent assessors. Further, neither my students nor I succeed until each of them not only shares my vision, but can translate it into action by producing the highest-quality assessments possible. I will not be the very best teacher I can be until every one of my students can hit the target *and knows it.*

We have many means at our disposal for setting students up for success in this way. For example, we may do any of the following:

- Bring them into the process of setting targets, such as defining content to be mastered, skills to be demonstrated, and problems to be solved.

- Engage them in designing, developing, administering, scoring, and interpreting the results of practice assessments.

- Have them play a role in developing the performance criteria and rating procedures to be used in carrying out performance assessments.

- Set them to work cooperatively to internalize standards of quality and evaluate their own and each others' achievement.

This list could go on and on. As we progress, we will consider many examples of practical ways to turn the assessment process over to learners, to put the standards of quality in their hands, to eliminate the mystery of success in school, and to make them full partners in the assessment process. For now, suffice to say, emphatically, that assessment is no longer merely a tool for collecting data.

Time for Reflection

Can you think of a time in your educational experience when your teacher involved you in the design of the assessment you would take? What role(s) did you play? What effect did this participation have on your motivation to succeed?

CHAPTER SUMMARY: SOUND ASSESSMENT BECOMES ESSENTIAL

Without question effective, efficient, productive instruction is impossible without sound assessment. The very fabric of the American educational system, from the classroom to the boardroom to the halls of educational policy at the highest levels, is held together by threads of assessment. While our purposes for assessing and our assessment methods may differ across levels, the decisions they lead to must be made with the best interests of students clearly in mind.

We have explored the array of differences between and among the assessments used at both classroom and policy levels. They arise from different needs, rely on different procedures, lead to different interpretations and uses, and vary greatly in scope and depth. Nevertheless, all are important. All are useful. All must meet standards of quality.

As educators, we have a strong tendency to be parochial in our point of view about assessment, attending only to our own special corner of the teaching and learning world. This chapter is intended to represent and encourage a more worldly view. Those of us who teach must realize that other decision makers at other levels also need assessment results. While their tests tend to be different in form and tend to have less direct impact on student learning, still they are worth doing for all the reasons given herein.

By the same token, those in positions of school management and policy making must also acknowledge the supremely important role of classroom assessment. Students, teachers, and parents are decision makers, too, and are therefore critical users of assessment information. Our assessment traditions have neither included nor valued such a multifaceted view of the assessment process and its role in instruction. As a result, our allocations of assessment resources have not reflected a balance of concern for both large-scale and classroom assessment.

When we permit the breadth and depth of our vision of assessment to stretch from students in the classroom to policy makers in the board room to legislators in the chambers of political power, we begin to understand why assessment competence is so critical for professional educators and why basic assessment literacy is so important for those who support the educational enterprise. Sound assessment at all levels is critical to student well-being, and to effective schools.

EXERCISES TO ADVANCE YOUR LEARNING

Knowledge Outcomes

1. Study Tables 3–2, 3–3, and 3–4 until you can reconstruct them from memory. Never lose this sense of the diversity of needs for assessment results at many levels for many purposes.

2. Reread the section comparing standardized and classroom assessment and construct a simple summary table in your own words listing the differences between the two.

3. List as many ways as you can for making assessment a part of the learning process—not just as a source of scores and grades.

Reasoning Outcomes

1. Professor Scates noted key differences between standardized and classroom assessment some fifty years ago. He pointed out the dangers of overlooking these differences and urged that attention be given to assuring the quality of both. Yet, over the decades, we have neglected the quality of classroom assessment in favor of the allocation of resources for high-quality standardized testing. Why do you think this has been the case?

2. Those who advocate doing away with standardized tests often argue that they fail to reflect important outcomes. Find a sample of a commercially published

standardized test battery, check its user's guide, and examine some test items. What outcomes are tested? Are they important, in your opinion? Why?

3. Identify as many reasons as you can why involving students in the process of developing, administering, scoring, and interpreting results of classroom assessment might enhance their motivation to succeed.

Affective Outcomes

1. Some contend that to assess student achievement at all is inhumane. "Judge not lest ye be judged," they might say. Others contend that the inhumanity arises out of poor-quality assessments and not out of the assessment act itself. With whom do you agree? Why?

2. Do you feel standardized tests are, in fact, overemphasized in our school culture and society? Why?

3. Do you think students can or should be made more prominent players in school assessment processes? Why?

CHAPTER 4

Specifying Achievement Targets

Chapter Objectives

As a result of studying the material presented in Chapter 4, reflecting upon that material, and completing the learning exercises at the end of the chapter, you will:

1. Master content knowledge:
   a. Know the important benefits of specifying clear and appropriate outcomes.
   b. State the risks of being explicit about outcomes.
   c. Identify five kinds of achievement targets valued in most classrooms.
   d. Identify sources of information and guidance in selecting and defining valued outcomes.
   e. State various ways to communicate about expected outcomes.
2. Be able to use that knowledge to reason as follows:
   a. Translate each of the five kinds of outcomes discussed in this chapter into real examples of significant targets from your own school experience.
   b. Understand the relationships that exist between and among the five kinds of achievement targets.
   c. Understand the impact on student well-being of trying to assess an outcome we, as teachers, do not understand.
3. Attain the following affective outcomes:
   a. Value as useful and worthy of development all levels of thinking, reasoning, and problem solving.

   b. Regard it as essential that all teachers develop or select a coherent defini-
       tion of the meaning of reasoning and problem solving in their classroom.

Note: The objectives of this chapter do not include the mastery of any process
skills or the creation of any products.

How is the journey progressing for you so far? I hope the context of classroom assessment is becoming clearer. Thus far, we have established that
these are times of both stability and change in the world of assessment.

Those things that will remain stable relate primarily to the purposes for
assessment (i.e., the manner in which assessments are integrated into the teaching
and learning process). Assessment results will continue to be used at a variety of
levels, with students, teachers, and parents heading the list of most important users.
The most prominent changes, on the other hand, include shifts in mission of
schools, in the meaning of sound assessment, and in the locus of assessment
responsibility.

As schools become performance-driven institutions and as responsibility for the
design and management of programs continues to shift to schools and classrooms,
the need for assessments reflective of specific learning outcomes will intensify. Assessments will serve to do far more than sort. Further, the responsibility for assessment will continue to shift from assessment specialists to teachers and those local
educators that support classroom instruction.

CHAPTER ROADMAP

In this chapter, we continue with the theme of change. We will address what is perhaps both the single most important key to sound assessment and the greatest stumbling block to achieving the quality assessments we need: the definition of the
achievement targets or educational outcomes to be assessed. Because we live in
times of rapid change in the definition of what it means to be a successful student,
it is becoming more and more imperative that we stay in touch with the evolution
of thinking about important targets.

In Chapter 1, we described high-quality assessments as those that arise from
clearly articulated achievement targets, reflect those targets with proper assessment
methods, sample student performance on the valued targets properly, and control
sources of interference that cause mismeasurement. Number one, both on this list
and in the practice of sound classroom assessment, is the specification of an appropriate achievement target. Our challenge is to come to consensus on a clear set of
achievement expectations for students.

Assessors who cannot define student characteristic(s) to be assessed will have
great difficulty picking a proper assessment method, defining a proper sample of
performance, and minimizing problems within the assessment itself. Neither can they

share a clear vision of success with their students or select promising instructional strategies. The achievement *target* is the heart of the matter!

For example, a teacher faced with the responsibility of evaluating student writing proficiency who lacks a clear vision of what good writing looks like will be ineffective. Regardless of the subject or level of education, only those with sharp visions of valued outcomes can effectively and efficiently assess student attainment of those outcomes.

For this reason, we will devote this entire chapter to defining achievement targets for purposes of assessment. More specifically, we will explore the following:

- the challenges and benefits of defining clear and specific achievement expectations
- the various types of achievement targets to be defined for assessment
- information sources to tap for assistance in defining our valued educational outcomes
- strategies and methods to use in sharing information about achievement targets, once defined

If you are ready, then, let us continue.

CHALLENGING OUTDATED VALUES ABOUT OUTCOMES

In previous decades, it might have been acceptable to define the valued outcomes of school as "readin', ritin', and 'rithmetic." As we plan schools for the twenty-first century, however, the three Rs, while remaining as important as ever, are insufficient as the definition of our hopes for student achievement.

As we have established already, the decade of the 1980s was a time of reexamining valued outcomes. That reexamination continues today, as schools, districts, states, and even nations debate their achievement expectations.

Three Difficult Challenges

In this context, educators are having to confront three challenges in defining outcomes. The first is public debates about what those outcomes should be. We are a pluralistic society, with diverse views regarding what should be the final product of schooling. As these debates rage on at many levels, as a classroom teacher or member of the instruction support team, you must keep one key point clearly in mind: your students cannot wait for the debates to end. They are counting on you to guide them to the targets that define success *now*. They are expecting you to either (a) know where they are going, or (b) know how to help them figure it out for themselves.

For this reason, and pending consensus about outcomes among our constituents, each of us must have a clear sense of what we believe our students need to know and know how to do. Later in this chapter, I will offer suggestions for achieving this. But for now, just remember, the students who show up in classrooms to-morrow cannot wait for our lofty public dialogue to be completed. They need to learn to read, write, speak, listen, do math, do science, speak second languages, run computers now—not sometime in the uncertain future.

The second challenge we face related to the definition of outcomes to be as-sessed, as mentioned in Chapter 2, is that educational targets are now perceived to be far more complex than previously realized. For example, we only recently have come to understand the multidimensional aspects of the reading, writing, and math-ematics problem-solving processes. For this reason, it is increasingly important that we strive to understand this complexity and learn to translate it into sound assess-ments and instruction.

The third challenge we face is an accelerating rate of change in both the num-ber and complexity of school outcomes. The current pace of technological change is mind boggling, and all indications are that its momentum will continue. We have little idea what people will be hired to do in the twenty-first century, when today's kindergartners graduate from high school. For this reason, we must strive to help our students become lifelong, self-assessing learners who can keep track of their own alignment with changing times. As Figure 4–1 illustrates, successful students are those who believe in their own capabilities.

Figure 4–1
The Meaning of Academic Success

In the face of all of these challenges, it becomes your responsibility as a teacher to address these fundamental questions:

- Do you know what it is you want your students to know and to be able to do?
- Can you clearly articulate your educational vision to yourself, your peers, and your community?
- Can you define success for your students in terms they understand?
- Can you provide an environment within which your students can understand their own success?

If your honest answer to all these questions is yes, you are ready to design assessments. If your response is no, or if you feel uncertain, you have more preparation ahead.

Time for Reflection

Take a few moments and reflect on the questions posed above. How clear is your vision of the various outcomes you will be expected to help students deliver? List the subjects you will teach by grade level and try to define a few of your achievement expectations in each area in concise language. Do you know what it means to be good at these things?

The Benefits of Clear and Appropriate Targets

Any energy you invest in becoming clear about those outcomes will pay big dividends at assessment time. Here are three benefits that will result if you can state your instructional responsibilities in clear terms.

Benefit 1: Limits to Teacher Accountability.   One major benefit of defining specific achievement targets is that you define the limits of your professional responsibility. These specific limits on your responsibility provide you with a standard by which to gauge your own success as a teacher. In short, it helps you control your own professional destiny.

With clearly stated outcomes in hand—outcomes that have been verified as appropriate by your supervisors—if all goes well, you will be able to say, "Look, I am a successful teacher. My students have attained the achievement targets that were assigned to me as my instructional responsibility." Hopefully, you will gain both the internal and external rewards of your own clearly defined and documented success.

From a slightly different point of view, in effect, this prevents you from being trapped with unlimited accountability; where, by default, you are held responsible for producing in your students virtually any human characteristic that anyone has ever defined as desirable! No one can hope to succeed under the weight of such expectations. There will always be someone out there pointing to some valued outcome, claiming that schools failed them. This is a trap to which many educators fall prey. Clear targets set limits and set teachers and schools up for success by defining and delimiting responsibilities.

Acknowledging the Risks.   However, we would be naive if we failed to acknowledge that the clear and public definition of outcomes carries with it potential downside risks for teachers. Accountability is a double-edged sword. To the extent that you are clear and specific about the outcomes that you take on as your instructional responsibility, you open yourself up to the possibility that some of your students may not be able to hit the target after instruction, and there will exist concrete, irrefutable assessment evidence of this. There will be no hiding. In effect, your supervisor may be able to use your own focused, high-quality classroom assessment to muster evidence that you did not succeed in doing what you were hired to do—produce achievement results.

As a community of professionals, I think we need to face this possibility: If I succeed as a teacher and my students hit the target, I want credit and reward for that success. If my students fail to hit the target I want to know it, and I want to know why they failed.

I can think of five possible reasons why my students might not learn:

1. They lacked the prerequisites needed to succeed.
2. I didn't understand the target to begin with, and so could not convey it appropriately.
3. My instructional methods—strategies and materials—were inappropriate.
4. My students lacked motivation.
5. Some force(s) outside of school and beyond my control interfered and inhibited learning.

As a professional educator whose students failed to hit the target, I must know which problem(s) operated in my case if I expect to remedy the situation. Only then can I make the kinds of decisions and take the kinds of action that will promote success for me and my students.

For example, if reason number one applies, I need to talk with my colleagues at lower grades to discuss how our respective curricula mesh. If reasons two or three apply, I have to take responsibility for needing some pretty serious professional development. If reason number four applies, I may need to combine investigation of why my students lack motivation with self-analysis of my own professional development in motivating students. If reason number five applies, I need to contact the community beyond school to seek solutions.

Time for Reflection

What other reasons can you think of to explain why students might fail? What action might you take to counter each if it came up?

Note that I can choose the proper corrective action if and only if I take the risks of (a) gathering dependable information about student success or failure using my own high-quality classroom assessments, and (b) becoming enough of a classroom researcher to ferret out the causes of student failure. If I as a teacher simply bury my head in the sand and blithely blame my students for not caring or not trying, I may doom them to long-term failure for reasons beyond their control. Thus, when they fail, I must risk finding out why. If it is my fault or I can contribute to fixing the problem in any way, I must act.

I believe that the probability of the downside risk ever coming into play is greatly reduced when I start out with clear and specific targets. If I can share the vision with my students, they can hit it! If *I* have no target, how can *they* hit it? When I have a vision of success, we both have a high probability of succeeding. This brings us to the next benefit.

Benefit 2: Limits to Student Accountability.   Only when I have a clear sense of the following am I in a position to share the meaning of success with my students:

- knowledge my students need to master
- kinds of problems they need to be able to solve
- skills they must be able to demonstrate
- products they are to create
- affective targets to be attained

If I can help them internalize those expectations, I set them up to take responsibility for their own success. The motivational implications of this for students can be immense.

Personalize this! Say you are a student facing a test. A great deal of material has been covered. You have no idea what will be emphasized on the test. You study your heart out—but, alas, you concentrate on the wrong material. Nice try, but you fail.

Time for Reflection

How do you feel when this happens? How are you likely to behave the next time a test comes up under these same circumstances?

Now, say you are facing another test. A great deal of material has been covered. But your teacher, who has a complete understanding of the field, points out the parts that are critical for you to know. The rest will always be there in the text for you to refer to when you need it. Further, the teacher provides lots of practice in applying the knowledge in solving real-world problems and emphasizes that this is a second key outcome of the course. You study in a very focused manner, concentrating on the important material and its application. Good effort—you succeed.

Time for Reflection

Again, how do you feel? How are you likely to behave the next time a test comes up under these circumstances?

Given clear requirements for success, students are better able to gauge the appropriateness of their own preparation and thus gain control over their own academic well-being.

Benefit 3: More Manageable Teacher Workload.   As previously mentioned in our research on the task demands of classroom assessment, my colleagues and I determined that typical teachers can spend as much as one-third to one-half of their available professional time involved in assessment-related activities. That's a lot of time! In fact, in many classrooms it is entirely too much time.

One of the keys to minimizing this time commitment is clear achievement targets. Here's why: Any assessment is a sample of all the questions we could have asked if the test could be infinitely long. But since time is always limited, we can never probe all important dimensions of achievement. So we sample, asking as many questions as we can within the allotted time. A sound assessment asks a representative set of questions, allowing us to draw inferences about student performance on the entire domain of material from that student's performance on the shorter sample.

If we have set clear limits on our valued target, then we have set a clear sampling frame. This allows us to sample with maximum efficiency and confidence (i.e., to gather just enough information on student achievement without wasting time over testing). Let me illustrate.

If I want my students to master specific content knowledge, I can devise the most powerful (representative and efficient) test of that knowledge most easily when I have (a) set clearly defined limits on the size of that domain, (b) established which elements of that knowledge are most important for them to master for later learning, and (c) sampled those elements.

Similarly, if I select an achievement target in the arena of reasoning and problem solving, I will be confident of student mastery of those skills most quickly (i.e., based on the fewest possible exercises) if I am crystal clear about my definitions of *reasoning* and *problem solving*. If my vision of success is vague, I will need more evidence gathered over a longer period of time before I feel certain that my students have achieved.

Further, when I have a clear sense of the desired ends, I can use the assessment methods that are most efficient for the situation. In the next chapter, we will discuss four alternative assessment methods. I will argue that different methods fit different kinds of targets. It will become clear that some methods produce certain kinds of achievement information more efficiently than others. Skillful classroom assessors match methods to targets so as to produce maximum information with minimum invested assessment time. This is part of the art of classroom assessment. Your skill as an artist increases with the clarity of your vision of expected outcomes.

There you have three compelling reasons to invest energy up front to become clear about the meaning of success in your classroom. To make it easier for you to define success for yourself and your students, let's set some limits for the range of possible targets.

TYPES OF ACHIEVEMENT TARGETS

I hope I have convinced you that clearly defined outcomes are essential. If so, you might now wonder, How do I specify my targets? What is it that I must describe about them? The first step in answering these questions is to understand that we ask our students to attain a variety of outcomes. Our challenge as teachers is to understand which of these is relevant for our particular students.

As my colleagues and I analyzed the task demands of classroom assessment, we tried to discern patterns of outcome definition that link assessment to instruction in comfortable ways—ways that seemed to make sense to teachers (Stiggins & Conklin, 1992). One such pattern emerged as we talked with teachers about their common dissatisfaction with district standardized testing programs. Published standardized tests, they contended, didn't begin to cover the full range of outcomes that they valued. Thus, linking results to instruction seemed impossible to them.

To better comprehend what they meant, we collected, studied, categorized, and tried to understand the various kinds of valued outcomes reflected in teachers' classroom activities and assessments. The following major categories or types of achievement targets emerged as important:

- student mastery of substantive subject matter *knowledge*
- student ability to use that knowledge to *reason* and solve problems
- the ability to demonstrate certain achievement-related *skills,* such as read aloud, speak in a second language, perform psychomotor acts
- the ability to create certain kinds of achievement-related *products,* such as samples of writing, reports, art products
- attainment of certain kinds of feelings or *affective* states, such as attitudes, interests, motivational predisposition

As you will see, these categories are quite useful in thinking about classroom assessment because they seem to include all possible valued outcomes, are easy to understand, are related to one another in some very interesting ways and—here's the important part—have clear links to different kinds of assessment.

But before we discuss assessment, let's understand these categories of targets, or outcomes, more thoroughly. We will discuss them in some detail now, and will devote a chapter to the assessment of each in Part 3 of this text.

Knowledge Targets

All achievement arises out of a basis of knowledge on the part of the problem solver or skillful performer. In all classroom reasoning contexts, success depends in part on the student's mastery of the facts, information, procedures, conceptual relationships, and so on needed to solve the problem; that is, it depends on mastery of some substantive subject matter knowledge.

We cannot, for example, solve math problems without a foundational knowledge of math facts, number systems, and/or problem solving procedures. Nor can we speak a foreign language without mastery of its vocabulary, syntax, and structure. It is impossible to write an essay in English without a practical knowledge of letters, words, sentences, paragraphs, and grammar, as well as knowledge of how to write in an organized manner. We cannot read with comprehension if we lack sufficient background knowledge about the material presented in the text. We cannot respond to an essay question on the Civil War in history without access to facts about that event. In every performance domain, there is a basis of knowledge underpinning all competence.

Let me hasten to add, however, that this foundation of knowledge is never sufficient for finding solutions to complex problems; the necessary knowledge must be combined with appropriate reasoning proficiencies to succeed. The point is, however, that there is no such thing as content-free thinking.

At any point in the instructional process, a teacher concerned about student attainment of the building blocks to competence might legitimately hold that the valued outcome is for students to master some important basic knowledge (i.e., facts and information). At such a time, assessment of student mastery of that knowledge might very well make sense.

Please notice that I did not say that the teacher might expect students to *memorize* knowledge. I said *master* important knowledge—meaning to gain control over the specified material. That control can be gained either through memorization or through the effective use of appropriate reference materials.

Here is a key thought to bear in mind as you plan educational outcomes for the twenty-first century: The world does not operate solely on memorized information. To see what I mean, just try to fill out your income tax form next year without looking at the reference guide.

This is the information age. We're generating new information in almost all fields of study at record rates. Globally, the amount of available information doubles every few years. It is quite literally impossible for anyone to keep up with it.

As a result, we have learned to use computers and other reference technologies to help us gain access to the most current knowledge *when* we need it. Our intent is to maintain access to the important material only for as long as we need it, then to let the knowledge go. This is an appropriate way of mastering (meaning gaining control over) some substantive subject matter knowledge in this day and age.

In short, this "knowledge" category of educational outcomes includes both those achievement targets (core facts, information, and relationships) that students memorize, and those targets that students tap as needed through research. Both are important. Both present special classroom assessment challenges.

Time for Reflection

Identify the area of academic performance which you regard as your greatest strength. How strong is your underlying knowledge base in that area? Think about your weakest area. How strong is your knowledge base there? How critical is a strong, basic content knowledge to academic success?

Reasoning Targets

Rarely do we (or should we) want students to master content just for the sake of knowing it. It is virtually always the case that we want students to be able to use that information to reason and solve certain kinds of problems. For example, we want them to analyze and solve story problems in math, compare political events or leaders of the past, reason inductively and deductively in science, and evaluate opposing positions on social and scientific issues. We want them to use what they know within the problem context to achieve a desired solution.

If we hold such outcomes as valuable for our students, it is incumbent upon us to define precisely what we mean by reasoning and problem solving. Some teachers create their own definitions of different patterns of reasoning. Others rely on one or more of the many conceptual frameworks scholars have generated to define the thinking and problem-solving processes. Precise definition lays the foundation for meaningful assessment.

One conceptual framework has been advanced by Marzano (1992). Under the heading "Extending and Refining Knowledge," one of five such categories in this framework, Marzano lists such patterns of reasoning as comparing, classifying, inducing, deducing, constructing support, and abstracting. In another framework, Norris and Ennis (1989) include references to such patterns as analyzing arguments, judging the credibility of information sources, identifying assumptions, and deciding on an action, all of which call for the application of knowledge previously obtained in some manner.[1]

These reasoning frameworks depict important outcomes of the schooling process. Therefore, if we can each take responsibility for internalizing one of these visions and if we can learn to translate it into sound assessment exercises, we are ready to devise our own assessments or to verify the quality of assessments developed by others. Until we understand and can translate, we cannot assess.

Skill Targets

In most classrooms, there are things teachers want their students to be able to *do*—instances in which the measure of attainment is the student's ability to demonstrate certain kinds of behaviors. For example, at the primary grade level, a teacher might expect to see certain fundamental social interaction behaviors or the earliest oral reading skills. At the elementary level, a teacher might observe student performance in cooperative group activities. In middle school or junior high,

---

[1]We will describe and discuss these and several other such frameworks in detail in Chapter 10.

manipulation of science lab apparatus might be important. And at the high school level, public speaking or the ability to converse in a second language might represent valued outcomes.

In all of these cases, success lies in "doing" well. The assessment challenge lies in being able to define in words, through example, or both, what it means to do well. In addition, we must provide opportunities for students to show their skills, so we can observe and evaluate while they are performing.

Note that two necessary conditions for performing skillfully are first, that the student master prerequisite procedural knowledge, and second, that the student have the reasoning power to use that knowledge appropriately in performance. Thus, knowledge and reasoning outcomes form the foundations of skill outcomes. However, it is critical that we understand that, in this category, the student's performance objective is to put all the foundational and reasoning proficiencies together and to be skillful. This is precisely why achievement-related skills often represent complex targets requiring quite sophisticated assessments.

Product Targets

Yet another way for students to succeed academically is through creating certain products—tangible entities that reveal through some kind of medium that the student has mastered foundational knowledge, requisite reasoning and problem-solving proficiencies, and specific production skills.

For example, a high school social studies teacher might have students prepare a term paper. A middle school shop teacher might have students build a wooden table. An elementary school teacher might challenge students to prepare their first science lab reports. A primary grade teacher might collect samples of student artwork. A classic example of this target that crosses grade levels is creation of writing samples—tangible products that contain evidence of proficiency within them.

In all cases, success lies in creating products that possess certain key attributes. The assessment challenge is to be able to define clearly and understandably in writing and/or through example, what those attributes are. We must be able to specify exactly how high- and low-quality products differ.

Note once again that successful performance arises out of student mastery of prerequisite knowledge and through the application of appropriate thinking and problem-solving strategies. In addition, the student will probably need to perform certain predefined steps in the process of creating the desired product. So certain achievement-related behaviors underpin the creation of quality products. But evidence of ultimate success lies in the product itself.

Affective Targets

This final category of valued outcomes is quite broad and complex. It includes those characteristics that go beyond academic achievement into the realms of affective and personal feeling states, such as attitudes, interests, motivation, academic self-concept, and the like.

Many teachers hold the hope, for example, that students will develop affective characteristics such as a positive self-concept, positive attitudes toward school and school subjects, clear and appropriate values, strong interests, and a strong sense of internal control over their own well-being. These can be defined in terms of three essential elements: Each kind of feeling is directed at some specific object, each has a positive or negative direction, and each has a level of intensity, from strong to weak.

For instance, attitudes, values, and interests don't exist in a vacuum. Rather, they are focused upon certain aspects of our lives. We have attitudes about self, school, subjects, people. We hold values about politics, work, learning. We are interested in doing, reading, discussing certain things. Thus, affect is directed toward certain objects.

Further, our feelings about things are positive, neutral, or negative. Our academic self-concepts are positive or negative. We hold positive or negative attitudes. Our values are for or against things. We are interested or disinterested. Thus, direction is important.

And, our feelings about things vary in their intensity. Sometimes we feel very strongly positive or negative about things. Sometimes we feel less strongly. Sometimes the intensity is too weak to ascertain its direction. Intensity varies.

When teachers are in touch with these affective characteristics of their students (either as individuals or in groups) and when teachers can put students in touch with their own feelings about important issues, positive learning experiences can result. Obviously, however, we cannot know student feelings about things unless we ask. This requires assessment.

Since these affective and social dimensions of learners are quite complex, thoughtful assessment is essential. Success in assessing them is defined in exactly the same way as is success in assessing achievement: sound assessment requires a crystal-clear vision or understanding of the characteristic(s) to be assessed. Only then can a proper assessment method be selected, a sampling procedure devised, and sources of extraneous interference controlled so as to accurately assess direction and intensity of feelings about specified objects.

Summary of Targets

We have discussed five different but interrelated types of outcomes or achievement targets. I find the almost hierarchical relationship among them to be both interesting and useful. Knowledge is the foundation.

Reasoning and problem solving require application of that knowledge. Knowledge and thinking are foundations of successful skill performance and/or product development. And affect is very often connected to success in both academic and skill performance.

Step one in planning instruction or designing assessments is to specify the type(s) of target(s) to be hit by students. As you will see later, once a target is defined, the process of designing assessments is quite easy. The toughest part by far is coming up with the clear vision! We already have discussed the benefits of investing the effort required to do so.

Time for Reflection

Think back through your experience as a student. Try to think of the one teacher in your life who placed major emphasis on each of the five kinds of outcomes we have discussed. You may think of one teacher who stands out as emphasizing all, or your list might include a different teacher for each kind of outcome. But strive to think of someone who emphasized mastery of knowledge, someone who made you concentrate on using knowledge to solve problems, an advocate of the development of skills, a teacher for whom the creation of quality products was paramount, and one who attended most to your attainment of affective outcomes. As you reflect back on each of these former teachers, how do you feel about the things you learned from each? Do you regard some as better teachers than others that you had? Do you recall some as having used better assessments than others?

SOURCES OF INFORMATION ABOUT ACHIEVEMENT TARGETS

Teachers can identify and set limits on the achievement targets that are to be their particular responsibility in three ways: through thorough professional preparation, community interaction, and thoughtful planning with colleagues. Let's explore each.

Professional Preparation

Solid professional preparation is the foundation of clear and appropriate achievement targets. Put simply, if you intend to teach something, you had better understand it inside and out! Maximum teaching effectiveness arises from having a complete sense of the meaning of quality performance, including a complete understanding of the foundational knowledge and kinds of reasoning and problem-solving skills students need to master if they are to achieve success.

In my years of work in the arena of writing assessment, I have come across many teachers who have been given the responsibility of teaching students to write, but who haven't the slightest idea what it means to write well. They feel uncertain, and their students struggle. On the other hand, I also have met many teachers who possess a refined vision of success in this performance domain and have seen their students blossom as young writers. These two groups of teachers prepared differently to meet this professional challenge, and that difference showed in student achievement.

Those who would teach science concepts must first understand those concepts. Those who aspire to being math teachers must first develop a highly refined mental picture of those concepts, and so on. Those who would assess in these or any other performance domains must first become masters of the required material themselves. Three ways for you to reach this goal are to think of yourself as a lifelong learner, participate in professional training, and remain current with the literature of your profession.

Lifelong Learning.   Become the same kind of lifelong learner you want your students to become. Take personal responsibility to become good at what you expect your students to be good at. If you seek to help them become good writers, for example, become one yourself. Study, practice, strive to publish your work. Become a proficient performer yourself and commit to your own ongoing improvement, regardless of the target(s) you hold as valuable for your students.

Time for Reflection

In your lifetime, have you ever consciously made a commitment to yourself to become the very best you could possibly be at something? Did you succeed? Was the arena of your development related to your teaching? What could happen if the next target you choose as this focus of your own excellence was the same as that of your students, and you set out together in search of that excellence?

Teacher Training.   If you are currently involved in an undergraduate or graduate-level teacher training program, be sure your methods courses reflect the latest thinking about definitions of academic success. Early on in each course, ask specific questions of your professors and evaluate their answers critically.

For example, ask them about their understanding of the alternative visions of student success that could govern teaching in this arena. They should be able to cite a number of options. Which of these alternatives do they hold as being most appropriate and why? They should be able to provide written descriptions of the visions they value, and they should be able to cite references from the professional literature to support the reasons they hold those particular values. How do your professors plan to assess your mastery of those visions of successful student achievement? They should be able to provide specific examples of the assessment instruments and procedures they plan to use.

Evaluate the meaning of student success conveyed by your professors. Does it make sense to you? Can you master this vision with sufficient depth to convey it to your students comfortably? I understand that I am asking you to do something that will require a stretch on your part to evaluate their responses to your queries. After all, you're there to learn about achievement targets. However, as a teacher, you must be able to evaluate ideas as you learn them.

I also realize that I am asking you to do something that will require diplomacy on your part, because you do not hold the power in this communication with your professors. But in one sense you do: their job is to help you become a successful teacher. They have dedicated their professional lives to that effort. If your professors are committed to student well-being, they will welcome your "critical consumer" inquiries. (In fact, among the professors I know personally, you will gain great respect just for asking!)

Professional Literature.   While the ultimate responsibility for your preparation as a teacher falls to you and you alone, excellent support is available. As I noted in Chapter 2, our emergence into the era of performance-based education has spurred a great deal of high-powered reexamination of the valued outcomes of the educational process. This is a boon to teachers. Because in virtually every field, you have at your disposal definitions of achievement targets that hold the promise of allowing you to produce better achievers faster now than ever before—in reading, writing, science, math, reasoning and problem solving, foreign language, and many more.

To tap this wisdom, you need only contact the appropriate national professional association of teachers. Most have assembled commissions of their members to translate current research into practical guidelines for teachers, and many regularly publish journals to disseminate this research. (Appendix A contains lists of many readings from this professional literature.) Work with the resource personnel in your professional library if you have one. Often they can route special articles and information to you when it arrives. College and university libraries represent additional repositories of valuable information and support personnel. Further, each region of the nation is served by a regional educational laboratory. Check with your district office to identify yours. These agencies often offer information services.

You can also find support in understanding outcomes through study of textbooks, text support materials, and curriculum guides and frameworks. These might represent state, district, school, or even departmental statements of valued targets.

Tap all of these sources to build your own sense of understanding and confidence in the field of study in which you teach. I cannot overstate how much this will help when it comes to generating high-quality classroom assessment. In fact, it has been my experience in over fifteen years of classroom assessment research that the single most common barrier to sound classroom assessment is the lack of vision of desired outcomes on the part of teachers.

Community Involvement in Setting Targets

As we proceed through the 1990s, one of the critical lessons we are learning is that schools are institutions that function in a larger social context. The tremendous challenge of understanding and meeting the many needs of youth today requires that educators collaborate with other service agencies. Thus, for our part, we in education must be in touch with our partners in the social service community as we establish the valued outcomes of schooling.

Another lesson we are learning is that students can benefit from the restructuring of school organizations away from top-down hierarchies and toward school-based management models. This practice empowers schools to be in closer touch with their communities about expected outcomes of schooling and it empowers local teachers and members of the instructional support team to take greater responsibility for and to feel greater control over student attainment of those valued outcomes.

When we combine these lessons with the fact that we want schools to provide more than just a rank order of students—that is, we want them to provide competent citizens—what emerges is a pattern in which educators across the nation are meeting with local social, civic, and business communities to hammer out the desired outcomes expected from schools in the larger context of their communities.

This is another good thing for teachers, because it adds focus to school programs and sets useful limits on student, teacher, and school accountability. In addition, it enhances the clarity of our picture of the outcomes that teachers and instructional leaders must translate into assessments. If these collaborative efforts have been started in your community, tap into them for valuable insights. If such local partnerships have not yet been established where you teach, take charge and play a role in initiating them. The richer sense that you will develop of what it takes to be a contributing member of the community will help immensely in your development of sound assessments of key proficiencies.

Figures 4–2 and 4–3 present two examples of final school outcomes generated through school/community collaboration. One arises from statewide efforts in Oregon, the other from local efforts in a Washington school district.

Foundation Skills

Think	Think critically, creatively, and reflectively in making decisions and solving problems.
Self-Direct Learning	Direct his or her own learning, including planning and carrying out complex projects.
Communicate	Communicate through reading, writing, speaking, and listening, and through an integrated use of visual forms such as symbols and graphic images.
Use Technology	Use current technology, including computers, to process information and produce high-quality products.
Quantify	Recognize, process, and communicate quantitative relationships.
Collaborate	Participate as a member of a team, including providing leadership for achieving goals and working well with others from diverse backgrounds.

Core Applications for Living

Deliberate on Public Issues	Deliberate on public issues that arise in our representative democracy and in the world by applying perspectives from social sciences.
Understand Diversity	Understand human diversity and communicate in a second language, applying appropriate cultural norms.
Interpret Human Experience	Interpret human experience through literature and the fine and performing arts.
Apply Science and Math	Apply science and math concepts and processes, showing an understanding of how they affect our world.
Understand Positive Health Habits	Understand positive health habits and behaviors that establish and maintain healthy interpersonal relationships.

Figure 4–2

Oregon Certificate of Initial Mastery Outcomes (Source: Final Draft from the State CIM Task Force, Oregon State Department of Education, December 1992. Reprinted by permission.)

It is our expectation that students exiting South Kitsap School District will demonstrate a core of basic knowledge in order to be

- *creative thinkers* who develop and use a variety of resources to identify, assess, integrate, and apply a basic core of knowledge to effectively make decisions and solve problems.
- *self-directed learners* who set priorities, establish goals, and take responsibility for pursuing and evaluating those goals in an ever-changing society.
- *active citizens* who take the initiative to contribute time, energy, and talent to improve the quality of life for themselves and others in their local, national, and global environments.
- *effective communicators* who receive information in a variety of forms and present in various ways to a wide range of audiences.
- *quality producers* who create innovative, artistic, and practical products which reflect originality, high standards, and the use of appropriate technologies.
- *collaborative workers* who use effective group skills to manage interpersonal relationships within diverse settings.

Figure 4-3
South Kitsap School District Outcomes (Source: South Kitsap School District, Port Orchard, Washington. Reprinted by permission.)

Any instructional team that has internalized these targets, determined the building blocks to competence, and divided responsibility for developing competence is preparing for student success.

Building a Team Effort

Once the goals have been established through community planning, education professionals must take control of the next step: we must analyze each goal to determine the enabling objectives, the attainment of which builds to the accomplishment of the ultimate goal. If we want students to be competent communicators, for example, what are the specific competencies to be attained? Some might be the ability to read, write, speak, listen. What does it mean to be a good reader? A good writer? We can learn the components of each of these from the professional literature and thus establish those critical building blocks of competence.

Once those building blocks are identified, then the various members of the professional team of educators must collaborate with one another to decide how to fit these into the curriculum at various levels of instruction and define how they will support the ultimate goal: the development of competent communicators. What teachers will have responsibility for supporting student attainment of which of the building blocks? How shall teachers communicate with each other and with parents and students about progress? How shall all involved devise and conduct the assessments that inform instructional decision making? These are the classroom-level issues that teachers and instructional support personnel must address together to lay the foundation for student success.

A Note of Caution

As a teacher, you may or may not practice your profession in a community that engages in the kind of planning outlined above. Further, you may or may not practice in a school in which staff collaborate in the articulation of achievement targets across levels. In short, you may or may not receive the kind of school and community support needed to do a thorough job of generating an integrated portrait of success for students.

Nevertheless, each of us has a responsibility to our particular students to be clear and specific about our achievement expectations. The point is, while all of the school and community planning work described above is being carried out (if it is conducted at all), tomorrow in your classroom, or as soon as you enter a classroom for the first time, there will be a group of students wanting and needing to master content knowledge, learn to solve problems, master important skills, create important products, and/or attain certain affective outcomes. They count on you to know what these things mean and to know how to teach and assess them. So when it comes to being clear about what it means to be successful in your classroom, the responsibility stops with you, regardless of what else is going on around you! Embrace that responsibility.

COMMUNICATING ABOUT VALUED ACHIEVEMENT TARGETS

If the driving force behind successful performance-based education is a *shared* vision of success, then we must constantly strive to find more creative and effective ways to communicate our expectations to others. Over the years, we have found many ways to accomplish this and, without doubt, the most common is by using lists of instructional goals and objectives.

While this is an excellent option, it is just one of many options for casting valued outcomes in forms that allow us to communicate about them. We also can use other means to communicate targets.

For instance, a science teacher friend of mine presented a two-week biology unit on cells. As the unit unfolded, she engaged her students in some productive assessment-related activities. At the end of each day, she asked her students to identify what they thought were the most critical content elements covered that day. Using her thorough knowledge of the field, the teacher screened the ideas to be sure the students really hit on the important stuff. As a class, they kept a growing list of these elements, adding a few each day. As the unit moved into week two, she made it clear to her students that these elements, among other things, were going to be covered on the unit test. She was making the target clear.

A writing teacher I know wanted her students to play a central role in defining their own achievement target in writing. So she gave them two samples of student writing selected from previous years to illustrate two vastly different levels of proficiency. Working together as partners, they read the two papers and carefully analyzed their differences. Why is one so much better than the other, they asked? What makes them different? She was using examples of achievement-related products in conjunction with student assessments of proficiency to communicate her expectations to her students.

The principal of a school I visited worked with her staff to devise a new program to help students apply their reasoning and problem-solving proficiencies. She knew the program would be challenging and that support from home would be essential, so she invited parents to school for an evening workshop. At that session, she posed for parents the same kinds of problems their children would be solving. In effect, she provided parents with an opportunity to come to understand their own and each other's thinking and problem-solving skills. As a result, parents came to understand the kinds of achievement targets their children would be hitting. Everyone left that evening supportive and ready and able to help. The staff had succeeded in making their expectations clear to key members of their school community.

The bottom line is that we need not rely only on a list of objectives to describe our valued outcomes. We also can rely on collections of summary statements of important learnings, examples of good work, and, indeed, the very assessment process itself as means of communicating our visions of valued outcomes to others.

Look for more examples of innovative ways to communicate expectations through the use of assessment as you read on. Assessment is not just for gathering data—it can be a valuable means for setting students up for success through clear thinking and effective communication about what it means to be successful.

Time for Reflection

If you expected your students to become proficient at assembling functional electrical circuits, which would be the most effective way to show them in advance what success looks like—reading them an instructional objective stating the outcome in behavioral terms or having them watch you do it successfully just once? In your opinion, why would one be more effective than the other?

CHAPTER SUMMARY: CLEAR TARGETS ARE KEY

In this segment of our journey into the realm of classroom assessment, we have seen that the quality of an assessment rests on the clarity of the assessor's understanding of the student characteristic(s) to be assessed. Five kinds of characteristic outcomes or targets were identified as useful in thinking about and planning for assessment and its integration into the instructional process:

- mastering content knowledge
- using that knowledge to reason and solve problems
- demonstrating certain kinds of skills

- creating certain kinds of products
- attaining valued affective outcomes

Each teacher faces the challenge of specifying desired outcomes in the classroom, relying on a commitment to lifelong learning, strong professional preparation, community input, and collegial teamwork within the school to support this effort.

I urge that you specify valued outcomes in your classroom in writing and that you publish them for all to see. And further, I urge that students play a role (to the extent possible and under your supervision as their teacher) in identifying at least some of those valued targets.

When we do these things, benefits accrue for all involved. Limits of teacher accountability are established, setting teachers up to succeed. Limits of student accountability are established, setting students up for success. And, the huge assessment workload faced by teachers becomes more manageable because assessments can be sharply focused.

EXERCISES TO ADVANCE YOUR LEARNING

Knowledge Outcomes

1. List the important benefits of specifying clear and appropriate outcomes.
2. Identify the major risk to the teacher of being explicit about outcomes.
3. List and define the five kinds of achievement targets presented in this chapter.
4. Identify available sources of information and guidance in selecting and defining valued outcomes.
5. List three specific ways to communicate about expected outcomes.

Reasoning Outcomes

1. Translate each of the five kinds of outcomes into a real example of a significant target that you hit during your own school experience.
2. Explain in your own words the relationships that exist between and among the five kinds of achievement targets.
3. What do you think might happen to student academic self-concept if we tried to assess an outcome we, as teachers, did not understand or tried to use an outcome assessment whose meaning is unclear to us?

Affective Outcomes

1. Some conceptual frameworks divide reasoning into higher-order and lower-order kinds. Recall, or knowledge-level, outcomes often are regarded as lower

order. If this implies "less important, less challenging," do you agree? Are some kinds of reasoning more important than others?

2. In our society today, heated debates continue regarding the kinds of outcomes our schools should help students attain. Opposing camps often include conservative and liberal political factions, religious communities of differing opinions, and business leaders seeking job competence in discussion with those who seek a broader view of the complete citizen. In your opinion, are these volatile exchanges of values good or bad for schools and students? Why do you feel that way? Do you think these differing points of view can be accommodated in our educational system? If so, how? If not, why not?

CHAPTER 5

Understanding the Assessment Alternatives

Chapter Objectives

As a result of studying the material presented in Chapter 5, reflecting upon that material, and completing the learning exercises at the end of the chapter, you will:

1. Master content knowledge:
   a. Know each of the four basic assessment methods.
   b. Identify the achievement targets best assessed with each method.

2. Be able to use that knowledge to reason as follows:
   a. In a real classroom assessment context, be able to select an assessment method that will make sense given the achievement target to be assessed.
   b. Understand why some assessment methods represent strong matches with achievement targets while others are weak.

3. Attain the following affective outcomes:
   a. Value all methods of assessment as useful and worthy of careful development and use.
   b. Value strong matches between achievement targets and assessment methods on all occasions in the classroom.

Note: The objectives of this chapter do not include the mastery of any process skills or the creation of any products.

Having introduced the range of possible purposes for classroom assessment and the variety of different kinds of achievement targets to be assessed, we now turn to the issue of selecting proper assessment methods.

The assessment method of choice in any classroom context is a direct function of the purpose and the target. There are many possible reasons to assess. Different uses require different results. Different results require different modes of assessment. Further, there are many possible achievement targets. Different targets require different modes of assessment, too. Thus, without knowledge of purpose and target, it is impossible to devise a sound assessment.

For example, an assessment of instrumental music proficiency is likely to look very different from an assessment of knowledge of history facts. One relies on the assessor to listen to and subjectively judge proficiency. The other requires the administration of a set of test items that are scored correct or incorrect, yielding a score reflecting proficiency. Different outcomes, different assessment methods.

Note also that an assessment of instrumental music proficiency for the purpose of planning the next lesson for a student demands a different kind of assessment from one to be used to determine who receives a scholarship to the conservatory. The former requires a narrowly focused, brief assessment, the latter a much larger, more diverse sampling of proficiency. As purpose varies, so does the definition of a sound assessment.

Once the requirements of a quality assessment are determined for a particular classroom assessment context (i.e., purpose and target have been specified), then and only then can a proper assessment method be selected, developed and administered, so as to yield sound results for the user. As Figure 5–1 illustrates, the process is much like assembling a jigsaw puzzle—only those pieces that belong together will fit properly.

In this chapter, we're going to introduce a broad range of alternative assessment methods available to meet our combined purpose and target needs in the classroom. In addition, we will examine how to connect methods with outcomes—how to pick a method that really will reflect the target you wish to assess.

As you read this chapter, strive to maintain a balanced perspective regarding the viability of the assessment options covered. For decades, one method has dominated—the objectively scored paper and pencil test. As a result, some very important achievement targets went unassessed, especially in the context of high-stakes assessments.

As we moved into the 1990s, we began to experience a backlash to those decades of domination. As pointed out earlier, we began to embrace a more complex array of valued outcomes, and this required the use of such alternatives as performance assessment methodology.

As a result of this swing in values, we face two dangers. If we are not cautious, we risk moving out of balance in our assessments once again, with the same kind of domination by a single (but different) assessment method. Or, we risk inadequate assessment of student achievement because we fail to understand or acknowledge the real costs of conducting sound performance assessments and thus end up doing a shoddy job of implementing this promising alternative.

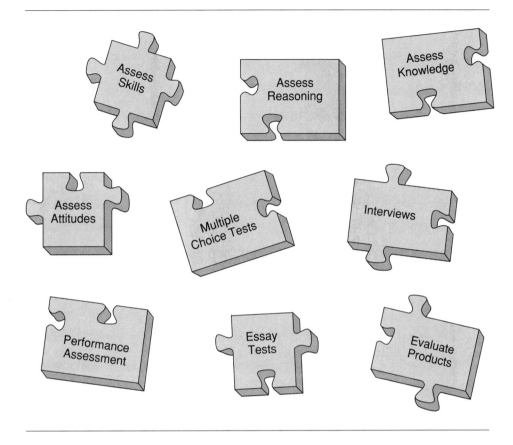

Figure 5-1
How Do the Pieces Go Together?

We can prevent such problems only by acknowledging that the challenge we face is difficult, and by meeting this challenge by effectively developing and using all of the assessment tools we have at our disposal.

CHAPTER ROADMAP

We're going to study four basic assessment methods, all of which are familiar to you, as a student and perhaps as a teacher:

- selected response assessments
- essay assessments
- performance assessments
- assessments that rely on direct personal communication with the student

	SELECTED RESPONSE	ESSAY	PERFORMANCE ASSESSMENT	PERSONAL COMMUNICATION
Know				
Reason				
Skill				
Product				
Affect				

Figure 5-2
A Plan for Matching Assessment Methods with Achievement Targets

Each provides its own special form of evidence of student proficiency. I will briefly introduce them in the next section of this chapter. Then, in Part 2, we will devote a chapter to each method, studying each in depth in terms of design, development, advantages, disadvantages, and keys to effective use in the classroom.

First, however, we are going to lay out the roadmap that will guide the remainder of our journey together. In the second half of this chapter, we will analyze how each of these four assessment methods aligns with the five kinds of achievement targets discussed in Chapter 4. In essence, we will see which methods make sense with each target and which do not. We will do this by filling in the cells of Figure 5–2 with commentary on viable matches.

THE ASSESSMENT OPTIONS

Selected Response Assessment

This is the classic objectively scored paper and pencil test. The respondent is asked a series of questions, each of which is accompanied by a range of alternative responses. The respondent's task is to select either the correct or the best answer from among the options. The index of achievement in this instance is the number or proportion of questions answered correctly.

Format options within this category include the following:

- multiple-choice items
- true/false items
- matching exercises
- short answer fill-in items

While I realize that fill-in-the-blank items do require a response that originates within the respondent, I include it in this category because it calls for a very brief answer that is counted right or wrong.

Standardized achievement test batteries often rely on selected response assessment methodology. So do the chapter tests that accompany many textbooks.

Time for Reflection

What is your most vivid memory of a selected response assessment from your school experience? What kinds of outcomes were assessed? How do you feel about these kinds of tests?

Essay Assessments

In this case, the respondent is provided with an exercise (or set of exercises) that calls for the preparation of an extended written answer. The student might be asked to answer a question or to provide an explanation of the solution to a complex problem. Open-ended math problems, where students are asked to show all work, also fall into this category. The originally constructed responses are read by the examiner, who judges the quality of the responses.

Evidence of achievement is seen in the conceptual content of the response (i.e., ideas expressed and the manner in which they are tied together). The index of achievement typically is the number of points attained out of a total number of points possible.

Time for Reflection

Have you worked with a teacher that relied heavily on the essay form of assessment? What kinds of outcomes did this teacher value most? How do you feel about these kinds of tests?

Performance Assessments

This label has become associated with assessments in which the respondent actually carries out a specified activity under the watchful eye of an evaluator, who observes performance and makes judgments as to the quality of achievement demonstrated. Performance assessments can be based either on observations of the process while skills are being demonstrated, or on the evaluation of products created.

In the first case, evidence of achievement is seen in the respondent's ability to carry out the proper sequence of activities or to do something in the appropriate manner. It is the doing that counts. The index of achievement typically is a performance rating or profile of ratings reflecting levels of quality in the performance.

Examples include evaluations of musical performance, assessments of foreign language speaking proficiency, and assessments of athletic performance.

In the case of product evaluations, the respondent creates a complex achievement-related product that is intended to have certain attributes. The assessor examines the tangible product to see if those attributes are indeed present. In this instance, it is not so much the process of creating that counts (although that may be evaluated, too) but rather the characteristics of the creation itself.

Again in this case, the index of achievement is the rating(s) of product quality. Art or craft products fall into this category. So do exhibits created for science fairs. The classic example is the writing assessment, in which students produce samples that are evaluated not solely in terms of the content presented, but in terms of proficiency in using written language.

Time for Reflection

What is the most important performance assessment you ever participated in? What kinds of achievement targets were assessed? How effective was this kind of assessment for you?

Personal Communication as Assessment

One of the most common ways teachers gather information about student achievement is to talk with them! We don't often think of this as assessment in the same sense of the multiple-choice test or a performance assessment. But upon reflection it will become clear to you that certain forms of personal communication definitely do represent assessments of student achievement.

These forms of personal communication include questions posed and answered during instruction, interviews, conferences, conversations, listening during class discussions, conversations with others (such as parents or other teachers) about student achievement, and oral examinations. The examiner listens to responses and either (a) tallies them right or wrong if correctness is the criterion, or (b) makes subjective judgments according to some quality criterion. Personal communication is a prominent means of assessment in the classroom.

Time for Reflection

Have you ever worked with a teacher who always seemed to be able to ask just the right question at just the right time to reveal your own wisdom to you—wisdom you didn't even know you had? Or have you worked with a teacher who could always ask just the question you didn't know the answer to—and then always called on you? What effect did this have on you?

Some Thoughts About Methods

If you're tuned into 1990s assessment, you may be saying, "Wait a minute, what happened to the rapidly emerging alternative called portfolio assessment? Doesn't that represent a fifth method?"

I regard portfolios as a wonderful idea, and discuss their use in assessment and instruction in Part 4. However, I do not regard portfolios as a separate assessment method. Rather, they represent an excellent means of gathering diverse bits of evidence of student achievement (probably gathered using a variety of the methods described above) into a coherent whole. In short, portfolios are a means of communicating about student growth and development—not a form of assessment.

Note that three of the four assessment methods described above call for complex responses on the part of the student. They require the preparation of extended written responses, the performance of complex skills, the creation of multidimensional products, or participation in one-on-one communication—all of which take more time to administer and certainly more time to score than a set of true-false test items. Thus, if the amount of assessment time is held constant, selected response assessments can provide a much larger sample of performance per unit of assessment time.

Given this reality, you might ask, why not just use the most efficient option—selected response—every time? The reason is that selected response assessment formats cannot accurately depict all of the kinds of achievement we expect of our students. Different kinds of assessment methods align well with different kinds of achievement targets. We shall explore these relationships now.

MATCHING METHODS WITH TARGETS

The art of classroom assessment revolves around the teacher's ability to blend five kinds of achievement targets, with all of the forms and nuances of each, with four kinds of assessment methods, with all of the variations in format that come with each method. Sounds like a pretty big job! But, as it turns out, the recipes for creating these blends are not that complicated.

We will explore the blending process by crossing the five kinds of outcomes with the four methods to create a chart depicting the various matches of targets to methods. The result is Figure 5–2 (p. 84). Within each cell of this table, we can explore the nature and viability of the match. The result, though not a simple picture, is both understandable and practical.

I present brief descriptions of the various matches in Table 5–1. Please turn to this table now and read through it. As you read, please keep three key points in mind. First, remember that the various kinds of achievement targets we are discussing are hierarchically related, each building on those that precede it. Knowledge is the foundation. Problem solving involves application of knowledge. Skills represent knowledge and problem solving at work. Quality products are created by using

Table 5–1
Aligning Achievement Targets and Assessment Methods

Achievement Target	Selected Response	Essay	Performance Assessment	Personal Communication
Mastery of knowledge	All formats can be used to assess content knowledge	Can serve to assess student mastery of complex structures of knowledge	Can be used to assess knowledge mastered via effective use of reference materials	Good for narrow domains of knowledge when short-term record keeping is required
Reasoning	Can assess some key kinds of reasoning—but not all kinds	Written descriptions of problem solutions can provide a window into reasoning	Can watch student in the process of problem solving and draw inferences regarding proficiency	Ask student to "think out loud" to examine problem-solving proficiency
Skills	Can test for mastery of prerequisite procedural knowledge—but not ability to do it	Again, can ask student to describe complex "how to" procedural knowledge but not ability to do it	Can observe and evaluate skills as demonstrated	A strong match when the skill in question is oral communication proficiency; can ask student to describe and discuss complex "how to" procedural knowledge
Products	Can test for prerequisite knowledge of the attributes of quality products	Might tap ability to describe the attributes of a quality product	Can assess (a) proficiency in carrying out the steps required to create a quality product, and (b) the product itself	Can probe procedural knowledge and/or knowledge of attributes of a quality product
Affective	Can develop highly structured questionnaire items	Can use open-ended questionnaire items	Can infer affect from observation of behaviors or examination of products	Can talk with student about his or her feelings

knowledge, thinking, and skills in the right ways. Teachers who are concerned with building competence might well need to assess any of these elements of success.

Second, remember that assessments provide us with external indicators of the internal mental states we call achievement. These indicators are visible manifestations that we can see and evaluate. In other words, we can't just lift the top of the student's head off and look inside to see if math problem-solving proficiency is in there. So, we administer an assessment in the form of several math problems to be solved to gather evidence of proficiency from which we infer mastery of the desired target. One important key to selecting an acceptable method for any particular form of achievement is to choose the method that permits us to draw the most accurate inference. Thus, the foundation for the selection of a method, once again, is a refined vision of the achievement target to be assessed.

And finally, as stated before, any assessment represents a sample of all the exercises we could have posed if the assessment were infinitely long. A sound assessment relies on a sample that is systematically representative of all the possibilities. We generalize from the sample to the infinite array. In effect, we can infer how much of the target students have mastered.

Our goal in assessment design is to use the most powerful assessment option we can. Power derives from the accuracy with which a method can reproduce our valued outcome and the efficiency with which it can represent that outcome. We always want the highest-resolution picture of that valued target we can get using the smallest possible sample of student performance—maximum information for minimum cost.

As you read Table 5–1, I hope you can see more clearly why it is crucial to understand the achievement target in order to select a proper assessment method. This cannot be overstated: *Different targets require different methods.*

A startling realization that came to me as I worked through the cells of this table—thinking about which methods matched what outcomes—was that virtually every cell offered a viable match at some level. Some matches are stronger than others; that is, some get to the heart of the valued outcome better than others. For example, without question, the best way to assess writing proficiency is to rely on performance assessment and have students create written products. But we also can use selected response or personal communication to determine if essential knowledge based on effective writing is missing among those who don't write well. These don't accurately depict writing, but for the teacher striving to create writers, they do provide accurate representations of key prerequisites to effective writing. Thus, for day-to-day classroom assessment and instructional purposes, they represent useful assessment alternatives.

The realization that all methods have the potential of contributing at least some useful information about most kinds of classroom outcomes is very good news, because it tells us that we have a wide variety of tools at our disposal to help us to assess student learning.

How, then, do we decide which one to use? In the best of all possible worlds where both your time to assess and your assessment resources are unlimited, you choose the cell that affords you the most accurate depictions of your desired outcome. But, in the real world, we must select the methods of assessment that come closest to representing our valued outcome and that at the same time fit into the resource realities of our classrooms. Though compromise is inevitable, we can work some pretty good tradeoffs between fidelity and cost of assessment if we know what we're doing.

To illustrate, let's move across the table left to right, one row at a time. Strive to see the big picture. We are looking at the forest. We will spend the rest of this book examining the trees in rich detail.

Assessing Mastery of Content Knowledge

We all know we can use selected response, objective paper and pencil tests to measure student memorization of facts and information. Typically, these assessments tend to test knowledge of elemental facts in isolation, such as facts about the Civil War, spelling, vocabulary, earth science, and the like. Since these tests are efficient to use, they fit into the resource realities of most classrooms.

When the domain of knowledge is defined not as separate facts in isolation but rather as larger structures of knowledge where elements are related in complex ways, we can test student mastery using the essay format. Examples of larger information chunks that students might be asked to know might include the causes of the Civil War or differences among igneous, metamorphic, and sedimentary rocks. The practical question we must address in selecting this option, however, is how we shall find the time to read and evaluate the responses.

With respect to using performance assessment as an index of student mastery of content knowledge, remember that I earlier stated the need for citizens of the twenty-first century to be able to retrieve information on demand. The point is that the world does not function on memorized facts and information. Rather, we must all become competent users of reference materials as one means of gaining control over useful knowledge.

For this reason, I have expanded my own thinking about mastery of content knowledge to include the ability to use reference materials when necessary to retrieve needed information. One can use performance assessment methodology—observing students in the process of using reference resources—to determine proficiency in this arena.

Using a product evaluation as the basis for assessing mastery of content knowledge presents a special kind of problem, having to do with the nature of the inferences one can draw based on student performance. In the case where the student creates a high-quality product, there certainly is ample evidence that the performer mastered the necessary foundational knowledge. But difficulties arise when we are confronted with a poor-quality product. Standing by itself, that product does not reveal what went wrong. There are three possible explanations for it. The student may not have mastered the foundation knowledge. Something may have gone wrong in the process of creating the product. Or perhaps the student possessed the requisite knowledge and understood the process, but just didn't try. If we were simply to infer that the problem arose from a lack of knowledge, we might well be wrong. Without followup assessment—using other assessment methods—we just don't know.

Why do we care about the underlying cause of failure? Because, in the classroom, our mission is to promote success! We need to know what went wrong so we can support students in their attempts to improve.

If followup assessment of student mastery of requisite knowledge—using selected response, essay, or personal communication–based assessment methods—reveals a lack of mastery, then we know what to do. On the other hand, if followup assessment reveals a lack of motivation to perform, then a completely different course of action is called for. Without the followup, we just don't know what to do.

I submit that a primary reason why large-scale standardized assessments—whether objective tests or performance assessments—have historically had so little impact on teachers in classrooms is that they leave them without explanations of the reasons for student failures. They reveal only high- or low-level performance, which from a public accountability point of view may be good enough. But, from the teacher's point of view, they fail to reveal which explanation for failure is correct. They fail to suggest actions the teacher can follow. *Only* sound classroom assessments can do this.

The final option for assessing mastery of knowledge is direct personal communication with the student—for example, asking questions and evaluating answers. This is a good match, especially with limited amounts of knowledge to be mastered, few students to be assessed, and in contexts where records of performance need not be stored for long periods of time.

The reason I impose these conditions is that this obviously is a labor-intensive assessment method. So if the domain of knowledge to be assessed is large, the user is faced with the need to ask a large sample of questions. That just doesn't fit the resource realities in most classrooms. Further, if the number of students to be assessed is large, this option may not allow enough time to sample each student's achievement representatively. And, if records of performance must be stored over an extended period of time, written records will be needed for each student over a broad sample of questions. This, too, eats up a lot of time and energy.

Assessment via personal communication works best in those situations when the teacher is checking student mastery of a few critical facts during instruction in order to make quick, ongoing adjustments as needed.

Assessing Reasoning and Problem Solving

In most classrooms, we want students to be able to use the knowledge they master in productive ways to reason and solve complex problems. There are many ways to define what it means to be a proficient problem solver. We will discuss many of these alternative conceptualizations and their assessment throughout this book. For now, let me cite two or three sample patterns of reasoning as a point of departure for discussing assessment in this important arena.

One kind of reasoning we value is evaluative or critical thinking—the ability to make judgments and defend them through rigorous application of standards or criteria. Just as movie or restaurant critics evaluate according to criteria, so students can evaluate the quality of a piece of literature or the strength of a scientific argument.

Another commonly valued pattern of reasoning is inferential thinking—the ability to reason inductively and deductively, to draw generalizations from the evidence, or to predict outcomes from a set of initial circumstances. Yet another pattern involves using foundational knowledge to compare and contrast things, to infer similarities and differences.

How does one assess these kinds of outcomes? Our four methodological choices all provide excellent options when used by teachers who possess both a clear vision of what they wish to assess and sufficient craft knowledge of the assessment methods.

For example, we can use selected response exercises to get at certain patterns of reasoning—but not all. We can use them, for example, to see if students can analyze things, compare them, or draw inferences; to evaluate math problem-solving proficiency; or to assess procedural knowledge, such as how to use technology in scientific contexts.

I continue to be surprised by how many educators believe that selected response exercises can test only recall of facts. While they do this very well, the format is more flexible than many people think, though of course there are limits. Evaluative thinking—expressing and defending a point of view—cannot be tested using multiple-choice or true/false items because this kind of thinking requires at least a written expression of the defense. Further, when the problem to be solved is multifaceted and complex, involving several steps, the application of several different patterns of reasoning, and/or several problem solvers working together—as real world problems often are—then more complex assessment methods must be used. But for some kinds of reasoning, selected response works.

Essay tests represent an excellent way to assess student reasoning and problem solving. Student writing provides an excellent window into student thinking. In fact, very often, students can be encouraged to look through this window and assess their own reasoning and problem solving. Teachers can devise highly challenging exercises that ask students to analyze, compare, draw complex inferences, evaluate, or to use some combination of these.

Of course, the key to evaluating the quality of student responses to such exercises is for the assessor to understand the kind of reasoning required and to be able to detect its presence in student writing. Clear and appropriate scoring criteria are essential.

Performance assessment represents yet another excellent option in this arena. We can watch students in the act of problem solving in a science lab, for example, and draw inferences about their proficiency. To the extent that they carry out proper procedures, they reveal their inner reasoning.

However, again, drawing inferences about reasoning proficiency on the basis of the quality of student products can be risky. Certainly, strong performance (a high-quality product) is evidence of sound reasoning. But for classroom purposes, where assessment is used to promote student development, we have difficulty explaining and helping with weak performance, with a low-quality product. Did the student fail to perform due to a lack of foundational knowledge, failure to reason productively, or lack of motivation? As previously stated, without followup assessment by other means, we just don't know.

If we don't follow up with supplemental assessment, and thereby infer the wrong cause of failure, at the very least our remedy is likely to be insufficient. We may waste valuable time reteaching material already mastered or teaching reasoning skills already developed.

One of the strongest matches between target and assessment method in Table 5–1 is the use of personal communication to evaluate student reasoning. Teachers can do any or all of the following:

- ask questions that probe patterns of reasoning
- have students ask each other questions and listen for evidence of reasoning in the response
- have students reason out loud, describing what they are thinking as they confront a problem
- have students recount their reasoning processes
- simply listen attentively during class discussions for evidence of sound, appropriate reasoning

Just talking informally with students can reveal so much, when we know what we're looking for! However, with this method, it will always take time to carry out the assessment and to keep accurate records of results.

Assessing Mastery of Skills

When our assessment goal is to find out if students can demonstrate achievement-related skills, such as speak in a second language, give a formal speech, or interact with classmates in socially acceptable ways, then there is just one way: observe them while they are exhibiting the desired behaviors and make judgments as to their quality—performance assessment. There is no other choice. Each of the other options falls short of this ultimate outcome.

But sometimes limited resources make it impossible to assess the actual skill. At those times, you may need to go for second best and come as close to the real target as you can. You have several options when you need to trade fidelity for greater efficiency in the assessment of skills. You can use selected response test items to determine whether the student can recognize the right behaviors. For example, given a number of performance demonstrations (on video, perhaps), can the respondent identify the best? Or, you may use a multiple-choice format to see if students know the proper sequence of activities to carry out when that is relevant to the outcome. Given several descriptions of a procedure, can the respondent identify the correct one? We can also use this method to ask if students have mastered the vocabulary needed to communicate about desired skills.

Realize, however, that such tests assess only prerequisites to effective performance—the building blocks to competence. They cannot assess that examinee's actual level of skill in performing.

With this same limitation, you could have students write essays about the criteria they might use to evaluate performance in a vocal music competition, knowledge that might well represent an important foundation for performing well in such a competition. But, of course, this will fall short of a real test of performance.

Finally, personal communication represents an excellent means of assessment of skills when the skills in question have to do with oral communication proficiency. For such an outcome, this is the highest-fidelity assessment option.

For other kinds of skills, however, personal communication can only serve as a means to get at proficiency in describing sound performance. It falls short of providing direct data on the ability to perform.

Assessing Proficiency in Creating Products

The same limitations discussed for skills assessment apply here. If our assessment goal is to determine whether students can create a certain kind of achievement-related product, there is no better way than to have them actually create one. In fact, performance assessment represents the *only* means of direct assessment. The best test of the ability to throw a ceramic pot is the quality of the finished product itself. The best test of the ability to set up scientific apparatus is the completed arrangement. The best test of the ability to write a term paper is the finished paper.

Again, you could use a selected response assessment format to see if a student can pick out a quality product from among several choices. Or, you could test knowledge of a quality product's key attributes. But these are limited substitutes for assessment that actually asks students to create the product.

It is also possible to have students write essays about or discuss, with their teacher or other students, the key attributes of a carefully crafted object, such as a cabinet in shop class. Again, students who could respond well to such an exercise might well possess the important prerequisite knowledge. But sometimes the real issue is whether students can create a carefully crafted cabinet. When that is the question, performance assessment is the answer.

Assessing Affective Outcomes

It is instructive to note that the entries in the last row of Table 5–1 include no weak matches. The range of assessment methods available to tap the various dimensions of affect is wide indeed.

Let's take a minute to review some of the student characteristics that fall under this heading. Affective dimensions of individuals that might be the object of classroom assessment include attitudes, values, interests, self-concept, and motivational disposition. Remember, as stated in Chapter 4, the focus of affective assessment is to determine the direction and intensity of student feelings about different school-related objects.

The key to success in affective assessment—as usual—is a clear and appropriate definition of the characteristic to be assessed. Given a clear understanding, could we translate such outcomes into selected response questions? You bet! But our collection of such items won't be a test per se—it would more properly be considered a questionnaire. Many selected response item formats are very useful for such highly structured questionnaires. For instance, we could offer students statements and ask if they agree, disagree, or are undecided. Or, we could ask them to select from among a list of adjectives those that most accurately apply to themselves or to some other object. This assessment realm is rich with useful options.

Essay questions are another viable option for tapping affective outcomes. Open-ended questionnaire items can be written in such a manner as to ask students to describe both the direction and intensity of their feelings about any particular object. After fifteen years of in-school and in-classroom research on classroom assessment practices, one of the most startling insights for me has been how rarely teachers use questionnaires to gather affective information from their students—information that could make everyone's job so much easier.

The match between affective targets and performance assessment is a bit more complex, however, because of the nature of the inferences that must be drawn. In this case, I urge caution. It certainly is possible to look at samples of student performance or at student-created products and draw some conclusions about attitudes, values, and motivational dispositions with respect to that particular project. If students demonstrate high levels of achievement, their attitude was probably strongly positive, they probably valued the project and their work, and they probably were disposed to work hard to perform well.

However, care must be exercised at the other end of the performance continuum. When performance is poor, there are many possible explanations, only one of which is a poor attitude and lack of motivation. Only additional followup assessment will reveal the real reason for failure to perform.

One excellent way in which to conduct such a followup might be direct personal communication with the student. In the right atmosphere, students will talk openly and honestly about the strength and direction of their feelings. The keys to success, of course, are to be able to establish that open environment and to know what kinds of questions to ask to tap important affect.

CHAPTER SUMMARY: TARGETS AND METHODS MUST MATCH

Sound classroom assessments arise from a clear and appropriate target and sample student performance with respect to that target using a proper assessment method. A strong assessment method is one that provides the most direct view of student performance—that permits the strongest inferences from the assessment results to the actual status of the achievement target.

In this chapter, we have described four assessment methods and discussed how they might be used selectively to tap student achievement on a wide range of school outcomes. A strong inference I would have you draw from now on is that the sound assessment of the full range of our valued school outcomes in the classroom will require applying *all* of the assessment tools we have at our disposal: selected response paper and pencil tests, essay exercises, performance assessments, and direct personal communication with students. No single method can serve all of our assessment needs. We must learn to use them all.

EXERCISES TO ADVANCE YOUR LEARNING

Knowledge Outcomes

1. List and define each of the four basic assessment methods. Identify any format options within each method.
2. Scan the chapter again and create a new version of Table 5–1 in your own words.

Reasoning Outcomes

1. If you had to select only one method for assessing each of the five kinds of achievement targets, which method would you choose for each and why?
2. Create another Figure 5–2 framework with empty cells. In each cell, if the combination of target and method represents a strong match, enter a plus sign. If the match is weak, enter a minus sign. What generalizations, if any, do you infer from the resulting pattern?
3. If our objective was to assess your teaching proficiency, what assessment method(s) should we use and why? (Reflect on the active ingredients of good teaching before answering.)

Affective Outcomes

1. Some in the education community condemn selected response tests as trivializing learning. Others condemn essay tests as too difficult to score dependably, as too subjective. Still others think performance assessment is too labor intensive and is as undependable as are essay tests. Then there are those who feel that personal communication is too biased a form of assessment because teacher-student personalities get in the way. If we listen to all of these critics, we will be left without viable assessment options of any sort. To whom should we listen? What methods should we use? Why?

PART TWO

Understanding Assessment Methods

I have had my solutions for a long time;
but I do not yet know how I am to arrive at them.
J.K.F. Gauss (1777–1855)

CHAPTER 6

Selected Response Assessment: Still Useful After All These Years

---

Chapter Objectives

As a result of studying the material presented in this chapter, reflecting on that material, and completing the learning exercises presented at the end of the chapter, you will:

1. Master content knowledge:
    a. Understand the roles of objectivity and subjectivity in selected response assessment.
    b. Know three steps in the selected response assessment development process, including substeps in each.
    c. Identify the kinds of achievement targets that can be reflected in selected response assessments.
    d. List classroom assessment context factors to consider in deciding whether or when to use selected response assessments.
    e. State considerations in sampling student performance with selected response exercises.
    f. Know advantages and disadvantages of four selected response format options: multiple-choice, true/false, matching, and short answer fill-in items.
    g. List specific guidelines for the construction of test items in these four formats.

2. Be able to use that knowledge to reason as follows:
    a. Identify major categories of content and thinking for your selected response assessments.
    b. Identify propositions that can form the basis of sound test items.
    c. Transform those propositions into high-quality selected response items.

3. Be proficient at the following skills:
   a. Be able to carry out the steps in the assessment development process.
   b. Evaluate previously developed selected response assessments to ensure their quality.

4. Create the following quality products:
   a. Selected response assessments that meet predefined standards.

5. Attain the following affective outcomes:
   a. Sense the importance of knowing about sound selected response assessment.
   b. Value selected response assessment as a viable option for use in the classroom.
   c. See selected response assessment as a valuable instructional tool in which students should be and can be full partners.
   d. See selected response assessment as a means of increasing instructional efficiency.

Consider the multiple-choice and true/false test—now there's a real test, the kind we've all come to know and love or fear, depending on our personal experiences. Have you ever noticed how many people contend that they "never were good test takers?" This usually is the kind of test to which they are referring. Yet, many of the most important tests we took in school asked us to select the one right answer.

For most of us, that process began with those once-a-year standardized achievement and/or intelligence tests. (Personally, I never seemed to finish those before my teacher called, "Time's up!" No one ever explained why they wouldn't let me finish. But rules were rules.) Soon, the score came back and went into our "permanent record," even though no one ever seemed to know what those scores meant. It was all rather mysterious.

As we grew older, we were taught to care deeply about grades and grade-point averages. As these aspects of the educational process grew in importance in our lives, our teachers tended to rely more and more on tests consisting of "right or wrong" items. Remember exchanging papers so we could score our neighbor's test as the teacher read the right answer? I guess they thought we'd cheat if we scored our own. And woe be unto the kid who happened to question a right answer— regardless of the reason!

Next came time for college admissions tests, and even greater mysteries. No one seemed to know what was coming as test time approached, least of all our teachers. Nevertheless, we knew we had better be "on" that day. A whole Saturday morning—literally hours—of nothing but multiple-choice test items. And when you had finished, you had no idea how well you had done. Remember? Then the scores came back and once again no one knew what they really meant—but they had to be high or your life was in ruins!

Once again, at this level, it all seemed so secretive. No one seemed to know what was really going on. Everyone seemed to operate on the blind faith that those in charge of testing knew best and could be counted upon to do the right thing.

This is the lore of selected response tests. We've all experienced them, we have plenty of emotions tied to them and, to this day, we have lots of questions about them. My goal in this chapter is to eliminate the mystery surrounding this assessment methodology. We'll cover the basics of the various selected response formats. Then, in later chapters, we'll explore a variety of classroom assessment and standardized test applications of these formats.

CHAPTER ROADMAP

We will discuss four specific kinds of selected response test formats:

- multiple-choice
- true/false
- matching
- short answer fill-in

The great strength of these methods lies in their ability to tap certain kinds of student achievement with accuracy and great efficiency, when carefully developed by skillful users. In this chapter, we will explore the origins of these strengths and what it means to develop and use them with care.

Further, we will consider the limitations of these formats. One such shortcoming, some contend, is that they tend to focus student attention on information in isolation by testing one element at time. The larger context and structure of relationships between and among elements can get lost. In addition, others say, they cannot tap the kinds of complex, multifaceted problem-solving proficiencies that are so relevant in the real world. We will probe these and other weaknesses. Selected response assessments are not the be-all and end-all of achievement testing, and never were. But they remain a viable option. We'll see why in this chapter.

As we journey through this aspect of assessment, in addition to understanding these strengths and limitations, you will come to do the following:

- understand the roles of objectivity and subjectivity in the design and use of selected response assessments
- see why it is important to understand this kind of testing
- know when to use selected response methods
- know how to develop a high-quality test using the four test formats listed above, avoiding the most common pitfalls
- understand how to integrate these kinds of tests into instruction by bringing students into the assessment development and use process as full partners

As we go, keep the big picture in mind. Figure 6–1 is a duplicate of Figure 5–2, which matched our five achievement targets with four modes of assessment. We will

	SELECTED RESPONSE	ESSAY	PERFORMANCE ASSESSMENT	PERSONAL COMMUNICATION
Know				
Reason				
Skill				
Product				
Affect				

Figure 6-1
Aligning Achievement Targets and Assessment Methods

be dealing in depth with the darkened cells. Then, as we move through Parts 2 and 3, we will cover more cells until our comprehensive assessment picture is complete.

SUBJECTIVITY IN SELECTED RESPONSE ASSESSMENT

You may have been wondering why I have chosen the label *selected response assessments* for these four formats. Certainly, a more common label for these kinds of assessments is "objective paper and pencil test." I have chosen a less common label, paradoxically, to promote clearer understanding. The traditional label can mislead by suggesting that there is no subjectivity involved in these tests—that everything associated with this format is "scientific," and there is little danger of bias due to assessor judgment.

Assessments are made up of (a) exercises designed to elicit some response from students, and (b) an evaluation scheme that allows the user to interpret the quality of that response. Let's be very clear about the fact that the "objectivity" in the selected response form of assessment applies *only* to the scoring system. It has nothing to do with the exercise side of the equation.

Well-written selected response test items frame challenges that allow for just one best answer or a limited set of acceptable answers. This leads to the "objective" evaluation of responses as being right or wrong. However, the process of developing exercises that form the basis of this kind of assessment includes a major helping of the test author's professional judgment or subjectivity. When the test items are written and/or when they are selected for inclusion on the final test, someone is making a subjective judgment as to the meaning and importance of the material to be tested.

My point is that all assessments, regardless of their format, involve judgment on the part of the assessor. Therefore, all assessments reflect the biases of that assessor. The key to the effective use of sound assessments as a part of the instructional process is to make sure those biases are clear and public from the outset, so that everyone has an equal chance to see and understand what it means to be successful.

Further, I have chosen the label *assessments* instead of *tests* to make the point that we are not talking only about traditional tests. Selected response item formats also can appear on quizzes, homework assignments, and practice exercises during instruction. For this reason, they can be used summatively as final tests documenting achievement or formatively to promote growth along the way. In Chapter 3, we established that both uses are critical to student well-being and thus demand sound assessment.

The Importance of Knowing How to Assess

There are three specific reasons why it is important for you to understand how to design and use selected response assessment formats, even in these times when performance assessment methodology is becoming so popular in school testing.

The first reason is the most obvious. There is a very good chance you will want to design and develop selected response assessments for use in your classroom. Virtually every teaching situation includes important achievement targets at some time during the school year that can be translated into selected response formats for assessment. When these times arise, you will need to know how to prepare and use such assessments.

The second reason for attaining a basic understanding of selected response assessment is that you may want to use tests developed by others. You will need to be able to evaluate the quality of these tests before using them.

For instance, you may want to use tests that come with your textbooks. Text publishers often ask their authors to develop tests to accompany their textbooks as an aid to the teacher and, frankly, as a marketing device to save teachers from the time-consuming work of developing their own tests. If these textbook-embedded tests are developed by those familiar with the achievement targets established for the book and knowledgeable about the development of sound tests, then everyone wins. The publisher sells books, the teacher saves time and effort, and students benefit from sound assessment during instruction.

Problems arise, however, when those who were charged with design and development of these tests did not understand the intended targets and/or were untrained in developing sound tests. When this occurs, unsound tests result and students are in danger of becoming victims of inaccurate assessment.

What is the likelihood that this will occur? As a teacher, you will never know the skill level of those who designed the assessments that come with your textbooks. This leaves you with two choices: trust the text author and publisher to have done a good job and proceed on the assumption that the tests are sound, or conduct your own quality control check on the tests. This choice should be an easy one; anyone who chooses option one simply is being naive or worse. But when you choose option two, you must be prepared to be a critical consumer and thoroughly carry out that quality control check.

Time for Reflection

If you are an experienced teacher, how often have you come across tests of inferior quality accompanying your textbooks? As you think back, what were the problems with these tests? Make a list of specific problems and save it for review later in the chapter.

Never forget that *you,* the teacher, are the last line of defense against the mismeasurement of student achievement using objectively scored paper and pencil tests. Whether you play the role of test developer or gatekeeper, in the final analysis, you are responsible for the quality of the tests used in your classroom.

The third reason why you need to be conversant with the meaning of quality as applied to selected response assessments is that you must be in a position to act in your own best interest when your achievement is being assessed. All undergraduate or graduate students face the prospect of taking tests. Even as a practicing teacher or administrator, at licensing or certification time, you may well find yourself confronted with selected response examinations. It is in your interest to know if these tests— which can influence your life in profoundly important ways—are sound or unsound.

When they are unsound, it is in your best interest and in the best interest of your classmates and others who will follow to point out any flaws in test design that are likely to render the score inaccurate as an estimate of real achievement.

I know this presents a challenge in diplomacy. It can be risky to point out these problems to those in power positions. But if we let obvious sources of mismeasurement go unchecked, not only do we allow ourselves to be mistreated, but we miss golden opportunities to strike a blow on behalf of higher levels of assessment literacy throughout the educational system. When the opportunity presents itself, you can take advantage of such "teachable moments" to diplomatically help your professors understand and adhere to accepted standards of quality.

Time for Reflection

Have you ever been involved in an experience where you knew an assessment of your achievement was unsound and you knew why? What did you do about it? Was your action productive?

MATCHING SELECTED RESPONSE ASSESSMENTS TO ACHIEVEMENT TARGETS

In Chapter 5, we touched on strategies for aligning our various assessment methods to the different kinds of achievement targets. Let's continue that discussion now by examining the kinds of targets that can be translated effectively into selected response formats.

Select the best answer:

Which of the test item formats listed below can be used to assess both student mastery of content knowledge and their ability to use that knowledge to reason and solve problems?
   a. Multiple-choice
   b. True/false
   c. Matching
   d. Short answer fill-in
   e. All of the above
   f. None of the above

The best answer is (e), all of the above. All four formats can tap both knowledge mastery and reasoning, two of the five basic kinds of outcomes discussed in earlier chapters. In addition, however, these formats also can shed at least some light on the other three kinds of performance: skills, products, and affect.

Matching Method to Target

Assessing Knowledge.   Selected response test items can be used to test student mastery of subject matter knowledge. Remember, students can master content knowledge in either of two ways: through memorization and through the effective use of reference materials. Clearly, selected response exercises can be used to test the former—memorized facts and information.

But don't be trapped into thinking that this is all they can do. I continue to find many educators across the land holding tenaciously to the misconception that all these kinds of items can do is test knowledge of facts. Multiple-choice, true/false, matching, and fill-in exercises are not just for testing recall of facts and information. When carefully constructed, they can do *much* more.

For example, we can use open-book versions of these tests to see if students know the organizational structure of content in a textbook or other reference document and can gain easy access to information contained therein. The ability to gain mastery of knowledge for later reference has become a very important life skill in the information age.

Assessing Reasoning.   Various reasoning and problem-solving outcomes also can be assessed with selected response formats. When students are presented with questions eliciting answers they have not previously memorized, they can demonstrate the ability to dip into their existing structures of knowledge, retrieve critical information, and use it in sophisticated problem-solving ways. For example, we can assess student ability to think comparatively by presenting true/false exercises depicting differences between two events or objects and asking them to judge the appropriateness of the comparisons. And we can use selected response exercises to test student ability to draw inferences. We do this on reading tests, for example, when we ask them to identify the main idea of a story.

Assessing Skills.   While we cannot use selected response test formats to assess student mastery of skills such as speaking, interacting socially, tuning an engine, and the like, we can use them to assess mastery of at least some of the procedural knowledge prerequisite to being able to demonstrate these kinds of skills. For instance, if a student fails on a performance assessment to communicate effectively in a second language, we might wish to follow up with a selected response test to see if the student knows the vocabulary. Or if a student fails to solve a math problem adequately, we might follow up with an assessment of the student's knowledge of the algorithm for solving such problems. If a student fails to carry out a science lab procedure correctly, we can ask whether the student knew the steps in the process.

All proficiency is based on a foundation of factual knowledge. A student cannot write in an organized manner unless and until that student has mastered (i.e., knows) a variety of organizational alternatives.

Assessing Products.   Still further, we can construct selected response exercises that test student knowledge of the attributes of a quality product that are prerequisite to being able to create such a product. Students who don't know the attributes of a good term paper are unlikely to be able to reflect those attributes in their own efforts. Or, students who cannot distinguish a quality product from others of inferior quality are unlikely to be able to produce quality. Selected response assessments can test all these things.

Time for Reflection

What are some of the things a student needs to know to be able to produce a quality term paper? List some of the procedural knowledge that may need to be covered during instruction to set students up for success on a term paper project. Further, what are some of the key attributes of a quality final product?

Please understand that these kinds of foundational knowledge typically are not sufficient as outcomes of instruction. Without question, ultimately, we are far more concerned with what students can do with what they know. But knowledge foundations *are* absolutely necessary as results of instruction. And, as a teacher charged with moving the student toward excellence, sometimes, you may need to verify the presence of prerequisite knowledge in the student's bag of tools.

Also understand that I am not saying you *must* assess knowledge foundations. My point is simply that you *can* if you wish—if it fits into your classroom context. And when you decide to do so, selected response formats can serve you well.

Assessing Affect. In a different vein, you can develop questionnaire items to tap student attitudes, values, motivational dispositions, and other affective states, items that ask the respondent to select from among a finite number of response options. Questions inquiring about preferred extracurricular activities, for example, might offer such choices. Attitude scales might offer a statement about a particular feeling, such as "School is a place where my academic needs are met," and then might ask students if they agree, disagree, or are undecided. These can represent excellent ways to tap both the direction and intensity of student feelings about important aspects of school or classroom life.

Please note that the remainder of this chapter deals only with the design of selected response assessment of student achievement. Design of assessment formats for use in the assessment of affect is covered completely in Chapter 12.

Summary of Target Matches

While we cannot reach all of the achievement targets we value with selected response exercises, we can tap parts of many. We can test student mastery of content knowledge, including that which is memorized and that which is secured through the effective use of reference materials. In addition, we can tap a variety of kinds of reasoning and problem solving, including analytical, comparative, and inferential thinking. And we can get at some of the underpinnings of successful performance in more complex arenas, assessing knowledge of appropriate procedures, and/or knowledge of the key attributes of quality products.

Thus, selected response assessment is versatile. In fact, it is a far richer and more useful methodology than most educators realize. This form of assessment is often misunderstood and misrepresented in its potential to help teachers and students. Some malign the multiple-choice format because it is the format used in standardized achievement test batteries. Critics sometimes contend that, since such tests are of little value in the classroom, the methodology must be flawed. This is not true, and represents a counterproductive, extreme position. In the classroom, where one important goal is to help students master the knowledge and thinking foundations of competence, the accurate and efficient assessment of that mastery can be a key to student growth and development. Selected response assessments have a role to play here; let us not discard the baby with the bathwater!

DEVELOPING SELECTED RESPONSE ASSESSMENTS

Assuming that selected response assessment is appropriate for the target(s) you wish to assess, there are other realities of life in classrooms that can and should contribute to your decision to use this option. We consider those assessment context factors here, and then turn to the actual test development process itself, highlighting some simple, yet powerful keys to sound assessment.

Context Factors

It is appropriate to consider using selected response formats under the following conditions:

- *You are absolutely certain students have a sufficiently high level of reading proficiency to be able to understand the exercises.* Students' mastery of the material being tested is always confounded with their ability to read the test items. Therefore, if a selected response test of knowledge mastery or problem solving is to be administered to the poor or nonreader, the examinee must be given some kind of support in overcoming the reading difficulty. It is only through such procedural adjustments that achievement and reading proficiency can be disentangled and an accurate estimate of achievement obtained.

- *A high-quality test already has been developed and is available for you to use.* Why waste time on new development when others already have done the work for you? But again, quality must be verified—it cannot and should not be assumed. Also be advised that some publishers have begun to produce computerized banks of test items out of which teachers can develop their own tests. If well written (read on to find out what this means), these can be very helpful.

- *The number of students to be assessed is large.* Once developed, the selected response test can be administered to large numbers of students at the same time and scored very quickly. These tests can be very efficient.

- *The scope of the achievement target is broad.* When there is much material to be mastered and tested, relatively large samples of test items will be needed to do it justice. These tests permit the administration of large numbers of items per unit of testing time.

- *Time permits students to respond to all test items.* In the old era of assessment, we ranked students on the basis of speed and accuracy. Very often, tests carried tight time limits by design. Not all students finished the test. However, as we are now concerned more about competence, assessment must focus on mastery of material, with less emphasis on speed. Test items not attempted fail to contribute useful information in this context. For this reason, we opt for "power" tests, which permit every student to at least attempt each test item.

- *Computer support is available to assist with item development, item storage and retrieval, test printing, and optical scan scoring.* Be advised that you can save immense amounts of time and effort through the thoughtful use of personal computer and optical scanning technology in the use of selected response assessments. Let me expand on this idea.

Using Technology in Assessment.   Technology is available to us today that can greatly ease the workload associated with selected response assessment. One time- and labor-saving device of immense potential is the personal computer. Many text publishers and other service providers have developed computerized item banks. The packages often include disks full of already developed exercises coded by content, type of reasoning involved, grade level, and subject. Software packages are also available to ease the word processing load of test construction, should you need to choose to create your own.

Ward (1991) provides a compilation of nearly one hundred currently available computerized test-item banking and test-analysis software packages. To illustrate the level of sophistication of this technology, IPS Publishing of Vancouver, Washington, has developed thousands of computer algorithms, or routines, capable of automatically generating millions of high-quality mathematics test items on command. Exercises generated reflect specific learning objectives cross-referenced to nearly all of the texts used across the United States and Canada in elementary arithmetic through calculus. They also make available an objective tracking system that allows teachers to identify target objectives, generate tests, automatically score tests, record results, and plan individualized instruction for students.

Another very interesting application of technology to the selected response assessment development process is *computer adaptive testing* (Legg & Buhr, 1992). In this case, the computer stores a bank of test items of varying difficulty covering a given achievement target. Essentially, the computer selects the items to be administered on the test. The examinee, responding to the computer through a keyboard, is given an item to answer. If the examinee gets it right, the computer jumps to a higher level of difficulty. The system continues to increase the difficulty until the examinee misses an item. The difficulty then begins to drop back until the examinee begins to answer correctly. In this way, the computer can assist in finding the student's functional level of competence while administering far fewer items faster than a conventional test.

One final application of technology that demands mention here is optical scanners—those scoring machines that produce results so quickly. The fact is that any teacher who uses selected response formats other than fill-in and is scoring by hand is wasting a great deal of time. Not only can these machines generate test scores, but in their currently available versions, they can analyze test items to tell you how your students did collectively on each item. If that is not diagnostic of your instruction and their learning, diagnosis will never be possible! Further, companies such as National Computer Systems (NCS) of Eden Prairie, Minnesota, have combined scanning technology with other computer hardware and software to link objectives, assessments, and student records in new and efficient ways. And the good news is that these scanners and the associated forms are now quite inexpensive.

I will continue to refer to applications of technology in classroom assessment as our journey progresses, particularly in Part 3, dealing with classroom applications. But for now, let's examine the nature of the test development process itself.

THE STEPS IN TEST DEVELOPMENT

Described in its simplest form, the selected response test is developed in three steps—each of which requires the application of special professional competence. Those three basic steps require that the developer do the following:

1. devise a test plan or blueprint that frames an appropriate sample of achievement

2. identify the specific elements of knowledge and thinking to be assessed

3. transform those elements into test items

The steps of test planning and identifying elements to be assessed are the same for all four test item formats, so we will deal with those together. Then we will discuss how to write quality test items using each individual format.

Step 1: Preparing a Test Plan

Building a test without a plan is like building a house without a blueprint. Two things are going to happen and both are bad! First, the construction process is going to take much longer than it would if you had a plan, and second, the final product is not going to be what you had expected or hoped for. In the development of selected response assessments, a carefully developed blueprint is, as you shall see, virtually everything. Plan well and the test will almost automatically develop itself.

Besides making the test development process easier and more efficient, test blueprinting offers an opportunity for teachers and students to clarify achievement expectations—to sharpen their vision of what it means to be successful. As you will see, this planning process absolutely requires that the test developer delve deeply into the material to be learned, so as to understand the deep structure of the knowledge to be mastered and the complexity of the problem solving to be accomplished using that knowledge. Without this clarity and depth of vision, it will be impossible to develop sound assessments.

We have two types of test plans from which to choose. One is called a *table of test specifications*. The other relies on a list of *instructional objectives* to guide test construction. Each holds the promise of providing the foundation for a sound test and of helping integrate selected response assessment into your teaching and learning process. Choose whichever you like—both work. They are essentially equally effective as test planning devices, as you shall see.

The Table of Specifications.   To explain how the table of test specifications works, we must begin with the basic unit of the objectively scored test—the individual test item. Any test item requires the respondent to do two things: to gain access to a specific piece of information (either from memory or reference materials), and to use that knowledge to carry out a cognitive operation (i.e., to solve some kind of problem).

For example, I might construct a test item based on knowledge of assessment methodology and ask the respondent simply to recall it:

List the critical attributes of a sound assessment.

Or I might ask the respondent to recall two elements of content knowledge about assessment and relate one to the other, as in this comparison item:

What is one similarity between multiple-choice and fill-in test items?

In this case, the respondents must dip into their reservoir of knowledge about assessment methods (prerequisite knowledge), analyze the component elements of each, and find elements that are similar (comparative thinking). So it is in

Table 6-1
Table of Specifications for Civil War Unit Test

Content Category	Number of Items			
	Recall	Compare	Infer	Total
Causes	2	2	1	5
Major battles	6	2	2	10
Effects	7	4	4	15
Total	15	8	7	30

the case of all such test items: elements of knowledge are carried into some thinking process.

Time for Reflection

Find a test you have developed or taken that relies on selected response items. Analyze five or ten items to determine the required knowledge elements and the kind of cognitive operation to be carried out.

The table of test specifications takes advantage of this combination of knowledge retrieval and its application to permit the development of a plan that promises to sample both in a predetermined manner. Table 6–1 is a simple example of such a table.

In this table, we find a plan for a unit test in history, focusing on the Civil War. The test is to include thirty items worth one point each.

On the left, we have subdivided the content knowledge into three basic categories: causes, major battles, and effects of the war. Each category obviously contains many elements of knowledge within it, some of which will be transformed into test items later. But for now, note in the last column that we have decided to include five items testing knowledge of causes, ten on battles, and fifteen on effects. These numbers reflect our sense of the relative importance of these three categories of material.

Time for Reflection

Please think about how a teacher might establish test item priorities. Why might some categories receive more items than others? List as many possible considerations as you can.

The differences in the number of items assigned to each category might reflect any or all of the following:

- the amount of instructional time spent on each
- the amount of material in each category
- the relative importance of material in each category for later learning

This is an important part of the art of classroom assessment: As a teacher, your special insights about the nature and capabilities of your students and the nature and amount of material you have covered must come into play in setting these priorities. Given this particular body of material, as a teacher/test developer, you must ask, What should be the areas of greatest emphasis if I am to prepare students for material to come later in their education?

To be able to answer this question—to develop this vision—you must know and understand the content and kinds of reasoning that form the foundations of your special arenas of instructional responsibility. You must be a master of the content and thinking to be learned. In the absence of such a vision of the meaning of success for students, how do you design instruction to promote that success and how do you devise assessments reflective of that success? You cannot.

Notice the columns in Table 6–1. Three kinds of thinking are listed—three different kinds of cognitive actions to be required of respondents: *recall* elements of knowledge, *compare* them, and draw *inferences* (meaning to draw generalizations using the knowledge in the reasoning process). Once again, outcome priorities are reflected on the bottom: fifteen recall items, eight comparison items, and seven inference items. If the test is to accurately and fairly test the results of instruction, students need to have been provided with opportunities to practice these patterns of thinking. That is, instruction should have reflected these priorities, too.

Once the categories are defined and row and column totals are specified (which does not take very long for a teacher who *knows* the material), you need only spread the numbers of items through the cells of the table so that they add up to the row and column totals. This will generate a plan to guide the writing of a set of test items that will systematically sample both content and thinking priorities as established.

But how do you decide how many rows and columns to include in a table of test specifications? How do you decide what those rows and columns should reflect? There are no rigid rules. You can include as many rows and columns as make sense for your particular unit and test. This aspect of the development process is as much art as it is science. You should consider the following factors with respect to content categories:

- Look for natural subdivisions in the material presented in a text, such as chapters or major sections within chapters. These are likely to reflect natural subdivisions of material generally accepted by experts in the field. Each chapter or section might become a row in a table of specifications.

- Be sure categories have clearly marked limits and are large enough to contain a number of important elements of knowledge within each. As you will see below, these elements are to be sampled during item writing and you need a clear sampling frame.

- Use subdivisions of content and kinds of thinking that are likely to make sense to students as a result of their studies. Ultimately, they must see the vision too if they are to meet your expectations.

With respect to reflecting the kinds of thinking to be assessed, categories included in the table should have the following characteristics:

- Categories should have clear labels and underlying meanings that are couched in accepted conceptions of cognition. There are many options out there that have been carefully researched and are highly refined. I will say more about these, and provide examples, in Chapter 10.

- Categories should be so familiar and comfortable that you can almost automatically pose exercises that demand student thinking in those terms.

- Each category should represent kinds of thinking and problem solving that occur in the real world.

- All categories should represent kinds of thinking students can understand and converse about as a result of experience and practice during instruction.

The bottom line is this: The categories of content, kinds of thinking tested, and proportion of items assigned to each should reflect the content priorities communicated to students during instruction. Remember, students can hit any target they can see and that holds still for them!

Instructional Objectives as Test Plans.   You can reach this same end of building a quality test plan by generating a list of instructional objectives, if you assume each objective, like each cell in a table of specifications, specifies the knowledge to be brought to bear and the action to be taken (recall it, analyze it, compare it, and so on) by the student. Here are examples of such objectives:

> *Given knowledge of the Civil War, the student will be able to compare and contrast the battle strategies of the Union and the Confederacy.*

> *The student will know (i.e., be able to recall) the causes of the Civil War.*

Note that each objective need not be written so as to define outcomes at a high level of specific detail. Rather, like cells in a table of specifications, they can set frames around categories that contain many possible test items within them. Sound objectives answer the question, What knowledge is to be used to perform what cognitive activity? Later, test items can be prepared that actually go inside and retrieve those combined knowledge and thinking elements and use them as their basis. But more about that below.

Plans Really Help.   For now, simply realize that the frames placed around content and thinking by tables of specifications and lists of instructional objectives are very important for three reasons. First and foremost, they define success for students, giving those students control over their own fate. They know that, if they master the material, they will score high. Those who know this going into the test are more likely to succeed. Let the spotlight shine on your expectations so all can see them.

Second, clearly written expectations in the form of tables of test specifications and lists of objectives set limits on teacher accountability for student learning. With thoughtful plans in place, for example, you are no longer responsible for seeing to it that every student knows every single fact about the Civil War. Rather, students need to know causes, battles, and effects, and know how to reason using that information. When all of your students can hit such a complex target, you are a supreme success as a teacher—and there can be no question about it.

Third, once the overall plan is assembled, it becomes possible for you to develop comparable forms of the same test. This can be very useful when you need to protect test security, such as when you need another form for students who were absent or who must retake the test for some reason. You can assemble another set of items that samples the same content and kinds of thinking, and develop a test of different items that you know represents identical material. This means that all students are provided with the same chances of success.

Summary of Step 1.   The first step in test development is to formulate a plan—a blueprint for the test, if you will. Sound plans can be developed only by those who themselves have attained complete mastery over the material (content and thinking) to be assessed. Given that foundation, you can either (a) design a table of test specifications, or (b) prepare a list of instructional objectives. Any cell of the table or any objective will represent the union of two essential elements: some content knowledge to be retrieved via memory or reference and some cognitive act to be carried out using that material.

Using tables of specifications or lists of objectives allows you to connect the test directly to instructional priorities. In this way, these plans also set limits on the meaning of student and therefore teacher success, thus maximizing the chances that you and your students will each achieve the levels of excellence that you seek.

Step 2: Selecting Elements to Be Tested

Once the table of specifications or list of objectives has been developed, the test designer faces the challenge of selecting the combined elements of knowledge and thinking to be tested. In Table 6–1, the cell crossing battles with recall requires the construction of six test items. The next key test development question is, Can these items test recall of *any* six battles during the Civil War? How does one decide which of the huge number of facts about Civil War battles to test?

There are two factors to consider in answering this question: the need to sample representatively the different components of material in the unit, and the relative importance of those components. Let me explain how these come into play.

Sampling Considerations.   As previously stated, any selected response assessment is really only a sampling from an ideal, infinitely long test. Clearly, if we were to test student mastery of every event of the Civil War, we'd be talking about an impossibly long test! The most efficient way to prevent this problem and create tests that fit into reasonable time limits is to select a sample of the important material, test it, and assume that the score on that sample reflects proportional student mastery of the total body of knowledge.

To understand this, think about commonly used polling techniques. Pollsters cannot afford to ask every citizen's opinion. So they select a sample of voters, ask them to express their opinion, and then estimate from this carefully selected sample how the general population feels on key issues.

In test development, we do exactly the same thing with test items. If we sample larger bodies of content and thinking (assessment specialists call these *domains*) in a representative manner, then performance on the sample can lead to inferences about the proportion of material in those larger domains that students have mastered.

But precisely what is it that we are to sample on our test on the Civil War, for example? Can we pick just any set of facts, test them, and then generalize? The answer is no—not just any facts. Here is another place where classroom assessment becomes an art. We must select a sample of all possible *important* elements of knowledge in combination with *important* cognitive challenges.

Who decides what is important, and how do they do it? If you are to develop the test, you do! If the textbook publisher developed the test and you are charged with evaluating it, you must establish the achievement target priorities in your classroom, so you can see if the text-embedded test covers your valued outcomes.

This is yet another reason why the assessor must possess a highly refined vision of the achievement target. Those who have immersed themselves in the material know what is important. But there are other places to turn to for advice in finding the important material. For example, the textbook's author will highlight and emphasize its most important material in lists of objectives and chapter summaries, as will any accompanying teacher's guides.

In addition, state, district, building, and/or department curriculum guidelines typically spell out priorities at some level. Sometimes, just taking time to talk with colleagues about instructional priorities can help.

Other valuable sources of guidance in articulating valued knowledge and thinking outcomes are the various national and state professional associations of teachers, such as of science, of mathematics, of English, and so on. Nearly every such association has assembled a commission within the past five years to identify and spell out in writing standards of excellence for student achievement in their domain. You should be familiar with any national standards of student performance held as valuable by teachers in your field.

Out of all of this *you* must decide what is important to test within each cell of your table of specifications or within each instructional objective you specify in your classroom. And so it is that, even though you might use an "objective test" format, the material tested is very much a matter of professional judgment on your part.

But please understand that this subjectivity is not a problem as long as you are in touch with priorities in your field and specify your valued outcomes very carefully. No one can do this work for you. You must possess the vision and it must be a sound and appropriate vision, given the students you teach and the latest thinking about the disciplines you teach and assess.

Identifying Important Propositions.   In this section, I offer a practical and efficient means of transforming your vision, whether expressed in a table of specifications or a list of objectives, into quality test items. This strategy promises to save you more test development time and have a greater impact on the quality of your tests than any other single test development suggestion in this chapter. Just be advised from the outset that this tactic is subtle—another aspect of the *art* of test development. But with practice, anyone can master it.

Capture the elements to be tested in the form of clearly stated sentences that reflect important elements of content and stipulate the kind of cognitive operation to be carried out. In the test development field, we call these statements *propositions*. As you shall see, propositions save time.

But before I illustrate their use, I need to ask you to accept something on faith now, which I will verify for you later through example: When you have identified and listed all of the propositions that form the basis of a test, the test is 95 percent developed! While the work remaining is not trivial, I promise you that it will go so fast it will make your head spin. When your goal is high-quality selected response tests, if you invest your time up front in identifying the important elements of success—finding those outcomes that top your list of things students should know and be able to do—the rest of the test development process will be automatic.

To collect these propositions, or basic units of test development, we begin by reviewing the material to be sampled on the test, keeping the table of specifications or instructional objectives close at hand.

Refer to Table 6–1 once again. We need fifteen recall test items in total. Two of these must address causes of the war. So as we review the material on causes of the war, we seek out and write down, say, five or six causes that we consider every student should know.

Remember, we don't need to gather a large number of cause/recall propositions, because we're only going to use two of them on the test. But those collected must reflect the most important material. As we collect propositions, we use clearly stated sentences:

> *One major cause of the Civil War was the desire of the north to abolish slavery.*

> *A contributing cause of the Civil War was conflicting economic priorities of the industrial north and the agricultural south.*

Once the cause/recall propositions have been written, we move on to find key elements of the battles/recall cell. Note from the blueprint that we need six of these. Given this expectation, we should try to find and state ten or twelve important propositions. That way, if we need to replace some later or if we want to develop two forms of the same test, we have our active ingredients (additional propositions) ready to go.

Besides, we want to have enough propositions for the test to give us confidence in the generalizations we plan to draw from student performance on the sample to their likely mastery of the universe of material we could have covered on the test. We know we can't ask everything. But we need to be sure to ask enough. It's a matter of judgment. If we err at all, we want to err in the direction of including too many rather than too few items for a given cell.

And so we would proceed through all nine cells of the table, seeking out and writing down more propositions than we will need. In effect, we are creating a list of important learnings. Note that we have attempted no test items yet.

Table 6–1 tells us we need a total of eight comparison propositions, two each on causes and battles and four on effects. Here's a possible battles proposition requiring comparative thinking:

> *The 1864 battles of The Wilderness and Cold Harbor were similar in that both brought generals Lee and Grant into direct confrontation and resulted in huge casualties on both sides.*

Here is an example requiring inferential thinking:

> *Superior weaponry and training were primary reasons for the ultimate victory of the Union Army in the Civil War.*

This proposition includes possible inferences about effects for that cell of the table of specifications. Please note that these inferences may not have been explicitly covered in class; that is, we may not have expected students to memorize them. Rather, they may represent the kinds of inferences we want them to be able to draw from their own knowledge of the Civil War. To test their ability to think on their feet, then, we must present cognitive challenges in test items that demand more than recall.

This idea bears further discussion, as it is critical to sound test development. As shown in Table 6–1, we need test items that reflect the student's ability to think comparatively (column 2) and to draw inferences (column 3). To reach this goal, a very special relationship must exist between the items that appear on the test and the preceding instruction: The item must, at test time, present a problem that calls for applying knowledge in a way not specifically covered during instruction. Thus, it must present a problem for which students have not systematically memorized the answer. They must be given the challenge of reasoning it out right there on the spot.

Certainly, students must dip into their reservoir of available knowledge—that is, must recall information—to reason productively. But the aim of some propositions should be to assess more than recall when the goal of instruction is more than recall. If we want students to make the leap, for example, from just knowing something to analyzing, comparing, or inferring—that is, to reasoning—we must rely on novel questions at test time to make them do so.

The most practical implication of this perspective on test development is that it makes it perfectly acceptable to include material on the test not explicitly covered in class, if we wish to tap student reasoning and problem solving. However, we also have an obligation to the students to be sure they have had the opportunity to (a) master the basic knowledge required to answer such test items, and (b) practice with similar kinds of reasoning and problem-solving propositions. I will say more about these issues in Chapter 10, where we will discuss assessing student thinking and problem solving.

Summary of Step 2.   Step two calls for selected response test developers to march back through the material to be tested, blueprint in hand, in search of the important learnings to be tested. These form the basis of propositions—sentences that capture the essence of things worth knowing and reasoning worth doing. These propositions will be translated into actual test items, discussed in step three, below.

But before making those translations, it is wise to step back from this list of propositions and review them one more time, asking yourself, Does this collection of sentences really provide a composite picture of what I think are the important knowledge and reasoning outcomes of this unit? If you really know and understand the material and know how the material relates to that which the student will confront in the future, weak propositions will jump out at you. If you find weak entries, replace them. When the list meets your highest standards of coverage, you are ready to make a selected response test.

Additional Thoughts on Steps 1 and 2

Without question, these are complex test development steps. I think it reasonable to expect you to be asking, How does he expect me to do all of this and teach, too? My answer is for you to stick with me through the final test development step, where it will become apparent why all of this planning saves you a great deal of time and effort.

Also be advised that this kind of test development process quickly becomes second nature to those who practice and master it. I promise you, if you are not confident that you have mastered all of the content or thinking processes before you start, by the time you finish designing some tests in this way, you will have mastered them. In this sense, the very process of test development is an excellent professional development experience.

And finally, let me plant a small seed of an idea in the following "Time for Reflection," so we can grow this idea together as we travel on.

Time for Reflection

If this test development process involves too much work for one teacher to do all alone, can you think of any helpers that might be brought into the process to lighten the workload associated with developing tables of specifications, lists of objectives, and propositions? Who could help you and what sort of work might they do? Jot down some thoughts now and we will come back to this later.

Step 3: Building Test Items from Propositions

Earlier, I stipulated that developing a high-quality test plan and specifying propositions represent 95 percent of the work in selected response test development. Complete the list of propositions and the test will almost develop itself from that point. The reason lies in the fact that the proposition form captures a complete and coherent thought. Professional test developers understand that the key to fast and effective item writing is to be sure to start with such a complete and coherent thought about that which is to be tested.

Once we have a proposition in hand, we can spin any kind of selected response item out of it that we wish. Let me illustrate with the following inference proposition. (Remember, I want my students to think through the answer to this. It was not explicitly covered in class.)

> *If the Union Army had followed up its defeat of Lee and his Army of North-ern Virginia at Antietam, the Civil War would have been shortened.*

To generate a true/false item out of this proposition that is true, we can simply in-clude the proposition on the test as stated! The proposition is a true true/false test item as written. This is true of all well-stated propositions.

If we want a true/false item that is false, we simply make one part of the propo-sition false:

> *A Union Army followup of its defeat of the Confederacy at Antietam would have had no effect on the outcome of the Civil War.*

To convert this proposition to a fill-in item, we simply leave out the phrase dealing with the effect and ask a question:

> *What would have happened if the Union Army had followed up its defeat of Lee's Confederate forces at Antietam?*

If we desire a multiple-choice item, we add a number of response options, only one of which is correct.

Mark my words: every well conceived and clearly stated proposition—whether requiring recall or some other kind of thinking—is an automatic source of test items.

Invest your time and effort up front learning the underlying structure of the ma-terial you teach, and finding the *important* propositions. These are the keys to the rapid development of sound selected response assessments.

Item Writing Tips.   Once you have identified the format(s) you plan to use, a few simple keys will aid you in developing sound test items. Some of these guidelines apply to all formats, some are unique to each particular format.

General Guidelines.   These tend to focus on the form of the presentation. The sim-plicity of their advice belies their power to improve your tests, believe me.

1. *Write clear and sharply focused test items.* Good item writing is first and fore-most an exercise in clear communication. Follow the rules of grammar—tests are as much a public reflection of our professional standards as any other prod-uct we create. Include only material essential to framing the question. Come to the point. Our goal is to test mastery of the material, not the student's ability to figure out what we're asking!

    Not this:

    When scientists use magnets they need to know about the poles, which are?

But this:[1]

What are the poles of a magnet called?
a. Anode and cathode
b. North and south
c. Strong and weak
d. Attract and repel

2. *Ask a question.* In the case of multiple-choice and fill-in, minimize the use of incomplete statements as exercises. When you force yourself to ask a question, you force yourself to express a complete thought in the stem or trigger part of the item, which usually promotes clear understanding by the respondent.

   Not this (these items might be presented with a graph depicting interest rate patterns):

   Between 1950 and 1965
   a. Interest rates increased
   b. Interest rates decreased
   c. Interest rates fluctuated greatly
   d. Interest rates did not change

   But this:

   What was the trend in interest rates between 1950 and 1965?
   a. Increased only
   b. Decreased only
   c. Increased, then decreased
   d. Remained unchanged

3. *Aim for the lowest possible reading level.* This is an attempt to control for the inevitable confounding of reading proficiency and mastery of the material in the student's score. Minimize sentence length and syntactic complexity and eliminate unnecessarily difficult vocabulary.

4. *Eliminate clues to the correct answer either within the item or across items within a test.* When grammatical clues within items or material presented in other items give away the correct answer, students get items right for the wrong reasons. The result is misinformation about the student's true achievement.

   Not this:

   All of these are examples of a bird that flies, *except* an
   a. Ostrich
   b. Falcon
   c. Cormorant
   d. Robin

---

[1]Item adapted from *Handbook on Formative and Summative Evaluation of Student Learning* (p. 592, Item A.4–2.211) by B. S. Bloom, J. T. Hastings, and G. F. Madaus, 1971, New York: McGraw-Hill. Copyright 1971 by McGraw-Hill, Inc. Reprinted by permission of the publisher.

Or this:

Which of the following are examples of birds that do not fly?
a. Falcon
b. Ostrich and penguin
c. Cormorant
d. Robin

5. *If you write the items, have them read at least once by a knowledgeable colleague.* This is especially true of the really high-stakes tests, such as big unit tests and final exams. No one is perfect. We all overlook simple mistakes. Having a willing colleague review your work just takes a few minutes and can save a great deal of time and eliminate problems in the long run. Don't get your ego so tied up in your test that you can't take some constructive criticism when it's needed.

6. *And please, double check the scoring key for accuracy before scoring.* 'Nuff said!

Multiple-choice Items.   Keep these few simple, yet powerful, guidelines in mind:

1. *Ask a complete question to get the item started, if you can.* This has the effect of placing the focus on the item in the stem, not in the response options. (See the interest rate example above.)

2. *If you find yourself repeating the same words at the beginning of each response option, reword the stem to move the repetitive material up there.* This will clarify the problem and make it more efficient for the respondent to read. (Again, see the interest rate example.)

3. *Be sure there is only one correct or best answer.* This is where that independent review by a colleague can help. Remember, it is acceptable to ask respondents to select a best answer from among a set of answers, all of which are correct. Just be sure to word the question so as to make the respondent's task clear.

4. *Word response options as briefly as possible and be sure they are grammatically parallel.* This has two desirable effects. First, it makes items easier to read. Second, it helps eliminate grammatical clues as to the correct answer. (See the second bird example above.)

Not this:

Why did colonists come to the United States?
a. To escape heavy taxation by their native governments
b. Religion
c. They sought the adventure of living among native Americans in the new land
d. There was the promise of great wealth in the new world
e. More than one of the above answers

But this:

Why did colonists migrate to the United States?
a. To escape taxation
b. For religious freedom
c. For adventure
d. More than one of the above

5. *Vary the number of response options presented as appropriate to create the item you want.*
    a. Offering two to five response options or more can still produce outstanding items. There is no single best number of responses.
    b. Vary the number of response options offered across items within the same test, when appropriate.
    c. Limit the use of "all of the above" or "none of the above" as a means to fill up spaces just because you can't think of viable incorrect answers. In fact, sound practice suggests limiting their use to those few times when they fit comfortably into the item context.
    d. Include more than one correct answer and ask the student to find all correct answers, when appropriate. Give credit for all correct answers.

By the way, here's a simple, yet crafty, multiple-choice item writing tip: If you compose a multiple-choice item and find that you cannot think of enough plausible incorrect responses, include the item on a test the first time as a fill-in item. As your students respond, those who get it wrong will provide you with the full range of viable incorrect responses you need to include it next time as multiple-choice!

True/False Items. You have only one simple guideline here: Make the item entirely true or false as stated. Complex "idea salads" including some truth and some falsehood just confuse the issue. Precisely what is the proposition you are testing? State it and move on.

Matching Exercises. Please note that matching exercises really represent complex multiple-choice items with a number of stems offered along with a number of response options. Therefore, all of the guidelines offered for multiple-choice apply here, too. In addition, observe the following guidelines:

1. *State the matching challenge up front* with a clear and concise set of directions specifying what is to be matched.
2. *Keep the list of things to be matched short.* The maximum number of options is ten. Shorter is better. This minimizes the information processing and idea juggling respondents must do to be successful.
3. *Keep the list of things to be matched homogeneous.* Don't mix events with dates or with names. Again, idea salads confuse the issue. Focus the exercise.
4. *Keep the list of response options brief in their wording and parallel in their construction.* Pose the matching challenge in clear, straightforward language.

5. *Include more response options than are needed and permit response options to be used more than once.* This has the effect of making it impossible for the respondent to arrive at the correct response purely through a process of elimination. If a student answers correctly using elimination and you infer that student has mastered the material, you will be wrong.

Fill-in Items.   Here are three simple guidelines to follow:

1. *Ask a question of the respondent and provide space for an answer.* This forces the expression of a complete thought on your part. The use of incomplete statements as item stems is acceptable. But if you use them, be sure to capture the essence of the problem in that stem.

2. *Try to stick to one blank per item.* Come to the point. Ask one question, get one answer, and move on to the next question. Simple language, complete communication, clear conclusions. Does the student know the answer or not?

3. *Don't let the length of the line to be filled in be a clue as to the length or nature of the correct response.* This may seem elementary, but it happens. Again, this can lead to misinformation about the student's real level of achievement.

The creative test developer also can generate some interesting and useful assessment exercises by mixing the various formats.

1. Mix true/false and multiple-choice formats to create exercises in which the respondent must label a statement true or false and select the response option that gives the proper reason why.
   Example:

   As employment increases, the danger of inflation increases.
   - a. True, because consumers are willing to pay higher prices
   - b. True, because the money supply increases
   - c. False, because wages and inflation are statistically unrelated to one another
   - d. False, because the government controls inflation

2. Mix multiple-choice or matching and fill-in to create a format in which the student must select the correct response and fill in the reason why it is correct. As a variation, we can ask why incorrect responses are incorrect too.

Time for Reflection

Can you recall any variations of these formats used by your own teachers that you found to be challenging, creative, or especially effective? Can you think of combinations of these formats that might be useful?

Here's another simple but effective test development idea: If you wish to use selected response items to assess student reasoning and problem-solving proficiency, but (a) you are not sure all of your students have the same solid background in the content, or (b) you want to see them apply content you don't necessarily want them to memorize, you can turn to what is called an *interpretive exercise*. In this case, you provide information to respondents in the form of a brief passage, chart, table, or figure and then ask a series of questions calling for the interpretation or application of that material.

Example:[2]

Here is a graph of Bill's weekly allowance distribution.

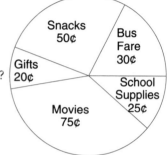

1. What is the ratio of the amount Bill spends for school supplies to the amount he spends for movies?
   A. 7:2
   B. 1:3
   C. 2:7
   D. 3:1
2. What would be the best title for this graph?
   A. Bill's weekly allowance.
   B. Bill's money graph.
   C. Bill's weekly expenditures.
   D. Bill's money planning.

And finally, here are a few simple guidelines for setting up the test as a whole that will improve the quality of the results:

1. *Provide clear directions and specific indications of the point value for each exercise.* This helps students use their time wisely.

2. *Start each test with some relatively easy items.* This will give students both some time and the means to get their test anxiety under control.

3. *Present all items of like format together.*

4. *Keep all parts of an item on the same page.*

5. *Make sure all copies are clear and readable.*

Summary of Step 3.   In this step, you transformed propositions into test items. This need not be a complex process. Regardless of the item format, you must write test items clearly and as simply as possible, ask questions whenever possible, eliminate inappropriate clues to the correct answer, seek one clearly correct answer whenever possible and appropriate, ask a colleague to review important tests, and follow just a few simple format-specific guidelines for item construction. These guidelines are collected for convenient use in Figure 6–2.

Further, we help students perform up to their potential when we provide clear and complete instructions, let students know how each exercise contributes to the total test score, start with easy items, and make sure the test is readable.

---

[2]Reprinted from "Measuring Complex Achievement: The Interpretive Exercise" (p. 198, Example III) in *Measurement and Evaluation in Teaching* (6th ed.) by N. E. Gronlund and R. L. Linn, 1990, New York: Macmillan. Copyright 1990 by Macmillan Publishing Co. Reprinted by permission of the publisher

Figure 6-2

Test Item Quality Checklist

General guidelines for all formats
___ Items clearly written and focused
___ Question posed
___ Lowest possible reading level used
___ Irrelevant clues eliminated
___ Items reviewed by colleague
___ Scoring key double checked

Guidelines for multiple-choice items
___ Item stem poses a direct question
___ Repetition eliminated from response options
___ One best or correct answer is provided
___ Response options are brief and parallel
___ Number of response options offered fits item context

Guideline for true/false items
___ Statement is entirely true or false as presented

Guidelines for matching exercises
___ Clear directions given
___ List of items to be matched is brief
___ List consists of homogeneous entries
___ Response options are brief and parallel
___ Extra response options offered

Guidelines for fill-in items
___ A direct question is posed
___ One blank is needed to respond
___ Length of blank is not a clue

Selecting from Among the Four Item Formats

An important issue we have yet to address is, How do we decide which selected response format—multiple-choice, true/false, matching, or fill-in—to use with each kind of outcome?

In general, the first three are preferable when scoring efficiency is an issue, especially when you have an optical scan machine scoring service available. When achievement targets fit these formats, students are old enough to respond by bubbling in answer sheets (generally from grade 4), and scoring can be automated, multiple-choice, true/false, and matching formats, which can be big time savers. Unfortunately, until computer technology allows us to scan and evaluate student writing, short answer fill-in items are going to take longer to score. (Incidentally, the technology exists today to scan actual student work into the computer. But its evaluation still requires the human eye and mind.)

On the other hand, fill-in exercises are preferable when we wish to control for guessing. And make no mistake about it, guessing can be an issue. If a student guesses an item right and we infer that the right answer means the student has mastered the material, we are wrong. This means we have mismeasured that student's real achievement.

Given a true/false test, respondents who rely on blind guessing alone will answer about half of the items correctly. With multiple-choice, it depends on the number of response options: four-choice tests yield a guessing score of 25 percent correct, five-choice, 20 percent. Notice that any respondent who can confidently eliminate two or three options in a multiple-choice item before guessing raises the odds of guessing correctly to those of the true/false item! With fill-in items, on the other hand, the chances of success through guessing alone are greatly reduced.

Your heart must go out to students who score below the chance or guessing score on a selected response test. Not only are such students misinformed, but they're unlucky!

Multiple-choice items are recommended when the author can identify one correct or best answer and at the same time identify a number of viable incorrect responses. On its surface, that might sound obvious. But think about it. If we formulate our incorrect responses carefully, we can use multiple-choice items to uncover common misunderstandings and to diagnose students' needs. Let me illustrate.

If we were to start with a math problem and solve it correctly, we have identified the correct response (response option 1). Next, we can solve that same problem making a common mistake on purpose. Say we carry that mistake all the way to an answer. This yields response option 2, and it will be incorrect. But if anyone chooses that incorrect response option when they take the test, we will know what mistake they made. Next, we solve the same problem making another kind of common mistake, and another viable incorrect response results (response option 3). We continue until we have as many incorrect response options as needed. Thus, each incorrect response can provide useful information about the students who choose it, if the item is developed in a thoughtful manner.

If we administer such a test and analyze how many students selected each response option (which can be done very easily with currently available optical scan test scoring technology and item analysis software packages), we gain clear insights into common misconceptions among our students. Multiple-choice exercises developed in this way can serve to identify student needs with a minimum of investment in testing time.

True/false exercises are most useful when we have a great deal of material to cover and want to ask a large number of questions per unit of testing time, or when we have much to cover and limited testing time. These items require very short response times. They also are usable when we either cannot think of or don't want to take the time to generate lists of viable incorrect response options for multiple-choice items.

The greatest strength of matching items lies in their efficiency. When carefully developed to include homogeneous elements, they are in effect several multiple-choice items presented at once. Each premise statement to be matched triggers a new multiple-choice test item and all items in a matching exercise offer the same set of multiple response options. They can be used to assess mastery of knowledge and/or thinking and problem solving, although most tend to center on recalling associations.

Working Backwards to Verify Test Quality

We have come a long way in this chapter depicting a "simple" three-step test development process, from blueprints to propositions to test items. Before we leave this topic, let's discuss a natural extension of this process. This is an idea you may already have considered.

We can reverse this entire process in order to evaluate previously developed tests, such as those that come with a textbook or those we have developed in previous years. To do this, we begin at the test item level: Do the items themselves adhere to the few critical guidelines presented above? If they do not, there is obvious reason for concern about test quality. If they do, we proceed to the next level of analysis.

At that next level, we can transform the items into the propositions that they reflect. This is accomplished by doing the following:

- Combining the multiple-choice item stem with the correct response
- Adding true true/false items to the list of propositions
- Making false true/false items true
- Matching up elements in matching exercises
- Filling in the blanks of short answer items

We then analyze the resulting list of propositions, asking, Do these reflect the priorities in our instruction? In addition, we can collect the propositions into like groups to generate a list of instructional objectives or to create a table of specifications depicting the overall picture of the test, including the proportional representation of content and thinking. Again we can ask, Do these reflect priorities as we see them?

This backward analysis can both reveal the flaws in previously developed tests and help us understand the nature of the revisions needed to bring the test up to important standards of quality.

Barriers to Sound Selected Response Assessment

Recall that, in earlier chapters, we listed five key attributes of a sound assessment: clear target, clear purpose, proper method, appropriate sample, and extraneous interference controlled. These also reflect the things that can go wrong, that can keep a student's test score from being an accurate reflection of that student's real level of achievement. Listed below, by way of summary, are many of the sources of mismeasurement touched on in this chapter. Also listed are actions we can take to prevent these problems. These remedies are offered in the service of helping you develop sound selected response assessments.

Potential Source of Error	*Remedies*
Lack of vision of the target	Carefully analyze the material to be learned to find the priority knowledge and thinking outcomes.
	Learn to find the truly important learning propositions.
Wrong method for the target	Use selected response methods to assess mastery of knowledge and appropriate kinds of reasoning only.
	Selected response can test prerequisites of effective skill and product performance, but not performance itself.
Inappropriate sampling: • Not representative of important propositions • Sample too small • Sample too large for time available	Know the material and plan the test carefully. Include more items. Shorten cautiously so as to maintain enough to engender confidence in generalizing to the total domain to be sampled.

Sources of Extraneous Interference
• Student-centered problems:
  Cannot read well enough to understand and respond
  Insufficient time to respond
• Poor-quality test items
 	
• Scoring errors
	
	Lower reading level or offer reading support.
	Shorten test or allow more time.
	Learn and follow both general and format-specific guidelines for writing quality items. Seek review by a colleague.
	Double check answer key.

INCLUDING STUDENTS IN THE SELECTED RESPONSE ASSESSMENT PROCESS

We have said right from the outset that classroom assessment can serve two important purposes. One is to provide information for teacher, student, and parent to use in informing the various decisions they must make. The other is as a teaching tool. Specific ways to weave selected response assessment development and use into the very fabric of your teaching and learning environment are presented in Figure 6–3. Many of these suggestions reflect an idea planted earlier in the chapter. Remember when I asked you who else might become involved in the process of assessment development and use, in order to lighten your classroom assessment workload? The coworkers to which I referred are your students.

- Develop a table of final test specifications for a final unit test *before* the unit is ever taught. A clear vision of the valued outcomes will thus be secured and instruction can be tailored to promote student success.

- Share a copy of that plan with every student. Review it carefully at the beginning of the unit and explain your expectations at that time. Now students and teacher share the same vision.

- Involve students in the process of devising the original plan, or involve them from time to time through the unit in checking back to the blueprint (a) to see together—as partners—if you might need to make adjustments in the test plan and/or (b) to chart your progress together.

- Once you have the test plan completed, develop a few test items each day as the unit unfolds. Such items certainly would reflect timely instructional priorities. Further, at the end of the unit, the final exam would be all done and ready to go! This eliminates the last-minute anxiety of test development and improves test quality.

- Involve students in writing practice test items. Think of the benefits: the students will have to evaluate the importance of the various elements of content, and they will have to become proficient in using the kinds of thinking and problem solving valued in that classroom. Developing sample test items provides high-fidelity practice in doing these things.

- As a variation on that theme, provide unlabeled exercises and have students practice (a) placing them in the proper cell of the test blueprint structure, and (b) answering them.

- As another variation, have students evaluate the quality of the tests that came with the textbook—do they match your plan developed for instruction?

- Have students use the blueprint to predict how they are going to do on each part of the test before they take it. Then have them analyze how they did, part by part, after taking it. If the first test was for practice, such an analysis would provide valuable information to help them plan their preparation for the real thing.

- Have students work in teams, with each one given responsibility for finding ways to help everyone in class score high in one cell, row or column of a table of specifications or one objective.

- Use lists of unit objectives and tables of test specifications to communicate with other teachers about instructional priorities, so as to arrive at a clearer understanding of how those priorities fit together across instructional levels or school buildings.

- Store test items by content and thinking category for reuse. If the item record also included information on how students did on each item (say, the percentage that got it right), you could revise instruction next time for items students had trouble with. Incidentally, this represents an excellent place to use your personal computer to advantage as a test item storage and retrieval system.

Figure 6-3
Strategies for Connecting Assessment to Instruction

Figure 6–3 represents only the beginning of a practically endless list. You can and should generate more and more ideas to add to it. These uses of the selected response assessment development process all contribute to one huge key to student success: *students can hit any target that they can see and that holds still for them.* These strategies serve to remove the mystery surrounding the meaning of academic success. They bring students into the process of defining that meaning and give them control over their own well-being.

Time for Reflection

Can you think of other specific ways to use assessment development, administration, scoring, or interpretation as an integral part of the teaching and learning process? Brainstorm more options. Did any of your own teachers integrate assessment into instruction? What did they do?

CHAPTER SUMMARY: PRODUCTIVE SELECTED RESPONSE ASSESSMENT

During this phase of our journey through the realm of educational assessment, we have considered multiple-choice, true/false, matching, and fill-in selected response test item formats. We established at the beginning of the chapter that these options often are labeled *objective* tests because of the manner in which they are scored. Answers are right or wrong—there is no judgment involved. However, subjective professional judgment does play a major role in all other facets of this kind of assessment, from test planning, to the selection of material to be tested, to the process of item writing itself. For this reason, it is essential that all selected response test developers adhere conscientiously to procedures for creating sound tests. Those procedures were the topic of this chapter.

We discussed the match between selected response assessment methods and the five basic kinds of achievement targets that are serving as signposts for our journey. These selected response formats can serve to assess student mastery of content knowledge, ability to reason in sophisticated ways, mastery of some of the procedural knowledge that underpins skills and the development of complex products, and presence of certain affective states.

As we examined the test development process itself, we explored several context factors that extend beyond just the consideration of match to target that must be taken into account in choosing selected response assessment. These included factors related to the student's reading abilities and to the kinds of support services available to the user.

Also under the heading of test development, we explored a three-step developmental sequence: test planning, identifying propositions to be tested, and test item writing. We reviewed a limited number of specific item and test development tactics within each step that promise to decrease test development time and increase test quality.

We closed with a list of specific ways to bring students into the assessment as full partners. Note that we are not referring simply to exchanging papers at test scoring time; rather, we are talking about a full partnership in assessment, with students assisting in identifying valued outcomes, designing assessments, creating those assessments, and interpreting and using assessment results. Note this last segment well! It presents a theme that will dominate the remainder of our travels together.

EXERCISES TO ADVANCE YOUR LEARNING

Knowledge Outcomes

1. Identify three reasons for knowing about selected response assessments.
2. Learn the three basic steps in test development and the substeps within each.
3. Identify the specific kinds of achievement targets that can be transformed into selected response formats and those that cannot.
4. Describe the factors to take into account when considering use of the selected response option.
5. Specify the key considerations in devising a sound sample of selected response items.
6. Make a chart listing the four selected response formats as rows and the following as columns: principle advantages, limitations, and when to use. Review this chapter and fill in the cells of the table.
7. Make a one-page chart listing your own tailor-made abbreviations of the general and format-specific guidelines for item writing presented in Figure 6–2. Keep them handy for easy reference if and when you consider selected response assessment.

Reasoning Outcomes

1. Identify ten important propositions from this chapter. When you have done so, review the list and ask yourself the following: (a) Do these represent the most important learnings from this chapter? (b) How would you identify which propositions represent the most and the least important information in the chapter?
2. Transform each of your propositions into true true/false, false true/false, fill-in, multiple-choice, and (where appropriate) matching items.

Skill Outcomes

1. Select a unit of instruction from the material you teach now, will teach, or have studied as a student that includes both content and thinking outcomes. Devise a table of specifications for this unit, find key propositions for each cell in your table, and construct items for your propositions.

Product Outcomes

1. Evaluate the test you created above in terms of the attributes of sound assessment.
2. Select a previously developed test, either from your files or from a text series you may have used, and apply these principles in evaluating it.

Have the guidelines been followed? Can you see how to fix whatever problems you find?

Affective Outcomes

1. Some have argued that these are times for performance assessment and that selected response assessments are remnants of bygone times—that selected response assessment formats have no place in the future of school testing. Do you agree? Why?

2. How do you feel about the idea of using selected response exercises and tests as teaching tools? Can they be helpful? If so, how? If not, why not?

3. I argue in this chapter that the suggested test development procedures would save you time in your test development process, if you use these kinds of assessment in your classroom. Do you agree? Why?

CHAPTER 7

Essay Assessment: Vast Untapped Potential

Chapter Objectives

As a result of studying the material presented in Chapter 7, reflecting on that material, and completing the learning exercises presented at the end of the chapter, you will:

1. Master content knowledge:
   a. State the roles of objectivity and subjectivity in essay assessment.
   b. Identify the kinds of achievement targets that can be reflected in essay assessments.
   c. List three steps in the essay assessment development process.
   d. Know classroom assessment context factors to consider in deciding whether or when to use essay assessments.
   e. State considerations in sampling student performance via essay exercises.
   f. Identify specific guidelines for the construction of essay exercises and scoring schemes.
   g. List specific ways to bring students into the essay assessment process as a teaching strategy.
2. Be able to use that knowledge to reason as follows:
   a. Identify content and reasoning targets for translation into essay assessments.
   b. Translate those outcomes into quality exercises and scoring criteria.
3. Become proficient at the following skills:
   a. Be able to carry out the steps in the assessment development process.
   b. Evaluate previously developed essay assessments to ensure their quality.

4. Be able to create quality products of the following sorts:
    a. Essay assessments that meet predetermined standards.

5. Attain the following affective outcomes:
    a. Understand the importance of knowing about sound essay assessment.
    b. Value essay assessment as a viable option for use in the classroom.
    c. See essay assessment as a valuable instructional tool in which students should be and can be full partners.
    d. See essay assessment as a viable alternative to performance assessment in those contexts where authentic performance assessment is not possible.

T he essay form of assessment may have the greatest untapped potential of any of the four assessment methods discussed in this book. The time has come for us to begin to take greater advantage of this rich assessment option.

As mentioned in Part 1, our changing social and economic circumstances and our increasingly technical world are demanding that schools assist students in attaining increasingly complex outcomes. As a result, we have sensed the insufficiency of selected response assessment. We have come to understand the need for richer assessment methods, such as performance assessment. At the same time, however, we now understand how expensive authentic performance assessments can be. Those expenses are detailed in Chapter 8.

Essay assessments may represent a compromise methodology under some circumstances. As you shall see in this chapter, essays permit us to tap at least some of our most highly valued, yet complex outcomes at a fraction of the cost of performance assessments. Further, as we begin to see students as partners in the assessment process in the sense of sharing some of the workload, we will come to regard labor-intensive assessment methods such as essays as more feasible than we have in the past.

For all of these reasons, we will come to see essay assessment as an increasingly useful alternative as we move through the 1990s. This chapter is devoted to exploring the untapped potential of the essay assessment alternative. This assessment methodology carries with it at least three major strengths:

- It can allow us to delve into student attainment of some complex and sophisticated achievement targets.

- The essay format allows us to assess these outcomes at a relatively low cost in time and energy.

- Essay assessments can be integrated into the teaching and learning process in a number of very productive ways.

Be advised, however, that this method of assessment brings risks with it too. The careless user might do any or all of the following:

- lack a sufficiently clear vision of the kinds of outcomes to be learned and therefore assessed

- fail to connect the essay format to the proper kinds of achievement targets
- fail to representatively sample the target domain
- fail to control for the many sources of bias that can invade subjective assessments

Those schooled in methods of avoiding these pitfalls, however, can use essay assessment to great advantage.

Time for Reflection

Please take a few minutes to reflect on your past experience with essay assessments. How often have your teachers relied on this method? If you teach currently, how much do you use this option? When you have come into contact with essay assessment as a student or teacher, what has the experience been like? Has it been positive or negative? Why?

CHAPTER ROADMAP

As with selected response assessments, each of us may face the development of our own essay tests, need to evaluate an essay test developed by others, and/or find ourselves on the examinee end of an essay test. For all of these reasons, it is important that we understand how issues of assessment quality relate to this form of assessment.

To assist you in facing these challenges, we will address four aspects of essay assessment in this segment of our journey:

- the critical role of subjective judgment in essay assessment
- the match of essay assessment to the five kinds of achievement targets: knowledge, reasoning, skills, products, and affect
- the essay assessment development process, covering both exercise development and the specification of scoring criteria
- strategies for drawing students into the essay assessment process as a means of raising both their levels of motivation to learn and their actual achievement

As we go, keep the big picture in mind. From our chart matching achievement targets with modes of assessment, we will be dealing with the cells darkened in Figure 7-1 as we proceed through this chapter.

But before we delve into the intricacies of essay assessment, let's take a quick look at this assessment option in action in the classroom.

	SELECTED RESPONSE	ESSAY	PERFORMANCE ASSESSMENT	PERSONAL COMMUNICATION
Know				
Reason				
Skill				
Product				
Affect				

Figure 7-1
Aligning Achievement Targets and Assessment Methods

ESSAY ASSESSMENT IN A PRODUCTIVE LEARNING ENVIRONMENT

A professor acquaintance of mine uses essay exercises exclusively for his final examinations in the classroom assessment course that he teaches for teachers and school administrators. He reports that he likes the essay format because it allows him to (a) present exercises that depict relatively complex real-world classroom assessment dilemmas, and (b) ask his students to use their knowledge of assessment methodology and their reasoning abilities to tell him in writing how they would resolve each dilemma if they were confronted with it in their classroom.

Obviously, he could obtain a more "authentic" assessment of their proficiency if he could place his students in a real classroom, have the problem appear in actuality, and observe their performance in solving it. But since that kind of authenticity is beyond reach in his context, he turns to an essay test and gains insight into achievement.

He samples the achievement of his students using ten essay exercises on each final exam. Those that appear on any one exam are selected from a pool of exercises the professor and his students have devised over the years to represent the broad array of classroom assessment challenges teachers face in real classrooms. Since time will not permit testing for all eventualities, the professor must compromise by administering a limited set of exercises and generalizing from each student's performance to the domain of material. He feels ten exercises are enough to give him confidence in making these inferences.

For each exercise, he has established performance expectations in advance by specifying either one best solution or a set of acceptable solutions to the classroom assessment problem presented. The professor carefully translates these expectations into a predetermined scoring scheme. His students are told up front how many points are associated with each exercise and they strive to attain as many of those points as they can.

A sample of one of his exercises is presented below, along with its scoring scheme. It reveals the kind of real-world complexity he can attain with this assessment format.

Sample Essay Exercise:
Assume you are a French teacher with many years of teaching experience. You place great value on the development of speaking proficiency as an outcome of your instruction. Therefore, you rely heavily on assessments where you listen to and evaluate performance. But a problem has arisen. Parents of students who attained very high scores on your written tests are complaining that their children are receiving lower grades on their report cards. The principal wants to be sure your judgments of student proficiency are sound and so has asked you to explain and defend your assessment procedures. Describe three specific assessment-related procedures you would want to follow in this instance and explain how you would defend each. (2 points for each procedure and rationale, total = 6 points.)

Criteria Used to Score Responses to This Exercise:
Assign points to each response as follows: Two points if the response lists any of these six procedures and defends each as a key to conducting sound performance assessments:

- specify clear performance criteria
- sample performance over several exercises
- apply systematic rating procedures
- maintain complete and accurate records
- use published performance assessments to verify results of classroom assessments
- use multiple observers to corroborate

Also award two points if the response lists any of these and defends them as attributes of sound assessments:

- specifies a clear instructional objective
- relies on a proper assessment method
- samples performance well
- controls for sources of rater bias

All other responses receive no points.

The professor claims that, over the years, these final exams have become very much a part of the teaching and learning process in his classes. I explain below how he has been able to achieve this.

The Procedure

These essay finals are take-home exams, so as to maximize the amount of time students spend reflecting and learning. His students report that they do, in fact, spend a considerable amount of time preparing their responses. Further, students receive the exercises a few at a time throughout the term, as the material needed to address the various problems is presented. This has the effect of making the achievement targets perfectly clear to the students, thus helping to focus learning and reduce some of the test anxiety. It also focuses study and spreads the extra learning time and effort over the entire term.

As take-home exams, these obviously are open-book exams. The professor covers a great deal of material about assessment in this course and reports that he does not expect them to memorize it all, any more than he expects his physician to memorize all of the treatment options she has at her disposal.

Rather, each student receives a full set of text materials assembled into an easy reference presentation format. Over the course of instruction and as they work on the exercises, students learn how to use these reference materials. Hopefully, after the course is over, they will keep their "library" of assessment ideas handy for classroom use. The open-book exam format encourages them to learn the overall organizational structure of these materials.

The Scoring

At the end of the term, when students hand in their final exam for scoring (all ten exercises come in together), the professor applies the predetermined scoring guides in evaluating each response to each exercise. Since enrollment can exceed fifty students per class, he has had to find ways to maximize reading and scoring efficiency. The single biggest time saver, he reports, is to have the scoring criteria clearly in mind before beginning the scoring process. Next is to score all responses to one exercise at one time and then move on to the next exercise. We'll review more time-saving ideas later in the chapter.

The Feedback

Students receive feedback on their results in the following forms:

- points assigned to each part of each response
- brief written rationale for the score, suggesting factors that might have been overlooked
- the total number of points summed over all exercises
- a grade based on comparing the total score to a predetermined set of cutoff scores for each grade

Students who attain grades that are lower than their expectations for themselves can rework any exercise(s) any time and resubmit their exam for reevaluation. If a reevaluation of their written work and a personal discussion with the professor reveals that they have completed more productive study and have attained a higher level of proficiency, the professor submits a change of grade at once. This procedure has the effect of extending the learning time beyond the limits of a single term when necessary.

Time for Reflection

If you took a course from a professor who practiced these assessment procedures (and perhaps you have), what would you expect to be the effect on your learning? Try to think of as many effects as you can.

The Impact

The professor reports that scoring all responses to a single exercise together helps him to integrate assessment into instruction in another important way. After reading fifty attempts to solve a relatively complex classroom assessment problem, he assures me that he knows which facets of instruction were effective and which were not. When his students are ready to resolve the classroom assessment dilemma presented in an exercise, he reports, it shows—almost all of them provide acceptable solutions. But when the professor has failed to set them up for success, it becomes painfully obvious in paper after paper. He knows without question which phase of instruction did not work. Next term, he revises instruction in the hope that his students will perform better on similar exercises.

The impact on students is clear, too. A high percentage of them do very well on these exams. They report that they spend more time on these exercises than on other exams, that they really have to study, analyze, and reflect deeply upon the material covered in class and required readings to find solutions to the problems presented. And, they welcome the opportunity to rework the material when necessary to score higher.

Context is Critical

Without question, this particular professor's assessment and grading procedures will not work in all contexts. In a very real sense, he works in what most teachers would regard as an ideal world: a manageable number of students and few preparations.

However, my point in telling you this story is *not* to convince you to adopt his procedures. Rather, it is to make the point that essay assessment can contribute to the effectiveness of a learning community in which teacher and students enter into a partnership with a mutual goal of maximum achievement.

We will explore how this might be done in your classroom, given your realities.

ENSURING THE QUALITY OF ESSAY ASSESSMENTS

Essay assessments represent the first of three assessment methods to be discussed over the next few chapters that are subjective by their very nature. You may recall that selected response assessments, we said, rely on matters of professional judgment in the setting of the target and design of the assessment exercises, but scoring typically is not a matter of judgment. By design, answers to well-constructed test items are right or wrong. The number of right answers produces a score that is not a matter of judgment, either. With essay assessments, professional judgment plays an even bigger role. Let's examine that expanded role.

Subjectivity in Essay Assessment

In the case of essay tests, professional judgment plays a role in both development and scoring. This means there are more ways for unwanted biases to creep into the assessment results, placing the attainment of meaningful scores in jeopardy. That, in turn, means that users of this methodology must be doubly vigilant against potential problems. However, we know how to create "subjective" (or judgmental) assessment tools in a systematic way that can ultimately make them one of the most versatile tools at our disposal.

Perhaps the most critical message of Part 2 of this book is this: *Assessments such as essays, that rely on professional judgment to evaluate student work, can produce quality results leading to effective instruction and high achievement only if they are carefully developed according to known rules of evidence using proper procedures.*

In the case of essay assessments, teacher judgment is involved in the following aspects:

- establishing the underlying achievement target
- selecting the component parts of that guiding target to be included in the assessment
- preparing essay exercises themselves
- devising scoring criteria
- conducting the scoring process itself

If teachers are not versed in this discipline of assessment and/or are not in command of the achievement targets to be assessed, they obviously run the risk of mismeasurement and it is their students who will feel the effects—frustration, misconceptions, and reduced learning.

In the case of essay assessment, as with any form of assessment, the responsibility for avoiding such problems and of assuring quality rests squarely with *you,* the teacher! Those who thoroughly comprehend the required material to be mastered are in an excellent position to plan exercises and scoring schemes that fit the valued outcomes of instruction. It is only through the development and use of strong exercises and appropriate scoring criteria that errors in measuring student achievement attributable to evaluator or rater bias can be avoided.

Let's look at specific ways to reach this goal.

Matching Method to Target

Essay assessments have a potential contribution to make in assessing key dimensions of student learning in all five categories of valued outcomes—knowledge, reasoning, skills, products, and affect.

Assessing Knowledge. Most experts advise against using essays to assess student mastery of subject matter knowledge, when the targets are conceived of as individual elements of content to be memorized. The primary reason is that we have better options at our disposal for tapping this kind of outcome. Selected response assessment formats provide a more efficient means of assessment that, at the same time, allow for a more precise and controlled sampling of the achievement domain.

Selected response test formats are more efficient than essays in this case for two reasons. First, you can ask more multiple-choice questions per unit of testing time than essay questions becaues multiple-choice response time is so much shorter. You can provide a broader sample of performance per unit of time with selected response items than with essay exercises. Second, scoring of selected response items is much faster than scoring of essays.

Selected response methods allow for a more confident sampling of student mastery of material in part because many more items can be included in the test, and in part because the inclusion of those items forces the student to address all key elements of knowledge within the target domain.

As an example, say we want to evaluate student spelling. If we do so by assessing their spelling as it appears in the papers they write, students can mislead us with respect to their real spelling achievement. Student writers are more likely to use words they are confident that they know how to spell. They will avoid words they are not sure about. Thus, left to their own devices, they can keep us from finding the words they cannot spell by leaving them out of their writing. In this way, a writing-based assessment of spelling will provide us with a biased sample of all the words they may need to know how to spell.

Selected response assessments counteract this problem by forcing the respondent to answer a set of items that systematically sample the target domain. Such assessments force the examinee to demonstrate mastery of all relevant material. If we ask students to attempt every word on the list (i.e., rely on a short answer fill-in test), we will find out which they can spell and which they cannot. In this way, selected response formats offer a greater degree of control over the sample of their spelling proficiency.

Even though all of this is true and important, however, I argue in favor of using the essay format for the assessment of student mastery of a specific, important form of content knowledge. Let me explain.

In discussing the design and development of selected response items, I described a planning process that began with a broad domain of content, divided that into categories for the table of specifications, and divided categories even further into collections of individual propositions, any one of which might be transformed into a specifically focused test item. In this scenario, elements of knowledge become quite small and individual (i.e., unrelated to one another).

However, this is not the only way to conceive of knowledge to be mastered. We may also conceive of units of knowledge that are larger, each containing several important smaller elements within it, all of which relate to one another in some important way. For example, we might want students to know all of the parts of a particular ecosystem in science and to know how they are related to one another. An essay assessment can help us evaluate student attainment of this kind of knowledge.

Below is an example of such an exercise that I might use on a final exam in my assessment course to find out if my students knew and understood test development.

> Describe the process of developing a selected response assessment, being sure to include all key steps, highlighting places where problems can arise, and specifying how you would prevent problems. (20 pts.)

We can use such exercises in an open-book exam too, if we wish to assess mastery of such complex knowledge through the use of reference materials. With essay assessments, we are seeking a readout of the more complex cognitive map of the learner. One of the most common complaints against the selected response form of assessment is that it compartmentalizes learning too much—knowledge is mastered but not integrated into a larger whole. Essay assessments can counter that problem effectively.

Assessing Reasoning.   Assessment experts agree that this is the real strength of essay assessment. At testing time, we can present complex problems that ask learners to bring their subject matter knowledge and reasoning skills together to find a solution. In instances where we cannot literally see this knowledge retrieval and reasoning process unfold, we ask students to describe the results of their reasoning. From this, we infer about the state of their knowledge and their ability to use it.

We can ask them to analyze, compare, draw inferences, and/or think critically in virtually any subject matter area. Furthermore, we can pose problems that require the integration of material from two or more subjects and/or the application of more than one pattern of reasoning. The key question we ask is, Do students know how and when to use the knowledge they have at their disposal to reason and solve problems?

Remember, however, the keys to the successful assessment of student thinking through the use of the essay format are the same as the keys to success with the selected response format:

1. Assessors must possess a highly refined vision of what they mean by the terms *thinking, reasoning,* and/or *problem solving.* (This is discussed in detail in Chapter 10.)

2. Assessors must know how to translate that vision into clear, focused essay exercises and scoring criteria.

3. The exercises must present problems to students that are new at the time of the assessment (i.e., problems for which students have not memorized a response).

We will discuss how to meet these standards later in this chapter.

Assessing Skills.   If the valued achievement target holds that students become proficient in demonstrating specific skills, then there is only one acceptable way to assess proficiency: observation of actual performance. For instance, say we want to find out if they can carry out certain complex behaviors, such as participating collaboratively in a group, communicating orally in a second language, or carrying out the steps in a science experiment. In these cases, standards of sound assessment require that students be given the opportunity to demonstrate group participation skills, speak the language, or conduct an actual lab experiment.

There is no way to use an essay test format to assess these kinds of performances. An essay exercise would not be "authentic"—it would not, could not accurately depict real performance.

However, there are some important skill-related outcomes that we can tap with the essay format. For instance, we can use the essay to assess mastery of some of the complex knowledge and even problem-solving skills that are *prerequisite* to performing the skill in question.

For example, if a student doesn't *know* how the functions of different pieces of science lab equipment relate to one another in an experimental context, there is no way that student will successfully complete the lab work. An essay question could be devised to see if the student had mastered that prerequisite knowledge.

Thus, we could use the essay format to assess student attainment of some of the building blocks of competence. The results of such assessments could be enlightening to a teacher planning future lessons aimed at helping students to attain ultimate competence.

Assessing Products.   Again in this case, if the valued target holds that students be able to create a specified kind of product that reflects certain attributes, the only high-fidelity way to assess the outcome is to have them actually create the product so it can be evaluated according to established standards of quality.

However, essays can provide insight into whether the student knows and understands the process of creating a quality product. Or, essays might provide insight into the respondent's awareness of the criteria or key attributes of a quality product. These might be useful assessments in a classroom context where the foundations of competence are being built. We can use essay assessments in these contexts, however, only if we remain constantly aware of the fact that being able to write about a good product and being able to create that product are different outcomes.

Assessing Writing as a Product.   One kind of product we often ask students to create is samples of their writing. We do this with essay tests, research report assignments, term papers, and so on. It is tempting to think of a term paper as just a long essay assessment tapping mastery of larger knowledge structures and/or complex thinking.

However, these bigger writing projects are different than responses to essay exercises, largely because of subtle but important differences in the nature of the criteria used to evaluate each.

When students write in response to an essay exercise, we evaluate in terms of criteria that focus on the respondent's mastery of the kind(s) of content and/or reasoning needed to answer the question adequately. Thus, it is the *substance* of the writing—the ideas expressed—that go under the microscope.

But when writing is the medium used to produce such a product as a term paper or research report, the criteria used to evaluate performance typically include issues of *form* as well as those of content and reasoning. When students use written language as a medium of communication, their writing can also be evaluated in terms of organization, sentence fluency, word choice, voice (i.e., the extent to which the writer's personality comes through to the reader), and other important factors.

Further, research reports and term papers can be evaluated in terms of presentation format, use of graphs and tables, and use and citation of references. When matters of form come into play, I think of writing as an achievement-related product and my list of key aspects of good performance begins to grow. We will discuss this more in Chapter 8.

Regardless, a key lesson to learn is that subjective assessment, whether of substance or form, requires clear thinking and effective communication of the performance criteria to be used to evaluate performance.

Assessing Affect. Student writing can provide a window into student feelings. When asked specific questions about the direction and intensity of their feelings toward focused aspects of the schooling process, in an environment of trust where it's clear that honesty is accepted, students can and will inform us about their attitudes, interests, values, and levels of motivation. Questionnaires containing open-ended questions can produce student writing that is full of profoundly important insights into the affective and social climate of a school or classroom.

Chapter 15 deals in detail with all issues and procedures related to the assessment of affective outcomes using this and other methods.

Summary of Target Matches. On the whole, essay assessment is a very flexible format. It can provide useful information on a variety of targets. We can use it to evaluate student mastery of larger structures of knowledge, whether memorized or mastered through the use of reference materials. We certainly can tap student reasoning and problem solving. We can assess mastery of the complex procedural knowledge that is prerequisite to skilled performance and/or the creation of quality products. And finally, we also can explore student affect in rich and useful ways through student writing.

But again, I caution that knowing what steps to take to appear skilled or to create a quality product, while necessary for attaining required levels of performance, may not be sufficient to guarantee success in actually demonstrating skill or creating that product.

Time for Reflection

We are about to begin the section of this chapter dealing with the design and development of sound essay exercises and scoring criteria. Before we do, I want you to attempt some development: Draft an essay exercise that could appear on a final exam on this chapter asking the respondent to describe the relationships between essay assessment and various kinds of achievement targets. Also, draft a proposed scoring scheme for your exercise. Keep these drafts handy, and refer to them as we discuss procedures for developing and scoring essay assessments.

DEVELOPING ESSAY ASSESSMENTS

The design and development process for essay assessments includes three steps:

1. assessment planning
2. exercise development
3. preparation to score

Test planning for this form of assessment is very much like planning selected response assessments, while exercise development is a bit easier, and preparation to score is much more challenging. After considering important context factors to take into account in deciding whether or when to use this option, we will turn to the test planning phase.

Context Factors

You will need to consider the classroom context factors delineated in Figure 7-2 before deciding whether the essay format is appropriate for the particular achievement target to be assessed. Attention to these factors will help you decide whether essays are appropriate.

Assessment Planning

The challenge, as always, is to begin with clearly articulated achievement targets. In this case, the target will reflect both the components of knowledge and the kinds of reasoning to be used by the respondent. Consequently, once again we have the option of starting with either a table of test specifications or a list of instructional objectives.

Tables of specifications for essay tests are like those used for selected response assessments in some ways, and different in others. The similarities lie in the basic framework. Table 7-1 is an example of such a table for an essay test covering some of the material in my course on assessment. As the developer of such a table, I must specify the domains of knowledge to be used on one axis and the kinds of reasoning or problem solving on the other. Row and column totals, and therefore entries in the cells of the table, once again, represent the relative emphasis assigned to each.

However, with the essay table of specifications, cells contain the number of points on the test that I have assigned to that content/reasoning combination, not the

- *The respondents' level of writing proficiency.* This is absolutely critical. If students lack writing skill, it is impossible to use this mode of assessment to gather useful information about their achievement. Writing proficiency is always confounded with achievement in this format. If that communication channel is closed, we must select another mode of assessment. It is the only fair way.
- *The availability of already developed high-quality essay exercises with associated scoring criteria.* If the work has already been done by you, your colleagues, or by the textbook author, and essays are ready to go, then go with them. Just be sure to verify quality.
- *The number of students to be evaluated.* The smaller the group, the shorter the overall time needed to do the scoring. The larger the group, the more scores you need.
- *The number of exercises needed to sample the material and the length of responses to be read and scored.* The smaller the number of exercises needed to provide an adequae sample of material and the shorter the responses, the less time will be needed for scoring. Most assessment experts recommend the use of more shorter exercises rather than fewer exercises requiring longer responses. The more exercises you use, the easier it is to sample the domain representatively.
- *The amount of person time available to read and evaluate responses.* This need not be only teacher time, although your time should be a major consideration. Sometimes, essay scoring support can come from students, teacher aides, or even from qualified parents. Be advised, however, of the two keys to being able to take advantage of such scoring assistance:
  1. Develop clear and appropriate scoring criteria and procedures.
  2. Train all scorers to apply those standards fairly and consistently.

Figure 7–2
Context Factors in the Use of Essay Assessments

numbers of individual test items, as was the case in Chapter 6. When I actually construct the test, I might spread those points over one or more exercises associated with each cell.

Given 100 points for the entire exam, this plan obviously emphasizes performance assessment relative to the other two, and on performance exercises requir-

Table 7–1
Table of Specifications for an Essay Test

Content	Recall	Inference	Evaluation	Total
Selected response assessments	10 pts	10	10	30
Essay assessments	10	10	10	30
Performance assessments	0	20	20	40
Total	20	40	40	100

ing inference and evaluation. If I were to use exercises valued at 10 points each, I would need ten exercises distributed so as to reflect these priorities.

These same values can be translated into instructional objectives, if we wish. Several are listed below. I list these sample objectives simply to illustrate a second way of capturing and communicating the meaning of academic success reflected in the cells of the table. You need not do both the table and the objectives. Select one or the other as a means of reflecting your valued outcomes.

- Students will know how to design selected response assessments to measure knowledge outcomes.
- Students will be able to draw inferences about the proper context within which to use essay tests.
- Students will be able to carry out a systematic evaluation of a previously developed performance assessment.

Sampling Student Achievement with Essays.   Just as with selected response items, essay exercises represent a sampling of two key elements: some knowledge to be retrieved (either from memory or reference) and some kind(s) of cognitive act to be carried out using that knowledge. In the case of essay exercises, the units of knowledge to be used are bigger, more inclusive entities than those that might form the basis of a multiple-choice test item.

Also as with selected response test plans, each cell in Table 7-1 or each instructional objective, establishes a sampling frame. That is, components of knowledge and examples of the application of kinds of thinking are captured within each. For instance, under the first objective above, we might ask about several types of test formats. For the second objective, the range of possible inferences and contexts within which to assess achievement is seemingly infinite. For the third objective, again, we have a great number of sample performance assessments that might be presented for evaluation.

Clearly, it would be impossible to include in one assessment all of the possible instances of the union of rows and columns as depicted in the table of specifications or in these kinds of objectives. If we did, we'd be talking about one *long* test!

Rather, the preferred method is to sample from all of these possibilities, picking a representative sample of the most important instances to present as exercises. And then based on student performance on this sample, we generalize to the domain of all possible exercises. If the student does well on these, that student would probably do well on any other set of similar exercises. Thus, in this sampling sense, essay tests are just like selected response tests.

But, who identifies the unions of knowledge and reasoning that really are important? This is *your* responsibility as the expert on valued outcomes in your classroom. Thus, you must possess an in-depth understanding of the full range of material that could be assessed. As soon as you have identified the range of possibilities, you are ready to select a representative sample of these for use in devising the exercises and scoring schemes that will comprise your test.

Note also that a table of test specifications designed to reflect the number of points allocated to each row, column, and cell can serve as the basis for an assessment made up of both selected response and essay exercises. While selected response items might count one point each, essay responses might count more.

Developing Essay Exercises

Essay exercises pose problems for students to solve. But what are the attributes of a sound exercise?

One of my students once described an exercise he received on a final exam at the end of his undergraduate studies. He had majored for four years in Spanish language, literature, and culture. His last final was an in-class essay exam with a three-hour time limit. The entire exam consisted of one exercise, which posed the challenge in only two words: "Discuss Spain."

Obviously, just a bit more detail would have been desirable. But haven't we all had experiences like this? One of the advantages often listed for essay tests relative to other test formats is that essay exercises are much easier and take less time to develop. I submit that many users turn that advantage into a liability by assuming that "easier to develop" means you don't have to put much thought into it—as evidenced in the above example.

Another common mistake teachers make is trying to turn an essay exercise into a demonstration of their creativity. A scientist friend offered an example from his experience as a college student: "Take a walk through a late Mesozoic forest and tell me what you see." This is better than "Discuss Spain." However, even more specification is needed to set the respondent up for success.

To succeed in the use of this assessment format, we must invest thoughtful preparation time in writing exercises that challenge respondents by describing a single complete and novel task. Sound exercises do three things:

1. *Identify the material to be brought to bear.* They specify the knowledge the student is supposed to command in preparing a response.

   Example: During the term, we have discussed both the evolution of Spanish literature and the changing political climate in Spain during the twentieth century.

2. *Specify the kind(s) of reasoning or problem solving to be carried out by the respondent.* Sound exercises specify what respondents are to write about.

   Example: During the term, we have discussed both the evolution of Spanish literature and the changing political climate in Spain during the twentieth century. Analyze these two dimensions of life in Spain, citing three instances where literature and politics may have influenced each other. Describe the mutual influences in specific terms.

3. *Point the direction to an appropriate response without giving away the store.* Good exercises list the key elements of good response without cueing the unprepared examinee as to how to succeed.

Example: During the term, we have discussed both the evolution of Spanish literature and the changing political climate in Spain during the twentieth century. Analyze these two dimensions of life in Spain, citing three instances where you think literature and politics may have influenced each other. Describe the mutual influences in specific terms. In planning your response, think about what we learned about prominent novelists, political satirists, and prominent political figures of Spain. (5 points per instance, total = 15 points.)

Let's analyze for content the example provided at the beginning of the chapter, reproduced below.

Assume you are a French teacher with many years of teaching experience. You place great value on the development of speaking proficiency as an outcome of your instruction. Therefore, you rely heavily on assessments where you listen to and evaluate performance. But a problem has arisen. Parents of students who attained very high test scores on your written tests are complaining that their children are receiving lower grades. The principal wants to be sure your judgments of student proficiency are sound and so has asked you to explain and defend your assessment procedures. Describe three specific assessment-related procedures you would want to follow in this instance and explain how you would defend each. (2 points for each procedure and rationale, total = 6 points.)

Here's the challenge to the student in a nutshell:

Demonstrate knowledge of:	performance assessment methodology
By using it to reason:	draw inferences about the proper applications of methods to a specific instance
Adhering to these standards:	list three and defend them

Time for Reflection

Please return to the essay exercise you developed at the beginning of this section of the chapter. Did you specify the knowledge to be used, kinds(s) of reasoning to be employed, and standards to be applied? Adjust your exercise as needed to meet these standards.

Another good way to check the quality of your essay exercises is to try to write or outline a quality response yourself. If you can, you probably have a properly focused exercise. If you cannot . . . you see what I mean.

Incidentally, when I use essays, I like to make it clear to my students that I care far more about the content of their answer than the form. I urge them to communicate their ideas as efficiently as they can, so I can read and score their responses as fast as possible. I urge them to use outlines and lists of ideas, examples, illustrations—whatever it takes to come to the point quickly and clearly. I do not require the use of connected discourse unless it is needed to communicate their solution to the problem. I explain that I do not want them beating around the bush in the hope that somewhere, somehow, they say something worth a point or two. Believe me, this suggestion makes scoring so much easier!

Figure 7-3 presents a checklist of factors to think about as you devise essay exercises. Answering these questions should assist you in constructing effective essay exercises.

In regard to the inclusion of the last point in Figure 7-3, don't offer choices: The assessment question should always be, "Can you hit the agreed-upon target or can you not?" It should never be, "Which part of the agreed-upon target are you most confident that you can hit?" This latter question always leaves a teacher uncertain about whether the student has in fact mastered the material covered in exercises not selected—some of which may be crucial to later learning.

Here is a final idea for exercise development: If you wish to use the essay format to assess reasoning skills, but you are not sure all students have a sufficient or equal grasp of the underlying body of knowledge, provide the knowledge needed to solve the problem and see if they can use it appropriately. This is another instance where you can use the interpretive exercise format discussed in Chapter 6. Simply provide a chart, graph, table, or paragraph of connected discourse and spin an essay or essays out of the material presented, as shown in the following example.

Map Skills: The Compromise of 1820.   Study the map. Then decide whether these statements are true or false. Explain your answers.

1. Most of the Louisiana Purchase was open to slavery.
2. Missouri was south of the line marked at 36° 30′.

Figure 7-3
Factors to Consider When Devising Essay Exercises

___ Do exercises call for *brief, focused responses?*

___ Are they written at the *lowest possible reading level?* Double check at the time of administration to ensure understanding—especially among poor readers.

___ Do you have the confidence that qualified *experts in the field would agree with your definition* of a sound response? This is a judgment call.

___ Would the elements in your scoring plan be *obvious to good students?*

___ Have you presented one set of exercises to all respondents? *Don't offer options* from which to choose.

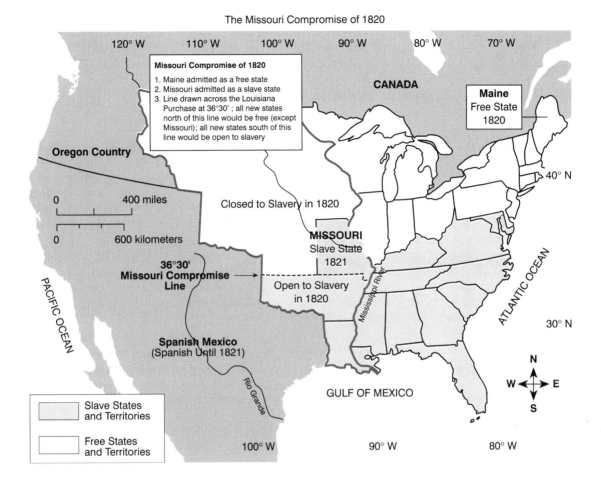

The Missouri Compromise of 1820

Missouri Compromise of 1820

1. Maine admitted as a free state
2. Missouri admitted as a slave state
3. Line drawn across the Louisiana Purchase at 36°30' ; all new states north of this line would be free (except Missouri); all new states south of this line would be open to slavery

3. Missouri was admitted to the United States as a slave state.
4. The Mississippi River divided the free and slave territories.
5. The southwest boundary of the United States in 1820 was the Rio Grande.[1]

Developing Essay Scoring Procedures

Many teachers score essays by applying what I call "floating standards," in which you wait to see what responses you get to decide what you wanted. The cynic in me

[1]Reprinted from *Explaining American History* (p. 303) by M. Swartz and J. R. O'Connor, 1986, Englewood Cliffs, NJ: Globe. Copyright 1986 by Globe. Reprinted by permission.

says users of this method of scoring simply adjust internally held standards and invisible score scales downward during scoring to produce scores that indicate high levels of achievement regardless of whether those levels were attained. The perceived benefits of this method, I fear, are that students always appear to have achieved, and no one will ever know otherwise—no one will be able to detect the underlying manipulation that occurred.

No one, that is, except the perpetrator! The only standards of ethical practice that will ever come to bear on your essay scoring practices are those that you hold for yourself. In that regard, I hope you will adhere to the instructional and assessment philosophy that has guided everything we have discussed up to this point: Students can succeed if they know what it means to succeed. That means we state the meaning of success up front, design instruction to help students succeed, and devise and use assessments that reflect those prestated standards. That includes formulating essay scoring criteria in advance and holding yourself and your students accountable for attaining those standards.

In other words, those floating standards that worked so well for us back in the old era of sorting, when we wanted a dependable rank order of students from highest to lowest achievers, now become antithetical to the very mission of performance-based classrooms and schools. They are as counterproductive today as they were convenient back then.

In fact, essay scoring is a classic example of evaluative, or critical, thinking. In evaluative thinking, we express an opinion about something and defend it through the logical application of specified criteria. Theater critics evaluate plays according to certain (rarely agreed-upon!) criteria and publish their reviews in the newspaper. Movie critics give thumbs up or down (an evaluative judgment) and use their criteria to explain why.

These are exactly the kinds of evaluative judgments teachers must make about responses to essay exercises as presented in this chapter and to observed performance and achievement-related products as discussed in Chapter 8. In all cases, the key to success is the clear articulation of appropriate performance criteria.

Scoring Options.   Typically, we convey the evaluative judgment in terms of the number of points attained on the exercises. Here are two acceptable ways to do this:

- *The Checklist Option*—Assign points to specific ingredients in an answer, and award points when the respondent includes those active ingredients.
- *The Rating Scale Option*—Define achievement in terms of one or more performance continuums in the form of rating scales; for example, a five-point scale defines five levels of performance and the rater subjectively places responses along that scale.

The French teacher example examined in this chapter illustrates the checklist option. A rating scale for the evaluation of more features of an essay response, such as *the quality of content and ideas,* might look as follows:

High score	5	The response is clear, focused and accurate. Relevant points are made (in terms of the kinds of reasoning sought by the exercise) with good support (derived from the content to be used, again as spelled out in the exercise). Good connections are drawn and important insights are evident.
	3	The answer is clear and somewhat focused, but not compelling. Support of points made is limited. Connections are fuzzy, leading to few important insights.
Low score	1	The response either misses the point, contains inaccurate information, or otherwise demonstrates a lack of mastery of the material. Points are unclear, support is missing, and/or no insights are included.

With a rating scale such as this, it is perfectly acceptable to leave points 2 and 4 for the evaluator to interpolate if the response falls in between two given scores.

The idea is to develop as many such scales as make sense for the evaluation of the particular material to be rated. Other criteria for ratings, for example, might include these factors:

- demonstrated mastery of content
- organization of ideas
- soundness of reasoning

Obviously the rating scale option is more subjective than the checklist option for awarding points. However, if you have done the following three things, your rating scales can serve as excellent tools for evaluating essay responses:

1. Define the meaning of student success in terms of such scales in advance of the assessment.
2. Provide examples to your students illustrating the differences between sound and unsound performance.
3. Provide practice in performing successfully according to those standards.

Experts in assessment urge also that you adhere to the additional guidelines presented in Figure 7-4 when developing essay scoring procedures.

Time for Reflection

Please return to the scoring scheme you developed with your exercise at the beginning of this discussion. Did you devise a clear and appropriate set of standards? Adjust them as needed.

Barriers to Sound Essay Assessment

To summarize, there are many things you can do to cause a student's score on an essay test to represent that student's real level of achievement with a high degree of

- Set *realistic expectations and performance standards* that are consistent with instruction and that promise students some measure of success if they are prepared.
- Check scoring guides against a few real responses to see if any *last-minute adjustments* are needed.
- *Refer back to scoring guidelines* regularly during scoring to maintain consistency.
- *Score all responses to one exercise* before moving on to the next exercise. This does two things: It promotes consistency in your application of standards, and speeds up the scoring process.
- Score all responses to one exercise *in one sitting without interruption* to keep a clear focus on standards.
- Evaluate responses *separately for matters of content (knowledge mastery and reasoning) and matters of form (i.e., writing proficiency).* They require the application of different criteria.
- Provide feedback in the form of *points and written commentary* if possible.
- If possible, keep the *identity of the respondent anonymous* when scoring. This keeps your knowledge of their prior performance from influencing current judgments.
- Although it is often difficult to arrange, try to have *two independent qualified readers score* the papers. In a sense, this represents the litmus test of the quality of your scoring scheme. If two readers generally agree on the level of proficiency demonstrated by the respondent, then you have evidence of relatively objective or dependable subjective scoring. But if you and a colleague disagree on the level of performance demonstrated, you have uncovered evidence of problems in the appropriateness of the criteria or the process used to train raters, and some additional work is in order. When very important decisions rest on a student's score on an essay assessment, such as promotion or graduation, double scoring is absolutely essential.

Figure 7-4
Guidelines for Essay Scoring

accuracy. Potential sources of mismeasurement are listed below, along with the action you can take to assure sound assessment.

Source of Error	*Counteraction*
Lack of target clarity:	
• Underlying knowledge unclear	Carefully study the material to be learned and outline the larger structures to be assessed. Use major categories to form one dimension of a table of specifications.

• Kinds of reasoning to be demonstrated unclear	Define kinds of reasoning to be used in clear terms in writing (see Chapter 10 for examples). Use kinds of reasoning to form a second dimension of a table of specifications.
Wrong target for essay	Limit use to assessing mastery of larger knowledge structures and complex reasoning.
Lack of writing proficiency on part of respondent	Select another assessment method or help them become more proficient writers.
Inappropriate sample of exercises	Select a representative sample of sufficient length to give you confidence, given your table of specifications.
Poor-quality exercises	Follow guidelines specified above.
Poor-quality scoring:	
• Inappropriate criteria	Redefine them to fit.
• Unclear criteria	Clarify them—in writing.
• Untrained rater	Train them!
• Insufficient time to rate	Find more raters (see Figure 7-5 for example), or use another method.

Integrating Essay Assessment into Instruction

With all assessment methods, the first and most obvious way to integrate assessment into the teaching and learning process is to match assessment to instruction by being sure that what is taught and learned is what is assessed. In the context of performance-based education, students deserve practice hitting the very targets for which they will be held accountable. Similarly, teachers deserve to be held accountable for their students' success in attaining those prespecified and agreed-upon outcomes.

Beyond this essential perspective, Figure 7-5 presents additional ways to integrate assessment with instruction by involving students as full partners in the process of assessing their own and each other's achievement.

This figure is intended to present enough ideas to prime the pump. This is just a start. The list of ways to bring students into the assessment equation is as endless as your imagination. Please reflect, experiment, and find more ways. Because these uses of the essay assessment development process all contribute to that huge key to student success: making the target crystal clear for them to see and hit. These strategies serve to remove the mystery surrounding the meaning of good performance on an essay and in the classroom. They put students in control of their own academic well-being.

- As with selected response assessment, develop a blueprint for an essay test before a unit is ever taught, share that plan with the students, and keep track of how well instruction is preparing them to succeed on the exam.
- Present students with unlabeled essay exercises and have them practice fitting them into the content and reasoning cells of the table of specifications.
- Have students join in on the process of writing sample exercises. To do so, they will need to begin to sharpen their focus on the intended knowledge and thinking targets—as they do this, good teaching is happening! Be careful, though; these might best be used as examples for practice. Remember, to assess student thinking, the exercises that actually appear on a test must present novel problems.
- Give students some sample exercises and have them evaluate their quality as test exercises, given the test blueprint.
- Have students play a role in developing the scoring criteria for some sample exercises. Give them, for example, an excellent response and a poor-quality response to a past essay exercise and have them figure out the differences.
- Bring students into the actual scoring process, thus spreading the work over more shoulders! Form scoring teams, one for each exercise on a test. Have them develop scoring criteria under your watchful eye. Offer them advice as needed to generate appropriate criteria. Then have them actually score some essays, which you double check. Discuss differences in scores assigned. Students find this kind of workshop format very engaging.
- Have students predict their performance in each cell in the table of specifications or objective and then compare their prediction with the actual score. Were they in touch with their own achievement?
- Collect essays and scoring criteria over the years to develop a pool for reuse. A personal computer can help with this. If you keep information on student performance on each record (say, average score), you can adjust instruction next time to try to improve learning.
- Exchange, trade, or compare tables of specifications and/or exercises and scoring criteria with other teachers to ease the workload associated with assessment development. Learn good ideas from each other and compare and adjust the instructional priorities within a school building or district.

Figure 7-5
Involving Students in the Assessment Process

CHAPTER SUMMARY: TAPPING THE POTENTIAL OF ESSAYS

We all have heard those stories about the same essays being given to several college professors, who assigned vastly different grades to the same pieces of work. These stories often are cited as indictments of the essay form of assessment. This is unfair.

The reasons the professors disagreed on the level of proficiency demonstrated were that they had no opportunity to discuss and arrive at common expectations—there was no development of a common view of what it meant to perform well, no communication, no preparation to devise sound exercises and to score dependably. As a result, there was no common basis for assigning grades.

These stories reflect supremely poor application of a potentially sound method. When placed in the hands of teachers and students who know what they are doing, essay assessments—like selected response assessments and the other methods that remain to be discussed—can unlock and promote effective teaching and learning.

In this chapter, we have explored ways to prevent these kinds of problems from arising. We began by exploring the prominent role of subjectivity and professional judgment in the essay assessment process. This prominence means that this method carries with it dangers of bias. We studied specific ways to prevent these dangers from becoming realities. One is to connect the essay assessment method to appropriate kinds of achievement targets. These include mastery of complex structures of knowledge, complex reasoning processes, some of the knowledge foundations of skill and product proficiencies, and affective outcomes.

However, the heart of the matter with respect to quality assessment is adherence to specific assessment development procedures. We studied these in three parts: assessment planning, exercise development, and preparation to score. In each case, we reviewed specific procedural guidelines.

And, as in Chapter 6, we closed with a broad array of strategies to engage students as full partners in the assessment process, from design and development of exercises, to scoring, to interpretation and use of essay assessment results. These strategies connect assessment to the teaching and learning process in ways that can maximize both student motivation to learn and actual achievement.

EXERCISES TO ADVANCE YOUR LEARNING

Knowledge Outcomes

1. List three reasons for knowing about essay assessments.
2. State the three basic steps in the essay assessment development process.
3. Specify the specific kinds of achievement targets that can be transformed into the essay assessment format and those that cannot.
4. What factors should one take into account in considering use of the essay assessment option?
5. Identify the key considerations in devising a sound sample of essay exercises.
6. Make a one-page chart with three columns listing your own tailor-made abbreviations of the information presented in Figures 7-3, 7-4, and 7-5. Keep this handy for easy reference when you use essay assessment.

Reasoning Outcomes

1. Write five essay exercises that tap dimensions of this chapter. When you have done so, review the list and ask yourself whether these really represent the most important learnings from this chapter.
2. Devise scoring schemes for each of your exercises.

Skill Outcomes

1. Select a unit of instruction from the material you teach, will teach, or have studied as a student that includes complex structures of content and reasoning. Devise a table of specifications, find key elements for each cell in your table, and construct essay exercises and scoring criteria.

Product Outcomes

1. Evaluate the test you created in the exercise above in terms of the attributes of sound assessment discussed in this and earlier chapters. How did you do?

2. Select a previously developed essay test, either from your files or from a text series you may have used, and apply the principles learned in this chapter in evaluating it. Have the guidelines been followed? Can you see how to fix any problems you find?

Affective Outcomes

1. Some have argued that these are times for performance assessment and that such paper and pencil assessments as essay tests are remnants of bygone times—that these assessment formats have no place in the future of school testing. Do you agree? Why?

2. Throughout the chapter, I argue that the assessment development procedures outlined here will help those who use these kinds of assessments to connect their essay assessments directly to their instruction. Having completed the chapter, do you agree? Why?

3. I also argue that the assessment development and use procedures suggested herein could save you time, if you use these kinds of assessment in your classroom. Do you agree? Why?

CHAPTER 8

Performance Assessment: An Old Friend Rediscovered

Chapter Objectives

As a result of studying the material presented in this chapter, reflecting on that material, and completing the learning exercises presented at the end of the chapter, you will:

1. Master content knowledge:
   a. Understand the roles of objectivity and subjectivity in performance assessment.
   b. Know the kinds of achievement targets that can be reflected in performance assessments.
   c. List three basic parts and nine design decisions that comprise the steps in performance assessment development.
   d. Specify classroom assessment context factors to consider in deciding whether or when to use performance assessments.
   e. State considerations in sampling student performance via performance exercises.
   f. Know specific guidelines for the construction of performance exercises and scoring schemes.
   g. Specify ways to bring students into the performance assessment process as a teaching strategy.
2. Be able to use that knowledge to reason as follows:
   a. Identify the kinds of skills and products that can form the basis of performance assessment exercises.
   b. Transform those important learnings into quality exercises and scoring criteria.

3. Become proficient at the following skills:
   a. Be able to carry out the steps in designing performance assessments.
   b. Evaluate previously developed performance assessments to determine their quality.
4. Be able to create quality products of the following sorts:
   a. Performance assessments that meet standards of quality.
5. Attain the following affective outcomes:
   a. Understand the importance of knowing about sound performance assessment.
   b. Value performance assessment as a viable option for use in the classroom.
   c. See performance assessment as a valuable instructional tool in which students can and should be full partners.
   d. Regard performance assessment with caution, valuing the need to adhere to rigorous standards of quality in development and use.

The education community has discovered performance assessment methodology! Across the land, we are in a frenzy to learn about and use this "new" assessment discovery. Performance assessments involve students in activities that require the demonstration of certain skills and/or the creation of specified products. As a result, this assessment methodology permits us to tap many of the complex educational outcomes we value that cannot be translated into paper and pencil tests.

With performance assessments, we observe students while they are performing, or we examine the products created, and we judge the level of proficiency demonstrated. As with essay assessments, we use these observations to make subjective judgments about the level of achievement attained. Those evaluations are based on comparisons of student performance to preset standards of excellence.

For example, a primary-grade teacher might watch a student interacting with classmates and draw inferences about that child's level of development in social interaction skills. If the levels of achievement are clearly defined in terms the observer can easily interpret, then the teacher, observing carefully, can derive information from watching that will aid in planning strategies to promote further social development. Thus, this is not an assessment where answers are counted right or wrong. Rather, like the essay test, we rely on teacher judgment to place the student's performance somewhere on a continuum of achievement levels ranging from very low to very high.

From a completely different context, a middle school science teacher might examine "mousetrap cars" built by students to determine if certain principles of energy utilization have been followed. Mousetrap cars are vehicles powered by one snap of a trap. One object is to see who can design a car that can travel the farthest by converting that amount of energy into forward motion. When the criteria are clear, the teacher can help students understand why the winning car goes furthest.

Performance assessment methodology has arrived on the assessment scene with a flash of brilliance unprecedented since the advent of selected response test formats earlier in this century. For many reasons, this "new discovery" has struck a chord among educators at all levels. Recently popular applications carry such labels as *authentic assessments, alternative assessments, exhibitions, demonstrations,* and *student work samples,* among others.

These kinds of assessment are seen as providing high-fidelity or authentic assessments of student achievement (Wiggins, 1989). Proponents contend that, just as high-fidelity music provides accurate representations of the original music, so too can performance assessments provide accurate reproductions of complex achievements under performance circumstances that stretch into life beyond school. However, some urge great caution in our rush to embrace this methodology, because performance assessment brings with it great technical challenges. They correctly point out that this is a very difficult methodology to develop and use well (Dunbar, Koretz, & Hoover, 1991).

CHAPTER ROADMAP

As with the other forms of assessment, there are three critical contexts within which your knowledge of performance assessment methodology will serve you well. First, you will design and develop performance assessments for use in your classroom in the future, if you are not doing so already. The quality of those assessments, obviously, is in your hands.

Further, the education literature, published textbooks, and instructional materials and published test materials all are beginning to include more and more examples of performance assessments, which you might consider for use in your classroom. Once again, you are the gatekeeper. Only you can check these for quality and appropriateness for use in your context.

And finally, as with other forms of assessment, you may find yourself on the receiving end of a performance assessment. Obviously, it is in your best interest to be sure these are as sound as they can be—as sound as you would want them if you were to use them to evaluate your own students. Be a critical consumer: If you find flaws in the quality of these assessments, be diplomatic, but call the problems to the attention of those who will evaluate your performance.

To prepare you to fulfill these responsibilities, our journey will begin with an explanation of the basic elements of a performance assessment, illustrated with simple examples; we continue by examining the role of subjectivity in this form of assessment; and then we will analyze the kinds of achievement targets performance assessments can serve to reflect.

Further, as we travel, we will do the following:

● Complete a detailed analysis of the assessment development process, including specific recommendations for actions on your part that can help you avoid the many pitfalls to sound assessment that accompany this alternative.

	SELECTED RESPONSE	ESSAY	PERFORMANCE ASSESSMENT	PERSONAL COMMUNICATION
Know				
Reason				
Skill				
Product				
Affect				

Figure 8-1
Aligning Achievement Targets and Assessment Methods

- Address strategies for devising the criteria by which to evaluate performance, suggestions for developing quality exercises to elicit performance to be evaluated, and ideas for making and recording judgments of proficiency.

- Explore the integration of performance assessment with instruction, not as a concluding section at the end of the chapter, but as an integral part of the entire presentation on performance assessment methodology.

In this way, we will be able to see the great power of this methodology in the classroom: its ability to place students in charge of their own academic well-being.

As you proceed through this chapter, keep the big picture in mind. The shaded cells in Figure 8–1 show the material we will be addressing herein.

Also as we proceed, be advised that this is just part one of a multipart treatment of performance assessment methodology. It is intended only to reveal the basic structure of performance assessments. The remaining parts are included in Part 3, on classroom applications. After we cover the basic structure and development of these assessments in this chapter, we will return with many more examples in Chapter 10, on assessing reasoning in all of its forms, and in Chapter 11, on using performance assessments to evaluate many skills and products. Your understanding of performance assessment methodology is contingent upon studying, reflecting upon, and applying material covered in all three chapters.

A Note of Caution

While I tend to be a proponent of performance assessment methodology because of its great potential to reflect complex and valuable outcomes of education, I urge caution on two fronts.

First, please understand that there is nothing new about performance assessment methodology. This is not some kind of radical invention recently fabricated by opponents of traditional tests to challlenge the testing industry. Rather, it is a proven method of evaluating human characteristics that has been in use for decades (Linquist, 1951), for centuries, maybe even for eons. For how long have we selected our leaders, at least in part, on the basis of our observations of and judgments about their performance under pressure? Further, this is a methodology that has been the focus of sophisticated research and development both in educational settings and in the workplace for a very long time (Berk, 1986).

Besides, anyone who has taught knows that teachers routinely observe students and make judgments about their proficiency. Admittedly, some of those applications don't meet accepted standards of assessment quality (Stiggins & Conklin, 1992). But we know performance assessment is common in the classroom and we know how to do it well. Our challenge is to make the assessment meet the standards.

Virtually every bit of research and development done in education and business over the past decades leads to the same conclusion: performance assessment is a complex way to assess. It requires that users prepare and conduct their assessments in a thoughtful and rigorous manner. Those unwilling to invest the time and energy needed to do it well are better off assessing in some other way.

Second, performance assessment methodology is not the panacea some advocates seem to think it is. It is neither the savior of the teacher nor the key to assessing the "real" curriculum. It is just one tool capable of providing an effective and efficient means of assessing some—but not all—of the most highly valued outcomes of our educational process. As a result, it is a valuable tool indeed. But it is not the be-all and end-all of the educational assessment process. For this reason, it is critical that we keep this form of assessment in balance with the other alternatives.

Although performance assessment is complex, and requires care to use well, it certainly does hold the promise of bringing teacher, students, and instructional leaders into the assessment equation in unprecedented ways. But the cost of reaching this goal can be high. You must meet the considerable challenge of learning how to develop and use *sound* performance assessments. This will not be easy! There is nothing here you cannot master, but don't take this methodology lightly—we're not talking about "assessment by guess and by gosh" here. There is no place in performance assessment for "intuitions" or ethereal "feelings" about the achievement of students. It is not acceptable for a teacher to claim to just "know" a student can do it. Believable evidence is required. This is neither a mystical mode of assessment, nor are keys to its proper use a mystery. It takes thorough preparation and meticulous attention to detail to attain appropriate levels of performance assessment rigor.

Just as with other modes of assessment, there are rules of evidence for sound performance assessment. Remember, sound assessments do the following:

- arise from clear and appropriate achievement targets
- serve a clearly articulated purpose
- rely on proper assessment methods
- sample performance appropriately
- control for all relevant sources of extraneous interference

Adhere to these rules of evidence when developing performance assessment and you can add immeasurably to the quality and utility of your classroom assessments of student achievement. Violate those rules—which is very easy to do in this case!—and you place your students at risk.

Time for Reflection

As you have seen, performance assessments are based on observation and judgment. Can you think of instances outside of the school setting where this mode of assessment comes into play? In the context of hobbies? In work settings? In other contexts? Please list five or six examples.

PERFORMANCE ASSESSMENT AT WORK IN THE CLASSROOM

To appreciate the extremely wide range of possible applications of performance assessment, we need to explore the many design alternatives that reside within this methodology. I will briefly describe and illustrate those now, and will then show you how one professor put this design framework to work in her very productive learning environment.

An Overview of the Basic Components

We initiate the creation of performance assessments just as we initiated the development of paper and pencil tests as described in the previous two chapters: We start with a plan or blueprint. As with selected response and essay assessments, the performance assessment plan includes three components. In this case, each component contains three specific design decisions within it.

First, the performance assessment developer must clarify the performance to be evaluated. Second, performance exercises must be prepared. And third, systems must be devised for scoring and recording results.

The immense potential of this form of assessment becomes apparent when we consider all of the design options available within this three-part structure. Let's explore these options.

Part 1: Clarifying Performance.   Under this heading, the user has the freedom to select from a nearly infinite range of achievement target possibilities. We can focus performance assessments on particular targets by making three specific design decisions, addressing the kind of performance to be assessed, identifying who will be assessed, and specifying performance criteria.

Nature of Performance.   This first design decision requires that we answer these basic questions: How will successful achievement manifest itself? Where will the evidence of proficiency most easily be found?

Performance might take the form of a particular set of skills or behaviors that students must demonstrate. In this case, we watch students "in process," or while they are actually doing something, and we evaluate the quality of their performance. The example given earlier of the primary-grade teacher observing the youngster in interaction with other students illustrates this kind of performance assessment. In that instance, success manifests itself in the actions of the student.

On the other hand, we also can define performance in terms of a particular kind of product to be created, such as the mousetrap car. In this application, the standards of performance would reflect important attributes of an energy-efficient car. The teacher would examine the car and determine the extent to which the criteria of efficiency had been met. Evidence of success is found in the attributes of the car as a product.

Some contexts permit or may even require the observation and evaluation of both skill and product. For example, you might watch a student operate a computer (skill) and evaluate the final product (the resulting program or other document) to evaluate that student's success in hitting both key parts of that achievement target.

Time for Reflection

Based on your experience as a student and/or teacher, can you think of additional classroom contexts where it might be relevant to assess both process and product?

Focus of the Assessment.   To address this design decision, we must understand that performance assessments need not focus only on individual student behaviors. They also can apply to the observation of and judgment about the performance of students functioning in a group.

In these times of cooperative learning, the evaluation of teamwork can represent a very important and useful application. Two kinds of observations are worthy of consideration. One focuses on the group interaction behaviors. The observer tracks the manner in which the group works as a whole. The group is the unit of analysis of performance, if you will. A sample performance assessment question might be, Given a problem to solve, does the group exhibit sound group problem-solving skills?

The other form of observation focuses on individual behaviors in a group context and summarizes those across individuals. For example, observers might tally and/or evaluate the nature of instances of aggressive and dangerous playground behavior. These can be very informative and useful assessments.

Performance Criteria.   Once we have decided on the performance and performer upon which to focus, the real work begins. Attention then shifts to (a) specifying in writing all key elements of performance, and (b) defining a performance continuum for each element so as to depict in writing what performance is like when it is of very poor quality, when it is outstanding, and all key points in between. These key elements or dimensions of performance are called the *performance criteria.*

In terms of the two examples we have been discussing, performance criteria answer the questions, What are the desirable social interaction behaviors for a primary-grade student? What are the specific attributes of an energy-efficient mouse-trap car?

Clear and appropriate performance criteria are critical to sound performance assessment. When we can provide sound criteria, we are in for an easy and productive application of this methodology. Not only will we be in focus on the expected outcomes, but with clearly articulated performance criteria, as you shall see, both students and teachers share a common language in which to converse about those expectations.

Time for Reflection

When you are evaluating a movie, what criteria do you apply? How about a restaurant? Write down criteria you think should be used as the basis for evaluating a teacher.

Part 2: Developing Exercises.   In designing performance exercises, we must think of ways to cause students to perform in a manner that will reveal their level of proficiency. How can we cause them to produce and present a sample product for us to observe and evaluate, for example? In this facet of performance assessment design, we decide the nature of the exercises, the number of exercises needed, and the actual instructions to be given to performers.

Nature of Exercises.   Performance assessment offers two exercise choices that, once again, reveal the rich potential of this methodology. Specifically, there are two ways to elicit performance for purposes of evaluation.

One option is to present a structured exercise in which you provide respondents with a predetermined and detailed set of instructions as to the kind of performance desired. They are completely aware of the assessment, they reflect upon and prepare for this assignment, and then they provide evidence of their proficiency. For example, they might be asked to prepare to give a certain kind of speech, perform some kind of athletic activity, write a term paper, or build a mousetrap car.

But also be advised that performance assessment offers another option not available with any other form of assessment. You can observe and evaluate some kinds of performance during naturally occurring classroom events and gather useful information about "typical" student performance. For example, the primary-grade teacher interested in the social interaction skills of one student obviously would disrupt the entire assessment by instructing the student, "Go interact with that group over there, so I can evaluate your ability to get along." Such an exercise would run completely counter to the very essence of the assessment. Rather, the teacher would want to stand back and watch the student's behavior unfold naturally in a group context to obtain usable information. Assessments that are based on observation and judgment allow for this possibility, while others do not. Just try to be unobtrusive with a true/false test!

It may have become apparent to you also that you can combine observations derived from administration of structured exercises and from the context of naturally occurring events to generate corroborating information about the same achievement target. For example, an English teacher might evaluate writing proficiency gathered in response to a required assignment and in the context of student daily writing journals done for practice. The combined information might provide insights about specific student needs.

Time for Reflection

Can you think of an instance outside of school in which observation of naturally occurring performance serves as the basis for an assessment? In the context of a hobby? In a work setting? In some other context? What is observed and judged and by whom?

Content of Exercises.   The final exercise-related design component is the actual content of the exercise. Like the essay exercise discussed in Chapter 7, instructions for structured exercises should include the kind(s) of achievement to be demonstrated, conditions under which that demonstration is to take place, and standards of quality to be applied in evaluating performance. Here is a simple example of a complete exercise:

Achievement: Your four-person team is to do the research requied to prepare a group presentation on the dwellings and primary food sources of the Native American tribe you have selected.

Conditions: The manner in which you carry out the background research and divide up responsibilities within the group is up to you. The focus of the evaluation will be your presentation. *(Note that the process will not be evaluated in terms of doing the background research or preparation, but it will be in the process of giving the presentation.)*

Standards: Your presentation will be evaluated according to the criteria we develop together in class, dealing with content (scope, organization, and accuracy) and delivery (use of learning aids, clarity, and interest value for the audience).

Number of Exercises.   Once the nature of the exercise is determined, you must decide how many exercises are needed. This is a sampling issue. How many examples of student performance are enough? As discussed, you must decide how many exercises are needed to provide a representative sample of all the important questions you could have asked given infinite time. If you want to know if students can speak French, how many times do they have to speak for you to be reasonably certain you could predict how well they would do given one more chance? How many samples of writing must you see to be confident drawing conclusions about writing proficiency? In fact, the answers to these questions are a function of the assessment context. To answer them, we must consider several factors, including the reasons for assessment and other issues. We will review these factors later in the chapter.

Part 3: Scoring and Recording Results.   Once performance has been clarified and exercises developed, procedures for managing results must be specified.

Level of Detail of Results.   First, the user must select one of two kinds of scores to generate from the assessment. Option one is to evaluate performance analytically, making independent judgments about each of the performance criteria separately. In this case, performance is profiled in terms of individual ratings. Option two is called holistic scoring. In this case, one overall judgment is made about performance that combines all criteria into one evaluation. The choice is a function of the manner in which assessment results are to be used. Some uses require the high-resolution microscope of the analytical system, while others require the less precise but also less costly holistic process.

Recording Procedures.   Second, designers must select a specific method for transforming performance criteria into usable information through a system of recording procedures. Once again, the great flexibility of performance assessment methodology comes through. Users have many choices here, too:

- checklists of desired attributes present or absent in performance
- various kinds of performance rating scales
- anecdotal records, which capture written descriptions of and judgments about performance
- mental records, which capture images and records of performance in the memory of the evaluator for later recall and use (to be used cautiously!)

Identifying the Rater.   And finally, performance assessment users must decide who will observe and evaluate performance. In most classroom contexts, the most natural choice is the teacher. Since performance evaluators must possess a clear vision of the desired achievement and be capable of the rigorous application of the performance criteria, who could be more qualified than the teacher?

Just be advised that you have other choices. You might rely on some outside expert to come to the classroom and participate. Or you might rely on the students to conduct self-assessments or to evaluate each other's performance.

The instructional potential of preparing students to apply performance criteria in a rigorous manner to their own work should be obvious. I will address this application in greater detail throughout the chapter.

Time for Reflection

As a student, have you ever been invited to observe and evaluate the skill or product performance of other students? What did you observe? What criteria did you use? Were you trained to assess? What was that experience like for you?

Summary of Basic Components.   Figure 8–2 lists the nine design decisions faced by any performance assessment developer. Also included are the design options available within each decision.

Design Factor	Options
1. Clarifying Performance	
Nature of performance	Behavior to be demonstrated
	Product to be created
Focus of the assessment	Individual performance
	Group performance
Performance Criteria	Reflect key aspects of the specific target
2. Developing Exercises	
Nature of exercises	Structured assignment
	Naturally occurring events
Content of exercises	Defines target, conditions, and standards
Number of exercises	Function of purpose, target, and available resources
3. Scoring and Recording Results	
Level of detail of results	Holistic
	Analytical
Recording procedures	Checklist
	Rating
	Anecdotal record
	Mental records
Identifying the rater	Teacher
	Outside expert
	Student self-evaluation
	Student peer evaluation

Figure 8-2
Performance Assessment Design Framework

ENSURING THE QUALITY OF PERFORMANCE ASSESSMENTS

If we are to apply the design framework shown in Figure 8–2 productively, we need to understand where the pitfalls to sound performance assessment hide. For instance, if we are not careful, problems can arise from the inherently subjective nature of performance assessment. Other problems can arise from trying to use this methodology in places where it doesn't belong.

Subjectivity in Performance Assessment

Professional judgment guides every aspect of the design and development of any performance assessment. For instance, as the developer and/or user of this method, you establish the achievement target to be assessed using input about educational priorities expressed in state and local curricula, your text materials, and the opinions of experts in the field. You interpret all of these factors and you decide what will be emphasized in your classroom—based on professional judgment.

Further, you select the assessment method to be used to reflect that target. Based on your vision of the valued outcomes and your sense of the assessment options available to you, you make the choices. This certainly qualifies as a matter of professional judgment.

In the classroom, typically you create the assessment, either selecting from among some previously developed options or generating it by yourself. If you generate it yourself, you choose whether to involve students or other parties in that design process. In the case of performance assessment, the first design issue to be faced is that of devising performance criteria, those detailed descriptions of success that will guide both assessment and instruction. This translation of vision into criteria is very much a matter of professional judgment.

So is the second design decision you must make: formulating performance exercises, the actual instructions to respondents that cause them to either demonstrate certain skills or create some tangible product, so their performance can be observed and evaluated. And finally, of course, this observation and evaluation process is subjective too. Every step along the way is a matter of your professional and subjective judgment.

For decades, the assessment community has afforded performance assessment the status of second-class citizenship because of the potentially negative impacts of all of this subjectivity. The possibility of bias due to subjective judgment has rendered this methodology too risky for many.

More recently, however, we have come to understand that carefully trained performance assessment users, who invest the clear thinking and developmental resources needed to do a good job, can use this methodology effectively. Indeed, many of the increasingly complex achievement targets that we ask students to hit today demand that we use performance assessments and use them well. In short, we now know that we have no choice but to rely on subjective performance assessment in certain contexts. So we had better do our homework as an education community!

Here I must insert as strong a warning as any presented anywhere in this book: In your classroom, *you* will set the standards of assessment quality. It is *your* vision that will be translated into performance criteria, exercises, and records of student achievement. For this reason, it is *not* acceptable for you to hold a vision that is wholly a matter of your personal opinion about what it means to be academically successful. Rather, your vision must have the strongest possible basis in the collective academic opinions of experts in the discipline within which you assess and of colleagues and associates in your school, district, and community.

Systematic assessment of student performance of the wrong target is as much a waste of time as a haphazard assessment of the proper target. The only way to prevent this is for you to be in communication with those who know the right target and the most current best thinking about that target, and for you to become a serious student of their standards of academic excellence. Strive to know the skills and products that constitute maximum proficiency in the disciplines you assess.

Time for Reflection

What specific sources can teachers tap to be sure they understand skill and performance outcomes?

Matching Method to Target

As the meaning of academic excellence becomes clear, it will also become clear whether or when performance assessment is, in fact, the proper tool to use. While the range of possible applications of this methodology is broad, it is not infinitely so. Performance assessment can provide dependable information about student achievement of some, but not all, kinds of valued outcomes. Let's examine the matches and mismatches with the five kinds of outcomes we have been discussing: knowledge, reasoning, skills, products, and affect.

Assessing Knowledge.   If the objective is to determine if students have mastered a body of knowledge through memorization, observing performance or products may not be the best way to assess. Three difficulties can arise in this context, one related to potential sampling errors, another to issues of assessment efficiency, and a third related to the classroom assessment and instructional decision-making context.

Consider, for example, asking students to participate in a group discussion conducted in Spanish as a means of assessing mastery of vocabulary and rules of grammar. While this is an apparently authentic assessment, it might lead you to incorrect conclusions. First, the students will naturally choose to use vocabulary and syntax with which they are most comfortable and confident. Thus they will naturally select biased samples of all possible vocabulary and usage.

Second, if this is an assessment of the level of knowledge mastery of a large number of students, the total assessment will take a great deal of time. This may cause you to collect too small a sample of the performance of each individual, leading to undependable results. Given this achievement target, it would be much more efficient from an achievement sampling point of view to administer a simple objectively scored vocabulary and grammar test. Then, once you are confident that the foundational knowledge has been mastered and the focus of instruction turns to real-world applications, you might turn to the group discussion performance assessment.

Consider this same issue from a slightly different perspective. If you use the performance assessment as a reflection of the knowledge mastery target, it will be difficult to decide how to help the student who fails to perform well. It will not be clear what went wrong. Is the problem a lack of knowledge of the vocabulary and grammar, and/or an inability to pronounce words, and/or anxiety about the public nature of the demonstration? Since all three are hopelessly confounded with one another, it becomes difficult to decide on a proper course of action. Thus once again, given this target and this context, performance assessment may not be the best choice.

When the knowledge to be memorized is to be sampled in discrete elements, a selected response format is best. When larger structures of knowledge are the target, the essay format is preferable. Both of these options offer more control over the material assessed.

However, if your assessment goal is to determine if students have gained control over a body of knowledge through the proper and efficient use of reference materials, then performance assessment might work well. For instance, you might give students the exercise of finding a number of facts about a given topic and observe the manner in which they attack the problem, applying performance criteria related to the process of using particular library reference services and documents. A checklist of proper steps might serve as the basis for scoring and recording results of the assessment.

Or, you might ask for a written summary of those facts, which might be evaluated on rating scales in terms of the speed with which it was generated, the efficiency of the search, and the accuracy and thoroughness of the summary. Observation and judgment might play a role here.

Assessing Reasoning. Performance assessment also can provide an excellent means of assessing student reasoning and problem-solving proficiencies. Given complex problems to solve, students must engage in thinking and reasoning processes that include several steps. While we cannot directly view the thought processes, we can use various kinds of proxy measures as the basis for drawing inferences about the reasoning carried out.

For example, we might give chemistry students unidentified substances to identify and watch how they go about setting up the apparatus and carrying out the study. The criteria might reflect the proper order of activities. Those who reason well will follow the proper sequence and succeed. Those whose reasoning is flawed will go awry. Some might classify this as a selected response test: students identify the substance correctly or they do not; right or wrong. While that is true in one sense, think about how much richer and more useful the results are when the assessment is conceived and carried out as a performance assessment—especially when the student fails to identify the substance accurately. A comparison of the reasoning actually carried out with the reasoning spelled out in the performance criteria will be very revealing, and instructionally relevant.

Performance assessments structured around products created by students also can provide insight into the reasoning process. The resulting product itself is a reflection of sound or unsound reasoning during its development. One simple example might be the production of a written research report by students who carried out the above experiment. That report would reflect and provide evidence of their problem-solving capabilities.

Another example of a product-based performance assessment would be the physics challenge of building a tower out of toothpicks that will hold a heavy load. One performance criterion certainly will be the amount of weight it can hold. But others might focus on whether the builder adhered to appropriate engineering principles. The product-based performance assessment can help reveal the ability to apply those principles.

In fact, the thoughtful development and use of this performance assessment can help students achieve such a problem-solving goal. For example, what if you gave students two towers built purposely to hold vastly different amounts of weight? They might be told to analyze each in advance of the load-bearing experiment to predict which would hold more. Further, you might ask them to defend their prediction with specific design differences. After the experiment reveals the truth, the students are more likely to be able to infer how to build strong towers. In essence, the problem-solving criteria will have been made clear to them.

Assessing Skills.   The great strength of performance assessment methodology lies in its ability to ask students to perform in certain ways and to provide a dependable means of evaluating that performance. Most communication skills fall in this category, as do all forms of performing, visual, and industrial arts. The observation of students in action can be a rich and useful source of information about their attainment of very important forms of skill achievement. We will review many examples of these as our journey continues.

Assessing Products.   Herein lies the other great strength of performance assessment. There are occasions when we ask students to create complex achievement-related products. The quality of those products indicate the creator's level of achievement. If we develop sound performance criteria that reflect the key attributes of these products and learn to apply those criteria well, performance assessment can serve us as both an efficient and effective tool. Everything from written products, such as term papers and research reports, to the many forms of art and craft products can be evaluated in this way. Again, many examples will follow.

Assessing Affect.   To the extent that we can draw inferences about attitudes, values, interests, motivational dispositions, and/or academic self-concept based either on the actions of students or on what we see in the products they create, then performance assessment can assist us here, too.

However, I urge caution. Remember, sound performance assessment requires strict adherence to a preestablished set of rules of evidence. Sound assessments must do the following:

- *Reflect a clear target*—We must thoroughly understand and develop sound definitions of the affective targets to be assessed.

- *Serve a clearly articulated purpose*—We must know precisely why we are assessing and what it is we intend to do with the result—especially tricky in the case of affective outcomes.

- *Rely on a proper method*—The performance must present dependable information to us about affect.

- *Sample the target appropriately*—We must collect enough evidence of affect to give us confidence in our conclusions.

- *Control for extraneous interference*—The potential sources of bias in our judgments about student attitudes, values, interests, and so on must be understood and neutralized in the context of our assessments.

When applying these standards of quality to the assessment of achievement outcomes—those content-based targets we are trained to teach—it becomes somewhat easier to see the translations. That is, hopefully, we have immersed ourselves far enough in a particular field of study to attain a complete understanding of its inherent breadth and scope. We should know when a sample of test items, a set of essay exercises, a particular performance assessment, or a product evaluation captures the meaning of academic success.

When it comes to affective outcomes, however, most of us have had much less experience with and therefore are much less comfortable with their meaning, depth, and scope. That means successfully assessing them demands careful and thoughtful preparation.

We can watch students in action and/or examine the things they create and infer about their affective states. But we can do this only if we have a clear and practiced sense of what it is we are looking for and why we are assessing it. I will address these issues in depth in Chapter 12.

Summary of Target Matches.   There are many important educational outcomes that can be translated into performance assessments. That is, if we prepare carefully, we can develop performance criteria and devise exercises to sample the following:

- use of reference material to acquire knowledge
- application of that knowledge in a variety of problem-solving contexts
- proficiency in a range of skill arenas
- ability to create different kinds of products
- feelings, attitudes, values, and other affective characteristics

In fact, the only target for which performance assessment is not recommended is the assessment of simple elements or complex components of subject matter knowledge to be mastered through memorization. Selected response and essay formats work better here.

DEVELOPING PERFORMANCE ASSESSMENTS

As with selected response and essay assessments, we develop performance assessments in three steps. Each step corresponds to one of the three basic design components introduced earlier. Developers must specify the performance to be evaluated, devise exercises to elicit the desired behavior, and develop a method for making and recording judgments.

Unlike other forms of assessment, however, this form permits flexibility in the order in which these parts are developed. But before we consider those issues, we will review context factors we should consider in deciding whether or when to adopt performance assessment methods.

Context Factors

Clearly, the prime factors to consider in the assessment selection process are the appropriateness of the achievement target for your students and the match of performance assessment methodology to that target. You must also ask yourself certain practical questions when deciding if performance assessment is the right choice for your particular context. These questions are posed in Figure 8–3.

Approximating the Best.   Remember, while performance assessment can be used to assess reasoning, we also can use selected response and essay formats to tap this kind of outcome. In addition, while performance assessment is the best option for measuring attainment of skill and product outcomes, again, we can use selected response and essay to assess student mastery of important prerequisites of effective performance. In this sense, they represent approximations of the best.

Further, as you will see in Chapter 9, sometimes we can gain insight into achievement by having students talk through hypothetical performance situations. Admittedly, these are second best when compared to the real thing. But they can provide useful information.

These "proxy" measures might come into play when we seek to size up a group of students very quickly for instructional planning purposes. In such a case, we might need only group performance information, so we could sample a few students from the group and assess just a few aspects of the performance of each. By combining information across students, we generate a profile of achievement that indicates group achievement strengths and needs. We can use such group information to plan instruction. Under these circumstances, it may be unnecessary to use costly, full-blown performance assessments of every student. Rather, we might turn to simpler, more efficient paper and pencil or personal communication–based approximations of the best assessment to get what we need.

In effect, you can use proxies to delve into the prerequisites of skill and product performance to determine individual student needs. Remember that the building blocks of competence include knowledge to be mastered and reasoning power—both of which can be assessed with methods that fall short of actual performance

- *Do you have the expertise required to develop clear and appropriate criteria?* Don't take this too lightly. If you have not developed a deep sense of important outcomes in the field and therefore don't have a highly differentiated vision of the target(s), performance assessment can present a very frustrating challenge. Understand the implications of teaching students to hit the wrong target! Solicit some help—an outside opinion—just to verify the appropriateness of your assessment. For instance, find a colleague or maybe a small team of partners to work with.

- *Are your students able to perform in the ways required?* Be sure there are no physical and/or emotional handicaps that preclude being able to do the work required. Primary among the possible performance inhibitors may be evaluation anxiety in those assessment contexts requiring public displays of proficiency.

- *What is the purpose for the assessment?* If high-stakes decisions hang on the assessment results, such as promotion, graduation, a critical certification of mastery, or the like, you need to be prepared to invest the time and energy sufficient to produce confident results. Such critical assessments require a higher degree of confidence than do periodic examinations that measure current student proficiency levels in an ongoing classroom situation.

- *How many students will you assess?* The more students you must assess, the more carefully you must think through where or how you are going to find the time required to do them all. There are many creative ways to economize—such as sharing the work with other trained and qualified judges . . . like your students, among others.

- *What is the scope of the achievement target to be assessed?* Scope influences two things: the amount of evidence required to judge achievement and the amount of time over which you sample performance. If the scope is narrow and the time frame short (e.g., the focus of one day's lesson), few exercises will be needed to sample it well. Broader targets, on the other hand, require more exercises (e.g., a semester's worth of material), and demand that you spread your sample of exercises out over an extended period.

- *Is the target simple or complex?* Complex targets require more exercises to cover the full range of applications. For example, we cannot label a student a competent or incompetent writer on the basis of one exercise, no matter what that exercise requires. Writing is complex, taking many forms and occurring in many different kinds of contexts. If the target is complex, exercises must sample enough relevant forms and contexts to lead to confident inferences about competence.

- *Are the materials required to perform successfully available in school and/or at home?* Anticipate what specific materials students will need to perform the task at hand. School resources vary greatly, as do resources available for students at home. Be sure all have an equal opportunity to succeed before you proceed.

- *What resources do you have at your disposal to conduct the observation and scoring required of your assessment?* Obviously, observing and evaluating students or their products is a labor-intensive activity that demands much time and effort. If there has been one deterrent to the broader use of this methodology, it is the time required to do it well. Teachers often get trapped into thinking that all that work must automatically fall on their shoulders. This is not so. Other resources can include the principal(!), teacher aides, parents, outside experts, colleagues, and last but by no means least, students themselves, evaluating their own or each other's performance. Think about the instructional implications of involving them in the process. But remember, you must train them to apply the criteria dependably.

- *Has the author of your textbook or workbook, a colleague, or someone else already developed sound performance criteria and associated exercises for you to adopt and use?* Verify the quality and train yourself to apply the criteria dependably and these ready-made assessments can save a great deal of development time. Also, consider revising them to more closely fit your needs.

Figure 8-3
Context Factors to Consider in Selecting Performance Assessment

assessment. Not only can proxy measures serve as a means of such formative assessment, but to the extent that you involve your students in the assessment process, they also can introduce students to the various prerequisites before they need to put them together.

Further, any time resources are too limited to permit a full-blown performance assessment, we might be forced to think of alternatives; to come as close as we can to the real thing, given our resources. While the resulting paper and pencil or personal communication assessments will fall short of perfection, if they are thoughtfully developed, they may give us enough information to serve our needs.

If you do decide to use approximations, however, never lose sight of their limitations: understand the outcomes they do and do not reflect.

Time for Reflection

Can you remember a paper and pencil test you have taken that was a proxy measure for an achievement target that would have been more completely or precisely assessed with a performance assessment? How close did it come to the real thing, in your opinion?

The Order of Development

In explaining the basic three-part design framework, I began by specifying performance, then turned to exercises, then scoring practices. However, this is not the only possible or viable order of development for performance assessments.

For instance, we might begin developing a performance assessment by creating rich and challenging exercises. If we can present complex but authentic, real-world problems for students to solve, then we can see how they respond during pilot test administrations and devise clear criteria for evaluating the achievement of subsequent performers.

On the other hand, it is difficult to devise exercises to elicit outcomes unless and until we have specified precisely what those outcomes are. In this case, we could start by selecting the target, translate it into performance criteria, and then develop performance rating procedures. Then, given a clear vision of the desired performance, we can devise exercises calculated to elicit samples of performance to which we can then apply the criteria.

In a sense, we have a chicken-or-egg dilemma here. We can't plan to evaluate performance until we know what that performance is—but neither can we solicit performance properly until we know how we're going to evaluate it! Which comes first, the performance criteria or the exercises?

As luck and good planning would have it, you can take your choice. Which you choose is a function of your level of understanding of the valued outcomes to be assessed.

When You Know What to Look For.   Those who begin the performance assessment development process with a strong background in the area to be evaluated probably possess a highly refined vision of the target and can develop performance criteria out of that vision. If you begin with that kind of firm grounding, you may be able simply to sit at your desk and spell out each of the key elements of sound performance. With little effort, you may be able to translate each key element into different levels of achievement proficiency in clear, understandable terms. If you have sufficient pedagogical knowledge in your area(s) of expertise, you can use the procedures discussed in this chapter to carry out the necessary professional reflection, spell out your performance criteria, and transform those into scoring and recording procedures. Then you will be ready to devise exercises to elicit the performance you want.

When You Have a Sense of What to Look for.   However, not everyone is ready to jump right in in this manner. Sometimes we have a general sense of the nature of the performance but are less clear on the specific criteria. For example, you might want your students to "write a term paper," but not have a clear sense about the standards of quality you want to apply.

When this happens, you need a different starting place. One option is to give students a general term paper assignment and use the resulting papers—that is, actual samples of student work—as the basis for defining specific criteria. You can select a few high-quality and a few low-quality papers to compare as a means of generating clear and appropriate performance criteria. One way to do this is to sort them into three or four piles of general quality, ranging from poor to excellent, then carefully and thoughtfully analyze why the papers differ. Why do some work, while others don't? In those differences are hidden the performance criteria you seek.

The major shortcoming of starting with general exercises, of course, is that it puts students in the unenviable position of trying to perform well—write a good term paper, for example—without a clear sense of what good performance is supposed to look like. But remember, you need do this only once. From then on, you will always have well-developed criteria in hand to share with students in advance.

You can avoid this problem if you can recover copies of previous term papers. The key is to find contrasting cases, so you can compare them. They needn't come from your current students. Or, if you are assessing a demonstrated skill, perhaps you can find videotapes of past performance, or can locate students practicing and observe them. One excellent way to find the right performance criteria, your vision of the meaning of academic success, is by "student watching." You can derive the critical elements of student success from actual samples of student work. But to take advantage of this option, you first need to get them performing somehow. That may mean starting with the development of exercises.

When You're Uncertain about What to Look For.   Other times, you may have only the vaguest sense of what you want students to know and be able to do within a particular discipline. In these instances, you can use performance assessment exercises to help identify the truly important learnings. Here's how this works:

Begin by asking yourself, What kinds of real-world challenges do I want students to be able to handle? What are some sample problems I hope students would be able to solve? Using creative brainstorming, you and your colleagues can create and collect numerous written illustrative sample exercises. When you have assembled enough such exercises to begin to zero in on what they are sampling, then step back from the array of possibilities and ask, What are the important skills that seem to cross all or many of these problems? Or, if products are to result, What do all or many of the products seem to have in common? In short, ask, What are these exercises really getting at?

In other words, we draw inferences about the underlying meaning of success by examining various examples of how that success is likely to manifest itself in real-world problems. Out of these generalizations, we can draw relevant and explicit performance criteria.

One thing I like about this strategy is the fact that the resulting performance criteria are likely to be usable for a number of similar exercises. Good criteria generalize across tasks. They are likely to represent generally important dimensions of sound performance, not just those dimensions that relate to one narrowly defined task. They capture and convey a significant, generalizable portion of the meaning of academic success.

Having acknowledged these various options in the order of assessment development, I will now outline a simple performance assessment development sequence starting with the criteria, adding in the exercises, and concluding with the development of scoring and recording procedures. You can mix and match these parts and use the development of one part to help you solve problems in the development of another part. This is the *art* of performance assessment development.

Phase 1: Defining Performance

Our goal in defining the term *performance* as used in the context of performance assessment is to describe the important skills to be demonstrated and/or the important attributes of the product to be created. While performance assessments also include evaluations of or judgments about the level of proficiency demonstrated, our basic challenge is to *describe* the underlying basis of our evaluations.

More specifically, in designing performance assessments, we work to find a vocabulary to use in communicating with each other and with our students about the meaning of successful performance. The key assessment question comes down to this: *Do you, the teacher, know what you are looking for in performance?* But the more important instructional question is this: *Do you know the difference between successful and unsuccessful performance and can you convey that difference in meaningful terms to your students?* Remember, students can hit any target they can see and that holds still for them. In performance assessment contexts, the target is defined in terms of the performance criteria.

Shaping Your Vision of Success.   As I have said repeatedly, the most effective way to be able to answer these two questions in the affirmative is to be a master of the skills and products that reflect the valued academic outcomes in your classroom. Those who teach drama, music, physical education, second languages, computer operations, or other skill-based disciplines, are prepared to assess well only when they possess a refined vision of the critical skills involved. Those who instruct students to create visual art, craft products, and various written products face both the teaching and assessment challenges with greatest competence and confidence when they are masters at describing the high-quality product to the neophyte.

Connoisseurs can recognize outstanding performance when they see it. They know a good restaurant when they find it. They can select a fine wine. They know which movies deserve a thumbs up, which Broadway plays are worth their ticket price. And connoisseurs can describe why they have evaluated any of these as outstanding. It is their stock in trade. However, because the evaluation criteria may vary somewhat from reviewer to reviewer, their judgments may not always agree. In restaurants, wines, movies, and plays, the standards of quality may be a matter of opinion. But, that's what makes interesting reading in newspapers and magazines.

Teachers are very much like these connoisseurs, in that they must be able to recognize and describe outstanding performance. But there are important differences between connoisseurs and teachers.

Not only can well-prepared teachers visualize and explain the meaning of success, but they can impart that meaning to others so as to help them *become* outstanding performers. In short, they are *teachers,* not just critics.

In most disciplines, there are agreed-upon skills and products that proficient performers must master. The standards of excellence that characterize our definitions of high-quality performance are always those held by experts in the field of study in question. Outstanding teachers have immersed themselves in understanding those discipline-based meanings of proficiency and they understand them thoroughly. Even when there are differences of opinion about the meaning of outstanding performance in a particular discipline, well-prepared teachers understand those differences and are capable of revealing them to their students.

It is this depth of understanding that must be captured in our performance expectations so it can be conveyed to students through instruction, example, and practice. Because they must be shared with students, our performance criteria cannot exist only in the intellect of the assessor. They must be translated into words and examples for all to see. And they must be capable of forming the basis of our judgments when we record the results of our assessments.

Finding Help in Shaping Your Vision.   In this regard, since we now have nearly a decade of significant new discipline-based performance assessment research and development behind us, many fields of study already have developed outstanding examples of sound criteria for critical performance. Examples include writing proficiency, foreign language, mathematics, and physical education. The most accessible source of information about these developments is the national association of teachers in each discipline. Nearly every such association has advanced written standards of student achievement in their field of study within the past five years. Any association that has not completed that work by now is conducting such studies at this time and will have them completed soon. I will provide examples of these in Part 3.

Not only will these associations probably have completed at least some of this work themselves, but they likely know others who have engaged in developing performance standards in their field. These may include university researchers and/or state departments of education. Check with your reference librarian for a directory of associations to learn how to contact those of interest to you.

Many contend that most of the important advances in the development of new assessment methods, including performance assessments, conducted over the past decade have been made by assessment departments of state departments of education. For this reason, it may be useful to contact your state personnel to see if they have either completed development of performance criteria in your discipline or know of other states that have. Again, I will share examples of these later.

And finally, consider the possibility that your local district or school curriculum development process may have resulted in the creation of some new performance assessment. Or perhaps a colleague, completely unbeknownst to you, developed an evaluation of a kind of performance that is of interest to you, too. You will never know unless you ask. At the very least, you may find a partner or even a small team to work with you in your performance assessment development.

Six Steps in Developing Your Own Criteria.   If you must develop performance criteria yourself, you must carry out a thoughtful task or product analysis. That means you must look inside the skills or products of interest and find the active ingredients. In most cases, this is not complicated.

A professor associate of mine decided to develop a performance assessment of her own teaching proficiency. The assessment would focus on the critical skills in the presentation of a class on assessment. Further, she decided to engage her students in the process of devising those criteria—to assure that they understand what it means to teach effectively. Let me describe how that went.

Please note that the examples presented in this description are real. They came directly from the work of the actual class depicted in this story. They are not intended to represent exemplary work or the best possible representation of the attributes discussed and should not be regarded as such. They are merely presented as illustrations from real classroom activities.

Step 1: Reflective Brainstorming.   The process of developing criteria reflecting teaching proficiency began with a brainstorming session. The professor talked with her students a few moments about why it is important to understand how to provide sound instruction in assessment methods, and then asked, What do you think might be some of the factors that contribute to effective teaching? They listed suggestions on the board, trying to capture the essence of each with the briefest possible label.

That list looked something like this:

know the subject	poised
use humor	flexible
organized	on schedule
enthusiasm	good support materials
fresh ideas	appropriate text

relevant content	monitor student needs
clear objectives	voice loud, clear, varied
be interactive	comfortable environment
use visuals well	refreshments!
be interesting	material connected
appropriate pacing	challenging
believe in material covered	personalize communication
professional	effective time management
credible information	in control

From time to time, the teacher would dip into her own reservoir of ideas about effective teaching and offer a suggestion, just to prime the pump a bit.

As the list grew, the flow of ideas began to dry up—the brainstorming process slowed. When it did, she asked another question: What specific behaviors could teachers engage in that would help them be effective—what could they do to maximize the chances of making instruction work? The list grew until everyone agreed that it captured most of what really is important. The entire process didn't take more than ten minutes.

Time for Reflection

Think about your experience as a student and/or teacher. What other keys to effective teaching can you think of?

Step 2: Condensing. Next, she told them that they needed to be able to take advantage of all of these excellent suggestions to evaluate her class and her effectiveness. However, given the immense list they had just brainstormed, they just wouldn't have time to evaluate on the basis of all those criteria. They would have to boil them down to the truly critical factors. She asked how they might do that.

Some students thought they should review the list and pick out the most critical entries, to concentrate on those first. Others suggested that they try to find a smaller number of major categories within which to group elements on the long list. To reach these goals, the professor asked two questions: Which of the things listed here on the board are most crucial? Or, What supercategories might we place the individual entries in, to get a shorter list?

At this point in the development process, it became important to keep the list of supercategories as short as possible. She asked the class if they could narrow it down to four or five—again capturing the essence of the category with the briefest possible label. (These supercategory headings need to represent truly important aspects of sound performance, because they form the basis for the performance criteria, as you will see.)

Here are the five supercategories the students came up with after about five minutes of reflection and discussion:

Content

Organization

Delivery

Personal characteristics

Classroom environment

Time for Reflection

Based on the list presented above, supplemented with your additions, what other supercategories would you suggest?

Remember, the goal throughout this entire activity is to build a vocabulary both students and teacher can use to converse with each other about performance. This is why it is important to engage students in the process of devising criteria, even if you know going in what criteria you want used. *When you share the stage with your students, they get to play a role in defining success and in choosing a language to describe it that they understand, thus connecting them to their target.* (Please reread that sentence. It is one of the most important in the entire book. It argues for empowering students, the central theme of this work.)

Step 3: Defining.   Next, class members collaborated in generating definitions of each of the five chosen supercategories, or major dimensions of effective teaching. The professor assigned responsibility for writing a concise definition of key dimensions to groups of students, one dimension per group. She advised them to consider the elements in the original brainstormed list by reviewing it and finding those smaller elements subsumed within each supercategory. This would help them find the critical words they needed to describe their dimension. When each group completed its draft, a spokesperson read their definition to the class and all were invied to offer suggestions for revising them as needed.

Here are some of the definitions they composed:

Content: appropriateness of presentation of research, theory, and practical applications related to the topic of assessment; appropriateness of course objectives

Organization: appropriateness of the order in which material is presented in terms of aiding learning

Delivery: deals with the presentation and interaction patterns in terms of conveying material and helping students learn it

Personal characteristics: appropriateness of the personal manner of the instructor in relating to the material, the students, and the interaction between the two

Class environment: addresses all physical aspects of the learning atmosphere and setting that are supportive of both students and teacher

The group work, sharing, and revision took about twenty minutes.

Step 4: Contrasting.   With labels and definitions for key performance dimensions in hand, they turned to the next challenge: finding words and examples to describe the range of possible performance within each dimension. They had to find ways to communicate with each other about what teaching looks like when it is very ineffective and how that changes as it moves toward outstanding performance. By establishing a sense of the underlying continuum of performance for each dimension of effective teaching (that is, to share a common meaning of proficiency ranging from a complete lack of it to totally proficient), they can observe any teaching and communicate about where that particular example should be rated on each key dimension.

In preparation for this activity, the professor dug up brief, ten-minute videos of two teachers in action, one faltering badly and the other hitting on all cylinders. She showed these videos to her students and asked the question, What makes one class work well while the other fails? What do you see that makes them different in terms of the five key dimensions defined earlier? They rewound and reviewed the examples several times while defining those differences for each dimension. This activity always helps participants zero in on how to describe performance, good and bad, in clear, understandable language. (Regardless of the performance for which criteria are being developed, my personal experience has been that the most effective method of articulating the meaning of sound and unsound performance is that of very carefully studying vastly contrasting cases. These developers used this method to great advantage to define the basis for their performance criteria.)

Step 5: Describing Success.   As the students began to become clear on the language and examples needed to describe performance, they searched for ways to capture and quantify their judgments, such as by mapping their continuum descriptions onto rating scales or checklists. (We'll learn more about this in the section below on scoring and recording.) The class decided to develop three-point rating scales to reflect their thinking. Figure 8–4 presents some of these scales. This phase of the work took about an hour.

Time for Reflection

See if you can devise a three-point rating scale for one or two of the other criteria defined above.

Step 6: Revising and Refining.   The professor was careful to point out that, when they arrived at a definition of academic success—whether as a set of performance criteria, rating scales, or whatever form it happened to take—the work was not yet done. They needed to practice applying their new standards to some teaching samples to see if they really fit—to see if they might need to more precisely define key aspects of performance. We can learn a general lesson from this: performance criteria should never be regarded as "finished." Rather, with time and experience in applying our standards to actual samples of student work, our vision of the meaning of success will grow and change. We will sharpen our focus. As this happens, we are obliged to adjust our performance expectations to reflect our most current sense of the keys to academic success.

Note the Benefits.   I hope you realized that the entire performance criteria development sequence we just reviewed represents far more than just a preparation to assess dependably. This sequence almost always involves participants in serious, highly motivated questioning, probing, and clarifying. In fact, assessment and instruction are indistinguishable when teachers involve their students in the process of identifying performance criteria.

Another Useful and Important Application.   However, for various reasons, you may not wish to involve your students. Perhaps the students are too young to comprehend the criteria or the process. Or perhaps the target requires the development and application of highly technical or complex criteria that would be out of reach of the students. I have seen student involvement work productively as early as the third grade for some simple targets. But it may not always be appropriate.

Content	3	outcomes clearly articulated challenging and provocative content highly relevant content on assessment for teachers
	2	some stated outcomes content somewhat interesting and engaging of some relevance to the classroom
	1	intended outcomes not stated content boring irrelevant to teachers and the classroom
Delivery	3	flow and pace moves well humor used checks for clarity regularly feedback used to adjust extensive interaction with students
	2	pacing acceptable some of the time material and/or delivery somewhat disjointed some checking for clarity some student participation
	1	pacing too slow or too fast delivery disconnected much dead time no interaction—one-person show no checking for clarity

Figure 8-4
Sample Score Scales for Effective Teaching

When this happens, at least consider another option for carrying out this same set of activities: Rather than engaging your students as your partners, devise criteria with a group of colleagues. If you do, you may argue about what is really important in performance. You might disagree about the proper language to use to describe performance. And you may fight with each other about key differences between sound and unsound performance. But I promise you these will be some of the most engaging and productive faculty meetings of your life. And out of that process might come long-term partners in the performance assessment process.

Even if everyone doesn't agree in the end, each of you will have reflected deeply on, and be able to defend, the meaning of student success in your classroom. We all need that kind of reflection regularly.

Summary of the Six Steps.   However, if it comes down to you devising your own performance criteria, you can rely on variations of these steps, listed again in Figure 8–5. And remember, when students are partners in carrying out these six steps, you and your students join together in a learning community.

These activities can provide clear windows into the meaning of academic success—they can give us the words and examples we need to communicate about that meaning. I urge you to share those words with all who have a vested interest in

---

Step 1. Begin by reflecting on the meaning of excellence in the performance arena that is of interest to you. Be sure to tap your own professional literature, texts, and curriculum materials for insights, too. And don't overlook the wisdom of your colleagues and associates as a resource. Talk with them! Include students as partners in this step too. Brainstorm your own list of key elements. You don't have to list them all in one sitting. Take some time to let the list grow.

Step 2. Categorize the many elements so that they reflect your highest priorities. Keep the list as short as possible while still capturing the essence of performance.

Step 3. Define each key dimension in clear, simple language.

Step 4. Find some actual performance to watch or examples of products to study. If this step can include the thoughtful analysis of a number of contrasting cases—an outstanding term paper and a very weak one, a flowing and accurate jumpshot in basketball and a poor one, a student who functions effectively in a group and one who is repeatedly rejected, and so on—so much the better.

Step 5. Use your clearest language and your very best examples to spell out in words and pictures each point along the various continuums of performance you use to define the important dimensions of the achievement to be assessed.

Step 6. Try your performance criteria to see if they really do capture the essence of performance. Fine tune them to state as precisely as possible what it means to succeed. Let this fine tuning go on as needed for as long as you teach.

Figure 8-5
Steps in Devising Performance Criteria

student success, most notably, with your students themselves. This, then, is the *art* of developing performance criteria.

Attributes of Sound Criteria.   Quellmalz (1991), writing in a secial issue of a professional journal devoted to performance assessment, provides us with a simple list of standards against which to compare our performance criteria in order to judge their quality. She points out that effective performance criteria do the following:

1. Reflect all of the important components of performance—the milestones in target attainment.

2. Apply appropriately in contexts and under conditions in which performance naturally occurs.

3. Represent dimensions of performance that trained evaluators can apply consistently to a set of similar tasks (i.e., not be exercise specific).

4. Are developmentally appropriate for the examinee population.

5. Are understandable and usable by all participants in the performance assessment process, including teachers, students, parents, and the community.

6. Link assessment results directly into the instructional decision making process.

7. Provide a clear and understandable means of documenting and communicating about student growth over time.

I would expand this list to include one additional standard: The development of performance criteria should be seen as an opportunity to teach. Students should play a role in the development of performance criteria whenever possible.

Figure 8–6 details rating scales that depict two key dimensions of good writing, organization and voice. Note the simple, yet clear and specific nature of the communication about important dimensions of good writing. With these kinds of criteria in hand, we definitely can help students become better performers.

Phase 2: Designing Performance Exercises

Performance assessment exercises, like selected response test items and essay exercises, frame the challenge for the respondent and set the conditions within which that challenge is to be met. Thus, they are a clear and explicit reflection of the desired outcomes. Like essay exercises, sound performance assessment exercises outline a complete problem for the respondent: achievement to be demonstrated, conditions of the demonstration, and standards of quality to be applied.

As specified earlier in this chapter, we face three basic design considerations when dealing with exercises in the context of performance assessment. We must determine the following:

1. the nature of the exercise(s), whether structured exercises or naturally occurring events

Organization

5   *The organization enhances and showcases the central idea or theme. The order, structure, or presentation is compelling and moves the reader through the text.*

- Details seem to fit where they're placed; sequencing is logical and effective.
- An inviting introduction draws the reader in and a satisfying conclusion leaves the reader with a sense of resolution.
- Pacing is very well controlled; the writer delivers needed information at just the right moment, then moves on.
- Transitions are smooth and weave the separate threads of meaning into one cohesive whole.
- Organization flows so smoothly the reader hardly thinks about it.

3   *The organizational structure is strong enough to move the reader from point to point without undue confusion.*

- The paper has a recognizable introduction and conclusion. The introduction may not create a strong sense of anticipation; the conclusion may not leave the reader with a satisfying sense of resolution.
- Sequencing is usually logical. It may sometimes be too obvious, or otherwise ineffective.
- Pacing is fairly well controlled, though the writer sometimes spurts ahead too quickly or spends too much time on the obvious.
- Transitions often work well; at times though, connections between ideas are fuzzy or call for inferences.
- Despite a few problems, the organization does not seriously get in the way of the main point or storyline.

1   *The writing lacks a clear sense of direction. Ideas, details or events seem strung together in a random, haphazard fashion—or else there is no identifiable internal structure at all. More than one of the following problems is likely to be evident:*

- The writer has not yet drafted a real lead or conclusion.
- Transitions are not yet clearly defined; connections between ideas seem confusing or incomplete.
- Sequencing, if it exists, needs work.
- Pacing feels awkward, with lots of time spent on minor details or big, hard-to-follow leaps from point to point.
- Lack of organization makes it hard for the reader to get a grip on the main point or storyline.

Figure 8-6
Sample Rating Scales for Writing (Reprinted from "Linking Writing Assessment and Instruction" in *Creating Writers* (104–106) by V. Spandel and R. J. Stiggins, 1990, White Plains, NY: Longman. Copyright 1990 by Longman. Reprinted by permission of Longman.)

2. the specific content of structured exercises, defining the tasks to be carried out by performers
3. the number of exercises needed to provide a sufficient sample of performance

We will now delve into each in some detail.

Voice

5   *The writer speaks directly to the reader in a way that is individualistic, expressive, and engaging. Clearly, the writer is involved in the text and is writing to be read.*

- The paper is honest and written from the heart. It has the ring of conviction.
- The language is natural yet provocative; it brings the topic to life.
- The reader feels a strong sense of interaction with the writer and senses the person behind the words.
- The projected tone and voice give flavor to the writer's message and seem very appropriate for the purpose and audience.

3   *The writer seems sincere, but not genuinely engaged, committed, or involved. The result is pleasant and sometimes even personable, but short of compelling.*

- The writing communicates in an earnest, pleasing manner. Moments here and there amuse, surprise, delight, or move the reader.
- Voice may emerge strongly on occasion, then retreat behind general, vague, tentative, or abstract language.
- The writing hides as much of the writer as it reveals.
- The writer seems aware of an audience, but often weighs words carefully, stands at a distance, and avoids risk.

1   *The writer seems indifferent, uninvolved, or distanced from the topic and/or the audience. As a result, the writing is flat, lifeless, or mechanical; depending on the topic, it may be overly technical or jargonistic. More than one of the following problems is likely to be evident.*

- The reader has a hard time sensing the writer behind the words. The writer does not seem to reach out to an audience, or make use of voice to connect with that audience.
- The writer speaks in a kind of monotone that tends to flatten all potential highs and lows of the message.
- The writing communicates on a functional level, with no apparent attempt to move or involve the reader.
- The writer is not yet sufficiently engaged or at home with the topic to take risks or share him/herself.

Figure 8-6, (*Continued*)
Sample Rating Scales for Writing

Nature of Exercises.   The decision about whether to rely on structured exercises, naturally occurring events, or some combination of the two should be influenced by several factors related to the outcome(s) to be assessed and the environment within which the assessment is to be conducted.

Focus of Assessment.   Structured exercises and naturally occurring events can help us get at slightly different targets. When a pending performance assessment is announced in advance and students are given instructions as to how to prepare, we intend to maximize their motivation to perform well. In fact, we often try to encourage best possible performance by attaching a grade or telling students that observers from outside the classroom (often parents) will watch them perform. When we take these steps and build the assessment around structured exercises, we set our conditions up to assess students' best possible performance, under conditions of maximum motivation to do well—a very important outcome.

However, sometimes our objective is not to see the student's "best possible" performance. Rather, what we wish is "typical" performance, performance under conditions of the students' regular, everyday motivation. For example, we want students to adhere to safety rules in the woodworking shop or the science lab all the time (under conditions of typical motivation), not just when they think we are evaluating them (maximum motivation to perform well). Observation during naturally occurring classroom events can allow us to get at the latter.

From an assessment quality control point of view, we still must be clear about our purpose. And, explicit performance criteria are every bit as important here. But our assessment goal is to be watching closely as students behave spontaneously in the performance setting.

Time for Reflection

Identify a few achievement targets you think might be most effectively assessed through the unobtrusive observation of naturally occurring events. In your experience as a teacher or student, have you ever been assessed in this way? When?

Time Available to Assess.   In addition to motivational factors, there also are practical considerations to bear in mind in deciding whether to use structured or naturally occurring events. One is time. If normal events of the classroom afford you opportunities to gather sound evidence of proficiency without setting aside special time for the presentation of structured exercises and associated observations, then take advantage of the naturally occurring instructional event. The dividend will be time saved from having to devise exercises and present and explain them.

Natural Availability of Evidence.   Another practical matter to consider in your choice is the fact that classrooms are places just packed full of evidence of student proficiency. Think about it—teachers and students spend more time together than do the typical parent and child or husband and wife! Students and teachers live in a world of constant interaction in which *both* are watching, doing, talking, and learning. A teacher's greatest assessment tool is the time spent with students.

This permits the accumulation of bits of evidence—for example, corroboration of past inferences about student proficiency and/or evidence of slow, gradual growth—over extended periods of time, and makes for big samples. It offers opportunities to detect patterns, to double check, and to verify.

Spontaneous Assessment.   Everything I have said about performance assessment up to this point has depicted it as rational, structured, and preplanned. But teachers know that assessment is sometimes spontaneous. The unexpected classroom event or the briefest of unanticipated student responses can provide the ready observer with a new glimpse into student competence. Effective teachers see things. They file those things away. They accumulate evidence of proficiency. They know their students. No other assessor of student achievement has the opportunity to see students like this over time.

But beware! These kinds of spontaneous performance assessments based on on-the-spot, sometimes unobtrusive observations of naturally occurring events are fraught with as many dangers of misassessment as any other kind of performance assessment. Even in these cases, we are never absolved from adhering to the basic principles of sound assessment: clear target, clear purpose, proper method, sound sample, and controlled interference.

You must constantly ask yourself: What did I really see? Am I drawing the right conclusion based on what I saw? How can I capture the results of this spontaneous assessment for later use (if necessary or desirable)? Anecdotal notes alone may suffice. The threats to sound assessment never leave us. So by all means, take advantage of the insights provided by classroom time spent together with your students. But as a practical classroom assessment matter, do so cautiously. Create a written record of your assessment whenever possible.

Time for Reflection

Can you think of creative, realistic ways to establish dependable records of the results of spontaneous performance assessments that happen during an instructional day?

Exercise Content.   Like well-developed essay exercises, sound structured performance assessment exercises explain the challenge to the respondent and set them up to succeed if they can, by doing the following:

- identifying the specific kind(s) of performance to be demonstrated
- detailing the context and conditions within which proficiency is to be demonstrated
- pointing the respondent in the direction of a good response by identifying the standards to be applied in evaluating performance

Here is a simple example:

Achievement: You are to apply your knowledge of energy converted to motion and simple principles of mechanics by building a mousetrap car.

Conditions: Using materials provided in class and within the time limits of four class periods, please design and diagram your plan, construct the car itself, and prepare to explain why you included the design features you chose.

Standards: Your performance will be evaluated in terms of the specific standards we set in class, including the clarity of your diagrammed plan, the performance and quality of your car, and your presentation explaining its design features. If you have questions about these instructions or the standards of quality, let me know.

In this way, sound exercises frame clear and specific problems to solve.

In a comprehensive discussion of the active ingredients of sound performance assessment exercises, Baron (1991) offers us clear and thought-provoking guidance. I quote and paraphrase below at length from her work because of the richness of her advice. Baron urges that we ask important questions about the nature of the assessment:

- "If a group of curriculum experts in my field and a group of educated citizens in my community were to use my assessment tasks as an indicator of my educational values, would I be pleased with their conclusions? And would they?" (p. 307)
- "When students prepare for my assessment tasks and I structure my curriculum and pedagogy to enable them to be successful on these tasks, do I feel assured that they will be making progress toward becoming genuine or authentic readers, mathematicians, writers, historians, problem solvers, etc.?" (p. 308)
- "Do my tasks clearly communicate my standards and expectations to my students?" (p. 308)
- Is performance assessment the best method to use given what I want my students to know and be able to do?
- "Are some of my tasks rich and integrative, requiring students to make connections and forge relationships among various aspects of the curriculum?" (p. 310)
- "Are my tasks structured to encourage students to access their prior knowledge and skills when solving problems?" (p. 310)
- "Do some tasks require students to work together in small groups to solve complex problems?" (p. 311)
- Do some of my tasks require that my students sustain their efforts over a period of time (perhaps even an entire term!) to succeed?
- Do some tasks offer students a degree of freedom to choose the course of action—to design and carry out the investigations—they will take to solve the problem?
- "Do my tasks require self-assessment and reflection on the part of students?" (p. 312)
- "Are my tasks likely to have personal meaning and value to my students?" (p. 313)
- "Are they sufficiently challenging for the students?" (p. 313)
- "Do some of my tasks provide problems that are situated in real-world contexts and are they appropriate for the age group solving them?" (p. 314)

These guidelines define the art of developing sound performance exercises.

Time for Reflection

What might a performance assessment exercise look like that could test your skill in developing a high-quality performance assessment? What specific ingredients would you include in the exercise?

The Number of Exercises—Sampling Considerations. How do we know how many exercises are needed within an assessment to give us confidence that we are drawing dependable conclusions about student proficiency? This is a particularly troubling issue in the context of performance assessment, because the amount of time required to administer, observe, and score any single exercise can be so long. Sometimes, we feel it is impossible to employ a number of exercises because of time and workload constraints.

However, this view can lead to problems. Consider writing assessment, for example. Because writing takes so many forms and takes place in so many contexts, defining proficiency is very complex. As a result, proficiency in one writing context may not predict proficiency in another. We understand that a proper sample of writing proficiency, one that allows generalizations to the entire performance domain, must include exercises calling for various kinds of writing, such as narrative, expository, and persuasive. Still, however, we find large-scale writing assessments labeling students as writers or nonwriters on the basis of a single twenty- to sixty-minute writing sample (Bond & Roeber, 1993). Why? Because that's all the assessment resources will permit!

Sampling always involves tradeoffs between quality of resulting information and the cost of collecting it. Few have the resources needed to gather the perfect sample of student performance. We all compromise. The good news for you as a teacher is that you must compromise less than the large-scale assessor primarily because you have more time with your students. This is precisely why I feel that the great strength and future of performance assessment lies in the classroom, not in large-scale standardized testing.

In the classroom, it is often helpful to define *sampling* as the purposeful collection of a number of bits of information about student achievement gathered over time. When gathered and summarized carefully, these bits of insight can form a representative sample of performance that can lead to confident conclusions about student achievement.

Unfortunately, there are no hard and fast rules to follow in determining how many exercises are needed to yield dependable conclusions. That means we must once again speak of the *art* of classroom assessment. I will share a sample decision rule with you now that depicts the artistic judgment in this case, and then I will review specific factors you can consider when exercising your judgment.

The sampling decision rule is this: You know you have presented enough exercises and gathered enough instances of student performance when you can predict with a high degree of confidence how well the student would do on the next one. Part of performance assessment sampling is science and part of it is art. Dealing first with the science, the more systematic part, one challenge is to gather samples of student performance under all or most of the circumstances in which they will be expected to perform over the long haul. Let me illustrate from life.

Let's say we want to assess for the purpose of certifying the competence of commercial airline pilots. One specific skill we want them to demonstrate, among others, is the ability to land the plane safely. So we take candidates up on a bright, sunny, calm day and ask them to land the plane—clearly an authentic performance assessment. Let's say all pilots do an excellent job of landing. Are you ready to certify them?

If your answer is yes, I don't want you screening the pilots hired by the airlines on which I fly. Our assessment only reflected one narrow set of circumstances within which we expect our pilots to be competent. What if it's night, not bright, clear daylight? A strange airport? Windy? Raining? An emergency? These represent realities within which pilots must operate routinely. So the proper course of action in sampling performance for certification purposes is to analyze relevant variables and put them together in various combinations to see how each candidate performs. At some point, the array of samples of landing proficiency (gathered under various conditions) combine to lead us to a conclusion that the skill of landing safely has or has not been mastered.

This example frames your performance assessment sampling challenge, too. How many "landings" must you see under what kinds of conditions to feel confident your students can perform according to your standards? The science of such sampling is to have thought through the important conditions within which performance is to be sampled. The art is to use your resources creatively to gather enough different instances under varying conditions to bring you and the student to a confident conclusion about proficiency.

In this context, I'm sure you can understand why you must consider the seriousness of the decision to be made in planning your sample. Some decisions bear greater weight than others. These demand assessments that sample both more deeply and more broadly to give you confidence in the decision that results—such as certifying a student as competent for purposes of high school graduation, for example. On the other hand, some decisions leave more room to err. They allow you to reconsider the decision later, if necessary, at no cost to the student—for example, assessing a student's ability to craft a complete sentence during a unit of instruction on sentence construction. When the target is narrow and the time frame brief, we need sample fewer instances of performance.

Figure 8–7 identifies four factors to take into account in making sampling decisions in any particular performance assessment context. Even within the guidelines these provide, however, the artistic sampling decision rule is this: You know how confident you are. If you are quite certain you have enough evidence, draw your conclusion and act upon it.

But your professional challenge is to follow the rules of sound assessment and gather enough information to minimize the chance that you are wrong. The conservative position to take in this case is to err in the direction of oversampling to raise your level of confidence.

If you feel uncertain about the conclusion you might draw regarding the achieve-

- *The reason(s) for the assessment.* The more critical the decision, the more sure you must be and the more information you should gather; a simple daily instructional decision that can be reversed tomorrow if necessary requires less confidence and therefore a smaller sample of performance than a high school graduation decision.
- *The scope of the target.* The broader the scope the more different instances of performance we must sample.
- *The amount of information provided by the response to one exercise.* Exercises can be written to produce very large samples of work, providing a great deal of information about proficiency; when we use these, we may need to use fewer exercises.
- *The resources available for observing and evaluating.* Put simply, the bigger your labor force, the more assessment you can conduct per unit of time. This may be something you can really take advantage of. Always remain aware of all the shoulders over which you can spread the performance assessment workload: the principal, teacher aides, colleagues, parents, outside experts, *students . . .*

Figure 8-7
Considerations in Performance Assessment Sampling

ment of a particular student, you have no choice but to gather more information. To do otherwise is to place the well-being of that student in jeopardy.

Time for Reflection

Based on your experience as a student, can you identify a skill achievement target that you think would take several exercises to sample appropriately, and another that you think could be sampled with only one, or very few, exercises? What are the most obvious differences between these two targets?

Phase 3: Scoring and Recording Results

Three design issues demand our attention at this stage of performance assessment development, if we are to make the entire plan come together:

1. the level of detail we need in assessment results
2. the manner in which results will be recorded
3. who will do the observing and evaluating

These are straightforward decisions, if we approach them with a clear target and a clear sense of how the assessment results are to be used.

Level of Detail of Results.   We have two choices in the kinds of scores or results we derive from our observations and judgments: holistic and analytical. Both require explicit performance criteria. That is, we are never absolved from responsibility for having articulated the meaning of academic performance in clear and appropriate terms.

However, the two kinds of scoring procedures use the criteria in different ways. We can either (a) score *analytically* and make our judgments by considering each key dimension of performance or criterion separately, thus analyzing performance in terms of each of its elements, or (b) make our judgments *holistically* by considering all of the criteria simultaneously, making one overall evaluation of performance. The former provides a high-resolution picture of performance but takes more time and effort to accomplish. The latter provides a more general sense of performance but is much quicker.

Your choice of score type will turn on how you plan to use the results (whether you need precise detail or a general picture) and the resources you have available to conduct the assessment (whether you have time to evaluate analytically).

Some assessment contexts demand analytical evaluation of student performance. No matter how hard you try, you will not be able to diagnose student needs based on holistic performance information. You will never be able to help students understand and learn to replicate the fine details of sound performance by teaching them to score holistically.

But on the other hand, it is conceivable that you may find yourself involved in an assessment where you must evaluate the performance of hundreds of students with few resources on hand, too few resources to score analytically. Holistic may be your only option.

(As a personal aside, I must say that I am minimizing my own use of holistic scoring as a single, stand-alone judgment of overall performance. I see few applications for such a score in the classroom. Besides, I have begun to question the meaning of such scores. I have participated in some writing assessments in which students whose analytical profiles of performance [including six different rating scales] were remarkably different ended up with the same holistic score. That gives me pause to wonder about the real meaning and interpretability of holistic scores. I have begun to think holistic scores mask the kind of more detailed information needed to promote classroom-level student growth. It may be that, in the classroom, the benefits of quick scoring are not worth the costs of sacrificing such valuable assessment information.)

When a holistic score is needed, it is best obtained by summing analytical scores, simply adding them together. Or, if your vision of the meaning of academic success suggests that some analytical scales are more important than others, they can be assigned a higher weight (by multiplying by a weighting factor) before summing. However, a rational basis for determining the weights must be spelled out in advance.

It may also be acceptable to add a rating scale that reflects "overall impression" to a set of analytical score scales, if the user can define how the whole is equal to more than the sum of the individual parts of performance.

Recording Results.   Performance assessors have the freedom to choose from among a wonderful array of ways to record results for later communication. These include checklists, rating scales, anecdotal records, and mental record keeping. Each of these is described in Table 8–1 in terms of definition, principal strength, and chief limitation.

Table 8-1

Options for Recording Performance Judgments

	Definition	**Strength**	**Limitation**
Checklists	List of key attributes of good performance checked present or absent	Quick; useful with large number of criteria	Results can lack depth
Rating scales	Performance continuum mapped on several-point numerical scale ranging from low to high	Can record judgment and rationale with one rating	Can demand extensive, expensive development and training for raters
Anecdotal records	Student performance is described in detail in writing	Can provide rich portraits of achievement	Time consuming to read, write, and interpret
Mental records	Assessor stores judgments and/or descriptions of performance in memory	Quick and easy way to record	Difficult to retain accurate recollections, especially as time passes

Note that checklists, rating scales, and anecdotal records all store information that is descriptive in terms of the performance criteria. That is, each element of performance checked, rated, or written about must relate to our judgments about student performance on established key dimensions.

In using mental record keeping, we can store either ratings or images of actual performance. I included it in this list to provide an opportunity to urge caution when using this notoriously undependable storage system! Most often, it is not a good idea to rely on our mental records of student achievement. When we try to remember such things, there are five things that can happen and four of them are bad. The one good possibility is that we *might* retain an accurate recollection of performance. The bad things are that we could do any or all of the following:

- forget, losing that recollection forever
- remember the performance but ascribe it to the wrong student
- unconsciously allow the memory to change over time due to our observations of more recent performance
- retain a memory of performance that serves as a filter through which we see and interpret all subsequent performance, thus biasing our judgments inappropriately

The chances of these problems occurring increase the longer we try to maintain accurate mental records and the more complex these records are.

For the reasons listed above, I urge you to limit your use of this filing system to no more than a day or two at most and to very limited targets. If you must retain the record of performance longer than that, write it down—as a checklist, a set of rating scales, or an anecdotal record!

Checking for Errors in Judgment.   Subjective scoring—a prospect that raises the anxiety of any assessment specialist—is the hallmark of performance assessment. I hope by now you see why it is that we in the assessment community urge caution as the education community moves boldly to embrace this option. It is fraught with potential danger and must be treated with great care.

We already have discussed many ways to assure that our subjective assessment process is as objective as it can be:

- be mindful of the purpose for assessing
- be crystal clear about the target
- articulate the key elements of good performance in explicit performance criteria
- share those criteria with students in terms they understand
- learn to apply those criteria in a consistent manner
- double check to be sure bias does not creep into the assessment process.

Testing for Bias.   There is a simple way to check for bias in your performance evaluations. Remember, bias occurs when factors other than the kind of achievement being assessed begin to influence our judgments, such as the gender, age, ethnic heritage, appearance, or prior academic record of the examinee. You can determine the degree of objectivity of your ratings by comparing them with the judgments of another trained and qualified evaluator who independently observes and evaluates the same student performance with the intent of applying the same criteria. If, after observing and evaluating performance, two independent judges generally agree on the level of proficiency demonstrated, then we have evidence that the results reflect student proficiency. But if the judges come to significantly different conclusions, they obviously have applied different standards. We have no way of knowing which is the most accurate estimate of true student achievement. Under these circumstances the accuracy of the assessment must be called into question and the results set aside until the reasons for those differences have been thoroughly explained.

Time for Reflection

It's tempting to conclude that it is unrealistic to gather corroborating judgments in the classroom—to double check ratings. But can you think of any helpers who might assist you in your classroom by playing the role of second rater of a performance assessment? For each, what would it take to involve them productively? What benefits might arise from their involvement?

Practical Ways to Find Help.   While this test of objectivity, or of evaluator agreement, promises to help us check an important aspect of performance assessment quality, it seems impractical for classroom use for two reasons: it's often difficult to come up with a qualified second rater, or we lack the time and expertise required to compare evaluations.

In fact, however, this process need not take so much time. You need not check all of your judgments for objectivity. Perhaps a qualified colleague could double check just a few—just to see if your ratings are on target.

Further, it doesn't take a high degree of technical skill to do this. Have someone who is qualified rate some student performance you already have rated, and then sit down for a few minutes and talk about any differences. If the performance to be evaluated is a product students created, have your colleague evaluate a few. If it's a skill, videotape a few. Apply your criteria to one and check for agreement. Do you both see it about the same way? If so, go on to the next one. If not, try to resolve differences, adjusting your performance criteria as needed.

Please understand that my goal here is not to have you carry out this test of objectivity every time you conduct a performance assessment. Rather, I want you to understand the spirit of this test of your objectivity. An important part of the art of classroom performance assessment is the ability to sense when your performance criteria are sufficiently explicit that another judge would be able to use them effectively, if called upon to do so. Further, from time to time it is a good idea to actually check whether you and another rater really do agree in applying your criteria.

On those occasions, however, when you are conducting very important performance assessments that have significant impact on students (i.e., for promotion decisions, graduation decisions, and the like), you absolutely must at least have a sample of your ratings double checked by an independent rater. In these instances, remember you do have access to other available evaluators: colleagues in your school or district, your building administrative staff, support teachers, curriculum personnel, experts from outside the field of education (when appropriate), retired teachers in your community, qualified parents, and others.

In addition, sharing your criteria with your students and teaching them to apply those standards consistently can provide you with useful insights. You can be assured that they will tell you which criteria they don't understand.

Just remember, all raters must be trained to understand and apply your standards. Never assume that they are qualified to evaluate performance on the basis of prior experience if that experience does not include training in using the criteria you employ in your classroom. Have them evaluate some samples to show you they can do it. If training is needed, it very often does not take long. Figure 8–8 presents steps to follow when training raters. Remember, once they're trained, your support raters are allies forever. Just think of the benefits to you if you have a pool of trained evaluators ready to share the workload!

More about Students as Partners

Imagine what it would mean if your helpers—your trained and qualified evaluators of process and/or product—were your students. Not only could they be participants in the kind of rater training spelled out in Figure 8–8, but they might even be partners in the process of devising the performance criteria themselves. And, once trained, what if they took charge of training some additional students, or perhaps trained their parents to be qualified raters, too? The pool of available helpers begins

- Have trainees review and discuss the performance criteria. Provide clarification as needed.
- Give them a sample of work to evaluate that is of known quality to you (i.e., which you already have rated), but not to your trainees.
- Check their judgments against yours, reviewing and discussing any differences in terms of the specifics of the performance criteria.
- Give them another sample of work of known quality to evaluate.
- Compare their judgments to yours again, noting and discussing differences.
- Repeat this process until your trainee converges on your standards, as evidenced by a high degree of agreement with your judgments.
- You and the trainees evaluate a sample of work of unknown quality. Discuss any differences.
- Repeat this process until you have confidence in your new partner(s) in the evaluation process.

Figure 8-8
Steps in Training Raters of Student Performance

to grow as more participants begin to internalize the meaning of success in your classroom.

Without question, the best and most appropriate way to integrate performance assessment and instruction is to be absolutely certain that the important performance criteria serve as the goals and objectives of the instruction. As we teach students to understand and demonstrate key dimensions of performance, we prepare them to achieve the targets we value. We prepare in sound and appropriate ways to be held accountable for student learning when we are clear and public about our performance criteria, and when we do all in our power to be sure students have the opportunity to learn to hit the target.

In addition, we can make performance assessment an integral part of the teaching and learning process by involving students in assessment development and use:

- Share the performance criteria with students at the beginning of the unit of instruction.
- Collaborate with students in keeping track of which criteria have been covered and which are yet to come.
- Involve students in creating prominent visual displays of important performance criteria for bulletin boards.
- Engage students in the actual development of performance exercises.
- Engage students in comparing contrasting examples of performance, some of which reflect high-quality work and some of which do not (perhaps as part of a process of developing performance criteria).
- Involve students in the process of transforming performance criteria into checklists, rating scales, and other recording methods.
- Have students evaluate their own and each other's performance, one on one and/or in cooperative groups.

- Have students rate performance and then conduct studies of how much agreement (i.e., objectivity) there was among student judges; see if degree of agreement increases as students become more proficient as performers and as judges.

- Have students reflect in writing on their own growth over time with respect to specified criteria.

- Have students set specific achievement goals in terms of specified criteria and then keep track of their own progress.

- Store several samples of each student's performance over time, either as a portfolio or on videotape, if appropriate, and have students compare old performance to new and discuss in terms of specific ratings.

- Have students predict their performance criterion by criterion, and then check actual evaluations to see if their predictions are accurate.

Time for Reflection

Have you ever been involved in any of these ways of assessing your own performance—as a partner with your teacher? If so, what was the experience like for you?

These activities will help increase students' control of their own academic well-being and will remove the mystery that too often surrounds the meaning of success in the classroom.

Barriers to Sound Performance Assessment

There are many things in the design and development of performance assessments that can cause a student's real achievement to be misrepresented. Many of the potential problems and remedies are summarized in Table 8–2.

CHAPTER SUMMARY: THOUGHTFUL DEVELOPMENT YIELDS SOUND ASSESSMENTS

This chapter has been about the great promise of performance assessment. However, the presentation has been tempered with the need to develop and use this option cautiously. Performance assessment, like other methods, brings with it specific rules of evidence. We must all strive to meet those rigorous standards.

We began with an overview of the three steps in developing performance assessments: clarifying performance (dealing with the nature and focus of the achievement to be assessed), developing exercises (dealing with the nature, content, and number of exercises), and scoring (dealing with kinds of scores, recording results, and identifying and training the evaluator). As we covered each step, we discussed how students could become full partners in performance assessment design, development, and use. The result will be better performers.

Table 8-2
Barriers to Sound Performance Assessment

Source of Problems	Remedy
Inadequate vision of the target	Seek training and help needed to clarify the vision. Collaborate with others in this process.
Wrong method for the target	Stick to process and product targets when using performance assessment.
Incorrect performance criteria	Compare contrasting cases to zero in on key differences. Tap into sources of quality criteria devised by others.
Unclear performance criteria	Study samples of performance more carefully. Seek qualified expertise whenever necessary.
Poor-quality exercises	Think about and specify achievement to be demonstrated, conditions, and standards to be applied.
Inadequate sample of exercises	Define the domain to be sampled as precisely as possible. Gather as much evidence as possible. Strive for professional confidence in your conclusions by finding a colleague who can corroborate your judgments.
Too little time to evaluate	Add trained evaluators—they are available!
Untrained evaluators	Use clear criteria and examples of performance as a starting point in training them.
Inappropriate scoring method selected (holistic vs. analytical)	Understand the relationship between holistic and analytical scoring and assessment purpose.
Poor record keeping	Strive for accurate written records of performance judgments. Don't depend on memory.
Keeping the criteria and performance assessment process a mystery to students	Don't!

To assure quality, we discussed the need to understand the role of subjectivity in performance assessment. We also analyzed the match between performance assessment and the five kinds of achievement targets, concluding that strong matches can be developed for mastery of knowledge through reference materials, reasoning, skills, and products. We discussed the key context factors to consider in selecting this methodology for use in the classroom, centering mostly on the importance of having in place the necessary expertise and resources.

We devised six practical steps for formulating sound performance criteria, urging collaboration with students and/or colleagues in the process. We set standards for sound exercises, including the need to identify the achievement to be demonstrated, the conditions of the demonstration, and the standards of quality to be applied. And finally, we spelled out scoring options, suggesting that analytical evaluation of student work is likely to be most productive, especially when students are trained to apply standards of quality to their own and each other's work.

As the decade of the 1990s unfolds, we will come to rely more and more on performance assessment methodology as the basis for our evaluation of student achievement, and as a means of integrating assessment and instruction. Let us strive for the highest quality, most rigorous assessments our resources will allow.

EXERCISES TO ADVANCE YOUR LEARNING

Knowledge Outcomes

1. Memorize the three basic parts and nine design decisions that guide the performance assessment development process.

2. List the aspects of performance assessment design that require professional judgment and the dangers of bias associated with each.

3. Specify the kinds of achievement targets that can be transformed into the performance assessment format and those that cannot.

4. Identify the factors to take into account in considering use of the performance assessment option.

5. Describe the key considerations in devising a sound sample of performance exercise.

6. Memorize the six steps in the design of performance criteria and the basic ingredients of sound exercises.

7. In your own words, list as many ways as you can to bring students into the performance assessment process as partners.

Reasoning Outcomes

1. Find an example of a performance assessment previously developed by you or others and evaluate it. Using the framework provided in this chapter, analyze the underlying structure of the assessment and evaluate each part to see if standards of quality have been met. Write a complete analysis of the assessment, detailing what you would do to improve it, if necessary.

Skill Outcomes

1. Select a unit of instruction from the material you teach, will teach, or have studied as a student, that includes skill or product outcomes. Go through the process of devising a performance assessment for one of those outcomes, including performance criteria, exercises, and a scoring and recording scheme.

Product Outcomes

1. Evaluate the assessment you created in the exercise above in terms of the attributes of sound assessment discussed in this and earlier chapters. How did you do?

Affective Outcomes

1. Some have argued that performance assessments are too fraught with potential bias due to evaluator subjectivity to justify the attention they are receiving these days. Do you agree? Why?

2. Throughout the chapter, I argue that the assessment development procedures outlined here will help teachers who use performance assessments to connect those assessments directly to their instruction. Having completed the chapter, do you agree? Why?

3. I also argue that the assessment development and use procedures suggested herein, while apparently very labor intensive, could save you valuable teaching time in the long run. Do you agree? Why?

Personal Communication: Another Window to Student Achievement

---

Chapter Objectives

As a result of studying the material presented in Chapter 9, reflecting on that material, and completing the learning exercises presented at the end of the chapter, you will:

1. Master content knowledge:
   a. Understand the roles of objectivity and subjectivity in assessments based on personal communication.
   b. State the kinds of achievement targets that can be reflected in personal communication–based assessments.
   c. Know strengths, limitations, and keys to effective use of five formats of personal communication assessment: instructional questions and answers, class discussions, conferences and interviews, oral exams, and conversations with others about students.
   d. Understand key considerations in sampling student performance via personal communication.
   e. List specific ways to engage students in the assessment process using personal communication.

2. Be able to use that knowledge to reason as follows:
   a. Understand when and where to turn to assessment based on personal communication.
   b. Detect potential contributors to mismeasurement when relying on personal communication and know how to control them.
   c. Given a purpose for assessment, an achievement target to be assessed, and a classroom context in which personal communication is to serve as

the assessment method, understand how to sample students and questions appropriately to satisfy information needs.

3. Become proficient at the following skills:
    a. Pose questions and interact with students in ways that permit the collection of quality information about mastery of knowledge and reasoning proficiency.

4. Become proficient in creating the following products:
    a. Record-keeping systems for storing information about student achievement gathered via personal communication.

5. Attain the following affective outcomes:
    a. Regard personal communication with caution, valuing the need to adhere to rigorous standards of quality in development and use.
    b. Value personal communication as an assessment option in the classroom.
    c. See assessment via personal communication as a valuable instructional tool in which students should be and can be full partners.

Teachers gather a great deal of valuable information about student achievement by talking with them. We don't often think of this as assessment, but it is. At different times during the teaching and learning process, we do the following:

- Ask questions during instruction, listen to answers, and evaluate achievement.
- Conduct conferences with students that, in effect, serve as interviews yielding information about achievement.
- Listen carefully for student contributions during class discussions to evaluate student reasoning.
- Conduct oral examinations to assess mastery of required material.
- Converse with others (students, teachers, and parents) to gather information about a student's achievement.

These five kinds of assessment, studied collectively and as individual assessment formats, are the focus of this chapter.

Those who teach understand that, while personal communication is a mode of assessment that virtually never informs the momentous decisions and will never command the attention of our highly visible standardized testing programs, it nevertheless always has been and will be a critical form of classroom assessment.

Time for Reflection

You have studied and reflected upon assessment enough by now to be able to anticipate some of the assessment issues about to be raised in this chapter.

Please take a few moments to list all of the things that you believe can go wrong with personal communication as assessment. What may render our conclusions about student achievement incorrect? What must we guard against to assure quality? Keep your list handy as you read on.

CHAPTER ROADMAP

To assist you in finding and avoiding the pitfalls to sound personal communication–based assessment, we will explore the practical meaning of quality classroom assessment in the context of personal communication.

- We begin with an illustrative application of personal communication in use in the classroom—relying on yet another strategy that brings students inside the assessment process in order to advance achievement.

- We then use that platform to conduct a careful analysis of issues of objectivity and dangers of bias with this mode of assessment.

- We next address issues related to the match of personal communication to the five kinds of achievement targets we have been discussing throughout this text.

- We then turn to a detailed analysis of each of the five formats of personal communications listed above: questioning, interviews, discussion, oral exams, and conversation with others.

- And finally, after reviewing some basic strategies for sampling student achievement through personal communication, we conclude with a summary of specific suggestions for integrating assessment into the teaching and learning process.

You will find that the tenor of this chapter is somewhat different from those of the three previous methodology chapters. My intent is not so much to provide extensive detail on concrete procedures as it is to inform you of factors to be aware of as you interact with students and draw inferences about their achievement based on what you hear from them. Interact with students in a focused manner, listen attentively, and be cautious in the conclusions you draw, and your interactions can provide a clear window into student learning.

In terms of our big picture, the shaded cells in Figure 9–1 indicate the material covered in this chapter.

	SELECTED RESPONSE	ESSAY	PERFORMANCE ASSESSMENT	PERSONAL COMMUNICATION
Know				
Reason				
Skill				
Product				
Affect				

Figure 9-1
Aligning Achievement Targets and Assessment Methods

PERSONAL COMMUNICATION AT WORK AS ASSESSMENT IN A COMMUNITY OF LEARNERS

The Potential Value

Our personal exchanges with students can be packed with useful information and thus can serve a variety of important and often interwoven purposes in the classroom. For example, sometimes our interactions with students simply provide information that corroborates or calls into question assessment results secured through other, more structured means. That is, some teachers use this form of assessment as a double check for another assessment. Sometimes, teachers use insights derived from questions and answers during instruction to find out if the class as a whole or individual students are on track or tuned in—to monitor and adjust, if you will. In addition, we often use various forms of personal communication to encourage and evaluate student reasoning and problem solving. Many teachers reflect on student achievement demonstrated through participation in classroom discussion at report card grading time. Clearly these represent uses of the personal communication assessment process that are very important to student well-being in the classroom.

When we use this form of assessment with care, we can tap dimensions of achievement not easily accessed through any means. For instance, an effective questioner can use properly sequenced questions to probe deeply into student reasoning *and* put students in close touch with their own problem solving proficiency at the same time.

Further, thoughtful questioners can link assessment to instruction with great efficiency and effectiveness. For example, we can uncover students' misconceptions very quickly through this mode of assessment and correct them at once.

The Need for Caution

By the same token, if we are not careful in our use of personal communication as assessment, we can mismeasure achievement every bit as easily with this mode as with any of the other modes. As you shall see, the list of potential pitfalls is as long as with performance or paper and pencil assessments. In fact, in some senses, the list of challenges to the effective use of personal communication assessment is even longer than those of other modes because this one often is carried out casually in an informal context, where bias can creep in without even being noticed. But the good news is that we know how to overcome these potential problems.

Nowhere is classroom assessment more of an art than in the use of personal communication to track student growth and development. Typically, there is no table of test specifications to match against our intended target. There are no test items to check for quality, no score results. We can't check for agreement among observers to see if judgments are consistent. These are the artifacts of preplanned, structured classroom assessments. Often, personal communication is not like that. It's more spontaneous, more personal.

Nevertheless, we must understand and appreciate the fact that even this more artistic mode of assessment carries with it specific rules of evidence. Understand and adhere to those rules and you can derive valuable information about the attainments of your students. Disregard those rules and—just as with other forms of assessment—you can do great harm. With this form of assessment, just as with the others, we must be vigilant in our pursuit of quality.

The Preparation to Assess

Let's begin this phase of our journey with an analysis of an instructional/assessment strategy called *scored discussions*. I read of this idea in an article by Zola (1992) and later had a chance to see it in action. Here's how it works when an outstanding teacher uses it:

The teacher's goal is to help students learn to make productive contributions to public discussions of important, social issues. Thus, the focus of assessment is group interaction skills during class discussion.

She begins by informing students that they will read a brief essay on a controversial social topic and then discuss it, analyzing key elements of the controversy and evaluating different points of view. She promises that the discussion may become "spirited" from time to time, as opinions are expressed and challenged. However, she demands that the interaction remain civil. (This, incidentally, represents an excellent cooperative learning strategy.)

To begin with, our teacher asks her students a question: From the perspective of personal interactions, what discussion skills are most likely to contribute to a productive class discussion? What positive behaviors are really effective discussants likely to exhibit? She and her students brainstorm, and come up with the following characteristics of good contributors:

- making high-quality contributions that are on the topic
- listening attentively when others are contributing
- acting purposely to bring others into the discussion
- asking clarifying questions
- not being afraid to take a position and defend it
- making their points clear and brief

When they run out of ideas, though they realize that their list is not exhaustive, she asks them to identify three or four of the listed interaction skills they feel are most crucial to achieving a productive discussion. They then select those of the remaining skills that they consider important, but not quite as important as the first set.

Next, she asks students to brainstorm personal interaction patterns that might be counterproductive in a discussion. This list includes the following:

- putting other discussants down for their ideas
- not participating
- not listening attentively
- interrupting others
- dominating the discussion
- making contributions that are off topic

Again, she asks them to set priorities among these counterproductive behaviors.

From these lists, they devise a scoring sheet that lists the important productive behaviors, each of which earns two points when exhibited. Next, they list the less important productive behaviors, giving these a point value of one. Counterproductive behaviors are then listed, with point values of minus two and minus one. Each discussant's goal, they agree, is to attain the highest (positive!) score they can during the ensuing discussion.

Time for Reflection

What might such a scoring sheet look like? Develop your own sheet using the items listed.

The Discussion and Assessment Process

Now here's a twist that I think is terrific: Students are paired randomly. One member of each team is labeled an "innie," the other an "outie." The students sit in two circles, outies sitting right behind their innie partners, scoring sheet in hand. Innies read a brief piece on a controversial topic (perhaps a newspaper editorial on a volatile political issue) and discuss it among themselves. Every time their partner exhibits one of the behaviors listed on the scoring sheet, the outie tallies it. Later, tallies are counted to find the frequency of occurrence of the various targets. These are multiplied by points to yield a score.

Innies and outies then reverse roles. Outies read an essay on a controversial topic and discuss. Their partners observe, evaluate, and summarize in exactly the same way, arriving at a profile of performance for later discussion.

The Feedback—via Personal Communication

When discussions are done, partners meet to share and discuss results. Their assignment is to talk with each other about the quality and impact of their contribution to the group interaction. They identify positive, productive patterns, as well as specific ways to improve. Partners are asked to provide specific examples of things that seemed to work well and those that did not. If any misinterpretation occurs, discussants have a chance to explain what they were trying to do. In short, partners provide feedback on results, not just as scores, but as personal communication about the assessment and its results.

Later, the class as a whole discusses the implications of this activity for attaining goals of civic responsibility. As they debrief this activity, of course, they strive to adhere to good discussion techniques!

As a variation on this idea, you may wish to use the scored discussions strategy as a group learning activity by videotaping group discussions before and after students brainstorm, devise the scoring sheet, observe each other, and provide focused feedback. Have students as a class view the resulting videos, and compare and contrast group performance. Was the discussion conducted at the end of the lesson more civil and productive than the prelesson discussion? Again, analyze why—always bring your lesson to a close with a thoughtful analysis.

Time for Reflection

Obviously, the scored discussions activity will span considerable time, with the preparation to assess, multiple discussions, partner feedback and debriefing, and whole class debriefing. If you were to plan this for your classroom over several days, what would your lesson plan look like? Please devise a sample plan—in writing.

ENSURING QUALITY ASSESSMENT USING PERSONAL COMMUNICATION

Assessment via personal communication is yet another assessment method that is subjective by its very nature. In this section, we explore the role of subjectivity in this form of assessment. We then deal with other practical quality control matters, including issues of match between personal communication and the five kinds of outcomes we've been exploring, classroom realities to take into account with this method, and more sampling considerations.

Subjectivity in Personal Communication

Professional judgment, and therefore subjectivity, permeates all aspects of assessments that rely on personal communication. Professional judgment guides all of the following:

- the achievement targets we set for students
- the questions we pose (and sometimes generate very quickly on the spot)
- the criteria we apply in evaluating answers (often without a great deal of time to reflect)
- the performance records we store (often in memory)
- the manner in which we retrieve results for later use
- interpretations we make of those results
- the various ways in which we use those results

For this reason, it is imperative that, as when using other assessment methods, you know and understand the achievement target and know how to translate it into clear and specific questions and other probes to generate focused information.

Potential Problems.   Let's be specific about the reasons not to take personal communication as assessment too lightly as a source of information and as a teaching strategy.

The Problem of Forgetting.   One reason for caution is that we must understand the fallibility of the human mind as a recording device. Not only can we lose things in there, but the things we put in can change over time for various reasons, only some of which are within our control. These are aspects of subjectivity to be aware of when using personal communication as assessment. We must act purposely to counter them. The scored discussion idea described above did so by carefully developing and using their scoring sheet.

Time for Reflection

Have you ever been the victim of an assessment in which you demonstrated some important proficiency, but because of your teacher's mental lapse, the record of your accomplishments was lost? If so, what was that experience like for you?

The Problem of Filters.   We also must remain aware of and strive to understand those personal and professional filters, developed over years of experience, through which we hear and process student responses. They represent norms or standards, if you will, that allow us to interpret and act upon the achievement information that comes to us through observation and personal communication. We have discussed them before—they are our personal biases.

These filters hold the potential of improving or harming assessment quality. On the good side, if we set achievement expectations based on a thorough understanding of a particular field of study and if we interpret the things students say with those clearly held and appropriate standards, we can use personal communication as a positive and productive form of assessment.

Further, if we set our expectations for an individual learner on the basis of accurate information about their current level of achievement, we maximize the chances that we will be able to assist them in achieving more. These represent appropriate uses of norms and expectations.

However, there is a dark side to these interpretive filters. They can be the source of inappropriate bias. If we set our expectations for students, not on the basis of a clear understanding of the discipline or not on the basis of careful assessment of student capabilities, but on the basis of stereotypes or other convenient categories of people that are in fact unrelated to real academic achievement, we risk doing great harm indeed. If, for example, we establish professional filters by holding predetermined expectations of learners according to gender, ethnic heritage, cultural background, physical appearance, linguistic experience, our knowledge of a student's prior achievement, or any of a wide variety of other forms of prejudice—things unrelated to actual achievement—we allow bias to creep into the assessment process. The scored discussion class described above countered these dangers by adhering to one of the basic rules of sound assessment: develop clear targets. They were careful to spell out the specific behaviors that were to be labeled productive and counterproductive.

Time for Reflection

As a student, have you ever been on the losing end of a biased assessment—where for some reason, your teacher's inappropriate personal or professional filters led to an incorrect assessment of your proficiency? What was that like? What effect did it have on your learning?

The Challenge of Sampling.   Just as with other forms of assessment, we can make sampling mistakes. One is to gather too few bits of information to lead to confident conclusions about proficiency. In the scored discussion example above, this problem would arise if the discussions were too short for everyone to have a chance to demonstrate the ability to contribute productively.

Another sampling mistake is to spend too much time gathering too many bits of information. This is a problem of inefficiency. We eventually reach a point of diminishing returns, where additional information is unlikely to change the conclusion about proficiency. This would occur in the scored discussion example if the group interactions went on longer than necessary.

To avoid such sampling problems, we must seek just enough information without overdoing it. In the classroom, this is very much a matter of subjective judgment. Thus, it represents another example of a place where the *art* of classroom assessment—your professional judgment—comes into play. More about this below.

Attribute of Quality	Defining Question
Arise from a clear and specific achievement target	Do my questions reflect the achievement target I want my students to hit?
Serve clear purposes	Why are we using personal communication to assess? How will results be used?
Assure a sound representation of that target	Can the target of interest to me be accurately reflected through direct personal communication with the student?
Sample performance appropriately	Do I have enough evidence?
Control for unwanted interference	Am I in touch with potential sources of bias, and have I minimized the effects of personal and professional filters?

Figure 9-2
Defining Issues of Quality for Personal Communication as Classroom Assessment

Avoiding Problems Due to Subjectivity. We can avoid problems due to the fallibility of the human mind and bias only by attending to those five ever-present, important, basic attributes of sound assessment as they apply in the context of personal communication. Whether we plan or are spontaneous in our personal communication with students, we must bear these quality standards in mind. Figure 9–2 reviews these standards as they apply to personal communication as assessment.

When these standards of quality are met, personal communication holds the promise of providing rich and useful data about student attainment of important educational outcomes. Obviously, as with other methods, one prominent key to our success is the match of our method to the various outcomes we need to assess. We discuss how to find sound matches next.

Matching Method to Target

Personal communication–based assessments can provide direct evidence of proficiency in three of the five kinds of targets we have been discussing and can provide insight into the student's readiness to deliver on the other two. This is a versatile assessment option.

Assessing Knowledge. This can be done with personal communication, but you need to be cautious. Obviously, you can question students to see if they have mastered the required knowledge through memorization and/or through the effective use of reference materials. To succeed however, you must possess a keen sense of the limits and contents of the domain of knowledge in question.

Once again, since you cannot ask all possible questions, especially using this labor-intensive method, you must sample and generalize. I'll say more about the critical importance of careful sampling below.

Assessing Reasoning.   Herein lies the real strength of personal communication as a means of assessment. Skillful questioners can probe student reasoning and problem solving both while the very thinking process is underway and retrospectively, to analyze how the student reached the solution. But even more exciting is that you can use the questioning process to help students understand and enhance their own reasoning.

For example, you can ask them to let you in on their thought processes as they analyze events or objects, describing component parts. You can probe their ability to draw meaningful comparisons, to make simple or complex inferences, or to express and defend an opinion or point of view. There is no more powerful method for exploring student reasoning and problem solving than a conversation while they are actually trying to solve the problem. By exploring their reasoning along with them, you can provide students with the kinds of understanding and vocabulary needed to converse with you and with each other about what it means to be proficient in this performance arena.

Asking students to "think out loud" offers great promise for delving deeply into their reasoning. Mathematics teachers often ask a student to talk about their thinking as they proceed step by step through the solution to a complex math problem. This provides a richness of insight into the student's mathematical reasoning that cannot be attained in any other way.

Further, as students talk through the process, you also can insert followup questions: Why were certain steps taken or omitted? What would have happened if you had . . . ? Do you see any similarities between this problem and those we worked on last week? When students are unable to solve the problem, tactical questioning strategies can tell you why. Did the student lack prerequisite knowledge of number systems? Analyze the problem incorrectly? Misunderstand the steps in the process? These probes permit you to find student needs and link the assessment to instruction almost immediately—there is no need to wait for the score reports to be returned!

Time for Reflection

One of the popular ways of assessing reading comprehension these days is to have the student retell a story they have just read. As the retelling unfolds, the teacher is free to ask questions about the story as needed to probe the student's interpretation. Why do you think this kind of assessment has become so popular? What does it offer that, say, a multiple-choice test of reading comprehension does not?

Assessing Skills and Product.   In the previous chapter, we established that the only way to obtain direct information about student skills or proficiency in creating quality products is to have them actually "do or create" and compare their work to pre-established standards of quality.

However, if you are a skilled teacher of "doing or creating" (i.e., a teacher who possesses a highly refined vision of such a target), you can ask your students to talk through a hypothetical performance, asking a few key questions along the way, and know with a certain degree of confidence whether the students are likely to be proficient performers, and what aspects of their performance are likely to fall short of expectations.

This can save assessment time in the classroom. Let's say, for example, the kind of performance to be assessed is complex and the cost of time and materials required to conduct a full-blown performance assessment is quite high, as in an assessment of repairing an expensive piece of electronic equipment in a technology education class. If this teacher has some question about a particular student's proficiency and, therefore, is hesitant about investing the time and equipment needed to carry out the assessment, she could simply sit down and talk with the student, ask a few critical questions of the student, and based on the level of achievement reflected in the student's answers, infer whether it would be proper to conduct the actual assessment or offer additional instruction and more time to prepare.

In this same performance-related sense, you can ask students strategic questions to examine the following:

- prior success in performing similar tasks
- confidence in their ability to deliver sound performance
- knowledge and understanding of the criteria to be used to evaluate performance (i.e., key skills to be demonstrated or key attributes of quality products)
- awareness of the steps that need to be taken to create quality products

Based on the results of such probes, you can infer about competence. But again, talking is not doing. Without question, some may be able to talk a better game than they can actually deliver. So clearly, personal communication is inferior to actual performance assessment when it comes to evaluating skill and product outcomes. But under certain circumstances, it can be an inexpensive, accessible, and instructionally relevant form of classroom assessment.

Assessing Affect.   Herein resides another strength of personal communication as a form of assessment. Perhaps the most productive way to determine the direction and intensity of students' school-related attitudes, interests, values, or motivational dispositions is to simply ask them. An ongoing pattern of honest exchanges of points of view between you and your students can contribute much to the creation of powerful learning environments.

The keys to making personal communication work in the assessment of student affect are trust and open channels of communication. If students are confident that it's all right to say what they really think and feel, they will do so.

Time for Reflection

What kinds of questions might you ask a student to tap the direction and intensity of that students' real, honest feelings about the learning environment in your classroom?

Context Factors

Obviously, in the hands of an experienced user, personal communication has much to offer as an assessment technique.

First, you can forge a clear and complete link between your questioning strategies and the focus of instruction. Even as the teaching and learning process is progressing, a few strategically placed questions can help you to monitor and adjust.

Second, unlike some other forms of assessment, a questioner who is startled or puzzled by a student response can ask followup questions to dig more deeply into student thinking. In other words, you can get beyond a particular response to explore its origins. If you find misconceptions, you can take action to correct them immediately.

Third, also unlike some other forms of assessment, personal communication can be spontaneous, allowing you to take advantage of unexpected opportunities to assess and promote achievement. That is, when you sense a need for a bit more information on student thinking, you can strike while the iron is hot and take advantage of a teachable moment.

Fourth, personal communication is almost infinitely flexible in its range of applications as classroom assessment. It can focus on a range of valued outcomes. It can focus the assessment microscope on individual students, or on students as a group. It can sample students and/or the material being covered. Students may volunteer to respond, or you can call on anyone. Interaction can be public or private. Questions and answers can come from either you or the student. Assessment can be structured or informal. Considering only the flexibility indicated here, you must agree that this is a versatile mode of assessment.

And fifth, to the attentive user, the student's nonverbal reactions can provide valuable insights into achievement and feelings about the material learned (or not learned). These indicators of confidence, uncertainty, excitement, boredom, comfort, or anxiety can serve as triggers leading you to probe more deeply into the underlying causes. This kind of perception checking can result in levels of student/teacher communication not achievable through other assessment means.

Other Factors to Consider.   However, even given these strengths, the fact that almost all classroom assessment using personal communication is not subject to outside verification means that no one but you will ever be able to check to see if you are doing a good job. The standards of sound practice here are yours, and yours alone. Remember, your students and their parents will assume that you are constantly applying the highest standards of professional practice.

In that regard, there are several potential pitfalls to sound assessment using personal communication about which you must remain constantly aware.

Common Language.   Teacher and student must share a common language. This factor has become more and more critical through the 1980s and 1990s, as ethnic and cultural diversity has increased markedly in our schools. By common language, I don't just mean a shared vocabulary and grammar, although these obviously are critical to communication. I also mean a common sense of the manner in which a culture shares meaning through verbal and nonverbal cues. Ethnicity and cultural heritage may differ between student and teacher. If you assess by means of personal communication, you must know how to make meaning in the language and culture of your students. When you lack that understanding, mismeasurement is assured.

Sufficient Verbal Fluency.   This is not the same as common language. If this method is to provide accurate information about achievement, students must be both willing and able to express themselves fluently. The danger of mismeasurement lies in both directions here. If the student is not fluent, you may misinterpret and draw incorrect inferences. And if the student is "too fluent" (if you know what I mean) you can be bamboozled—Beware!

Appropriate Personality Characteristics.   Shy, withdrawn students simply may not perform well in this kind of assessment context, regardless of their real achievement. To make these methods work, two people must connect in an open, communicative manner. For some students, this simply is too risky—often for reasons beyond your control.

This coin has two sides: There also is the danger that students with very outgoing, aggressive personalities will try to lay down a "smoke screen" to mislead you with respect to their real achievement. But, this only works with assessors who have not prepared carefully, and who cannot stay focused. You fall prey to the dangers of bias in assessment when you allow yourself to be distracted by irrelevant factors.

Sufficient Time.   There must be enough time available to carry out this one-on-one form of assessment. When the target is narrow in scope and few students are to be assessed, time may not be a factor. A question or two may suffice to provide a quick glimpse into achievement. No problem.

However, as the target broadens and the number of students increases, two time dimensions become more important. First, there must be enough time to permit you to interact with each student whose achievement is to be assessed in this manner. Second, there must be sufficient time available with each student to allow you to properly sample achievement. If this time is not available, it is better to turn to another strategy that does not require such intense one-on-one contact.

Safe Environment.   Personal communication works best as assessment when students feel they are learning in a safe environment. There are many ways to interpret this. One kind of safety permits them to succeed or fail in private, without an embarrassing public spotlight. Another kind of safety takes the form of a peer environment sensitive to the plight of those who perform less well and supportive of their attempts to grow. Still another kind of safety comes from having the opportunity to learn more and perform again later with the promise of a higher level of success. Nowhere is personal safety more important to sound assessment than when that assessment is conducted through public personal communication.

Students Understand the Need for Honesty.   Personal communication works best as assessment when students understand that sometimes their teacher needs an honest answer—not their attempt at a best possible answer or the answer they think their teacher wants to hear. This mode of assessment provides its best information most efficiently when a sound interpersonal relationship exists between you and your students. Again, the key is trust. Students must know that if they give you the "socially desirable" response to a question—a response that misrepresents the truth about their achievement or feelings—then you will be less likely to help them.

A Means to Keep Accurate Records.   Because there are no tangible results with assessments conducted via personal communication, records of achievement can be lost. Over a span of a few moments or hours when the communication focuses on narrow targets, this may not be a problem. But when the context includes many students, complex targets, and a requirement of extended storage, you absolutely must maintain more tangible records—written or taped records of some kind. If you have no means or hope of doing so when necessary, you would do better to revise your assessment plans.

Figure 9–3 summarizes the five benefits of and seven practical keys to the effective use of assessment by means of personal communication discussed above.

Time for Reflection

Can you think of any additional classroom realities that might need to be considered in selecting personal communication as a means of assessment?

More about Sampling

Remember, any assessment represents only a sample of an ideal assessment of infinite length. The key to successful sampling in the context of personal communication is to ask a representative set of questions, one that is long enough to give confidence in the generalizations drawn to the entire performance domain.

Example of an Easy Fit.   Here's a scenario in which it is easy to meet these standards of quality: A teacher is about to initiate a new science reading activity on fish with his third graders. As a prereading activity, he wants to be sure all students have sufficient information about fish to understand the reading. He checks the story very carefully for vocabulary and concepts that might be stumbling blocks for his students. Then he begins to ask questions of his students, probing understanding of those words and ideas. As he samples their prior knowledge through questions and

Benefits:

- Personal communication can be quick and efficient.
- Immediate connections are possible between assessment and instruction.
- The user can be opportunistic—taking advantage of teachable moments.
- The method is flexible.
- Assessment can attend to nonverbal responses, too.

Things to investigate:

- Do teacher and students share a common language?
- Have students attained a sufficiently high level of verbal fluency to interact effectively?
- Do students have personalities that permit them to open up enough to reveal true achievement?
- Is there sufficient time for assessment?
- Do students see the environment as safe enough to reveal their true achievement?
- Do students understand the need to reveal their true achievement?
- Can accurate records of achievement be kept?

Figure 9-3
Factors to Consider in the Use of Personal Communication as Assessment

answers, he takes great care to see that those who didn't know the meaning when asked understand that meaning before beginning to read.

In this scenario, the performance arena is quite small and focused: vocabulary and concepts from within one brief science story. Sampling by means of personal communication is simple and straightforward, and there are no real record-keeping challenges presented. The teacher simply verifies understanding on the part of each student before proceeding. After that, most records of performance can be put on the back burner. The teacher might make a mental note to follow up with those students who had the most difficulty, but all other records can be "deleted."

Example of a More Challenging Fit.   Now here's a scenario in which the assessment challenges are more formidable: A high school health teacher who relies extensively on small- and large-group discussion of health-related social issues as her instructional technique wants to encourage student participation in class discussions. To accomplish this, she announces at the beginning of the year that twenty-five percent of each student's grade will be based on the extent and quality of their participation in class. She is careful to point out that she will call on people to participate and expects them to be ready.

This achievement target is broader in two ways: it contains a great deal more elements (the domain is much larger), and it spans a much longer period of time. Not only does the teacher face an immense challenge in adequately sampling each individual's performance, but her record-keeping challenge is much more complex and demanding. Consider the record-keeping dilemma posed by a class schedule that includes, say, four sections of eleventh-grade health, each including thirty students! And remember, mental record keeping is not an option: When we try to store such information in our gray matter for too long, bad things happen. These are not unsolvable problems, but they take careful preparation to assess. In this sense, they represent a significant challenge to the teacher.

These two scenarios capture the essence of the quality control challenge you face when you choose to rely on personal communication as a primary means of tracking student achievement. You must constantly ask yourself: Is my achievement target narrow enough in its scope and short enough in its time span to allow for conscientious sampling of the performance of individual students or students as a group? If the answer is yes, in your opinion, proceed to the next question: Is the target narrow enough in its scope and short enough in its time span to allow me to keep accurate records of performance? If the answer again is yes, proceed. If the answer to either question is no, choose another assessment method.

Time for Reflection

A PE teacher is about to start a new game with a class of thirty fourth graders. She thinks the rules are familiar to all, but decides to check just to be sure. So she picks a student and asks what that student should do, according to the rules, if a particular situation arises. The student answers correctly. She calls on another, seeking a second interpretation. Correct again. She infers that the class knows the rules. Soon, the game falls into disarray due to rules violations. What mistake(s) did the teacher make? What should she have done?

Assessing Individuals or the Whole Class.   Personal communication assessments are useful in tapping the level of achievement of students both individually and as a class or group. Experienced teachers know how to sample a class of students by (a) selecting a small number representative of the various levels of achievement in the group, and (b) asking a small but representative sample of key questions of this "test" group, so as to infer about student mastery of material just covered. Results of such assessments of group status can tell teachers whether to reteach or move on.

But to make this work, we must remember that the samples of students and achievement must both be representative and have sufficient depth to justify our conclusions. The PE teacher in the "Time for Reflection" above did not. She checked the knowledge of too few students to support her inference about the knowledge level of the class as a whole. And, she asked too few questions about the rules of the game to correctly infer about student knowledge of all the rules. Both problems conspired to misinform her about her students' readiness to play the game.

Time for Reflection

What could the PE teacher have done to sample student achievement more dependably?

Before leaving sampling issues, let me restate in explicit terms a critical point in sampling individual student achievement through personal communication: Beware of the natural tendency to undersample. Often a teacher will pop two or three quick questions at a student, hear wrong answers, and make a snap judgment about overall achievement. Two questions is a pretty short test!

When relying on personal communication to assess—especially when using this mode—be sure to take time to gather enough information. Remember that tip I offered earlier about the art of determining when you have enough information to decide? You know you have asked enough questions and heard enough answers to infer about student achievement when you can anticipate with a high degree of confidence how the student would do if you gave them one more. Keep this tip in mind and don't sell your students short.

Summary of Quality Control Issues

Personal communication in its many forms can supply useful information to teachers about a variety of important educational outcomes, including mastery of subject matter knowledge, reasoning and problem solving, procedural knowledge that is prerequisite to skill and product creation proficiency, and affective outcomes. To create effective matches between this method of assessment and these kinds of targets, however, the user must start with a clear vision of the outcomes to be attained, know how to translate that vision into clear, focused questions, share a common language and open channels of communication with students, and understand how to sample performance representatively. But none of these keys to success is powerful enough to overcome the problems that arise when teachers' interpretive filters predispose them to be inappropriately biased in deciphering communication from students.

THE MANY FORMS OF PERSONAL COMMUNICATION AS ASSESSMENT

Throughout the above discussion of quality control, we have addressed personal communication as a class of assessment formats. We now conduct a thorough analysis of five formats of personal communication: questioning, conferences and interviews, class discussions, oral exams, and conversation with others. In each case, we will define it and identify several keys to its effective use in the classroom.

Please bear with me through this section, as I rely heavily on lists as a concise form of presentation. They allow me to share many thoughts in little space.

Instructional Questions and Answers

This has been a foundation of education since before Socrates. As instruction proceeds, either the teacher or the students themselves pose questions for others to answer. This activity promotes thinking and learning, and also provides information about achievement. The teacher listens to answers, interprets them in terms of internally held standards, and draws inferences as to the level of attainment of the respondent.

These keys to successful use will help you take advantage of the strengths of this as an assessment format, while overcoming weaknesses:

- Plan key questions in advance of instruction, so as to assure proper alignment with the target and with student capabilities.

- Ask clear, brief questions that help the student focus on a relatively narrow range of acceptable responses.

- Probe various kinds of reasoning, not just recall of facts and information.

- Ask the question first and then call on the person who is to respond. This will have the effect of keeping all students on focus.

- Call on both volunteer and nonvolunteer respondents. This, too, will keep all students on task.

- Keep mental records of performance only for a few students at a time and over no more than a day or two. Written records are essential for large numbers of students over longer periods.

- Acknowledge correct or high-quality responses; probe incorrect responses for underlying reasons. Also regarding incorrect or low-quality responses, remember that the public display of achievement (or the lack thereof) links closely to self-concept. Strive to leave the respondent with something positive to grow on.

- After a question is posed, wait three to five seconds for a response.

While this last suggestion turns out to be surprisingly difficult to do, research reviewed and summarized by Rowe (1978) reveals many benefits. These effects appear to be most positive when we give traditionally low-achieving students time to respond:

- The length of student responses increases.

- The number of unsolicited but appropriate responses increases.

- Failure to respond decreases.

- Student confidence increases.

- The incidence of creative, speculative responses increases.

- Student-centered interaction increases, while teacher-centered teaching decreases.

- Students defend inferences better.

- The number of questions asked by students increases.

- Slow students contribute more.

- Discipline problems decrease.

- Teachers tend to view their class as including fewer academically weak students.

- Teachers are less likely to expect only their brighter students to respond.

If we can force ourselves *not* to fill the silence with the sound of our own voices and can wait for responses to brief, clearly focused questions, not only do we derive sound assessment information from responses, but in effect we integrate assessment deeply into the instructional process.

Conferences and Interviews

Some student-teacher conferences serve as structured or unstructured audits of student achievement, in which the objective is to talk about what the student has learned and has yet to learn. The teacher and student talk directly and openly about levels of student attainment, comfort with the material to be mastered, specific needs, interests, and desires, and/or any other achievement-related topics that contribute to an effective teaching and learning environment. In effect, teachers and students speak together in the service of understanding how to work effectively together.

And remember, interviews or conferences need not be conceived as every-pupil, standardized affairs with each event a carbon copy. You might meet with only one student, if it fills a communication need. And, interviews or conferences might well vary in their focus across students who have different needs. The keys to successful use of conference and interview assessment formats are these:

- Both participants must be open to honest communication and willing to examine the real, important aspects of teaching and learning.
- Interview questions must be sharply focused on the achievement target(s) and the purpose for meeting.
- Questions should be carefully thought out and planned in advance. Remember, students can share in the preparation process.
- Plan for enough uninterrupted time to conduct the entire interview or conference.
- Be sure to conclude an interview with a summary of the lessons learned and their implications for how you and the student will work together in the future.

One important strength of the interview or conference as a mode of assessment lies in the impact it can have on the student-teacher relationship. When conducted in a context where the teacher has been up front about expectations, students understand the achievement target, and all involved are invested in student success, the conference has the effect of empowering students to take responsibility for at least part of the assessment of their own progress. Conducted in a context where everyone is committed to success and where academic success is clearly and openly defined, interviews are both informational and motivational in their outcomes.

Class Discussions

When students participate in class discussions, as in the example at the beginning of this chapter, the things they say reveal a great deal about their achievements and their feelings. Discussions are teacher- or student-led group interactions in which the material to be mastered is explored from various perspectives. Teachers listen to the interaction, evaluate the quality of student contributions, and draw inferences about individual student or group achievement. Clearly, class discussions have the simultaneous effect of promoting both student learning and their ability to use what they know.

To take advantage of the strengths of this method of assessment, while minimizing the impact of potential weaknesses, follow these keys to successful use:

- Prepare questions or discussion issues in advance to focus sharply on the intended achievement target.

- Involve students in the process of preparing, being sure their questions and key issues are part of the mix.

- Rely on debate formats or other team formats to maximize the number of students who can be directly involved. Pay special attention to involving low achievers.

- Formalize the discussion format to the extent that different roles are identified, such as moderator, team leader, spokesperson, recorder, and so on, to maximize the number of students who have the opportunity to present evidence of their achievement.

- Remember, the public display of achievement represents a risk that links that achievement (or the lack thereof) to self-concept. Be aware of those times when that risk must be controlled a bit for student good.

- Provide those students who have a more reserved personal style with other equally acceptable means of demonstrating achievement.

- In contexts where achievement information derived from participation in discussion is to influence high-stakes decisions, such as a grade, dependable written records of performance are required.

The great strength of class discussion as assessment is in its ability to reveal the depth and quality of students' thinking—their ability to analyze, compare, infer, and defend their points of view. The great danger of this method is the difficulty in sampling student performance in a complete and equitable manner. Care must be taken to structure discussions thoughtfully if we are to use them as assessments.

Oral Examinations

In European educational traditions and current assessment practices, the oral examination still plays a strong role. Teachers plan and pose exercises for their students, who reflect and provide oral responses. Teachers listen to and interpret those responses, evaluating quality and drawing inferences about levels of achievement.

In a very real sense, this is like essay assessment, discussed in Chapter 7, but with the added benefit of being able to ask followup questions.

While the oral examination tradition lost favor in the United States with the advent of selected response assessment, it still represents a form of assessment that has great potential for use today—especially given the increasing complexity of our valued educational outcomes and the complexity and cost of setting up higher fidelity performance assessments.

You can take advantage of the strengths of this format by adhering to some simple keys to the successful use of this method. You accomplish this in effect by adhering to all of the quality control guidelines listed in Chapter 7 for the development of quality essay assessments:

- Develop brief exercises that focus on the desired outcome.
- Rely on exercises that identify the knowledge to be brought to bear, specify the kind of thinking to be used, and identify the standards that will be applied in evaluating responses.
- Develop written scoring criteria in advance of the assessment.
- Be sure criteria separate content and thinking outcomes from facility with verbal expression.
- Prepare in advance to accommodate the needs of any students who may confront language proficiency barriers.
- Have a checklist, rating scale, or other method of recording results ready to use at the time of the assessment.
- If possible, record responses for later reevaluation.

Clearly, the major argument against this format of assessment is the amount of time it takes to administer oral exams. However, you can overcome part of this problem by bringing students into the assessment process as partners. If you adhere to the guidelines listed above and spread the work of administering and scoring over many shoulders, great benefit can be derived.

Conversations with Others

You can derive useful information about student achievement by talking with others about the achievement of the student in question. However, this form of personal communication must be used very carefully to produce quality information.

If you ask the right questions of those who have reason to know about the achievement of a particular student, then they may be able to provide insights you are unable to generate on your own. Possible sources may include other students, other teachers, other school staff, parents, and siblings. Since these people might have sampled student performance in ways you have not, in effect, you broaden your awareness of achievement and add confidence to your assessments if you add their inferences to your information base.

If you rely on conversations with others to derive information about the achievement of your students, be sure to attend to these keys to success:

- Be a critical consumer of this information: probe the nature and quality of the evidence mustered by the information provider. Be sure you share a common understanding of the meaning of the valued achievement targets. Be sure that they used sound assessment methods, sampled appropriately, and controlled for their own biases. In other words, ask only those who are in a position to know about the achievement of your students.

- In contexts where critical decisions hang in the balance, solicit information from more than just one other source, to guard against hidden bias.

INTEGRATING ASSESSMENT VIA PERSONAL COMMUNICATION INTO INSTRUCTION

Since instruction is conducted in large part through personal interaction between teacher and student, integrating this form of assessment into the teaching and learning process is not difficult. Restatements of the important ideas from this chapter follow, as well as additional ideas for involving students in the assessment process:

- Minimize the number of questions posed that simply require yes or no answers. Seek more complex responses as a matter of routine, so students come to expect it.

- Tap the full range of kinds of reasoning, not just recall of facts.

- Wait for a response. Let students know that you expect an answer and will not let them off the hook by allowing them to remain silent. Once they speak, the channels of communication are open.

- Keep the whole class involved by calling on nonvolunteers, asking students to add to what someone just said, and asking them to signal if they agree or disagree.

- Turn responsibility for questioning over to students; they can ask them of each other or of you (put your own reasoning power on the line in public once in a while).

- Ask students to paraphrase each other's questions and responses.

- Ask students to address key questions in small groups, so more students can be involved.

- Offer students opportunities to become discussion leaders, posing questions of their own.

- Ask students to keep track of their own performance, such as through the use of tally sheets and diaries.

- Designate one or two students to be observers and recorders during discussions, noting who responds to what kinds of questions and how well; other teachers can do this too.

- Engage students in peer and self-assessment of performance in discussions.

- Schedule regular interviews with students, one on one or in groups.

- Schedule times when your students can interview you about your impressions about how well things are going for them as individuals and as a group.

Time for Reflection

Have you studied with teachers who relied heavily on some form of personal communication as described above? How did they assess? Did they do it well?

CHAPTER SUMMARY: ASSESSMENT AS SHARING, PERSON TO PERSON

The key to success in using personal communication as assessment of student achievement is to remember that, just because assessment is sometimes casual, informal, unstructured, and/or spontaneous, does not mean we can let our guard down with respect to standards of assessment quality. In fact, we must be even more vigilant than with other forms of assessment, because it is so easy to allow personal filters, poor sampling techniques, and/or inadequate record keeping to interfere with sound assessment.

When we attend to quality standards, we use our interactions with students to reach important achievement targets, including mastery of knowledge, reasoning, knowledge and reasoning prerequisites of skill and product development competence, and affective outcomes. Thus, like the other three modes of assessment, this one is quite flexible. Even though we typically don't refer to personal communication as assessment, if we start with a clear and appropriate vision, translate it into thoughtful probes, sample performance appropriately and attend to key sources of bias, we can generate quality information in this manner.

So can students. Whether in whole class discussions, smaller collaborative groups, or working with a partner, students can be assessors, too. They can ask questions of each other, listen to responses, infer about achievement, and communicate feedback to each other. Beware, however. The ability to communicate effectively in an assessment context is not "wired in" from birth. It must be learned and practiced both by you and your students to be honed as an assessment skill.

EXERCISES TO ADVANCE YOUR LEARNING

Knowledge Outcomes

1. Specify the roles of objectivity and subjectivity in assessments based on personal communication.
2. Identify the kinds of achievement targets that can be reflected in personal communication–based assessments.
3. List the strengths, limitations, and keys to effective use of five formats of personal communication assessment: instructional questions and answers, class discussions, conferences and interviews, oral exams, and conversations with others about students.

4. Identify the key considerations in sampling student performance via personal communication.

5. Specify ways to engage students in the assessment process using personal communication.

Reasoning Outcomes

1. Assume that, as a first-grade teacher, you are about to read a story about volcanoes. To assure that your students will understand the story, you want to be sure they know the meanings of several key words used by the author. You decide to ask a few questions of the class before beginning. How would you handle this assessment situation? Would personal communication play a role? If so, how? How might achievement be sampled appropriately?

2. Assume you are a high school chemistry teacher needing to verify student adherence to safety rules in the science lab. How would you do so? What role might assessment via personal communication play? How might performance be appropriately sampled here?

3. In the scored discussion example at the beginning of the chapter, the teacher turned assessment and feedback responsibility over to the students. Students worked together to devise a set of expectations, observe each other, and share feedback. Do you think, therefore, that this represented a high-quality assessment? Why?

4. Identify three specific purposes for assessment, achievement targets, and classroom contexts in which you would turn to personal communication as your method of assessment (identify three of each).

5. For each instance identified in exercise four above, identify any potential sources of interference that might lead to mismeasurement. How would you control each?

Skill Outcomes

1. Enlist a colleague, friend, or classmate as a subject for this activity. Find a topic of mutual interest, such as a piece of literature, a hobby, a professional activity, or a favorite place. Plan and conduct an interview of your subject to find out how much that person really knows about this topic. Prepare your specific questions and/or other interaction ideas in advance. Your goal is to elicit information about their knowledge and their ability to use that knowledge to reason effectively. Before the interview, think of any potential problems that could arise and take action to prevent them. Keep a list of both ideas and problems. Conduct your interview, then analyze your work. Were you able to collect quality information from your interaction? Why?

Product Outcomes

1. Devise a method for recording the results of your interview. Include records of responses and of the inferences you draw about knowledge and reasoning proficiency.

Affective Outcomes

1. Some have argued that assessments that arise out of personal communication are too fraught with danger of bias due to subjectivity to justify their use as a source of classroom assessment information. Do you agree? Why?

2. Do you feel that assessment based on personal communication could be beneficial to students, to their well-being and learning in the classroom? If so, how? Please be specific.

PART THREE

Classroom Applications

Everyone complains of his memory, and no one complains of his judgment.

La Rochefoucald (1613–1680)

CHAPTER 10

Assessing Reasoning in Its Many Forms

CHAPTER OBJECTIVES

As a result of studying the material presented in Chapter 10, reflecting on that material, and completing the learning exercises presented at the end of the chapter, you will:

1. Master content knowledge:
   a. List the criteria to apply in selecting or developing a vision of reasoning and problem solving to use in your classroom.
   b. Know some of the conceptual frameworks advanced in the past as possible visions for you and your students.
   c. State various elements of the reasoning and problem-solving process.
   d. Specify assessment formats that can serve to reflect different kinds of reasoning and problem solving.
   e. Identify keys to the effective translation of various patterns of reasoning into assessment exercises and scoring criteria.
   f. State specific ways to integrate the assessment of reasoning into day-to-day classroom teaching and learning.

2. Be able to use that knowledge to reason as follows:
   a. Analyze, compare, and evaluate various visions of reasoning and problem solving in order to select or develop one for your classroom.
   b. Translate various kinds of reasoning and problem solving into assessment methods.

3. Become proficient at the following skills:
   a. Perform the steps of creating assessments that tap various forms of reasoning and problem solving.

4. Become proficient in creating the following products:
   a. Assessments that meet the five standards of quality.
5. Attain the following affective outcomes:
   a. See all kinds of thinking and reasoning as valuable, including mastery of content knowledge.
   b. Appreciate the importance of being able to gain mastery over content knowledge in two ways: through memory and through the effective use of reference materials.
   c. Value reasoning power as essential for all.
   d. See focused, high-quality assessments of reasoning and problem solving as essential for all.

Virtually every national analysis of and commentary on the state of education completed in recent years has referred to the need to develop proficient problem solvers if we are to be competitive in the world economy of the twenty-first century: the National Commission on Excellence in Education's 1983 report, *A Nation at Risk,* the Secretary's Commission on Achieving Necessary Skills' 1991 report, *What Work Requires of Schools: A SCANS Report of America 2000,* former President Bush's 1991 *America 2000* proposal, and the National Commission on Testing and Public Policy's 1991 report, *From Gatekeeper to Gateway: Transforming Testing in America.* For this reason, the 1980s and 1990s have become the decades of the reasoning and problem-solving curriculum.

Educational psychologists have analyzed reasoning and problem solving, curriculum developers have integrated reasoning into the curriculum, text authors have built reasoning challenges into their books, and issues related to the assessment of reasoning and problem solving have emerged in full color. This is yet another of those many valued educational outcomes that revealed itself to us in far richer detail during the 1980s than ever before.

As a result of a great deal of outstanding work by the educational research and development community and educational practitioners over the past decade, we are now in a position to help more students become more effective and proficient thinkers and problem solvers than ever before. To reach this goal, however, all teachers must do the following:

- develop a highly refined vision of the kinds of reasoning and problem solving to be demonstrated in their classrooms
- know how to translate that vision into a variety of quality assessments
- be able to integrate those assessments into the teaching and learning process

In this chapter, we explore all three parts of this equation.

CHAPTER ROADMAP

We will explore ways to form a community of problem solvers in the classroom by examining four different visions or conceptual frameworks of the reasoning and problem-solving process: those developed by Bloom (1956), Norris and Ennis (1989), Marzano (1992), and Quellmalz (1987).

As you will see, each framework includes several kinds of reasoning. Together, they reveal the diversity of conceptual framework options available to you. However, they do not delimit those options. Our professional literature includes others. Your responsibility is to review the alternative frameworks and to select or adapt one for use in your teaching context. We will explore how to do that together. But please be advised that the four frameworks reviewed here are intended to be illustrative—not prescriptive. I urge you to take your responsibility very seriously. Search out and explore as many options as you can before you settle on the best one for you and your students.

Time for Reflection

From the student's point of view, it probably would be best if all or most teachers on the same instructional team or in the same department, building, or maybe even district could adopt a common vision of successful problem solving. This would provide students with more practice in a wider variety of contexts, thus increasing their chances of experiencing academic success in the reasoning and problem-solving arena. How might you and your colleagues collaborate in evaluating the options and selecting a satisfactory framework? What might be the steps in that process?

As you review the frameworks available to you, and as you evaluate whether each is appropriate for you and your students, keep the following three criteria in mind. (Incidentally, this selection process represents a classic example of critical or evaluative reasoning, defined as using a set of criteria to select from among a number of choices.)

1. Select or develop a vision of a reasoning curriculum that you can internalize and be committed to—a framework with which you can become so comfortable that you can effortlessly integrate those valued reasoning processes into all events in your classroom.

2. The patterns of reasoning reflected in your curriculum should make sense in the real world. That is, they should reflect the manner in which adults solve important problems in everyday life.

3. The patterns of reasoning in your framework should be cast in a form that can make sense to your students. You must be able to translate the reasoning and problem-solving process into terms they can understand and internalize, too.

And so, in this chapter, we will explore options, investigating the translation of the various patterns of reasoning conveyed in these frameworks into various forms

	SELECTED RESPONSE	ESSAY	PERFORMANCE ASSESSMENT	PERSONAL COMMUNICATION
Know				
Reason				
Skill				
Product				
Affect				

Figure 10-1
Aligning Achievement Targets and Assessment Methods

of assessment. Through this process, it will become clear that all four basic forms of assessment—selected response, essay, performance assessment, and personal communication—have important contributions to make. A variety of important kinds of reasoning can be translated comfortably into selected response formats. Still others can be triggered by carefully crafted essay exercises, performance exercises, or thoughtful dialogue with students. We will examine examples of all of these.

As you begin this chapter, again, keep the big picture in mind. The shaded cells in Figure 10–1 indicate the achievement target and assessment methods that are of concern in this chapter.

Guiding Principles

As we proceed through this phase of our journey, please bear four guiding principles in mind.

Principle 1: Of all the kinds of achievement targets discussed in this book, none places a greater premium on a sharp vision of the valued outcome than does reasoning. Each of us must enter our classroom with a refined conceptual understanding of the reasoning process, the vocabulary needed to communicate effectively about our vision, and the strategies needed to share both the vision and its vocabulary with our students. Without such a clear sense of the kinds of reasoning to be mastered, both teacher and students will remain adrift in uncertainty about their success. Here's why:

Remember how the various kinds of achievement targets discussed herein build on one another? Knowledge forms the foundation. Only when requisite knowledge is available within a particular content domain can students use that knowledge to solve problems in that arena. Further, with knowledge and reasoning proficiencies in place, important and complex skills can be developed. And finally, sometimes we ask students to use their knowledge, reasoning, and skills to create quality achievement-related products.

The interrelationship among these four achievement targets makes each indispensable. In essence, they all grow together. As students gain access to ever more complex and differentiated arrays of knowledge, they can solve more and more complex problems, permitting them to master increasingly sophisticated skills and to create products of increasing complexity.

Thus it becomes clear that *reasoning,* conceived of either as retrieving essential knowledge or the use of that knowledge, represents a critical building block in the development of academic competence.

Principle 2: The common practice of differentiating between higher- and lower-order thinking is counterproductive. When we differentiate in this manner, unfortunately, the honor of being labeled "lower order" always goes to the mastery of content knowledge. As a result, content mastery has come to be seen as a less cognitively challenging and therefore less valuable educational outcome. Not only is this demeaning to the foundation of reasoning and therefore academic competence (see Principle 1 above), but the retrieval of useful knowledge can be even more cognitively challenging than other forms of reasoning.

This habit of labeling thinking higher- or lower-order has had an unfortunate impact, in my opinion. It has led some curriculum staff and teachers to deemphasize mastery of subject matter knowledge to the extent that students don't gain access to the kinds of knowledge foundations they need to solve complex problems. In my opinion, that pendulum has swung too far.

But, you might argue, our overemphasis on memorization to the exclusion of other forms of reasoning needed to be corrected. I must agree. But that does not mean we should go out of balance in the other direction, emphasizing complex reasoning to the exclusion of concern for mastery of essential knowledge. Rather, we should continue to place great curricular emphasis on the development of complex reasoning power but never lose sight of the fact that knowledge must be mastered (via memory or through the use of reference materials) if students are to solve problems—and there is nothing "lower order" about it! We need balanced attention to all outcomes.

Principle 3: We don't need to teach most students to think. The majority of students are natural thinkers from the time they arrive at school. That is, they possess the thought processes needed to survive and even prosper in school and beyond. They are capable of interacting purposefully with their world, confronting problems, reflecting upon solutions, solving problems, and deriving or constructing personal meaning from the experience. Further, most students will naturally continue to use their inherent abilities as long as we don't discourage them and/or prevent them from doing so.

Given this as a starting point, our instructional challenge is to help them understand how to organize or pattern those thought processes so as to be able to reason effectively in the various problem-solving contexts that life presents. If we can help them master a conceptual understanding and a vocabulary that will permit them to converse with us and with each other about their reasoning and problem-solving proficiencies, successes, and difficulties, we set them up to become the kinds of independent problem solvers they will need to be as productive adults.

Thus, from this point forward, we will define our achievement target of interest as *reasoning,* the practical appliction of thinking processes to solve significant problems.

Time for Reflection

Find some preschoolers engaged in play. Just watch them. See if you can identify some of the kinds of reasoning and problem solving they use. From your observations, what inferences do you draw about the thinking tools they bring with them to school?

Principle 4: Teachers do not have to take complete responsibility for the assessment of students' reasoning proficiencies. Given conceptual understanding of reasoning processes and a way to converse about their thinking, students can monitor their own and each other's reasoning, enjoy being part of the process and learn a great deal along the way! Our job as teachers is to begin with a vision of how one organizes reasoning in productive ways, share that vision with our students, teach them to monitor their own reasoning, and offer positive support as they come to terms with that reasoning.

UNDERSTANDING THE OPTIONS

Over the past decade, many educational researchers, psychologists, and philosophers have reflected on the reasoning and problem-solving process, putting forth a dazzling array of useful ways of describing it. Unfortunately, space limitations will not permit presenting all available conceptual descriptions of reasoning. Four of these descriptions, the Bloom, Norris and Ennis, Marzano, and Quellmalz frameworks, are detailed below in terms of their vision of student reasoning and the transformation of that vision into assessment methods. In addition, I have selected examples of ideas and methods illustrative of the assessment possibilities with each framework.

Once again, I emphasize that as a teacher or member of the instructional support team, you absolutely must take responsibility for following up with whichever of these you choose to investigate further. Seek out the appropriate references and become a student of the various models. Only then can you make an informed choice, and effectively implement your selected vision for your students.

The Bloom Taxonomy

For several decades, almost all assessment of "higher-order thinking" centered on Bloom's taxonomy of the cognitive domain (Bloom, 1956). This framework holds that thinking can be subdivided into six levels of cognitive operation—knowledge, comprehension, analysis, application, synthesis, and evaluation—each of which was said to represent a higher level of challenge than the ones that precede it. These levels are listed and defined in Table 10–1.

Teachers who seek to assess these dimensions of student thinking are advised to pose questions that reflect the various levels. Examples are listed in Table 10–1, along with a list of trigger words which, if used in paper and pencil tests or performance assessment exercises, can elicit evidence of respondents' reasoning proficiencies. Later in the chapter, we'll see examples of the kinds of scoring criteria you would need to develop to evaluate student responses to essay exercises or performance assessments.

Note the hierarchical ordering of levels. The "knowledge" level is regarded as the lowest level and the "evaluation" level the highest. Each successive level is regarded as presenting a more difficult cognitive challenge. As you may have inferred from the principles discussed above, I find that I cannot accept this part of this particular vision of the reasoning process. I think that we can pose very complex "knowledge" and "comprehension" exercises that far outstrip simple "analysis" and "synthesis" tasks in terms of their level of cognitive challenge. However, many educators don't share my discomfort with this facet of the Bloom framework. In any case, you should be aware of the hierarchy and its implications for assessment.

Matching Method to Target.   All of Bloom's levels but "evaluation" can be assessed using selected response formats. And virtually all levels can be assessed using essay, performance assessment, and personal communication methods. The list of trigger words in Table 10–1, if used in the exercise, can result in assessments of the Bloom levels. Beware, however. Using these trigger words does not guarantee success. Certain conditions must be satisfied to be sure you are assessing the levels of thinking in question. We will discuss these conditions in detail throughout the rest of this chapter.

Recently, new frameworks have stretched our vision of the reasoning process both in breadth and specificity. Please understand that I share these with you, not to make you proficient teachers or assessors of each, but merely to provide a path to greater understanding of the range of options. You must follow up and read the references listed and practice with each, if you wish to become proficient. (Have I said this enough times now so that you will begin to take this assignment seriously?)

The Norris-Ennis Framework

Norris and Ennis (1989) reveal to us their special set of steps that comprise the "critical thinking" process:

1.   clarify the issue by asking critical questions

2.   gather critical information about the issue

3.   begin to reason through the various sides or points of view

Table 10-1
Bloom's Taxonomy—The Cognitive Domain (Freely adapted from *Measurement and Evaluation in Teaching* (pp. 506–507) by N. E. Gronlund and R. L. Linn, 1989, New York: Macmillan. Copyright 1989 by Macmillan. Adapted by permission.)

Level	Definition	Sample Trigger Words	Sample Probe
Knowledge	Can remember terms, facts, procedures, relationships, concepts (lowest level)	list, label, name, outline, reproduce, define, describe	List the names of the main characters in the story.
Comprehension	Understands the meaning of material learned, can interpret and restate in own words (one step above knowledge recall)	explain, interpret, restate, translate, paraphrase, summarize	What was the main idea of the story?
Application	Can use material learned in novel, real-world contexts (demonstrates a higher level of understanding through comprehension)	demonstrate, manipulate, operate, modify, use, produce	Using what you know about the structure of the stories read in class, write a new story of your own.
Analysis	Understands the component parts of things and can categorize elements in sensible ways; understands elements and how they fit together	subdivide, differentiate, categorize, classify, break down, distinguish	Break the story down into its separate parts, describing how they relate.
Synthesis	Can combine separate knowledge, concepts, and understanding into a unified and novel whole	combine, relate, categorize, reassemble, reorganize	By combining these two stories about whales, what would you predict about the future of the whale population on earth?
Evaluation	Can judge the value or appropriateness of something by applying proper criteria in a logical manner	evaluate, appraise, judge, justify, defend	Is this a well written story, in your opinion? Why?

4.   gather further clarifying information and conduct further analysis as needed

5.   make and communicate the decision

In addition, Norris and Ennis expand our notion of the effectively functioning thinker and problem solver by including in their model an important array of dispositions that define a "critical spirit," or the propensity to use critical thinking abilities when needed. Let's consider both the abilities and disposition sides of this framework.

Critical Abilities.   Norris and Ennis (1989) amplify their vision: "Critical thinking is reasonable and reflective thinking that is focused upon deciding what to do or believe" (p. 3). Critical thinking is reasonable in that it is not arbitrary—it does not lead to just any conclusion but to the best conclusion for the critical thinker. And it is reflective in that the thinker consciously and assertively seeks the best possible solution. Thus, critical thinking, according to Norris and Ennis, is focused in the sense that it is consciously directed at a goal: it is purposeful. That critical thinking goal is to evaluate the best action or belief.

Thus, Norris and Ennis focus their framework on the thinking processes involved in gathering information about and applying proper criteria to judge different courses of action or points of view. This sounds a great deal like Bloom's evaluative thinking level. But other forms of reasoning come into play, too. The Norris and Ennis framework is presented in Table 10–2, in the form of a five-step reasoning process.

Time for Reflection

Following the steps in Table 10–2, especially the practical example, proceed through the critical thinking process to pose the important questions in deciding this issue: Should primary grade teachers be encouraged to use performance assessments in their classrooms? When you have finished with that, try a science issue: Should the United States continue developing a space station? And finally, think through the questions contained within any issue of special importance to you.

Does the Norris and Ennis framework represent a useful process for deciding on a proper course of action or belief, in your opinion? (Think critically!)

The Critical Spirit.   Those with a critical spirit, Norris and Ennis (1989) tell us, demand sound thinking from those around them, strive to stay well informed from the most credible sources, remain open minded, and take personal pleasure in dealing in an orderly manner with complex problems, among other personal attributes. Since these kinds of dispositions represent affective outcomes, we will address their assessment in Chapter 12. However, Norris and Ennis make the strong point that intellectual tools can go to waste in the absence of a sense of responsibility to use them.

Table 10-2
Norris and Ennis's Critical Thinking Framework (Adapted from *Evaluating Critical Thinking* (n.p.) by S. P. Norris and R. H. Ennis, 1989, Pacific Grove, CA: Midwest Publications. Copyright 1989 by Midwest Publications. Reprinted by permission of the publisher.)

Step in the Process	Thinking Required	Practical Example
Carry out elementary clarification of the problem	Understand the issue at hand	Should I stay home and study or visit friends?
	Analyze the points of view or positions	If I stay home, that means . . . If I go, that means . . .
	Ask and answer questions that clarify and challenge	What are the benefits of each action? What are the costs of each?
Gather basic information	Judge the credibility of various sources of information	Who can most effectively help me?
	Gather and judge information	When asked, my friends said . . . When asked, my parents said . . .
Make inferences	Make and judge deductions using available information	If I go, these will be the implications: If I stay, these will be the implications:
	Make and judge inductions	How can I meet both sets of needs?
	Make and judge value judgments	Which set of needs is most important?
Carry out advanced clarification	Define terms and judge definitions as needed	What does punishment mean? What does friendship mean?
	Identify assumptions	Study is good. I have to study now. Friends are important.
Come to best conclusion	Decide on an action	You decide!
	Communicate decision to others	And tell everyone.

Time for Reflection

What do you think might be some of the instructional keys to helping each of your students develop a "critical spirit?" How might you help them in a manner that puts them in touch with their own critical dispositions?

Matching Method to Target.   The Norris and Ennis framework represents complex, multipart reasoning in that it calls for the integrated use of various thought processes. Because of this complexity, it does *not* lend itself to selected response assessment.

However, we could use an essay format to gain information about student mastery of the steps in complex reasoning and their understanding about how those parts interrelate. In addition, we could use essay assessment as a vehicle for students to describe for us the reasoning processes they went through in dealing with a complex academic issue, such as "Was the United States justified in invading Vietnam?"

Based on their responses, we could evaluate not only the quality of criteria they consider and the support they muster for their point of view, but the nature and quality of the inferences they draw, and their ability to select credible sources of information and identify underlying assumptions, among other reasoning powers.

In addition, of course, performance assessment could serve us well here. We could pose an issue for students to address individually or in groups and observe the process from a distance with clear "critical thinking skills" performance criteria in mind. Examples of these criteria are presented later in the chapter.

We might probe their reasoning via personal communication with a few strategically placed questions as they work through an issue. Or we could have students reason aloud as we listen and evaluate them.

Or better yet, we could engage students in devising essay scoring criteria, performance assessment scoring criteria, or a checklist of key steps in the Norris and Ennis critical thinking process. We could turn at least some of the responsibility for the evaluation of their own and each other's reasoning over to our students. As they internalize the vision and reflect upon their own work, they will become critical thinkers.

Marzano's Dimensions of Learning

Like the Norris and Ennis vision, the conceptual framework offered by Marzano (1992) includes both cognitive and affective components. The cognitive dimensions of his relatively complex array of reasoning processes are presented in Table 10–3, with labels, definitions, and brief examples. The affective dimensions hold that students should develop and maintain both positive attitudes and perceptions about learning and a sense of personal responsibility for sound reasoning, or the skills they possess may go to waste. Again, we will address assessment of these kinds of attitudes in Chapter 12.

The great strength of this framework is the fact that each kind of thinking specified translates naturally and very comfortably into questions or probes that seem applicable to all subject matter areas. Further, each question seems unique and relevant in the real world. The key classroom assessment question is, How shall we translate these probes into various modes of assessment?

Time for Reflection

Using the questions posed in the righthand column of Table 10–3 as your model, select a content area of meaning to you and pose a series of questions you might use to probe your students' understanding of that area. Do you find this to be an easy or difficult translation? What problems arise, if any?

Table 10-3

Marzano's Dimensions of Learning (Adapted from *A Different Kind of Classroom: Teaching with Dimensions of Learning* (n.p.) by R. J. Marzano, 1992, Alexandria, VA: Association for Supervision and Curriculum Development. Copyright 1992 by ASCD. Reprinted by permission of the publisher.)

Label	Thinking Process	Sample Questions
1. Acquiring and integrating knowledge		
A. Declarative knowledge	Constructing meaning Organizing new knowledge Storing knowledge	How does this relate to something you already know? Can you see an underlying structure within this? What is it? How have you connected this new knowledge to your existing knowledge?
B. Procedural knowledge	Constructing procedures	Can you describe the procedures for doing this as you understand them?
	Altering procedures to personalize them	How can you change procedures to fit your needs and way of thinking?
	Internalizing procedures	Could you apply the procedures to this problem?
2. Extending and refining knowledge		
A. Comparing	Articulating similarities and differences	How are these things alike? How are they different?
B. Classifying	Grouping things into categories	Into what groups would you organize these? How are groups defined?
C. Inducing	Inferring principles from evidence	Based on these facts, what would you conclude?
D. Deducing	Applying principles to draw conclusions	Based on this principle, what should happen next?
E. Analyzing errors	Critiquing own thinking	What errors have been made in this reasoning?
F. Constructing support	Supporting assertions	What evidence would support this claim?
G. Abstracting	Articulating underlying theme	What pattern underlies this information?
H. Analyzing perspectives	Articulating personal views about issues	What is the reasoning behind your perspective?
3. Using knowledge meaningfully		
A. Decision making	Using criteria to select from options	Which course of action is best in this case and why?
B. Investigating	Gathering information	What information do you need to solve this problem?
C. Experimenting	Seeking explanations	Can you explain why this solution is best?
D. Problem Solving	Overcoming obstacles	Can you see a way around this obstacle and solve the problem?
E. Invention	Finding a better way	How could this solution be improved on?
4. Habits of the mind		
A. Self-regulated thinking	Being aware of one's own thinking	Can you describe how you solved the problem?
B. Critical thinking	Mustering support and defending clearly	How can you support that position?
C. Creative thinking	Persistent striving for new ways	How many different solutions can you identify?

244

Matching Method to Target.   In the Marzano framework, each of the four major cognitive categories seems to bring with it its own special assessment challenge. For instance, the spirit of part one of Table 10–3, "acquiring and integrating new knowledge," suggests assessments that rely on personal communication. While selected response and essay formats can tell us if required procedural or declarative knowledge has been mastered, Marzano seems interested in far more than whether students learn it per se. He also seems interested in how that new material is assimilated into the learner's existing structures of knowledge.

Since learning is an active process of constructing meaning—a personal process—I think Marzano wants us to discuss with students how that process is unfolding within them. Just as math teachers today are interested in far more than whether the problem solver gets the right answer, so too does Marzano want us to probe inside the student's own learning experience, using problems like those in part one of Table 10–3.

On the other hand, the probes associated with Table 10–3, part two, "Extending and refining knowledge," lend themselves far more to selected response modes of assessment. Identifying similarities and differences, being able to categorize, drawing inductive or deductive inferences, and finding underlying themes are all excellent foundations for multiple-choice test exercises, for example. Table 10–4 provides some simple illustrations.

This is not to say that an essay format couldn't work well here. It definitely could. As a matter of fact, entries 2F and 2H of Table 10–3, "Constructing support" and "Analyzing perspectives," require original reasoning communicated through essays or personal communication. But the point is that we could use selected response modes very comfortably here if circumstances required it. It seems consistent with the spirit of this section.

This is also not to say performance assessment couldn't work here. Once again, it could. Figure 10–2 provides an example of an excellent "comparison" performance

Table 10-4

Translating Marzano's "Extending and Refining" into Test Items (Using assessment knowledge as the base)

Kind of Thinking	Illustration
Comparing	Which of the options listed below represents a difference between essay assessment and performance assessment? (choices listed)
Classifying	Classify each of the sample test exercises below in terms of the kind of thinking it demands of students. (matching exercise)
Inducing	Based on the evidence presented below (a case is described), this teacher developed and used a sound assessment. (true or false)
Deducing	Given what you know about sound assessment strategies, which of the exercises presented below would you place on a test? (options follow)
Analyzing Errors	Find the flaw in the multiple-choice test item presented below. (item follows)
Abstracting	Of the choices listed below, which statement best summarizes the key to the effective assessment of student thinking? (choices follow)

Exercise:

You have volunteered to help out at your local library with their literacy program. Once a week after school, you help people learn how to read. To encourage your student to learn, you tell her about the different kinds of literature you have read, including poems, biographies, mysteries, tall tales, fables, and historical novels. Select three types of literature and compare them using general characteristics of literature that you think will help your student see the similarities and differences. Be ready to present a visual presentation of the comparison. You will be assessed [based on these criteria]:

Scoring Criteria:

A. Selects appropriate items to be compared.

    4 Selects items that are very well suited for addressing the basic objective of the comparison, and that show original or creative thinking.

    3 Selects items that provide a means for successfully addressing the basic objective of the comparison.

    2 Selects items that satisfy the basic requirements of the comparison, but create some difficulties for completing the task.

    1 Selects items that are inappropriate to the basic object of the comparison.

B. Selects appropriate characteristics on which to compare the selected items.

    4 Selects characteristics that encompass the most essential aspects of the items that are compared. In addition, the student selects characteristics that present some unique challenge or provide some unique insight.

    3 Selects characteristics that provide a vehicle for meaningful comparison of the items, and that address the basic objective of the comparison.

    2 Selects characteristics that provide for a partial comparison of the items and may include some characteristics that are extraneous.

    1 Selects characteristics that are trivial or do not address the basic objective of the comparison. Selects characteristics on which the items cannot be compared.

C. Accurately identifies the similarities and differences between items on the identified characteristics.

    4 Accurately assesses all identified similarities and differences for each item on the selected characteristic. Additionally, the student provides inferences from the comparison that were not explicitly requested in the task description.

    3 Accurately assesses the major similarities and differences in the identified characteristics.

    2 Makes some important errors in identifying the major similarities and differences in the identified characteristics.

    1 Makes many significant errors in identifying the major similarities and differences in the identified characteristics.

Figure 10-2

Performance Assessment Exercise Tapping Respondent's Ability to Compare (Reprinted from "Appendix B: Task/Situation Specific Rubrics" from *Performance Assessment Using Dimensions of Learning* (exercise p. 98, criteria, pp. 112–113) by R. J. Marzano, D. J. Pickering, and J. McTighe, 1993, Aurora, CO: Mid-continent Regional Educational Laboratory. Copyright 1993 by McREL. Reprinted by permission of the publisher.)

assessment exercise and sample scoring criteria from the Marzano, Pickering, and McTighe (1993) collection.

But these more complex assessment options carry a higher cost with little gain in the quality of the information that results for part two, "Extending and refining knowledge," of Table 10–3. For economy's sake, selected response formats are worth considering here.

However, as we turn to parts three and four of Table 10-3, "Using knowledge meaningfully" and "Habits of the mind," Marzano leads us to outcomes of greater complexity in the kinds of reasoning required, and that triggers serious thoughts of performance assessments. We must give students (working alone or in teams) decisions to make, investigations or experiments to conduct, problems to solve, or invention challenges, and watch them work. As long as we can agree in advance on what it means to perform effectively and as long as students have ample opportunities to practice, performance assessments based on teacher judgment can serve effectively here.

To see what that means in real assessment terms, refer to Figure 10–3, another example from Marzano, Pickering, and McTighe (1993), illustrating "experimental inquiry."

Thus, as we progress down the list of patterns of reasoning in Table 10–3, we find valued outcomes that permit the use of the broad range of assessment methods we have at our disposal. Just remember our five standards of assessment quality as you proceed.

Time for Reflection

What are those five attributes again?

The Quellmalz Framework

Quellmalz (1987) provides us with yet another excellent vision of the reasoning process. This version is relatively simple and straightforward, and is very easy for teachers and students to internalize and use.

After reviewing all of the educational, psychological, and philosophical frameworks presented in the professional literature over the decades, Quellmalz found that they usually contained these basic elements: recall, analysis, comparison, inference, and evaluation.

All of the various descriptions studied, she reports, operate on the principle (mentioned above) that there is no such thing as "content-free thinking." Rather, all thinking and problem solving arises out of a knowledge base. Without prerequisite knowledge, no problem can be solved. Thus, she began with "recall" as the first entry in her framework.

In addition, Quellmalz found that many of the scholars she studied used the following definitions:

- *analytical* thinking is thinking in terms of ingredients and component parts of something.

Exercise:

Identify interesting behavior you have noticed while riding in an elevator. Explain this phenomenon using accepted sociological and psychological principles. Based on your understanding of the principles involved, make a prediction that can be tested. Set up an experiment that will test your prediction and help explain the principles you have discovered. Describe whether the experiment proved or disproved your hypothesis and whether the principles you've described still hold true. When you present your findings to the class, you will need to support your oral presentation with a demonstration.

Scoring Criteria:

A. Accurately explains the phenomenon initially observed using appropriate and accepted facts, concepts, or principles.

   4 Provides an accurate explanation of the phenomenon. The facts, concepts, or principles used for the explanation are appropriate to the phenomenon and accurately applied. Additionally, the student's response reflects thorough and careful research or understanding.

   3 Provides an accurate explanation of the phenomenon. The facts, concepts, or principles used for the explanation are appropriate to the phenomenon and accurately applied with no significant errors.

   2 Explains the phenomenon but misapplies some facts, concepts, or principles, or omits some facts, concepts, or principles that are important for understanding the phenomenon.

   1 Leaves out key facts, concepts, or principles in explaining the phenomenon, or does not use appropriate facts, concepts, or principles to explain the phenomenon.

B. Makes a logical prediction based on the facts, concepts, or principles underlying the explanation.

   4 Makes a verifiable prediction that reflects insight into the character of the phenomenon. The prediction is entirely appropriate to the facts, concepts, or principles employed to explain the phenomenon.

   3 Makes a prediction that follows from the facts, concepts, or principles used to explain the phenomenon. The student's prediction can be verified.

   2 Makes a prediction that reflects a misunderstanding of some aspects of the facts, concepts, or principles used to explain the phenomenon, or makes a prediction that presents difficulties for verification.

   1 Makes a prediction that cannot be verified.

(Additional criteria are offered by the authors. However, those given here are sufficient to illustrate the kinds of judgments made.)

Figure 10-3

Sample Performance Assessment for "Using Knowledge Meaningfully in Experimental Inquiry" (Reprinted from "Appendix B: Task/Situation Specific Rubrics" from *Performance Assessment Using Dimensions of Learning* (exercise p. 109, criteria, pp. 127–128) by R. J. Marzano, D. J. Pickering, and J. McTighe, 1993, Aurora, CO: Mid-continent Regional Educational Laboratory. Copyright 1993 by McREL. Reprinted by permission of the publisher.)

- *comparative* thinking is reasoning in terms of similarities and differences between and among things.
- *inferential* thinking is defined in terms of inductive and deductive reasoning.
- *evaluative* thinking is expressing and defending an opinion or point of view.

As with previous frameworks, we can use simple probes to illustrate the assessment challenges presented by each of Quellmalz's kinds of reasoning. These appear in Table 10–5, along with simple definitions and trigger words or action verbs that can point exercises toward the various types of reasoning.

Insights into the Quellmalz Framework.   Here are a few refinements to hone your understanding of the Quellmalz framework:

- All four kinds of reasoning beyond recall require the application of knowledge—all reasoning and problem solving arises from a knowledge base. And remember, the appropriate knowledge base can be tapped through memory or through the use of reference materials.

- Analysis, as defined in this framework, is more than simply rote reading of a memorized list of components. It involves reflectively restructuring knowledge in new ways. I will amplify this point below.

- Comparison can be comparison or contrast—similarities or differences. Complex comparisons require analysis of the things to be compared to find elements that are alike.

Table 10–5
The Quellmalz Framework

Kind of Reasoning	Cognitive Process	Sample Trigger Words	Sample Probe
Recall	Master foundational knowledge	Define, list, label, name, identify	Can you restate or paraphrase the essential knowledge?
Analysis	Reason in terms of ingredients or component parts	Break down, subdivide, categorize, differentiate	What are the essential ingredients, components, or elements and how do the parts relate to the whole?
Comparison	Reason in terms of similarities and/or differences	Compare, contrast, relate, distinguish	How are these things alike or different?
Inference	Reason inductively or deductively	Anticipate, predict, hypothesize, deduce, induce	Given what you know, what would happen if we did the following?
Evaluation	Express and defend an opinion or point of view	Evaluate, judge, appraise, defend	In your opinion, which would be the best course of action? Why?

- Inference questions have one or more right answers. The questioner can frame the anticipated inference or set of inferences in advance. There may be more than one defensible inference, but the array of possibilities is finite. The questioner must know that array before asking the question.

Having said this, I hasten to point out that we must always remain open to the possibility that our students might outthink us! They may come up with solid defensible inferences that we had not considered. When this happens, they should be given credit for their insight.

- Evaluation probes always ask the students to express and defend an opinion. The focus of the evaluation is not whether the students hold the right opinion, but whether they can defend the opinion they hold. In short, the assessor must ask, Have the criteria taught and learned in class been applied in a logical manner in this response?

Time for Reflection

In the real world, complex problems rarely are solved using just one of these patterns of reasoning. More often than not, several patterns will need to be linked together to reach the goal. Identify a recent real-life problem you have confronted that required that you employ at least three of the Quellmalz reasoning patterns in combination to find a solution. Which patterns were they, and how did they relate to one another?

Matching Method to Target.   All four of the assessment methods discussed in this book can be used to assess the five kinds of reasoning in the Quellmalz framework. Table 10–6 offers simple examples, using the content knowledge of classroom assessment methods as the basis for reasoning.

The table does identify two poor-quality matches. One mismatch occurs at the union of evaluative reasoning and the selected response assessment format. The assessment of this kind of reasoning requires constructing and presenting an original defense. A right/wrong test item format will not permit this. For this reason, assessment of evaluative reasoning requires the use of one of the other three formats.

Another poor-quality match arises when we endeavor to assess recall with performance assessment. While this match can work, it makes little sense. Selected response and essay formats work far better for this kind of outcome. This is an inefficient use of a complex, labor-intensive assessment method.

A Critical Insight.   Did you notice the similarity between the recall and analysis exercises across Table 10–6? They all seem to get at component parts. What, then, is the difference? Essentially, the difference lies in the relationship between each exercise and the instruction that precedes it. In fact, this is true of any of the Quellmalz, Bloom, and Marzano patterns of reasoning that go beyond recall. Let me explain.

Let's say we've been studying various forms of government and ask our students to reflect across the various forms and brainstorm a generalized list of func-

Table 10-6
The Quellmalz Framework Transformed into Assessment Exercises

	Selected Response	Essay	Performance Assessment	Personal Communication
RECALL	What is a performance assessment?	Describe the underlying structure of a performance assessment, being sure to include all critical parts.	(Not a good option; other options fit better.)	Do you know the parts of a performance assessment? Tell me what they are.
ANALYSIS	Place each achievement target listed below into the proper category of outcomes.	Here is a sample performance assessment. How does it reflect the basic ingredients of all such tests?	Starting with this 40-item test, work backward to create a table of test specifications.	Have you ever thought about all the functions of assessment in schools? Brainstorm a list of them.
COMPARISON	Name one difference between a norm-referenced standardized test and a performance assessment.	Write an essay discussing the differences between sound and unsound assessments.	Make two parallel 10-item multiple-choice tests consisting of different items but that test the same material.	Think out loud about how performance assessment and personal communication are alike as assessment methods.
INFERENCE	If you wanted to improve this test item, which of the following actions would you take first? (List some alternative actions.)	You have been asked to evaluate your local teacher evaluation system for soundness as performance assessment. How would you proceed?	If you were to ask the student author to rewrite this essay, what three improvements would you suggest? (Present a sample essay.)	What do you think would be three likely effects of eliminating standardized tests in your community?
EVALUATION	(Not an option; constructed response required)	Which form of assessment is most prone to misuse, in your opinion? Why?	Your community believes students can't write. Here are ten samples of student writing. Is the community right? Defend your answer with analyses.	Which assessment method do you think would be most useful? Tell me why you think so.

tions of government. As they do so, we write their ideas on the chalkboard. This is clearly a personal communication–based assessment of inferential reasoning—right? Students are tapping into their knowledge of government structures, always scanning what they know about different forms to find commonalties and inferring about functions apparently common to several. An excellent complex reasoning exercise.

But then, let's say we step back from the chalkboard where the results of the brainstorm are listed, tell our students how important that list of functions is, and inform them that they had better learn it because it will be on the final next week. When this same exercise, which tapped rich inferential reasoning during class, appears as an essay exercise on the final, what kind of reasoning is it assessing?

I hope your answer is "recall." Any time prior instruction focuses students on memorizing responses, the assessment of those responses taps recall—regardless of what the exercise looks like. So how do we get beyond recall at testing time? By posing questions that the students have never seen before. These are the only kinds of exercises that engage the wheels of the problem-solving process.

The in-class brainstorming task described above assessed more than recall because the students were forced to do more than simply recall what they knew about government. When the challenge is new, the respondents must dip into their reservoir of knowledge, retrieve the right information, and use it in practiced, productive reasoning. If they have seen the question before, there is no guarantee that these steps will be required.

Please do not infer from this that turning an in-class reasoning exercise into recall items on a test is necessarily a bad idea. Sometimes, you may indeed find results of such classroom activities that are worth knowing outright. If so, put them on the test—but as recall exercises, nothing else.

An Application of the Quellmalz Framework.   Quellmalz and Hoskyn (1988) offer us relevant help in assessing student reasoning as demonstrated in their writing, by providing performance criteria developed to evaluate analytical, comparative, inferential, and evaluative thinking as presented in that writing. An example appears in Figure 10–4, depicting inferential reasoning rating scales (Hoskyn & Quellmalz, 1993).

When students are given writing exercises that require this kind of reasoning, these criteria can prove useful. Both students and teachers can learn to apply them: students when they write and evaluate their own writing, and teachers in evaluating and providing feedback on student writing.

An application of these criteria is presented in Figure 10–5, showing an example of student work and a set of ratings of that sample using the criteria given in Figure 10–4. The student was given a passage to read about a Native American boy who had found a wounded bear cub, nursed it back to health, and then released it. The boy missed the cub, so went with his grandfather to try to see if the cub was doing well. This student was then asked to infer and write about the mood that the author was trying to create, citing information from the text supporting her conclusion.

Before you read on, be sure to complete the Time for Reflection exercise on page 254.

Inference essays are evaluated according to six features: (1) stating a valid conclusion; (2) presenting evidence in support of the conclusion; (3) explaining why the evidence supports the conclusion; (4) explaining why knowing the general type of conclusion or the specific one is important (So what?); (5) presenting the interpretation in an organized, logical manner; and (6) when appropriate, considering alternative interpretations. The sixth feature is optional in evaluating students' written work, although it should routinely be considered in the lesson discussion.

Each feature is rated on a scale from 1 (low) to 4 (high). A score of one generally indicates that the feature is absent or inaccurate, while a score of four indicates that the feature is fully developed. Do not score the essay if it is off task. An explanation of the basis for each score point follows:

Conclusion/Generalization

4 The essay states a valid, acceptable conclusion. The conclusion is specific and accurate. The statement of the conclusion is elaborated by a fuller introduction that may include background, context, importance, or the types of information or evidence to be presented as support.

3 The essay simply states a specific, valid conclusion.

2 The essay implies the conclusion or generalization, but does not state it. Wrong conclusion with some evidence.

1 The conclusion is either not stated at all or it is inaccurately stated.

Supporting Evidence/Information

4 The essay presents evidence of information that is specific, accurate, relevant, and more than sufficient to support the conclusion.

3 The essay presents just enough evidence or information to support the conclusion. There may be some general descriptions of evidence or something slightly questionable. Most of the evidence is specific, accurate, relevant, and adequate to support the conclusion.

2 The evidence is not strong enough to support the conclusion. Some of the evidence may be specific, but most of it may be general or vague. Some evidence may be questionable. Evidence supports wrong conclusion.

1 Little or no evidence supports the conclusion. The evidence may be mostly vague, confusing, and inaccurate.

Explanation

4 The essay explains clearly, accurately, and thoroughly why the evidence presented supports the conclusion. Explanatory statements may summarize the relevance of the body of evidence, or may explain each type of evidence.

3 The essay presents some explanations of why most of the evidence supports the conclusion.

2 The essay may attempt an explanatory statement, but clear reasons are not given for the relevance of the evidence to the conclusion.

1 No explanations are offered, or they are confusing or inaccurate.

Figure 10–4

Criteria for Assessing Inference in Student Writing (Reprinted from *Multicultural Reading and Thinking Program Resource Notebook* (n.p.) edited by J. Hoskyn and E. Quellmalz, 1993, Little Rock, AR: Arkansas Department of Education. Copyright 1993 by Arkansas Department of Education. Reprinted by permission of the publisher.)

continued

Alternative Interpretations

4 The essay discusses how additional evidence or the same evidence may lead to different conclusions.

3 The essay states one or more alternative interpretations that may derive from the same or additional evidence; however, there is no discussion.

2 The essay asserts that there may be alternative interpretations, without specifying what they are.

1 No mention is made of alternative interpretations or the alternative offered seems completely inappropriate.

(The authors also offer scales for the remaining inference criteria. However, those listed here will suffice to illustrate the kinds of judgments made.)

Figure 10-4, *continued*

Time for Reflection

Find a colleague or classmate to work with on this activity. Both of you study and discuss the criteria spelled out in Figure 10–4 until you are quite sure you understand them. Help each other to see their meaning. Then cover up the ratings at the bottom of Figure 10–5 and independently read the sample of student writing. Each of you rate this student's reasoning performance according to the Figure 10–4 criteria, again working independently. Then compare your ratings. Do they agree? Explore any differences you find. Why did they occur? Check your work against the ratings listed at the bottom of Figure 10–5. Do they agree? What does this exercise suggest to you about how to successfully apply this subjective kind of assessment?

INVOLVING STUDENTS IN ASSESSING REASONING

To reiterate a point made earlier, our challenge is not to teach students to be thinkers. They come to us already doing it—it's wired in, so to speak. Our job is to point out how those natural reasoning processes can be used to advantage in school and beyond. The way to do this is to put students in touch with their own reasoning by providing them with (a) an understanding of their reasoning processes, (b) a vocabulary with which to communicate about those processes, and (c) the tools they need to evaluate their own reasoning.

To reach this goal, students must understand the kinds of reasoning that characterize the conceptual framework of the reasoning process used in their classrooms. They must master the language needed to converse about that process and they must develop the ability to reflect upon their own thinking and problem solving. And, perhaps most importantly, as Norris and Ennis (1989) have shown us, we must help them to take charge of their own reasoning and problem-solving proficiencies—to have a "critical spirit."

I list below several options for accomplishing this. Note that some elaborate on ideas presented in previous chapters.

- Have students think aloud when problem solving. This allows them to hear their thought processes, and makes those processes easier to reflect upon and talk about.

- Be sure your students learn to label and understand the kinds of thinking you emphasize. This provides a language to use in self-reflection and in communication about reasoning. As a matter of classroom routine, constantly model, label, and explain the kinds of reasoning being applied.

- Ask students to probe each other's reasoning. The process of searching for the proper question helps us understand our reasoning more completely.

- Offer students repeated opportunities to participate in developing sample test items that tap different kinds of reasoning, and to interpret test results in terms of the information they provide on performance in different problem-solving contexts.

- When asking questions that require reflection and thought, be sure to wait for a response. Reasoning takes time.

- Avoid questions during instruction that call for yes or no answers. Pose questions that require more complete thought and communication.

- Use "concept mapping" (Novak & Gowin, 1984) to assess analytical reasoning proficiency. In this approach, students create bursting diagrams to convey their understanding of concept relationships. Figure 10–6 shows a sample concept map about assessment. These maps reflect the complexity and ingredients in students' structures of knowledge, and efficiently evaluate analytical reasoning.

- Have students devise essay or performance assessment exercises that require the application of various kinds of reasoning. Encourage them to develop and apply scoring criteria to evaluate responses to these exercises.

- Keep the whole class involved in the thinking process as thinkers and reflectors on reasoning by calling on nonvolunteers, asking them to paraphrase, and asking them to add on to each other's thinking and to tap each other's thinking in small groups.

- Set up a classroom display reflecting the kinds of reasoning valued, including sample questions illustrating the valued outcomes.

- Have students keep journals describing the effectiveness of their reasoning and problem solving. This provides experience using the language of reasoning and in being reflective.

- Most importantly, remember that the assessment of the ability to reason and solve significant problems requires the presentation of novel challenges at assessment time. This means we must set students up for success by being sure they have access to essential knowledge via memory or reference material and by providing practice with essential reasoning processes. But then, at assessment time, we must present brand-new exercises, so they can put their reasoning tools to work.

I am infering the mood of a story about an Indian boy looking for a cub. I think the mood is joyful. Here is why.

First, it said Red Bird could hardly control his excitment, a sign of happiness can be noticed by ones excitement.

Next, it said that the singing of the birds echoed the singing of the Red Birds heart, Pink, yellow, and blue flowers danced in the breeze. That tells me that it was cheerful all around them.

Last, it said grandfather's eyes twinkled as they turned back toward the village. This meant that he was happy or joyful inside.

I think other conclusions are possible. I could have chosen peaceful. But I think there is more evidence that this story is joyful.

It is important to know the mood of the story so I can have a better understanding of the story and I can become a better reader.

Integration: 3+
The essay synthesizes strong evidence, and explanations to support a valid interpretation of mood of the story. The writer attempts discount an alternative interpretation and gives general reasons why inferring the mood of a story is important.

Conclusion: 4–
The writer briefly describes the story and states a valid conclusion, based on the evidence available in the story.

Evidence: 3+
Of the descriptions available in the text, the writer cites evidence which is sufficient, accurate and relevant.

Explanation: 4
The writer provides convincing explanations why each citation implies happiness.

Alternative Interpretation: 3–
The writer proposes a plausible alternative interpretaion; however, s/he does not explain why the alternative is not as good.

Figure 10-5
Sample of Student Writing with Inference Ratings (Reprinted from *Multicultural Reading and Thinking Program Resource Notebook* (n.p.) edited by J. Hoskyn and E. Quellmalz, 1993, Little Rock, AR: Arkansas Department of Education. Copyright 1993 by Arkansas Department of Education. Reprinted by permission of the publisher.)

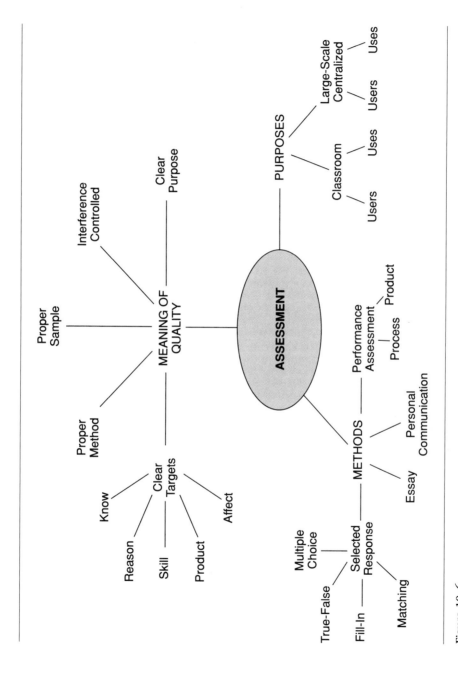

Figure 10-6
A Bursting Concept Map of Assessment

CHAPTER SUMMARY: FINDING THE PATH TO REASONING POWER

If students are to hit important reasoning and problem-solving targets—if they are to become confident, competent users of their own reasoning power, predisposed to put that power to work—they must be in touch with their capabilities in this critical performance arena. We need not teach them to think, but we must help them understand and organize their thinking so they can use it to maximum advantage. We must remember that the mind does not come with a user's guide. We can, and must, provide the needed guidance.

If we are to assist students, each of us must establish the vision of the proficient problem solver that will guide instruction in our classroom. To the extent that we can agree on this target across classrooms and grade levels, we maximize the chances of developing student proficiency over time.

So how do we choose? Back to those three criteria mentioned earlier: First, we must decide which framework makes the most sense for our students in our classroom. You need a conceptual definition of reasoning that you are willing to master completely—so completely that it becomes second nature to you in teaching and in assessing. You might wish to combine elements of different frameworks or adjust one to fit your own context. That's fine. Just become committed to whatever framework you adopt.

Second, your framework needs to make sense in the real world. Many frameworks can be translated into real-life reasoning and problem-solving contexts. Your challenge is to find a framework that allows *you* to make that translation comfortably. You will need many examples to share with your students of ways real-world problems can be resolved using whatever kinds of thinking you choose. It is only through these applications that you can help your students to both see the relevance of becoming more capable thinkers, and be motivated to take responsibility for their own reasoning and problem solving.

Third, your framework must be one that you can bring to life for your students. It must be made up of component parts that students can understand and those parts must be translated into a vocabulary they can use in conversation with you and with each other. One excellent way to share the meaning of success as thinkers with students is to teach them to reflect upon, understand, and evaluate their own reasoning, such as comparisons, inferences, or evaluations.

There are many refined conceptual frameworks out there for you to use in this endeavor. Several excellent choices were reviewed in this chapter. You must select one or some combination of these to guide your work. Consult the references cited in this chapter to learn more about these four frameworks. For further information on the assessment of reasoning, refer to the additional readings on this topic listed in Appendix A.

Our professional development challenge in preparing to assess reasoning is to understand how to translate the reasoning models we value into appropriate forms of assessment. All four basic methods—selected response, essay, performance assessment, and personal communication—can reflect valuable kinds of reasoning, if users understand and adhere to the key attributes of sound assessments: Start with a complete vision of the kind of reasoning to be assessed, select an appropriate method, sample student reasoning with enough exercises to give us confidence in assessment results, control for all those sources of extraneous interference discussed in earlier chapters, and be sure your assessments align with clear purposes for assessing.

EXERCISES TO ADVANCE YOUR LEARNING

Knowledge Outcomes

1. What criteria should educators apply in selecting or developing a vision of the reasoning process to use in their classrooms?

2. Identify and outline the elements of four conceptual frameworks described in this chapter as possible visions of the reasoning process.

3. Define ten specific examples of elements of reasoning and problem solving as presented in this chapter.

4. Identify an appropriate assessment format for each of the examples identified under number three above.

5. List three procedural keys to the effective assessment of various forms of reasoning in the classroom.

6. List as many different ways as you can to integrate the assessment of reasoning into day-to-day classroom teaching and learning.

Reasoning Outcomes

1. Given what you now know of the four conceptual frameworks presented in this chapter, analyze and compare them. What similarities and differences do you see between and among them?

2. Select a content area of interest to you, in which you have developed a strong background. Within that context, develop an exercise to tap each of the levels of Bloom's taxonomy, each of Marzano's dimensions of learning, and each of the kinds of reasoning spelled out by Quellmalz.

3. In the content area you chose in exercise two above, select an important issue about which there might be differences of opinion and analyze that issue according to Norris and Ennis's conceptual framework.

Skill Outcomes

1. Select a unit of instruction that you currently teach or will teach in the future that calls for student attainment of reasoning outcomes. Analyze the intended outcomes so you can define them in clear and specific terms that both you and your students will understand. Select proper methods for reflecting those outcomes and devise sample assessments. Keep a journal in which you reflect

upon this process as you go. What problems do you encounter? What parts go smoothly? How might you make this process easier next time? Share your analysis of outcomes, products, and journal with a colleague or classmate. Discuss the experience.

Product Outcomes

1. Evaluate the assessments you created in the skill exercise above in terms of the five standards of sound assessment.

Affective Outcomes

1. Throughout this chapter, I have argued that all kinds of thinking and reasoning, including mastery of content knowledge, are of equal importance—that, while reasoning challenges may vary in their complexity, there is no such thing as higher- and lower-order thinking. Do you agree or disagree? Why?

2. As we look to the future and anticipate the continuing explosion in the amount of available knowledge and information-processing capability, which means of mastering content knowledge will become most useful: mastery through memorization or mastery through use of reference materials? Why will this be the case, in your opinion? (Note: It is tempting to respond quickly to this question. Please resist that temptation, and reflect critically on the implications of both sides of this issue.)

3. It has been common in schools in the past to make "higher-order reasoning" a special emphasis of talented and gifted programs. It has rarely been a special thrust of remedial programs. Do you think such differentiation across program lines is appropriate for students in the future? Why?

CHAPTER 11

Performance Assessment of Skill and Product Outcomes

Chapter Objectives

As a result of studying the material presented in Chapter 11, reflecting on that material, and completing the learning exercises presented at the end of the chapter, you will:

1. Master content knowledge:
   a. Specify keys to the development of quality performance criteria.
   b. State limitations of performance assessment.
   c. Know the range of achievement targets that can be reflected in performance assessments.
   d. State the range of forms performance assessments can take in practice.

2. Be able to use that knowledge to reason as follows:
   a. Identify the kinds of skills and products that can form the basis of performance assessment exercises.
   b. Transform those important outcomes into quality exercises and scoring criteria.
   c. Understand how the attributes of sound assessment come into play in the evaluation of performance assessments.

3. Become proficient at the following skills:
   a. Be able to carry out the steps in the performance assessment development process.

4. Be able to create the following products:
   a. Devise new performance assessments that meet standards of quality.

5. Attain the following affective outcomes:
    a. Value performance assessment as a viable option for use in the classroom.
    b. See performance assessment as a valuable instructional tool in which students can and should be full partners.
    c. Regard performance assessment with caution, valuing the need to adhere to rigorous standards in development and use.

N o assessment method can surpass performance assessment for flexibility and range of useful classroom applications. Its potential for tapping valuable yet extremely complex outcomes is immense indeed. But perhaps its greatest value lies in its potential for bringing assessment into the instructional process. We began to explore the broad applicability of performance assessment in the previous chapter with a few examples of assessing reasoning. In this chapter, we will continue our exploration with more examples of teacher-developed performance assessments.

CHAPTER ROADMAP

In this chapter, we will review many performance assessment examples developed by educators from coast to coast. The darkened cells in Figure 11-1 indicate the aspects of our topic on which we will be concentrating. The primary emphasis will be placed on parts 1 and 3 of Figure 11-2, on the heart of the performance assessment matter: the developer's specification of the achievement targets (in the form of performance criteria) and corresponding scoring procedures. The examples provided vary greatly in context, ranging from reading and writing to vocal music and foreign language, including skills and products assessed from preschool through high school. You will see examples of different kinds of performance criteria and rating procedures, and reflect upon their integration into instruction. Additional comments are offered on exercises where needed.

An Example

I begin by sharing an example of skill-based performance assessment used as a powerful classroom teaching tool by a professional associate in her classroom assessment course. Her students are challenged to solve an assessment problem and present their solution to a mock school board for evaluation. The instructor's goal is to evaluate students' ability to communicate in an assessment context, among other things. Here is the assignment:

> You have been assigned to a districtwide committee whose responsibility is to plan a comprehensive assessment policy for your school system. Plan the ingredients of your policy, being sure your policy (a) guides practice both in large-scale and classroom asssessment, and articulates the rationale for your

	SELECTED RESPONSE	ESSAY	PERFORMANCE ASSESSMENT	PERSONAL COMMUNICATION
Know				
Reason				
Skill				
Product				
Affect				

Figure 11-1
Aligning Achievement Targets and Assessment Methods

inclusion of each component part. Prepare to describe your proposed district-wide assessment policy to the school board and answer their questions. Your presentation to a simulated board will be evaluated in terms of content, strength of rationale, understanding of assessment's role in instruction, and clarity and confidence of communication.

The performance criteria cover these key elements:

- Content of the policy: Does it adhere to the key attributes of a sound policy as discussed in class? Are all important elements of such a policy included?
- Soundness of rationale for including each element: Is the rationale for including each section of the policy clearly appropriate and logically applied?
- Understanding of assessment's role in instruction: Does the policy attend to all relevant purposes for assessment?
- Clarity of communication: Does the presenter provide a jargon-free, understandable explanation of the meaning of quality assessment?
- Confidence in communicating: Is the presenter confident and assertive in responding to questions?

A major segment of class time is devoted to helping students prepare for this assignment. In one instructional segment, they are divided into committees and each team is given the assignment of devising a specific rating scale for one criterion.

When criteria have been drafted, students and teacher prepare to evaluate presentations by viewing and assessing previous videotaped presentations. As they practice applying the criteria, sometimes they find they have to adjust them, and sometimes individuals need to adjust personal biases in the interest of securing consistency in ratings across evaluators. When all are trained and prepared, class members give their presentations and are evaluated.

Time for Reflection

1. Given this kind of preparation, how well do you think these students do with their presentations? Why? 2. If the instructor has a very large class in a given term, can you think of time- and labor-saving ways she might transform this assessment to make it feasible within her available resources?

This is just one of literally hundreds of such classroom applications of performance assessment developed by educators in recent years. The purpose of this chapter is to share many more examples.

Important Reminders

As you proceed down the performance assessment road for the second time in this book, please bear some important thoughts in mind. In Chapter 8, you will recall, we developed a three-part performance assessment design framework addressing performance to be evaluated, exercises, and scoring and recording procedures. That design plan is reproduced in part in Figure 11-2. Before we proceed, see if you can fill in the design alternatives available within each element on the left. After you try, check your work against Figure 8-2. Keep this design framework in mind as you study this chapter.

Standards of Quality.   Remember the key attributes of sound performance criteria given by Quellmalz (1991). Sound criteria are those that have the following characteristics:

1. reflect all of the important components of performance—the milestones in target attainment

2. reflect keys to successful performance in contexts and under conditions in which performance occurs in the real world

3. represent dimensions of performance trained evaluators can apply consistently to a set of similar tasks (i.e., they are not exercise specific)

4. are developmentally appropriate for the examinees

5. are understandable and usable by all participants in the performance assessment process, including teachers, students, parents, and the community

6. link assessment results directly into the instructional decision-making process

7. provide a clear and understandable means of documenting and communicating about student growth over time

Design Factor	Design Options
1. Clarifying Performance	
Nature of performance	1. _____
	2. _____
Focus of the assessment	1. _____
	2. _____
Performance Criteria (What is the proper focus?)	_____ _____
2. Developing Exercises	
Nature of exercises	1. _____
	2. _____
Content of exercises (What are the key elements?)	_____ _____
Number of exercises (What is this a function of?)	_____ _____
3. Scoring and Recording Results	
Level of detail in scores	1. _____
	2. _____
Recording procedures	1. _____
	2. _____
	3. _____
	4. _____
Identify the rater	1. _____
	2. _____
	3. _____
	4. _____

Figure 11-2
Performance Assessment Design Framework Revisited

As you read, evaluate the extent to which the examples provided in this chapter meet these standards.

Cautions.   This chapter includes a variety of creative and high-quality applications of performance assessment. As you read about them, keep the following important cautions in mind.

First, the examples provided do not begin to cover the broad array of possible applications, nor can these illustrations teach you everything you need to know about the vast topic of performance assessment. Rather, they are intended to trigger your imagination, stimulate your curiosity, and encourage you to learn more about this methodology.

Second, while these appear to be and in most cases are highly refined applications, still, think of them as works in progress. One of the great lessons we are learning from our experiences in designing and developing performance assessments is that the very process of devising exercises and performance criteria helps us to refine our vision of the meaning of academic success. As a result, it is best to think of any set of performance criteria as the latest version of an ever-sharpening portrait of that success.

Third, the examples provided below are evidence of the pace of development of high-quality performance assessments. In this context, it is important to take advantage of already completed work and adopt assessments developed by others. As you do so, however, remember your students. It is very important that they develop a sense of both understanding and ownership of the performance criteria. This argues against the wholesale installation of other people's criteria in the classroom. Rather, even when using criteria developed by others, it is wise to "lead" students to your adopted standards of quality through the use of the student-centered performance assessment development procedures specified in Chapter 8.

Time for Reflection

Please reread pages 181–186 in Chapter 8 on the development of performance criteria and then deal with this challenge: Assume you knew in advance the criteria you wanted your students to master. How could you adapt those Chapter 8 procedures to permit students a role in devising criteria and yet still arrive at your preselected destination? Describe your procedures.

Another important lesson we are learning as we use these assessments in the classroom is that a clear image of academic success is not enough. In other words, a refined and appropriately focused set of performance criteria is a necessary but not sufficient condition from which to derive a quality performance assessment. The other key ingredient is the meticulous preparation of raters.

Dependable performance assessors are trained, not born. And training them is very challenging work—whether they're Olympic figure skating judges, assessors of student writing, evaluators of learning disabled students, or students preparing to evaluate their own performance. Not only must the achievement target be crystal clear and the trainer experienced and qualified, but trainees must be open and willing to learn. Unless these conditions are satisfied and quality training is provided, we cannot expect our observations of and judgments about student performance to be dependable, regardless of the quality of the performance criteria.

As you read this chapter, see *possibilities*. As you reflect on what you read, think, "This will take hard work." But remember, there are many who can share the workload, enjoy the process, and learn a lot!

And finally, remember that performance assessment represents just one of four viable methods of assessment that we have at our disposal. We can use selected response, essay, and personal communication formats to tap student mastery of many of the important dimensions of procedural knowledge prerequisite to becoming skillful in performance. In addition, we can use the essay format as a proxy measure for some very sophisticated forms of performance, at a fraction of the cost. Classroom teachers faced with growing assessment challenges and shrinking resources cannot overlook these options. With these guiding thoughts in mind, then, let's explore some real-world applications of performance assessment.

PRESCHOOL PLAY-BASED ASSESSMENT

In her book, *Transdisciplinary Play-Based Assessment,* Linder (1990) provides a functional approach to working with young children. Essentially, she offers a comprehensive set of performance criteria for documenting the physical and intellectual development of preschoolers. This performance assessment is based on observations conducted in naturally occurring contexts. First, the child is placed in a rich play environment full of objects to manipulate and activities to carry out. However, no specific directions are provided. Trained and experienced assessors then carefully observe the child's actions to profile strengths and needs.

Teachers I have spoken with who have used the Linder performance assessment system report that it helps in making school readiness decisions, identifying students with special educational needs early, and placing children in proper instructional environments. They report that, with practice, they become proficient at observing and evaluating very young learners.

The dimensions of development covered and level of detail used to describe each are illustrated in Figure 11-3, presenting two of her performance expectations for "sensorimotor development," one of ten performance arenas evaluated in this system. The figure details two of fifteen subcategories of performance rated under the sensorimotor heading.

Note that judgments regarding performance take the form of checklists of skills demonstrated or not. Standards of expected performance are conveyed for comparison purposes in the form of months.

Specific procedures also are offered for transforming checklist results into inferences about development to be used in completing the summary sheet, shown in Figure 11-4. Note the overlaid directions for completing the summary. This represents a detailed and refined performance assessment scheme.

Time for Reflection

If a group of teachers decided to adopt and use an assessment system like Linder's, how could they go about training themselves *and* verifying that they had become proficient and dependable judges?

ANN ARBOR FIRST GRADE ASSESSMENT

The Ann Arbor (Michigan) Public Schools have developed early elementary performance assessments that promise to deliver academic "Success for All Students" (their

Mobility in Standing

5-6 mo.	Bounces in standing
6–12 mo.	Pulls to stand at furniture
8–9 mo.	Lower extremities more active in pull to stand Pulls to stand through kneeling, then half-kneel
8 mo.	Cruises sideways Rotates the trunk over the lower extremities
8–18 mo.	Walks with two hands held
9–10 mo.	Cruises around furniture, turning slightly in intended direction
9–13 mo.	Pulls to stand with legs only, no longer needs arms
11 mo.	Walks with one hand held Reaches for furniture out of reach in cruising Cruises in either direction, no hesitation
9–17 mo.	Takes independent steps, falls easily
10–14 mo.	Walking—stoops and recovers in play
12 mo.	Equilibrium reactions present in standing

Development of Manipulative Prehension

18–25 mo.	Separates pop beads Snips paper with scissors
18–41 mo.	Strings three to four beads
22–30 mo.	Folds paper in half
24–29 mo.	Uses forearm rotation to turn door knob
24–35 mo.	Unbuttons large buttons
28–35 mo.	Snips on line using scissors
30–35 mo.	Cuts paper in half with scissors
30–47 mo.	Buttons one or two buttons alone
36–47 mo.	Holds paper with one hand while writing with the other hand
36–59 mo.	Uses scissors to cut paper on a line
42–47 mo.	Cuts circle with scissors
48–59 mo.	Places paper clips on paper Opens small padlock with key
60–71 mo.	Colors within lines

Figure 11-3

Linder's Age Range Expectations (Reprinted from *Transdisciplinary Play-Based Assessment, A Functional Approach to Working with Young Children* (p. 243) by T. W. Linder, 1990, Baltimore, MD: Paul H. Brookes. Copyright 1990 by Paul H. Brookes Publishing Co., Inc. P.O. Box 10624, Baltimore, MD 21285-0624. Reprinted by permission of the publisher.)

Name _____ Age _____ Date _____

OBSERVATION CATEGORIES	STRENGTHS	RATING	JUSTIFICATION	NEED
General Appearance of Movement				
Muscle Tone/Strength/Endurance				
Reactivity to Sensory Input				
Stationary Play Positions				
Mobility in Play				
Other Developmental Achievements				
Prehension and Manipulation				
Motor Planning				

SUMMARY SHEET INSTRUCTIONS

Definitions of scoring criteria:

+   Child demonstrates:
1. skill within an appropriate range of development, based on age charts or other references; *and*
2. typical behavior patterns, based on professional judgment and expertise; *and*
3. good quality of performance, based on professional judgment and expertise.

−   Child demonstrates:
1. delay in development based on age charts or other references; *or*
2. deviation from normal behavior patterns; *or*
3. poor quality of performance.

√   Insufficient information was obtained. Further evaluation is required.

NA Not applicable due to the age of the child, handicapping condition, or other factors.

NO No opportunity to observe, but further evaluation is not recommended.

Procedures:

1. For each of the *Observation Categories* in the left column, indicate strengths the child exhibited within the area.
2. For each of the *Observation Categories* in the left column, indicate whether the child receives a rating of [+], [−], [√], [NA], or [NO].
3. Under the column heading *Justification*, write a brief explanation of why the child received the rating of [−] or [√]. Documentation of reason for [−] rating will assist in the identification of the child's areas of need. Documentation of reason for [√] rating may aid in selection of future assessment procedures.
4. Under the column heading *Need*, if [+] was marked, no comments are necessary. If [−] was marked, identify specific needs for intervention or support. If [√] was marked, indicate the type of evaluation needed.

Figure 11-4
Linder's Summary Sheet for Sensorimotor Guidelines (Reprinted from *Transdisciplinary Play-Based Assessment: A Functional Approach to Working with Young Children* (p. 56) by T. W. Linder, 1990, Baltimore, MD: Paul H. Brookes. Copyright 1990 by Paul H. Brookes Publishing Co., Inc., P.O. Box 10624, Baltimore, MD 21285-0624. Reprinted by permission of the publisher.)

program title). Their assessment vision is seen clearly in their first grade assessments described below. In Chapter 15, we'll see the communication system they have devised to report the results of such assessments to parents.

Ann Arbor teachers started by devising clear visions of valued achievement targets as shown in Figure 11-5. And then, first-grade faculty worked diligently, relying heavily on the most current professional literature, to devise explicit five-point rating scales for each important outcome. Examples of these scales are provided from the domain of reading, in Figure 11-6, and writing, in Figure 11-7. Note the precise language and examples used to describe points on the scales of attainment. This example reveals the great success teachers can experience when working collaboratively to devise criteria. It also clearly illustrates the use of rating scales to describe and evaluate student performance.

But remember, sound performance expectations are never simply a matter of the collective local opinions of a group of teachers or curriculum directors. Rather, those expectations must also reflect the best, most current thinking about the meaning of success as defined by the leading thinkers in the field. It is the responsibility of those who wish to devise local criteria to tap the appropriate professional literature on their own or through a qualified consultant to assure a tight connection to the discipline to be evaluated.

Evaluations of this assessment system among Ann Arbor primary-level teachers reveal them to be positive about the amount of information and level of detail they can derive about student achievement.

EXAMPLES OF MATH PERFORMANCE ASSESSMENT

Recent refinements of math outcomes by the National Council of Teachers of Mathematics (NCTM) (1989) have given rise to an impressive array of experiments in performance assessment in this achievement domain. NCTM contends that all students must attain appropriate levels of mathematical literacy by meeting five basic standards:

- learn to value mathematics
- become confident in their ability to do mathematics
- become mathematical problem solvers
- learn to communicate in mathematics
- learn to reason mathematically

We will review three examples of innovative assessments of these kinds of math outcomes, because each example offers a glimpse of a key part of the performance assessment development puzzle. The state of Vermont responded to the math assessment challenge implicit in these outcomes by devising and pilot testing a mathematics portfolio assessment program. The state of Oregon responded by developing analytical performance rating scales for use in evaluating student solutions to

- By the end of first grade, *all* students will independently demonstrate the achievement of all of the outcomes (bold print).
- By the end of first grade, students will demonstrate appropriate growth or mastery of the desired outcomes (regular print).

Reading

Comprehension
   *1. Chooses and enjoys books independently.
   *2. Analyzes a " ++ picture book" *read to them* by identifying the story elements.
   *3. Uses pictures and words to construct meaning of an unfamiliar story.
   4. Distinguishes whether a story is realistic or fantasy using evidence *from the story.*

Fluency
   5. Reads a fictional narrative fluently.

Word Identification
   *6. Names and matches all upper and lower case letters.
   *7. Recognizes 100–120 words by sight.
   *8. Recognizes sound/symbols for consonants and digraphs at the beginning and ending of words.
   9. Sounds out three-letter words with CVC (consonant-vowel-consonant) pattern in and out of context.
   10. Uses context of sentence, paragraph, or story to identify an unknown word.

Writing

Process
   11. Identifies and uses some pre-writing strategies.
   *12. Rereads a recent draft with consistency of meaning.
   13. Responds with positive comments to another child's shared writing.

Product
   *14. Composes a draft of two or more thoughts on a topic using temporary spelling but completely understood by the writer.

Attitude
   *15. Has a positive view of own writing

*Outcomes to be assessed in the fall.

Figure 11-5
Ann Arbor Public Schools First-Grade Language Outcomes (Reprinted from "Success for All First Grade Students" (n.p.) by Department of Research Services, Ann Arbor Public Schools, 1993, Ann Arbor, MI: Author. Reprinted by permission of the publisher.)

1. Chooses and enjoys books independently.

Emerging	Developing	Achieving
Such as:	*Such as:*	*Criterion:*
Needs to have teacher select book.	Chooses appropriate book with teacher direction.	Independently chooses books to read or look at.
Flips through pages while giving attention elsewhere.	Independently chooses books used in class instruction.	*Such as:*
May refuse to select book or read book.	Spends a short time with books before directing interest elsewhere.	Spends a reasonable time with books.
Book remains on desk unopened.	Reads only with a partner.	Expresses enjoyment by talking about book ideas with teacher and/or peers.
Still reads book back-to-front.		During free time, chooses to read.
Finds other things to do in place of reading.		Enjoys books with and without a partner.

2. Analyzes a "++ picture book" *read to them* by identifying the story elements.

Emerging	Developing	Achieving
Such as:	*Criterion:*	*Criterion:*
Is learning to give full attention to the story being read.	Having heard a story, identifies two thirds of the following information (*story elements*) with prompting if necessary:	Having heard a story, identifies all of the following information (*story elements*) with prompting if necessary:
Does not attend to the story.	• Where? When? (*setting*)	• Where? When? (*setting*)
Only identifies the characters; cannot identify any other story element.	• Who? (*characters*)	• Who? (*characters*)
When asked questions about the story:	• What is the problem?	• What is the problem?
• does not respond	• What happens? (*most major events*)	• What happens? (*most major events*)
• answers are off subject.	• How is the problem solved? (*resolution*)	• How is the problem solved? (*resolution*)

Such as:

When questioned:
- gives general gist of information but not specifics.
- responds with one/two word answers.

Such as:

Communicates story information through any of the following:
- oral retelling,
- written retelling,
- responding to direct questions,
- role playing/dramatization,
- puppets,
- drawing/visual representation.

Retells story in correct sequence—beginning, middle, and end.

3. Uses picture clues and words to construct meaning of an unfamiliar story. (Note: Not all picture books can be used for this assessment; e.g., some pictures do not reflect the text.)

Emerging	Developing	Achieving
Such as:	*Such as:*	*Criterion:*
Does not look at pictures.	Struggles with decoding, then looks at the pictures.	Checks back and forth between words and pictures to build a more complete meaning than either the words or the pictures alone could provide.
When looking at pictures, does not make connections with the text.	Uses picture clues after the teacher has suggested using them.	
Teachers needs to model the use of picture clues.	Frequently makes incorrect inferences from pictures.	*Such as:*
Makes illogical inferences.	Carefully constructs meaning through pictures only.	Reads words rather than paraphrasing or picture reading.
Flips through pages without reading.	Can decode words but does not construct meaning.	Looks at pictures before and during reading, without teacher prompt.
Reads back to front of book.		Uses pictures to help decode words.
Struggles to decode words and gets no meaning.		Makes correct inferences from the pictures.

Figure 11-6

Sample of Ann Arbor's First-Grade Language Assessment Criteria (Reprinted from "Success for All First Grade Students" (n.p.) by Department of Research Services, Ann Arbor Public Schools, 1993, Ann Arbor, MI: Author. Reprinted by permission of the publisher.)

13. Responds with positive comments to another child's shared writing. (Note: This can be demonstrated in large or small groups, or in pairs.)

Emerging	Developing	Achieving
Such as:	*Such as:*	*Criteria:*
Reluctant to share own writing with peers.	Occasionally willing to share own writing with peers.	Comments relate positively to another child's writing and/or illustration, not the delivery.
Unable to find anything positive to say about another child's writing.	Comments may:	Cites a reason to support comments (e.g., "Jamal, I like the way you talk about your dog." [Why?] "Because you tell how naughty he is").
Never volunteers ideas.	● relate to the delivery only (e.g., "La-Toya was funny when she read her story").	
	● not be relevant to child's writing (e.g., Billy writes about his pet dog. Student responds "Billy and I went to the park").	*Such as:*
	● refer to child's topic but not the writing (e.g., Susie wrote about her cat. Student responds, "I have a cat, too").	Kinds of comments may reflect:
		● descriptive adjectives (color, size)
		● particularly interesting words (fluffy)
		● feelings (happy, angry, scared)
		● opinions (like, dislike)

14. Composes a draft of two or more thoughts on a topic using temporary spelling but completely understood by the teacher.

Emerging	Developing	Achieving
Such as:	*Such as:*	*Criterion:*
Writes with pictures, scribbles, letter strips.	Needs some teacher prompting.	Independently composes two or more connected thoughts on a topic using temporary spelling.
Cannot begin task.	Composes a draft following a sentence pattern:	
Finds distractions to avoid the task.	*"I like apples." "I like oranges."*	*Such as:*
Writes lists of words.	Illustration does not match the text.	Examples of connected thoughts:
Copies from books, classroom print, other student's writing.	Only writes one thought.	*"I like apples. They grow on trees."*
Teacher needs to assign a topic.	Needs help selecting a topic.	Illustration, if present, matches the text.
Uncomfortable/unwilling to use temporary spelling.	Willing to use temporary spelling, even though difficult.	Initiates own topic from pre-writing activity.
		Uses temporary spelling with ease.

15. Has a positive view of own writing.

Emerging	Developing	Achieving
Such as:	*Such as:*	*Criterion:*
Does not attempt to draw or write independently.	Willing to write but needs reassurance and support.	Confidently and independently demonstrates a positive attitude toward own ability to write.
Frequently says *"I can't write."*	Willing to share writing—with encouragement.	*Such as:*
Does not want others to see, hear, or read his/her writing.	Occasionally shows pride in writing.	Eagerly begins to write when directed.
Groans when asked to write.		Seeks opportunities to share writing with others.
		Shows pride in own writing:
		"I can write."
		"Look at this!"
		"See my story."

Figure 11-7

Sample of Ann Arbor's First-Grade Writing Assessment Criteria (Reprinted from "Success for All First Grade Students" (n.p.) by Department of Research Services, Ann Arbor Public Schools, 1993, Ann Arbor, MI: Author. Reprinted by permission of the publisher.)

open-ended math problems. The QUASAR project was launched to use student responses to complex problems to assess ability to solve problems, reason, and communicate mathematically. All three assessments were developed by teachers and offer the basic ingredients needed to forge close links to instruction.

The Vermont Assessment

Vermont teachers were the key players in the development of their statewide math assessment (Vermont Department of Education, 1990), thus assuring its relevance for the classroom. Knowing that the evaluation would be based on the examination of student work as presented in a portfolio, teacher committees spent six months devising criteria for evaluating the quality of the products contained in those portfolios. The project report provides an excellent description of a group of educators working collaboratively to devise performance criteria.[1]

> The committee began with a discussion of the emphasis for the portfolio content. The discussion focused on problem solving, communication, conceptual understanding, and math empowerment/disposition. Committee members worked to come to a common understanding of each of these terms, attempted to illustrate the concepts with examples of student work, and identified the elements of each concept that are critical to instruction.
>
> The committee's work was grounded in the products of Vermont classrooms. During these six months, the committee members reviewed samples of student work from their own classrooms, and worked with their colleagues to produce possible portfolio entries. They looked for evidence for each of the criteria, and identified what distinguished work of higher quality from other work with respect to the criteria. These qualitative differences were used to define the scale points for each criterion.
>
> The development process built on itself. As draft criteria and scales emerged, the committee applied the criteria to actual student products. Committee members returned to their classes and developed new tasks that would produce the kinds of information needed to fairly assess student skills with respect to criteria. They experimented with better ways of capturing more of the student's approach and decision making. Committee members shared the revised criteria with colleagues, and helped them capture examples of student learning that could be evaluated in terms of criteria.
>
> At each subsequent committee meeting, the criteria were applied to new samples of student work. Revisions to criteria were made, and ways were recorded to help teachers improve their assessment of student problem solving, to capture more of the "how and the why" of problem solving, and to make the process more manageable. The scoring criteria and the recommendations for program change articulated in this report reflect the work of this committee of Vermont educators. (p. 3)

Among the design decisions made during this process were that part of the evaluation would be based on best pieces of student work, and those pieces would be

---

[1]The following quotations are reprinted from "Looking Beyond 'The Answers': The Report of Vermont's Mathematics Portfolio Assessment Program," by the Vermont Department of Education, 1990 (Pilot Year 1990–1991) Montpelier, VT: Author. Reprinted by permission of the publisher.

evaluated in terms of the level of problem solving and communication proficiency exhibited. These two performance criteria were further subdivided as follows:

Problem-Solving Skills

>   PS1. Understanding of the Task
>
>   PS2. Selection of Approaches/Procedures/Strategies
>
>   PS3. Use of Reflection, Justification, Analysis, Verification in Problem Solving
>
>   PS4.–Findings, Conclusions, Observations, Connections, Generalizations

Mathematical Communication Skills

>   MC1. Language of Mathematics
>
>   MC2. Mathematical Representations
>
>   MC3. Clarity of Presentation (p. 4)

This meant that each of these seven elements had to be transformed into rating scales. One of the seven developed scales, PS2, is reproduced below to illustrate the richness of its description of success.

> Most problems have multiple ways in which they can be solved. Over time, students develop a repertoire of approaches, procedures, or strategies to solve problems. Strategies can include simple guessing, guessing and checking, systematic listing, using some form of manipulative, using Venn diagrams, using grids to record possible combinations, using formulas, and applying algorithms. There should not be just one way to solve a problem. Math teachers now recognize that it is more important to teach students multiple approaches to problem solving, and to let them choose methods that work for them.

> Although many different ways should be valued, selection of a strategy that can lead to an answer remains a goal. Students who select "guess and check" as a strategy for a problem that will take years to solve in that way should be able to evaluate the strategy and recognize that it is not viable, and they should select another approach.

> The rating scale for Quality of Approaches is:

> 1.   Inappropriate or unworkable approach or procedure
>
> 2.   Appropriate approach/procedure some of the time
>
> 3.   Workable approach
>
> 4.   Efficient or sophisticated approach or procedure

> At the first level, the student has chosen an approach or procedure that will not lead to a solution for the task. The second level allows for the complexity of some tasks which will call on students to complete multiple tasks within the exercise. In the event that the approach or procedure is workable for some of the task, but not all, then the response is a level 2.

> If the approach or procedure is viable and can lead to a solution, the piece is rated at a level 3. There are many routes to a solution, and each of these is treated as an equally acceptable strategy for this criterion. The most common approaches, as well as others, seemingly more cumbersome or inefficient responses, earn a rating of 3. There will be times when students provide very sophisticated strategies to solve a problem.

When rating a piece for the approach or procedure we tend to look at the demonstration, the description of approach, and the actual student products or drafts, scratch paper, and other artifacts of the problem-solving process. Problem solving cannot be "right answer" focused; the key to effective problem solving lies in the strategies one uses to attack the problem and the skills one uses to reflect on the process, to check one's work, and to verify one's decisions. In order to communicate the importance of the process, this criterion, which we sometimes refer to as the "how" of problem solving, emphasizes the approach and the viability of the strategies adopted by the student.

We recognize that students do not always record the procedures they follow, and we believe we must work toward increasing the attention students give to the process, as opposed to "the answer." We need to ask students, "What are you doing?" and have them describe the process in precise terms. The importance of process in problem solving suggests that process is the answer to many of these tasks. It is also important to note that students do not always label their strategies (nor should they, necessarily), and raters must try to follow and label the student's approach based on the record of work that students keep. It falls to professional judgment to infer what the student adopted as an approach. (p. 6)

Imagine six more scales like this designed for application in evaluating best pieces of student work. In combination, these represent key components of a high-resolution assessment of mathematical power. As a result, the Vermont assessment offers the potential of stretching student, teachers, and parents far beyond "number or percent correct" as a definition of mathematical power!

Remember our opening caution about these assessments representing "works in progress?" A careful analysis of the degree of agreement among raters independently evaluating these Vermont math portfolios revealed a lack of agreement among them regarding students' levels of proficiency (Koretz, McCaffrey, Klein, Bell, & Stecher, 1992). This same analysis also suggests that math exercises collected in the portfolios were not sufficient to permit confident generalizations to the larger domain of student math problem-solving proficiency. As a result, Vermont is instituting procedures to refine their sampling, performance criteria, and rater training systems.

As this work is completed, the utility of this system for classroom assessment can be established. To reach this goal, teachers (and subsequently their students) ultimately must be trained to internalize and apply the generalizable criteria dependably and efficiently. Followup analyses suggest that they are doing so, as Vermont refinements are improving assessment quality (Koretz, Klein, McCaffrey, & Stecher, 1993).

Time for Reflection

If you were in charge of this assessment and found a lack of agreement among raters of the math portfolios, what procedures would you implement to increase agreement? Where might the problems be? Be specific, listing as many possible causes as you can and procedures you might take to correct them.

The Oregon Experience

For over a decade, the state of Oregon has pioneered the development of analytical writing assessment schemes and has led efforts to integrate such performance assessments into instruction. They continue in this leadership role by being among the first to generalize this technology into the realm of math performance assessment. Like Vermont, Oregon used the NCTM standards as their vision of success, assembled experienced math teachers, and engaged them in devising performance assessment criteria to be used in evaluating written student solutions to complex, open-ended math problems.

They are currently pilot testing four such criteria: understanding the problem, mathematical procedures, problem-solving strategies, and mathematical communication. The definitions of these criteria are shown in Figure 11-8, and two of the asso-

---

Understanding the Problem

Understanding the problem includes the ability to interpret the problem and choose appropriate information while applying a strategy for a solution.

Students demonstrate conceptual understanding when they provide evidence that they can use models, diagrams, or varied representations of concepts; when they compare, contrast, or integrate related concepts; or when they interpret the assumptions.

Mathematical Procedures

Mathematical procedures are the ability to demonstrate appropriate use of mathematics. It is the mathematics the student chooses to use and the selection and correct application of appropriate procedures.

Students demonstrate procedural knowledge when they use numerical algorithms in an efficient manner; read and produce graphs and tables; execute geometric constructions; verify and justify the correctness of a procedure; or when they extend or modify the problem.

Problem-Solving Strategies

Problem solving requires the use of many skills, often in certain combinations, before the problem is solved.

Students demonstrate problem-solving strategies with clearly focused, good reasoning that leads to a successful resolution of a problem.

Mathematical Communication

Mathematical communication is the use of symbols and terms which attain specific, and sometimes different, meanings to common words. Effective communication is essential to learning and knowing mathematics.

Students demonstrate communication through the meanings they attach to the concepts and procedures in their response. Also through their fluency in explaining, understanding, and evaluating the ideas expressed in mathematics.

Figure 11-8

Oregon Dimensions of Problem Solving (Reprinted from "Dimensions of Mathematics Scoring Guide" (n.p.) by the Oregon Department of Education, July, 1993, Salem, OR: Author. Copyright 1993 by Oregon Department of Education. Reprinted by permission of the publisher.)

ciated rating scales are presented in their entirety in Figure 11-9 as illustrations. These represent additional examples of five-point rating scales with points 1, 3, and 5 specifically defined. Scores of 2 and 4 are available for use also, if the rater determines that a response lies between two points on the score continuum.

Criteria such as these permit the creation of the same kind of collaborative environment in math classrooms that we find these days characterizing writing instruction. Students can be given complex, open-ended math problems to solve, are taught to understand and apply these kinds of performance criteria, and then go to work solving problems, evaluating their own and each other's work while the teacher plays the role of coach and advisor.

The QUASAR Project

This national project is funded by the Ford Foundation to promote the acquisition of thinking and reasoning skills in mathematics, particularly among middle

---

Conceptual Understanding

Conceptual Understanding includes the ability to interpret the problem and select appropriate information to apply a strategy for solution. Evidence is communicated through making connections among the problem situation, relevant information, and logical/reasonable responses.

5 FULL CONCEPTUAL UNDERSTANDING: The student uses all relevant information to solve a problem.
- The student's answer is consistent with the question/problem.
- The student is able to translate the problem into appropriate mathematical concepts.
- The student uses all relevant information in the problem to solve the problem.

3 PARTIAL CONCEPTUAL UNDERSTANDING: The student is able to extract the "essence" of the problem but is unable to use this information to solve the problem.
- The student is only partially able to make connections between/among the concepts.
- The student's solution is not fully related to the question.
- The student understands one portion of the task completely, but not the complete task.

1 LACK OF CONCEPTUAL UNDERSTANDING: The student's solution is inconsistent or unrelated to the question.
- The student translates the problem into inappropriate mathematical concepts.
- The student uses incorrect procedures without understanding the concepts related to the tasks.
- The student's focus is on the solution.

Figure 11-9
Oregon Dimensions of Problem Solving—Dimensions of Mathematics Scoring Guide (Reprinted from "Dimensions of Mathematics Scoring Guide" (n.p.) by the Oregon Department of Education, July, 1993, Salem, OR: Author. Copyright 1993 by Oregon Department of Education. Reprinted by permission of the publisher.)

school students in disadvantaged communities (Silver, 1991). To assess program impacts, project staff developed the QUASAR Cognitive Assessment Instrument (Lane, 1993), consisting of open-ended exercises like the example shown in Figure 11-10 to be evaluated using the five-point holistic rating scale depicted in Figure 11-11.

In this case, note that the holistic scale includes common elements across levels. This enhances classroom applicability because teachers can devise analytical scales that reflect each of the common elements, if they wish. Such adjustments can permit more detailed feedback to students if needed.

SCIENCE ASSESSMENT

Citing reform in the science curriculum favoring hands-on problem solving and a refined sense of the student's active role in constructing meaning from learning experiences as raters, Shavelson, Baxter, and Pine (1991) have begun to experiment with "hands on" assessment of science achievement.

Problem-Solving Skills and Strategies

Problem solving requires the use of many skills, often in certain combinations, before the problem is solved. Students demonstrate problem-solving strategies with clearly focused, good reasoning that leads to a successful resolution of a problem.

5 EVIDENCE OF THOROUGH/INSIGHTFUL USE OF SKILLS/STRATEGIES: The skills and strategies used show some evidence of insightful thinking to explore the problem.
  • The student's work demonstrates some originality.
  • The student's work is clear and focused.
  • The skills/strategies used are appropriate and demonstrate some insightful thinking.
  • The student gives possible extensions or generalizations to the solution or the problem.

3 EVIDENCE OF ROUTINE OR PARTIAL USE OF SKILLS/STRATEGIES: The skills and strategies used do have some focus but clarity is limited.
 • The student applies a strategy which is only partially useful.
 • The student's strategy is not fully executed.
 • The student starts the problem appropriately, but changes to an incorrect focus.
 • The student's work is clear and focused, but not applicable to the problem.
 • The student recognizes the pattern or relationship, but expands it incorrectly.

1 LIMITED EVIDENCE OR SKILLS/STRATEGIES: The skills and strategies used lack a central focus and the details are sketchy or not present.
  • The procedures used are not recorded (i.e., only the solution is present).
  • Strategies are used randomly.
  • The student does not explore the problem fully looking for concepts, patterns, or relationships.
  • Organization is haphazard and disjointed.
  • The student fails to see alternative solutions and the problem requires them.

Figure 11-9, *continued*

Task 1: Mathematical Content: Data Analysis/Statistics
(Graph Reading and Interpretation)

Below is a graph of the activities that make up an average school day for Ellen.

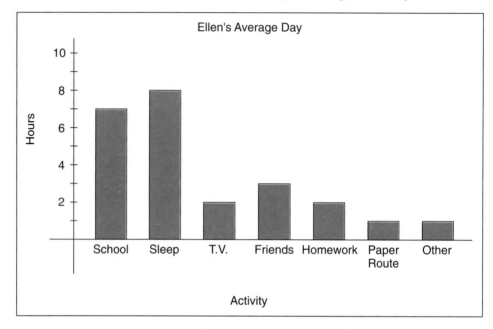

Write a story about one day in Ellen's life based on the information in the graph.

Desired Responses:

We would expect a student to write a story that incorporates both dimensions of the graph—the various activities in Ellen's day and how long each one takes. The student should express the situation in realistic terms such as placing the events in chronological order. For example:

Ellen woke up one hour early to do her paper route before going to school. After school, she and her friends went to the mall for 3 hours. Ellen wanted to watch her favorite shows on T.V. that night, so when she got home from the mall, she went right to her room to do her homework. It took her 2 hours to do her homework which left her plenty of time to see her shows. After watching T.V. for 2 hours she got ready for bed, tired after a long day.

Figure 11-10

Sample Assessment Tasks and Possible Student Responses (Reprinted from "The Conceptual Framework for the Development of a Mathematics Performance Assessment Instrument" by S. Lane, 1993, *Educational Measurement: Issues and Practice, 12*(2), pp. 16–23. Copyright 1993 by National Council on Measurement in Education. Reprinted by permission of the publisher.)

Score Level 4

Mathematical knowledge: Shows understanding of the problem's mathematical concepts and principles; uses appropriate mathematical terminology and notations; and executes algorithms completely and correctly.

Strategic knowledge: May use relevant outside information of a formal or informal nature; identifies all the important elements of the problem and shows understanding of the relationships between them; reflects an appropriate and systematic strategy for solving the problem; and gives clear evidence of a solution process, and solution process is complete and systematic.

Communication: Gives a complete response with a clear, unambiguous explanation and/or description; may include an appropriate and complete diagram; communicates effectively to the identified audience; presents strong supporting arguments which are logically sound and complete; may include examples and counter-examples.

Score Level 3

Mathematical knowledge: Shows nearly complete understanding of the problem's mathematical concepts and principles; uses nearly correct mathematical terminology and notations; executes algorithms completely; and computations are generally correct but may contain minor errors.

Strategic knowledge: May use relevant outside information of a formal or informal nature; identifies the most important elements of the problems and shows general understanding of the relationships between them; and gives clear evidence of a solution process, and solution process is complete or nearly complete, and systematic.

Communication: Gives a fairly complete response with reasonable clear explanations or descriptions; may include a nearly complete, appropriate diagram; generally communicates effectively to the identified audience; presents supporting arguments which are logically sound but may contain some minor gaps.

Score Level 2

Mathematical knowledge: Shows understanding of some of the problem's mathematical concepts and principles; and may contain serious computational errors.

Strategic knowledge: Identifies some important elements of the problems but shows only limited understanding of the relationships between them; and gives some evidence of a solution process, but solution process may be incomplete or somewhat unsystematic.

Communication: Makes significant progress towards completion of the problem, but the explanation or description may be somewhat ambiguous or unclear; may include a diagram which is flawed or unclear; communication may be somewhat vague or difficult to interpret; and arguments may be incomplete or may be based on a logically unsound premise.

Score Level 1

Mathematical knowledge: Shows very limited understanding of the problem's mathematical concepts and principles; may misuse or fail to use mathematical terms; and may make major computational errors.

Figure 11-11

General Mathematics Rubric (Reprinted from "The Conceptual Framework for the Development of a Mathematics Performance Assessment Instrument" by S. Lane, 1993, *Educational Measurement: Issues and Practice, 12*(2), pp. 16–23. Copyright 1993 by National Council on Measurement in Education. Reprinted by permission of the publisher.)   *(continued)*

Strategic knowledge: May attempt to use irrelevant outside information; fails to identify important elements or places too much emphasis on unimportant elements; may reflect an inappropriate strategy for solving the problem; gives incomplete evidence of a solution process; solution process may be missing, difficult to identify, or completely unsystematic.

Communication: Has some satisfactory elements but may fail to complete or may omit significant parts of the problem; explanation or description may be missing or difficult to follow; may include a diagram which incorrectly represents the problem situation, or diagram may be unclear and difficult to interpret.

Score Level 0

Mathematical knowledge: Shows no understanding of the problem's mathematical concepts and principles.

Strategic knowledge: May attempt to use irrelevant outside information; fails to indicate which elements of the problem are appropriate; copies part of the problem, but without attempting a solution.

Communication: Communicates ineffectively; words do not reflect the problem; may include drawings which completely misrepresent the problem situation.

Figure 11-11, *continued*

The actual assignment given students included three different kinds of paper towels and asked them to find which kind absorbed the most and which the least amount of water. To solve this problem, students were provided with these materials, in addition to the paper towels:

a scale for weighing	three flat trays
tweezers	a pitcher of water
a ruler	two funnels
three water glasses	an eye dropper
a timer	a pair of scissors
three small dishes	

The scoring scheme is reproduced in Figure 11-12. Note that the scoring criteria in this case take the form of checklists of descriptors. The rater's task is to find the descriptor that most closely aligned with the performance observed. This turns out to be a quick way to rate performance on multiple criteria. In a sense, it represents the "objectively scored" version of performance assessment. With checklists, attributes of performance are present or they are not. Also note the simple procedures spelled out at the bottom of Figure 11-12 for converting checklist performance into letter grades.

By all accounts, students find these kinds of hands-on science exercises both engaging and challenging. As a result, the atmosphere surrounding assessments of these kinds is generally quite positive. Motivation to perform well can be very high.

Student_____ Observer_____ Score_____

1. Method for Getting Towel Wet
   A. Container   **B.** Drops   **C.** Tray (surface)   **D.** No Method
Pour water in/put towel in   Towel on tray/pour water on
Put towel in/pour water in   Pour water on tray/put towel in
1 pitcher or 3 beakers/glasses

2. Saturation   **A.** Yes   **B.** No   **C.** Controlled (same amount of water—all towels)

3. Determine Result
   A. Weigh towel
   B. Squeeze towel/measure water (weight or volume)
   C. Measure water in/out
   D. Count number of drops until saturated
   E. Irrelevant measurement (i.e., time to soak up water, see how far drops spread out, feel
      thickness)
   F. Other_____

4. Care in Saturation and/or Measuring   Yes   No   A little sloppy (+/−)

5. Correct Result   Most   Least

Grade	Method	Saturate	Determine Result	Care in Measuring	Correct Answers
A	Yes	Yes	Yes	Yes	Both
B	Yes	Yes	Yes	No	One or both
C	Yes	Controlled	Yes	Yes/No	One or Both
D	Yes	No *or*	Inconsistent	Yes/No	One or Both
F	Inconsistent *or*	No *and*	Irrelevant	Yes/No	One or Both

Figure 11-12
Scoring Scheme for Science Assessment (Reprinted from "Performance Assessment in Science" by R. J. Shavelson, G. P. Baxter, and J. Pine, 1991, *Applied Measurement in Education* (Special Issue, 1991), (n.p.). Copyright 1991 by Lawrence Erlbaum Associates, Inc. Reprinted by permission of the publisher.)

ASSESSMENT IN THE ARTS

During the late 1980s, a project emerged in the Pittsburgh, Pennsylvania schools that both sharpened our thinking about the meaning of success in the arts and started us down the road to rigorous, student-centered art assessment. The project, called "Arts Propel," operates on the assumption that learning requires interaction among production, perception and reflection.[2]

---

[2]The quotation is reprinted from *Arts Propel: A Handbook for Music* by Lyle Davidson, Carol Myford, Donna Plasket, Larry Scripp, Spence Swinton, Bruce Torff, & Janet Waanders. Copyright 1992 by Educational Testing Service, Princeton, NJ (on behalf of Project Zero, Harvard Graduate School of Education). Reprinted by permission of the publisher.

Production [is] a perspective taken by the music maker or performer. This involves two strands: knowledge of the domain (how to play an instrument or critique a performance) and what we call authorship, or a willingness to take personal responsibility for work in that domain (ranging from eager citizenship in the ensemble to original or prolific arranging, improvising, or composing).

Perception [is] a broad-based dimension that includes the perspective of the active listener as well as the maker of art. The perceptual skills of the active listener involve particular aural skills (e.g., ability to match pitch, or hearing that a pitch or rhythm is incorrect) applied to one's own performance or that of others. Perception is also more general (e.g., awareness of form and style or sensitivity to interpretations) and even extends to one's social perception (e.g., understanding critiques of one's work or listening and then planning revisions of work with others).

Reflection also has a broad meaning. It includes reflection as the perspective of the evaluation of productions and perceptions and as the interpersonal aspect of understanding work in the domain. Reflection is thinking over what one has grasped perceptually. It involves both self-knowledge ("What am I after?") and self-assessment ("Did I get there?"); and self-correction in a content of knowledge of the materials of music ("How do I get closer?").

This philosophy led these educators to define key elements of sound performance (pun intended!) and to share that definition with performers for purposes of self-assessment. Figure 11-13 shows a sample Arts Propel rating sheet. Again we see the precise use of language to describe performance, this time in the context of an individual music lesson.

CALIFORNIA HISTORY–SOCIAL SCIENCE ASSESSMENT

One strength of performance assessment is its potential for assessing student achievement in those contexts where educators are integrating different curricular areas. By centering on important aspects of student performance in one complex assessment, we strive to more closely align the school experience to life beyond school, where many proficiencies might be needed at one time, and to assess with maximum efficiency by gathering information on a number of proficiencies at once.

Another strength of performance assessment is its flexibility to focus evaluation on group achievement in addition to individual performance. In these times of cooperative learning, we value group interaction outcomes, too. Since it makes no sense to give multiple-choice tests on mastery of cooperative group interaction skills, we are compelled to turn to performance assessment.

The California Assessment Program History-Social Science Group Performance Assessment (California Department of Education, 1991) provides a rich example of an assessment that combines these values for integrated curriculum and cooperative learning.

The assessment arises out of exercises that call upon students to study materi-

DOMAIN PROJECT: INDIVIDUAL LESSON

ENSEMBLE OR CLASS: _____ [VOICE] GRADE LEVEL(S):_____ (7-90 VERSION)	TEACHER SCORING STUDENT PERFORMANCE		
	1	2	3
DATE: _____			
TEACHER: _____ DATE:			
STUDENT: _____ CONDITION:			
VOCAL PERFORMANCE EXECUTION DIMENSIONS MUSIC PERFORMED: SCORE = NA IF NOT APPLICABLE			
Pitch Production* [1.0-1.9] = seldom performs pitches accurately or securely; [2.0-2.9] = sometimes performs with accurate pitch but with frequent or repeated errors; [3.0-3.9] = mostly accurate and secure pitches but with few isolated errors; [4.0-4.9] = virtually no errors and very secure pitches;			
Rhythm/Tempo Production* [1.0-1.9] = seldom performs durations accurately or with a steady tempo; [2.0-2.9] = sometimes performs durations accurately but with erratic pulse or frequent durational errors; [3.0-3.9] = mostly accurate rhythm and pulse with few durational errors; [4.0-4.9] = secure pulse and rhythmically accurate;			
Diction* [1.0-1.9] = seldom able to regulate vowel colors or consonants; [2.0-2.9] = generally consistent vowel color with some attempt to regulate consonant sounds; [3.0-3.9] = consistent vowel colors with increased control of consonants; [4.0-4.9] = maintains consistent control of diction;			

Figure 11-13

Sample Arts Propel Rating Sheet (Reprinted from *Arts Propel: A Handbook for Music* (n.p.)
by Lyle Davidson, Carol Myford, Donna Plasket, Larry Scripp, Spence Swinton, Bruce Torff,
& Janet Waanders. Copyright 1992 by Educational Testing Service, Princeton, NJ (on behalf
of Project Zero, Harvard Graduate School of Education). Reprinted by permission of the
publisher.)   *(continued)*

Dynamics (if applicable)* [1.0-1.9] = seldom able to control dynamics; [2.0-2.9] = generally controls dynamics with some responses to score markings; [3.0-3.9] = consistent dynamics and responses to score markings;			
Timbre or Tone Quality* [1.0-1.9] = uncontrolled tone production throughout all registers of voice; [2.0-2.9] = occasionally controls timbre in one register; [3.0-3.9] = generally controls timbre in more than one register; [4.0-4.9] = maintains consistent control throughout registers;			
Posture (if applicable) (Observed by Teacher During Performance) [1.0-1.9] = seldom attempts to use appropriate posture or diaphragm support; [2.0-2.9] = poor posture or support sometimes interferes with sound production; [3.0-3.9] = mostly consistent posture or support only within limited range; [4.0-4.9] = maintains consistent control and support throughout registers;			
Breath Control* [1.0-1.9] = no use of support mechanism; [2.0-2.9] = inconsistent use of support mechanism; [3.0-3.9] = consistent use of support mechanism; [4.0-4.9] = manipulates support mechanism for a variety of musical effects.			
[*Most conservative scoring = assign lowest possible score based on any or all of the factors listed]	(make additional comments on back)		

Figure 11-13, *continued*

als, interact, and prepare a resulting written document. California's exercise development guidelines hold that the group exercise must do the following:

1. be based on history-social science content
2. require higher-order thinking skills
3. involve discussion and activities by groups
4. include written exercises

An exercise description follows:

> All students will have an ISSUE or a theme (CONTENT) for which they will offer a response or SOLUTION, using a HISTORICAL PERSPECTIVE, through a COLLABORATIVE PROCESS, that will be assessed COLLECTIVELY and will include some INDIVIDUAL writing.
>
> This class will be divided into small groups to analyze primary and secondary source materials that reflect different points of view. After reading and discussing the documents, each group will decide on a position that it will share orally with the entire class. The evaluators and students will ask the small groups questions about their position.
>
> Follow-up activities will include individual writing of a short memorandum or a paragraph and then a culminating activity. For this, students will respond to a specific prompt about the issue. In these writings, students will support or oppose a view expressed in the presentations or state a personal viewpoint which is substantiated with facts and examples drawn from their knowledge of history-social science and participation in the group task.
>
> In some instances, instead of an essay, students can have the option of creating a drawing or cartoon to which they attach a brief one-paragraph explanation. (p. 6)

As the group interaction unfolds, an observer watches and evaluates according to criteria such as those detailed in Figure 11-14. Note that these particular criteria permit the rater to translate student performance into a precise gradient of points. These are registered on a score report, a sample of which is shown in Figure 11-15. Note also that the number of points available varies across the four major performance criteria. These differences reflect the relative importance of each for successful overall performance. Such differential weighting of criteria is perfectly acceptable if it adds precision to the resulting vision of success.

FOREIGN LANGUAGE ASSESSMENT

It is advisable when creating performance assessments to generate performance criteria that can be used to evaluate student achievement across a range of possible exercises. This permits the user to sample student performance across multiple con-

	LEVEL I (1-3 points)	LEVEL II (4-6)	LEVEL III (7-9)	LEVEL IV (10-12)	LEVEL V (13-16)	LEVEL VI (17-20)
COLLABORATION	Exclusive reliance on one spokesperson Little interaction Sporadic discussions Some students are disinterested or distracted	Strong reliance on spokesperson Only one or two persons interact Brief discussions Discussion not entirely centered on topic	Some reliance on spokespersons At least 2 students encourage interaction Discussion focuses mostly on documents and topic	At least half the students confer or present ideas Group shows some ability to interact Attentive reading and discussion of documents and listening Some evidence of discussion of alternatives	At least 3/4 of group actively participates Students show adeptness in interacting Lively discussion centers on the topic and alternatives	All students: Enthusiastically participate and share responsibility for task Refer to other opinions or alternatives in presentation and answers Show forethought and preparation in questions and answers
CRITICAL THINKING	(1-5) Little understanding or comprehension of task Uses only some of basic information provided Relies on own opinions Forms minimal conclusion based on only one or two pieces of information No mention of consequences	(6-10) Shows partial understanding of task Focuses on a single issue Uses basic information provided May include opinion as well as fact Forms conclusion after limited examination of evidence and little concern for consequences	(11-15) Shows general understanding of task Main focus on one issue but discusses at least one other idea Uses information provided and attempts to add to it Conclusion refers to some evidence and consequences	(16-20) Demonstrates good understanding of task and more than one view Uses main points of information provided and at least two other ideas Conclusion includes information and consideration of general consequences	(21-25) Demonstrates clear understanding of scope of task and several main issues Goes beyond documents and adds several relevant ideas Builds conclusion on examination of major evidence Considers several alternatives and possible consequences	(26-30) Demonstrates thorough understanding of many issues Uses extensive knowledge that is factually relevant, accurate, and consistent Conclusion shows analysis of evidence, reasonable alternatives, and a number of consequences

COMMUNICATION OF IDEAS	(1-3)	(4-6)	(7-9)	(10-12)	(13-16)	(17-20)
	Position is vague	Offers general position	Offers a specific position	Offers a clear, plausible position	Takes a well-defined position	Takes a strong, convincing position
	Presentation is brief with unrelated general statements	Presentation has only minimal organization	Presentation has basic organization	Organized argument with adequate evidence	Organized argument with good supporting evidence	Well-organized, persuasive argument with accurate, supporting evidence
	View on issue is not clear	Uses generalities to support position	Limited evidence applied to general conclusion	Considers several ideas or aspects of the issue	Discusses the major issues and shows some understanding of relationships	Discusses all significant issues with understanding of important relationships
	Statements tend to wander or ramble	Considers only one aspect of issue	Considers more than one idea or aspect of the issue			Examines the problem from several positions

KNOWLEDGE & USE OF HISTORY	(1-5)	(6-10)	(11-15)	(16-20)	(21-25)	(26-30)
	Reiterates facts without complete accuracy	Draws only on basic facts with some inaccuracies	Adds somewhat to basic facts with a fair degree of accuracy	Accurately relates other sources of information to the issue	Provides a variety of evidence	Incorporates many sources of evidence
	Barely indicates any previous historical knowledge	Refers to information to explain generally at least one part of issue	Refers to information to explain main issue and attempts to apply it to another issue	Analyzes information to explain at least one issue or concept with substantive support	Provides additional concepts for major issues	Explores major and minor historical concepts
	Almost total reliance on information provided	Limited reference to previous historical knowledge	General use of previous historical knowledge with fair degree of accuracy	Uses general ideas from previous historical knowledge with few errors	Accurately uses previous historical knowledge to examine issues involved	Extensively uses previous historical knowledge
		Strong reliance on the information provided				Shows in-depth understanding of the issue
						Relates issue to past and possible future situations

Figure 11-14

Group Performance Assessment Task—Scoring Guide (Reprinted from draft of "History-Social Science Group Assessment in California" (n.p.) by California Assessment Program, California Department of Education, 1991, Sacramento, CA: Author. Reprinted by permission of the publisher.)

Teacher_____ Period_____

☐ United States History ☐ World History

	GROUPS	POINTS	COMMENTS
1. Group and Collaborative Learning (20 points)			
Degree to which group members . . .			
adhere to task	I		_____
are involved in task	II		_____
pay attention to documents	III		_____
listen and willingly discuss differing views	IV		_____
extract, express, and share ideas and opinions	V		_____
2. Critical Thinking (30 points)			
Degree to which students . . .			
define and clarify issues	I		_____
analyze information related to the issue	II		_____
develop a position	III		_____
draw conclusions based on historical data	IV		_____
develop ideas and alternatives	V		_____
understand consequences of their position			
3. Communication of Ideas (20 points)			
Degree to which students . . .			
take a clear position	I		_____
support position with evidence in an organized and persuasive manner	II		_____
ask insightful questions	III		_____
answer questions in a concise, convincing manner	IV		_____
	V		_____
4. Knowledge and Use of History (30 points)			
Degree to which students . . .			
demonstrate knowledge and understanding of historical facts, issues, concepts, and relationships	I II		_____
use documents and other historical information to solve a problem or support a point of view	III IV		_____
refer to relevant historical data in answering questions	V		_____

LEVEL	1	2	3	4	5	6
TOTAL POINTS	16	32	48	64	82	100

_____
Evaluator

Figure 11-15
Group Performance Assessment Task—Scoring Form (Reprinted from draft of "History-Social Science Group Assessment in California" (n.p.) by California Assessment Program, California Department of Education, 1991, Sacramento, CA: Author. Reprinted by permission of the publisher.)

texts and draw more confident generalizations about proficiency. In other words, performance criteria that are exercise specific may reflect a target that is too narrow in scope.

Perhaps the best examples of generalizable performance criteria I have seen are those devised by the American Council on the Teaching of Foreign Languages (ACTFL) for use with their Oral Proficiency Interview (ACTFL, 1989). The Oral Proficiency Interview is a standardized procedure for the global assessment of functional speaking ability that relies on a trained examiner to carry on a conversation with the examinee, rating oral proficiency during the interaction, as well as afterward via audiotape recording.

The most unique and special feature of this assessment is that the proficiency guidelines that guide the rating process, developed originally by the government's Interagency Language Roundtable Testing Committee, are generic. That is, the same criteria can be applied to the evaluation of language proficiency in many languages. In fact, ACTFL currently offers training in the application of the criteria in eleven languages: Arabic, Chinese, English as a second language, French, German, Hindi, Italian, Japanese, Portuguese, Russian, and Spanish.

Another useful feature of the ACTFL rating system is that it begins with four major levels of proficiency, as depicted in Figure 11-16. As you can see, each level is defined in a straightforward manner, as seen in Figure 11–17. Then each is divided into sublevels to create a continuous eight-point rating scale. All four levels of speaking proficiency are presented along with subheads to illustrate the precise language used to judge performance in this case. Proficiency guidelines also are available from ACTFL to cover skills in listening, reading, and writing languages.

Although foreign language proficiency is a complex achievement target, these teachers and assessors have captured that complexity with thoughtful, clearly descriptive language. These kinds of criteria represent far more than rating scales. They represent the basis for communication and shared meaning between teacher and student.

Time for Reflection

Let's say you wanted to create a student-friendly version of the ACTFL criteria. What might it look like? (You needn't create the entire set. Start at the lowest level and try translating it for high schoolers who are just beginning to learn to speak a foreign language.)

TOWNSHIP DISTRICT'S SPEAKING ASSESSMENT

Teachers in the Township High School District 214 in Arlington Heights, Illinois have devised a similarly clear and well thought-out example of performance assessment in their speaking assessment. This example illustrates how a faculty can begin with an outcome clearly stated in the form of a set of goals, translate the goals into performance criteria, and then turn those visions of competence into easy-to-use rating scales. The authors of this assessment scheme report that they relied heavily on advice from Gray (1991), who had written about speaking assessment in the state of Illinois.

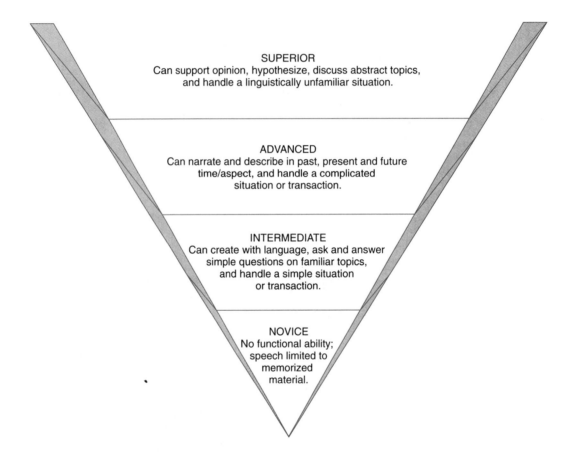

Figure 11-16
ACTFL Proficiency Levels (Adapted form *Oral Proficiency Interview: Tester Training Manual* (n.p.) by The American Council on the Teaching of Foreign Languages. Copyright 1989 by The American Council on the Teaching of Foreign Languages. Reprinted by permission.)

Novice	The Novice level is characterized by the ability to communicate minimally with learned material.
Novice-Low	Oral production consists of isolated words and perhaps a few high-frequency phrases. Essentially no functional communicative ability.
Novice-Mid	Oral production continues to consist of isolated words and learned phrases within very predictable areas of need, although quality is increased. Vocabulary is sufficient only for handling simple, elementary needs and expressing basic courtesies. Utterances rarely consist of more than two or three words and show frequent long pauses and repetition of interlocutor's words. Speaker may have some difficulty producing even the simplest utterances. Some Novice-Mid speakers will be understood only with great difficulty.
Novice-High	Able to satisfy partially the requirements of basic communicative exchanges by relying heavily on learned utterances but occasionally expanding these through simple recombinations of their elements. Can ask questions or make statements involving learned material. Shows signs of spontaneity although this falls short of real autonomy of expression. Speech continues to consist of learned utterances rather than of personalized, situationally adapted ones. Vocabulary centers on areas such as basic objects, places, and most common kinship terms. Pronunciation may still be strongly influenced by first language. Errors are frequent and, in spite of repetition, some Novice-High speakers will have difficulty being understood even by sympathetic interlocutors.
Intermediate	The Intermediate level is characterized by the speaker's ability to: • create with the language by combining and recombining learned elements, though primarily in a reactive mode; • initiate, minimally sustain, and close in a simple way basic communicative tasks; and • ask and answer questions.
Intermediate-Low	Able to handle successfully a limited number of interactive, task-oriented and social situations. Can ask and answer questions, initiate and respond to simple statements and maintain face-to-face conversation, although in a highly restricted manner and with much linguistic inaccuracy. Within these limitations, can perform such tasks as introducing self, ordering a meal, asking directions, and making purchases. Vocabulary is adequate to express only the most elementary needs. Strong interference from native language may occur. Misunderstandings frequently arise, but with repetition, the Intermediate-Low speaker can generally be understood by sympathetic interlocutors.
Intermediate-Mid	Able to handle successfully a variety of uncomplicated, basic and communicative tasks and social situations. Can talk simply about self and family members. Can ask and answer questions and participate in simple conversations on topics beyond the most immediate needs; e.g., personal history and leisure time activities. Utterance length increases slightly, but speech may continue to be characterized by frequent long pauses, since the smooth incorporation of even basic conversational strategies is often hindered as the speaker struggles to create appropriate language forms. Pronunciation may

Figure 11-17

ACTFL Foreign Language Proficiency Guideline for Speaking (Reprinted from *Oral Proficiency Interview: Tester Training Manual* (n.p.) by The American Council on the Teaching of Foreign Languages. Copyright 1989 by The American Council on the Teaching of Foreign Languages. Reprinted by permission.)

(continued)

	continue to be strongly influenced by first language and fluency may still be strained. Although misunderstandings still arise, the Intermediate-Mid speaker can generally be understood by sympathetic interlocutors.
Intermediate-High	Able to handle successfully most uncomplicated communicative tasks and social situations. Can initiate, sustain, and close a general conversation with a number of strategies appropriate to a range of circumstances and topics, but errors are evident. Limited vocabulary still necessitates hesitation and may bring about slightly unexpected circumlocution. There is emerging evidence of connected discourse, particularly for simple narration and/or description. The Intermediate-High speaker can generally be understood even by interlocutors not accustomed to dealing with speakers at this level, but repetition may still be required.
Advanced	*The Advanced level is characterized by the speaker's ability to:* • *converse in a clearly participatory fashion,* • *initiate, sustain, and bring to closure a wide variety of communicative tasks, including those that require an increased ability to convey meaning with diverse language strategies due to a complication or an unforeseen turn of events,* • *satisfy the requirements of school and work situations; and* • *narrate and describe with paragraph-length connected discourse.*
Advanced	Able to satisfy the requirements of everyday situations and routine school and work requirements. Can handle with confidence but not with facility complicated tasks and social situations, such as elaborating, complaining, and apologizing. Can narrate and descibe with some details, linking sentences together smoothly. Can communicate facts and talk casually about topics of current public and personal interest, using general vocabulary. Shortcomings can often be smoothed over by communicative strategies, such as pause fillers, stalling devices, and different rates of speech. Circumlocution which arises from vocabulary or syntactic limitations very often is quite successful, though some groping for words may still be evident. The Advanced-level speaker can be understood without difficulty by native interlocutors.
Advanced-Plus	Able to satisfy the requirements of a broad variety of everyday, school, and work situations. Can discuss concrete topics relating to particular interests and special fields of competence. There is emerging evidence of ability to support opinions, explain in detail, and hypothesize. The Advanced-Plus speaker often shows a well-developed ability to compensate for an imperfect grasp of some forms with confident use of communicative strategies, such as paraphrasing and circumlocution. Differentiated vocabulary and intonation are effectively used to communicate fine shades of meaning. The Advanced-Plus speaker often shows remarkable fluency and ease of speech but under the demands of Superior-level, complex tasks, language may break down or prove inadequate.
Superior	*The Superior level is characterized by the speaker's ability to:* • *participate effectively in most formal and informal conversations on practical, social, professional, and abstract topics; and* • *support opinions and hypothesize using native-like discourse strategies.*

Figure 11–17, continued.

Superior	Able to speak the language with sufficient accuracy to participate effectively in most formal and informal conversations on practical, social, professional, and abstract topics. Can discuss special fields of competence and interest with ease. Can support opinions and hypothesize, but may not be able to tailor language to audience or discuss in depth highly abstract or unfamiliar topics. Usually the Superior-level speaker is only partially familiar with regional or other dialectical variants. The Superior-level speaker commands a wide variety of interactive strategies and shows good awareness of discourse strategies. The latter involves the ability to distinguish main ideas from supporting information through syntactic, lexical, and suprasegmental features (pitch, stress, intonation). Sporadic errors may occur, particularly in low-frequency structures and some complex high-frequency structures more common to formal writing, but no patterns of error are evident. Errors do not disturb the native speaker or interfere with communication.

To begin with, following is the district-level statement of purpose[3] that underpins this Township District assessment (p. 4):

> Students will demonstrate they can use spoken language effectively in formal and informal situations to communicate ideas and information and to ask and answer questions by:
>
> A. Speaking clearly, expressively, and audibly
>   1. Using voice expressively.
>   2. Speaking articulately and pronouncing words correctly.
>   3. Using appropriate vocal volume.
>
> B. Presenting ideas with appropriate introduction, development, and conclusion
>   1. Presenting ideas in an effective order.
>   2. Providing a clear focus on the central idea.
>   3. Providing signal words, internal summaries, and transitions.
>
> C. Developing ideas using appropriate support materials
>   1. Being clear and using reasoning processes.
>   2. Clarifying, illustrating, exemplifying, and documenting ideas.
>
> D. Using nonverbal cues
>   1. Using eye contact.
>   2. Using appropriate facial expressions, gestures, and body movement.
>
> E. Selecting language suited to a specific purpose
>   1. Using language and conventions appropriate for the audience.

Out of these goals, faculty arrived at relatively detailed definitions of critical elements of effective communication, such as the following (pp. 2–3).

---

[3]The following material is reprinted from "District 214's Speech Assessment Rating Guide," (n.d.) by Township High School District 214, Arlington Heights, IL. Reprinted by permission of the district.

Vocal Expression: This element usually has three sub-elements that enter into the judgment about the use of the voice in an oral message.

Expressiveness refers to the extent to which the voice usage ranges from monotonous to interesting and enthusiastic.

Clarity refers to the distinctness of the articulation and pronunciation of words. This refers to the voice rather than to meaning. The rating is an evaluation of the clearness of the expression, not the understandability of the meaning of the word being used.

Audibility refers to appropriateness of the vocal volume used by the speaker. At one extreme, the speaker either could not be heard at all or bellowed throughout the entire presentation. At the other extreme, the speaker was clearly understandable throughout and used volume appropriate to the meaning of the message and the setting.

Organization: Generally, the arrangement or structure of oral messages is judged in three ways.

Order refers to the sequencing of main points within the message. No order would be extremely confusing to listeners, while effective order helps them both to follow and to anticipate ideas.

Focus (purpose) refers to the extent to which the central thesis is clear and the subpoints are related to this thesis.

Transition refers to the extent to which the speaker provides internal summaries and signal words ("in the first place," "finally," etc.) for the listener.

These definitions then provide the basis for the development of the twelve six-point rating scales that appear in Figure 11-18. Note that these rating scales have been placed on an optical-scan coding sheet for ease of computer processing. This kind of technology is relatively easy to develop and use to advantage in classroom performance assessment applications.

CHAPTER SUMMARY: PERFORMANCE ASSESSMENT, A DIVERSE AND POWERFUL TOOL

These performance assessment examples, combined with the illustrations presented in Chapter 8 on the methodology itself and in Chapter 10 on the assessment of reasoning, reveal the immense flexibility and potential of performance assessment. They remind us, too, of the great depth of information we can generate about student attainment of complex skill and product outcomes. And they remind us of the keys to quality assessment:

- Assesment starts with a vision of success in attaining an important outcome.
- It relies on teachers using carefully crafted language to articulate that vision for all concerned.
- It analyzes performance in terms of several key elements of success.
- It describes each element in the form of a performance continuum, all points of which are defined.

Features of Speech:	Absent (1)	(2)	Developing (3)	Adequate (4)	(5)	Fully Developed (6)
Vocal Expression Degree to which student articulates clearly, is audible, and includes vocal variation (pitch, rate, and phrasing) in performance.	Cannot be heard		Generally audible			Audible throughout
	Poor articulation		Generally clear			Clear throughout
	Monotonous		Some variation			Interesting/ enthusiastic
Physical Expression Degree to which student uses eye contact, gestures, and body movement.	Avoids eye contact		Some eye contact			Involves audience with eye contact
	Stiff or erratic		Some appropriate movement			Focuses attention and interest with movement
Organization Degree to which ideas are presented in effective order, central idea is clear, and student provides internal summaries and transitions.	No order		Some order			Effective order
	Unclear focus (purpose)		Clear focus (purpose)			Focus (purpose) ideas well related
	No transitions		Some transitions			Effective transitions/ summaries

Figure 11–18, *continued*

Sample Speaking Assessment (Reprinted from "District 214's Speech Assessment Rating Guide" (n.d., n.p.) by Township High School District 214, Arlington Heights, IL. Reprinted by permission of the publisher.)

(continued)

Features of Speech:	Absent	Developing	Adequate	Fully Developed
Support and Elaboration Degree to which ideas are clarified, illustrated, documented; clarity of reasoning process.	(1) No support	(2) (3) Some elaboration	(4)	(5) (6) Full/effective elaboration with documentation
	(1) Reasoning unclear	(2) (3) Reasoning clear	(4)	(5) (6) Reasoning clear and effective
Adaptation to Audience Degree to which student uses language and conventions appropriate for audience.	(1) Inadequate (unclear meaning, inappropriate style)	(2) (3) Adequate (appropriate use, clear meaning)	(4)	(5) (6) Effective (appropriate and effective style)
Integration	(1)	(2) (3)	(4)	(5) (6)

Figure 11-18, *continued*

- It relies completely on carefully trained teachers and/or students to judge achievement.

Further, understand that many of these examples come from professional literature available to all educators. Professional journals are presenting more and more performance assessments, including descriptions of exercises and performance criteria. Thus, very often, those who wish to assess performance need not start from scratch. Help may be readily available from colleagues and associates across the country who may already have designed exercises and devised scoring criteria. Check the references listed in Appendix A for more discussion and examples.

Also remember, if you don't have the time or other resources available to develop and use a full-blown performance assessment, sometimes proxy measures, such as the essay format described in Chapter 7, can help you come very close to your intended outcome. In addition, Shavelson et al. (1991), discussing performance assessment in science, also offer advice regarding the use of student notebooks and computer simulations as proxies. Notebooks provide students with an opportunity to write about their thinking, and computer simulations can offer an economical means of applying problem-solving skills. Although these options may not be as "authentic" as real performance assessments, they, too, can provide a clear view of important forms of student achievement.

And finally, remember that students can be full partners in designing, developing, and using performance assessments like those presented above in their classrooms. And when they do play key roles in the assessment process, they will think of creative and engaging exercises, and will define performance criteria that have value for them. They may well need guidance and leadership from their teacher. But with that help, they *can* contribute, and can enjoy doing so.

EXERCISES TO ADVANCE YOUR LEARNING

Knowledge and Reasoning Outcomes

1. List the key attributes of sound performance criteria. Analyze four or five of the examples provided in this chapter. Did they meet these standards?

2. Review the examples of performance assessments provided in chapters 8, 10, and 11 and analyze the following:
    - the range of targets covered
    - how many assess skills; products
    - how many assess individuals; groups
    - how many rely on structured exercises; natural events
    - how many yield holistic scores; analytical scores
    - how many transform results into rating scales; checklists
    - how many rely on criteria that the student could learn to apply (If it depends, what does it depend on?)

What generalizations can you make about performance assessment from these analyses?

Skill and Product Outcomes

1. For further practice, develop two additional performance assessments for use in your classroom, using the design framework in figure 11–2.

2. Find an example of a previously developed performance assessment in a discipline familiar to you. Evaluate it in terms of the attributes of a sound assessment. Is it a quality assessment?

Affective Outcomes

1. Some have argued that performance assessments are too subjective and potentially biased to justify the attention they are receiving these days. Now that you have studied the methodology itself and many examples of its application for classroom use, do you think it is possible to devise assessments that are free of bias? How might you convince skeptics?

2. I have argued that, even when a teacher is adopting or adapting other people's assessment criteria and procedures, that teacher can connect the performance assessments directly to instruction by involving students in development of the criteria, guiding in the right direction as needed. Do you think this represents sound practice? Why?

CHAPTER 12

Assessing Affective Outcomes

Chapter Objectives

As a result of studying the material presented in Chapter 12, reflecting on that material, and completing the learning exercises presented at the end of the chapter, you will:

1. Master content knowledge:
   a. State reasons why all teachers should attend to student affect.
   b. List attributes of high-quality assessments of affect.
   c. Understand differences between assessments of achievement and assessments of affect.
   d. Know ground rules for the productive assessment of student feelings in the classroom.
   e. State definitions of specific affective targets.
   f. Specify alternative methods of assessing those targets, detailing strengths, limitations, and keys to effective use of each.
   g. List specific ideas for developing and using each method.
2. Be able to use that knowledge to reason as follows:
   a. Transform affective outcomes into probes that tap both direction and intensity, using paper and pencil formats, performance assessment, and direct personal communication with students.
   b. Evaluate affective assessments developed by others to determine if they meet standards of quality.
3. Become proficient at the following skills:
   a. Carry out the steps required to develop sound affective assessments.

4. Be able to create the following products:
   a. Questionnaires, performance assessments, and interview protocols that meet standards of quality.
5. Attain the following affective outcomes:
   a. See affect as an important outcome of classroom instruction and as a key contributor to high levels of student achievement.
   b. Value high-quality assessment of affective outcomes if and when they are assessed.

Throughout our work together, we have spoken of the assessment of five kinds of targets. Four deal with key dimensions of academic achievement. When we assess mastery of subject matter knowledge, we seek to know how much of the material the student has learned. When we assess reasoning, we seek to know how effectively the student can use that knowledge to solve problems. When we assess skills, we evaluate what a student can do. When we assess products, we evaluate the quality of the things the student creates.

This chapter will address the fifth target: *Affect*. This is the term we use to identify the feeling dimensions of consciousness—the inward emotions, dispositions, or desires that influence our thoughts and our actions. Like achievement, affect is a multidimensional human characteristic, including such subcategories as attitudes, values, and interests. We will discuss these and more dimensions of affect in detail below. In this chapter, we will deal with student feelings about school-related issues. Students have feelings about teachers, classmates, school subjects, extracurricular activities, instructional methods, themselves as learners, and much else besides. Those feelings vary in their direction, from positive through neutral to negative. And they vary in intensity. Some feelings are very strong, some are moderate, and others are very weak. Our assessment challenge is to capture the direction and intensity of those feelings as they focus on specific aspects of school and the schooling experience.

I have learned many of my lessons about the challenge of assessing affect from Lorin Anderson's book, *Assessing Affective Characteristics in the Schools* (1981). I will share some of his most practical ideas with you in this presentation, along with a number of other useful suggestions for assessing these important outcomes.

We must begin this part of our journey with a sense of limits, however. If entire books have been written on the topic of affective assessment, we obviously will only be able to scratch the surface in this one chapter. Nevertheless, I have tried to assemble enough straightforward discussion and simple classroom assessment ideas to permit you to tap at least some of the feelings of your students. There will be much more for you to learn about this topic in the future.

	SELECTED RESPONSE	ESSAY	PERFORMANCE ASSESSMENT	PERSONAL COMMUNICATION
Know				
Reason				
Skill				
Product				
Affect				

Figure 12–1
Aligning Achievement Targets and Assessment Methods

CHAPTER ROADMAP

In terms of our overall picture, this chapter deals with all four assessment methods as they relate to affective outcomes in our table matching methods to targets. Figure 12–1 depicts that coverage.

More specifically, our mission in this chapter is together to do the following:

1. Take affective outcomes out of the realm of the mystical and into the light of day, so you can come to see them as real, understandable, and accessible.

2. Suggest a few simple strategies for assessing affective outcomes in your classroom, while adhering to standards of sound assessment.

This means, of course, that we must attend to issues of assessment quality in this chapter, just as in previous chapters.

REASONS FOR CONCERN ABOUT AFFECT

There are two reasons for each of us to be concerned about student affect. First, affective outcomes represent important outcomes of the schooling process in their own right. Second, student feelings are tightly intertwined with, and therefore have great influence on, academic achievement.

Affect as an Important Outcome

As outcomes of instruction, affect is every bit as important to student well-being as are knowledge, thinking, skills, and product outcomes. For example, we do little good to teach students to be competent writers if, in the end, they hate writing. We do not help them become competent readers if we fail to impart reading's great learning potential. In fact, we do them a distinct disservice if our educational environments leave them feeling as though they are not capable of learning. Regardless of their real level of competence, if they do not perceive themselves as in charge of their own academic well-being, they will not become the lifelong learners our future society will demand them to be. These are but a few examples of the kinds of affect that represent critical educational outcomes. These are important targets of instruction in and of themselves.

Affect as a Link to Achievement

Beyond this, affective outcomes represent critical dimensions of the classroom instruction process, because they are so tightly intertwined with achievement. Students who have positive attitudes, the motivation to try, and a sense of internal control of their own academic well-being are more likely to achieve at high levels than those who are negative, lack desire, and see themselves as victims of a hostile school world. Very often, students fail not because they cannot achieve, but because they don't want to achieve. They are not motivated to learn. Why? Because they don't understand the work, find it too hard to do, lack prerequisite achievement, and so on. So they fail, and that failure robs them of motivation. This becomes a vicious cycle. They feel powerless to control their own fate. Soon they come to believe that they cannot do it (negative academic self-concept) and that drives their motivation to try even lower. You can see the downward spiral that can result from the complex interaction of achievement and affect.

Clearly, there are many forces in a student's life that exert great influence on attitudes, values, interests, self-concept, and so on. Primary among these are family, peer group, church, and community. But school belongs on this list of contributors, too, especially when it comes to feelings about learning-related things. To the extent that you wish to help students attain affective outcomes and/or wish to take advantage of affect as a driving force to greater achievement, it will be important for you to know how to define and assess it well.

Time for Reflection

From a personal point of view, which of your school-related feelings (positive or negative) seem to have been most closely associated with your achievement? Were there subjects you liked or disliked? Instructors who motivated or failed to motivate? Positive or negative values that you held? How has your affect related to your achievement?

The Meaning of Quality

If your assessments of affective outcomes are to be as sound and as useful as your assessments of academic achievement, they too must arise from clear targets and reflect those targets with proper methods.

In fact, as you shall see, everything you have learned about quality assessment up to this point remains relevant for assessing affect:

- Start with a clear vision of the affective outcome to be assessed.
- Establish a clear purpose.
- Rely upon proper assessment methods.
- Sample appropriately.
- Control for extraneous interference.

Further, I hope you will be pleased to learn that the range of available assessment methods is the same as it is for achievement targets. You can opt for paper and pencil methods (selected response or essay), performance assessments, and/or personal communication. While the assessments themselves may look different in format, the basic methodology remains constant, as do the attributes of sound assessment.

A Critical Difference

There is one very important difference between achievement and affective outcomes, however, and it has to do with the reasons for assessing—the ways in which we use assessment results. It is perfectly acceptable to hold students accountable for the mastery of knowledge, reasoning, skill, and/or product outcomes. In this context, we assess to verify that students have met our expectations.

However, it is *not* acceptable to hold students accountable in the same sense for the attainment of affective outcomes. It is never acceptable, for example, to lower a student's grade because of an attitude that we regard as negative or because a student has a poor academic self-concept. Nor is it acceptable to raise a student's grade just because of a positive attitude, regardless of achievement.

Time for Reflection

In your experience as a student, have you ever had a report card grade greatly influenced (i.e., raised or lowered) by some dimension of your affect? What was that experience like? What impact did it have on you?

Rather, we assess affect in the hope of finding positive, productive attitudes, values, sense of self, and such among our students. If and when we find the appropriately strong positive academic values, positive attitudes about particular subjects, strong interests in particular topics, and things students say they like to do and can do well, we can take advantage of these to promote achievement gains.

But if our assessments reveal negative affect, then we have an obligation to plan educational experiences that will result in the positive affect we hope for. In fact, such experiences may or may not succeed in producing the affective outcomes we desire. But, if we do not succeed in this endeavor, we cannot place sanctions on students with negative affect in the same way we can for those who fail to achieve academically. We cannot hold them accountable for positive affect in the same way we do for positive achievement.

On the contrary, I think responsibility for school-related affect should rest with us educators. As a teacher, I hold myself accountable for the attitudes and values my students develop about classroom assessment during our time together. If we strive to find better ways to help students have good attitudes, the overall positive impact of the schooling experience will be enhanced.

Three Ground Rules

Before we begin to define and to discuss ways to assess affective outcomes, let's pause briefly and agree on three important ground rules for dealing with these outcomes in the classroom.

Ground Rule 1.   Always remain keenly aware of the sensitive interpersonal nature of student feelings and strive to promote positive affect through your assessment of these outcomes. The process of assessing feelings yields vulnerability on both sides. When you assess, you ask students to risk being honest in a controlled environment where honesty on their part has not always been held at a premium. They may well be reticent to express honest feelings because of a lack of experience in doing so and because of the risk that the results somehow could be used against them. It takes a teacher who is a master of human relations to break through these barriers and promote honest expression of feelings in classrooms. One way I have done this is to permit respondents to your questions to remain anonymous.

And for your part, you risk asking for honesty in a place where the honest response may not turn out to be the one you had hoped to hear. Negative feedback is never easy to hear and act upon. Nevertheless, if you ask how students are feeling about things in your classroom, listen thoughtfully to the answers, and act on the results in good faith, the reward will be worth the risk you take. The result will be a more productive student-teacher relationship—a working partnership characterized by greater trust.

Time for Reflection

Under the best of circumstances, teachers become anxious when the time comes to ask students what they think about their teaching. Can you think of specific actions a teacher might take in preparing for, conducting, and interpreting the results of such an assessment to minimize the personal risk? List as many ideas as you can. Discuss them with colleagues or classmates.

Ground Rule 2.   *Know your limits when dealing with affective dimensions of instruction.* There are two important interrelated sets of limits of which you should be aware.

First, as you come to understand and assess affective educational outcomes, you will occasionally encounter students who are deeply troubled, personally and/or socially. Be caring but cautious in these instances. These are not occasions for you to become an amateur psychologist. If you find yourself in a situation where you feel uneasy with what you are learning about a student or about your ability to help that student deal productively with feelings or circumstances, you may well be reaching the limits of your professional expertise. Listen to your instincts and get help.

The most caring and responsible teachers are those who know when it is time to contact the principal, a counselor, a school psychologist, or a physician to find competent counseling services for students. Do not venture into personal territory for which you are not trained. You can do great damage if you fail to respond appropriately—even with the most positive intentions.

The second set of limits is a corollary to the first. I urge you to focus your attention on those classroom-level affective outcomes over which you are likely to, and in fact should, have some influence. When assessing and evaluating student feelings, stick with those feelings as they relate to specific school-related objects: attitudes about subjects or classroom activities, interests they would like to pursue, preferences for activities, self-concept as a learner in an academic setting, and so on. These have a decidedly school-oriented bent and they represent affective outcomes families and school communities are likely to agree are important as parts of the schooling experience.

I urge you to avoid those aspects of personal circumstance or personality that stretch beyond the classroom, such as family values, anxiety, or personal self-concept. These can either take you beyond your capacity as a professional, or take you into value arenas that your students' families or communities may regard as out of bounds for school personnel.

Please understand this: You need not go too far over those classroom-related limits before members of your community may begin to see your actions on behalf of positive, productive affect as invading their turf. Some families and communities are very protective of their responsibility to promote the development of certain strongly held values and will not countenance interference from schools. This is their right.

Time for Reflection

How might a teacher, or even an entire school, work with the community to establish parameters for dealing with affective outcomes—to divide responsibility for assuring positive student feelings about school and school-related topics without stepping out of bounds? What specific strategies come to mind for heading off problems in advance?

You must decide how to deal with these limits within your community. Just be advised that the conservative approach is to focus in your classroom on those di-

Figure 12-2
Ground Rules for Assessing Affect in the Classroom

- Deal with affect honestly to promote trust.
- Know your limits and stay within them:
  —as a professional educator
  —as a member of a larger community
- Act assertively on behalf of positive school-related affect.

mensions of affect that we all agree are the legitimate purview of the teacher—attitudes about school-related activities. As the chapter progresses, you will attain a clearer sense of what this means.

Ground Rule 3. *If you care enough to understand affective outcomes and to develop quality assessments of them, then care enough to take the results seriously and change your instruction when needed.* In other words, don't ask how students are feeling about things just to appear to care. The more you act on the results of these assessments, the greater the potential that students will share feelings in the future that will allow you to improve the nature and quality of your learning environment. When done well, assessment of school-related affective outcomes can be a productive classroom activity for students and teachers. It can lead to specific actions on the part of teachers and students that promote constructive learning and maximum achievement.

To assist you in keeping these critical guidelines clearly in mind, Figure 12–2 presents a concise summary.

DEFINING AFFECTIVE OUTCOMES

To make sense of the range of possible outcomes that might be included under this heading, I will follow Anderson's (1981) lead and discuss several kinds of affect that have relevance in the school setting:[1]

- attitudes
- interests
- motivation
- school-related values
- preferences
- academic self-concept
- locus of control

---

[1]All quotations from and references to Anderson's work in this chapter are from *Assessing Affective Characteristics in the Schools* by L. W. Anderson, 1981, Needham, MA: Allyn and Bacon. Used by permission of the publisher.

These represent significant dimensions of classroom affect, all are relatively easy to define and understand, and all can be assessed in the classroom using relatively straightforward procedures.

However, be advised that these are not the only forms of affect referred to in the professional literature. Sometimes, for example, educational goals may refer to such attributes as *interpersonal sensitivity, honesty, morality, responsibility,* and *self-assurance,* among others. In this chapter, we will not delve into all of these forms of affect for three reasons: our available space is limited, the definitions of these additional options are not as clear and sharp as those listed above, and sometimes these kinds of affect can take us dangerously close to the limits of our professional and community responsibility (in my opinion). We will therefore limit our discussion to the seven kinds of affect listed.

Defining Kinds of Affect

If we are to assess these affective characteristics, we must begin with clear and specific definitions. In this section, we will learn some basic definitions that will suffice for you to be able to design simple assessments for use in your classroom. However, please realize that our education literature contains a large body of knowledge about each of the various kinds of outcomes defined here. The more deeply you can tap into that literature and understand these concepts, the easier it will be for you to address them in your assessment and instruction. Please take seriously your professional responsibility to become a student of the kinds of affect you seek for your students.

Attitudes.   Anderson defines attitudes as "feelings that . . . can be either unfavorable or favorable, positive or negative, and are typically directed toward some specific object. The association between the feelings and a particular object are learned. And once learned, the feelings are consistently experienced in the presence of that object" (p. 33).

Obviously, the range of attitudes we can hold is as broad as the number of objects to which we might react. In schools, students might have favorable or unfavorable attitudes about each other, teachers, administrators, school subjects, instructional activities, and so on.

Interests.   These represent feelings that can range from a high level of excitement to no excitement at all at the prospect of engaging in, or while engaged in, some particular activity. Once again, the relationship between the object and level of interest is learned. A student might be very interested in drama, but completely disinterested in geography.

Motivation.   We will define this form of affect as the strength of the need within a student to achieve or to act favorably toward school activities and/or school-related work. It is the willingness to follow through, the disposition to seek success, to avoid failure, to aspire to performance norms and expectations. For example, students can be highly motivated or not motivated at all to participate in some learning activity or to pursue some direction of study.

Values.   Anderson thoughtfully defines these feelings, stating that, first, "values are beliefs as to what should be desired, what is important or cherished and what standards of conduct or existence are personally or socially acceptable. Second, values influence or guide things: behavior, interests, attitudes, satisfactions. . . . Third, values are enduring. That is, values tend to remain stable over fairly long periods of time" (p. 34). Again, the objects of our values can range far and wide, and are learned. They seem to have anchors deep in our being.

Preferences.   Preferences reflect our desire or propensity to choose one object over another. Anderson points out that these may be manifestations of attitudes (one is more favorable than the other), interests (one is more interesting), and/or values (one has greater value). The essence of preference is that these accumulated feelings lead to a choice on the part of the student.

Academic Self-Concept.   No affective characteristic is more school-related than this one. It is the sum of all evaluative judgments one makes about one's success and/or productivity in an academic context. In essence, it is an attitude (favorable or unfavorable) about one's self (the object) when viewed in a classroom setting. Academic self-concept, writes Anderson, is a learned vision that results largely from evaluations of self by others over time.

Locus of Control.   This represents a very important part of academic self-concept. In this case, the characteristic of interest is the student's attributions or reasons for academic success or failure. One kind of attribution is defined as internal: "I succeeded because I tried hard." Another possible attribution is external, where chance rules: "I sure was lucky to receive that A!" Yet another attribution also is external, but someone else rules: "I performed well because I had a good teacher." At issue here is students' perceptions of the underlying reasons for the results they experienced. This, too, is a learned self-perception arising from their sense of the connection of effort with academic success.

Variations within Kinds of Affect

As mentioned in the introduction, all types of affect vary along three important dimensions. They deal with feelings about different objects. Some, like attitudes and values, can focus on an infinite range of objects. Others, like academic self-concept and locus of control, are more limited in their focus.

They also can vary in direction. Think of affect as stretching from a neutral point outward in both directions along a continuum from positive to negative.

And finally, feelings vary in their intensity, from strong to moderate to weak. As you visualize the above-mentioned continuum for each type of affect, as you move further and further away from neutral, think of feelings as increasing in intensity. In the extremes, feelings become strongly positive or negative.

Table 12-1

Range of School-related Affect (Adapted from *Assessing Affective Characteristics in the Schools* (n.p.) by L. W. Anderson, 1981, Needham, MA: Allyn and Bacon. Copyright 1981 by Allyn and Bacon, Inc. Adapted by permission of the publisher.)

Unfavorable	←*Attitude*→	Favorable
Disinterested	←*Interest*→	Interested
Weak	←*Motivation*→	Strong
Unimportant	←*Value*→	Important
Choice A	←*Preference*→	Choice B
Negative	←*Academic Self-Concept*→	Positive
Assign responsibility else-where	←*Locus of Control*→	Accept responsibility

One final generalization that we must always bear in mind as we assess and consider affect in instruction is that feelings can be very volatile—especially among the young. Student feelings can quickly change both in direction and intensity for a large number of reasons, only some of which are rational, or understandable by adults. I mention this only to point out that it may be important to assess affect repeatedly over time to keep track of it. The results of any one assessment may have a very short half life.

Anderson provides a simple table depicting these variations, reproduced in Table 12–1. Given our discussion so far, I'm sure you can begin to understand why our assessment challenge is to focus student attention on the school-related objects of interest and to gather information on the direction and intensity of the relevant feelings. This turns out to be quite possible to do in the classroom, if we understand and apply some relatively straightforward assessment tactics.

Time for Reflection

Read through the entries in Table 12–1, and for each line, think of some current aspect of your life that comes close to each end of each continuum: something you have a very positive attitude about and something about which your attitude is very negative; something you're very interested in and something in which you have little interest; and so on, all the way to the bottom. Your students have feelings too—just as strong as yours. The key question is, how can we harness those feelings in the service of maximum achievement?

ASSESSMENT OPTIONS

So, how do we tap the direction and intensity of feelings about school-related objects? Just as with achievement outcomes, we rely on one or a combination of our standard four types of assessment: paper and pencil methods that rely on selected response or essay, performance assessment, and personal communication with students.

In this case, I group selected response and essay into a paper and pencil form of assessment because the two options represent different forms of questions that can appear on one of our basic affective assessment tools: the questionnaire. We can ask students questions about their feelings on a questionnaire and either offer them a finite range of response options from which to select, or ask them open-ended questions and request brief or extended written responses. If we focus our questions on affect about particular objects, we can interpret responses in terms of both the direction and intensity of feelings.

Performance assessment of affective outcomes is just like performance assessment of achievement outcomes. We conduct systematic observations of student behavior and/or products with clear criteria in mind and draw inferences about the direction and intensity of their feelings. So, once again, observation and professional judgment provide the basis for this form of affective assessment.

Assessments of affect that rely on personal communication typically take the form of interviews, either with the student or with others who know about the student. These can be highly structured or very much more casual, such as a discussion or conversation with the student. The questions we ask and the things we talk about reveal the direction and intensity of feelings.

The remainder of the chapter is devoted to examining each of these basic assessment options and to exploring how each can help you tap the seven kinds of affective outcomes defined for this discussion.

MATCHING AFFECTIVE TARGET WITH ASSESSMENT METHOD

Each of the methods for tapping student affect can be cast in many forms and each carries with it specific advantages, limitations, keys to success, and pitfalls to be avoided. We examine these, then review a few tips for the effective development and use of each. As we go, I will try to illustrate how the various forms of questionnaires, performance assessment, and personal communication can be used to tap our seven defined kinds of affect.

Table 12–2 shows an overview analysis of the assessment methods. As you can see, each method offers its own special set of strengths. These can help you fit each into your context as needed. Notice also that the keys to success and potential pitfalls are consistent across the bottom part of the table. Students who fail to understand and appreciate the purpose for the assessment and/or are feeling vulnerable are less than likely to communicate honestly. By the same token, it is critical that they understand that their task is not to formulate their responses so as to please their teacher. There are no "right" answers, only honest answers. This can be a surprisingly difficult concept to get across to students whose only experience has been to strive to be correct.

Table 12-2
Tools for Assessing Affect

	Selected Response (Structured) Questionnaire	Open-ended (Nonstructured) Questionnaire	Performance Assessment	Personal Communication
Strengths	Can be sharply focused Easy to administer Easy to summarize results Results comparable across respondents Can be anonymous Can sample consistently over time	Focus can be sharp Relatively easy to develop Relatively easy to administer Reasons for feeling can be probed Can be anonymous Can sample consistently over time	Inferences can be drawn by observing behavior or products Can focus on nonverbal cues Can be unobtrusive Can observe groups or individuals	Can be highly focused Can be casual, nonthreatening Can be highly structured or not Can attend to verbal and non-verbal cues Can ask followup probes Respondents like attention Can produce greater depth
Limitations	No followup probes Reasons for feelings may not be apparent Reading proficiency required	No followup probes Labor-intensive processing of results Scorer can misinterpret Reading proficiency required Writing proficiency required	Can unwittingly observe atypical behavior (i.e., nonrepresentative sample) Sometimes may not be anonymous Can misinterpret behaviors seen Can be time consuming	Withdrawn student may not communicate Interviewer can misinterpret Cannot be anonymous Can be time consuming
Best Results When	Purpose is clear Affective target defined Students understand and value the purpose Administration is relaxed Instructions are clear Questions worded clearly	Purpose is clear Affective target defined Students understand and value the purpose Administration is relaxed Instructions are clear Questions worded clearly Students are proficient writers	Purpose is clear Criteria are clear and appropriate Multiple observations are made Students understand and value the purpose Instructions are clear	Purpose is clear Affective target defined Students understand and value the purpose Interaction is relaxed Instructions are clear Questions worded clearly
Pitfalls to Avoid	Students don't take it seriously or feel threatened Students offer socially desirable response Too long Ambiguous questions Leading questions	Students don't take it seriously or feel threatened Students offer socially desirable response Too long Ambiguous questions Leading questions	Unclear criteria Too few observations Assessment triggers socially desirable behaviors that misrepresent real affect	Students don't take it seriously or feel threatened Students offer socially desirable response Too long Ambiguous questions Leading questions

Time for Reflection

What specific actions can a teacher take to help students understand the meaning of a "socially desirable response" and to see why truly honest answers are more appropriate under some circumstances?

In addition, the assessment should not be so long that motivation lags among respondents. And it should not include questions that "lead" students to the response you want to receive. Here are two out-of-balance items that lead the respondent:

You really do like math, don't you?

or

Which response best reflects your attitude toward math?
   a. I love it
   b. I like it a lot
   c. I find it very challenging
   d. I really enjoy it

You should instead ask focused questions in a value-neutral manner:

How confident are you that you can solve this kind of math problem appropriately: (fill-in some math problem-solving challenge)?

And, you should offer response options that combine direction and intensity:

   a. Very confident
   b. Quite confident
   c. Somewhat confident
   d. Not confident at all

We will now consider procedural guidelines for questionnaire, performance assessment, and interview planning and design that can enhance their quality.

Questionnaires That Assess Affect

Questionnaires represent one of the most convenient means of tapping important student feelings. And yet, in a decade and a half of classroom assessment research, I cannot remember more than a handful of teachers who used this method in their classrooms. There are many possible reasons. Perhaps for some the risk of tapping student feelings within the learning environment is too high. Others may lack confidence in questionnaire development. Still others may think of achievement as so important that they give no time to affective outcomes. Some may simply feel that students won't take it seriously.

The best way I know to get students to take questionnaires seriously (i.e., to provide complete and honest responses) is to let them know that they have everything to gain and nothing to lose by being honest. That means focusing on topics students care about and establishing a reputation for acting on results in ways that benefit them.

Within the questionnaire itself, we must strive to ask questions that are relevant—about which students are likely to have an informed opinion. We must avoid ambiguity in the questions, and seek to ask brief, precise, complete questions and to offer response options that make sense.

Whenever I develop a questionnaire, I strive to combine all of these ideas in a way that enlists the support of the respondent as an ally, a partner in generating sound information. Sometimes that means permitting responses to be offered anonymously, to reduce the risk to the respondent. Sometimes it means promising to share results or promising to act purposefully and quickly based upon those results. Sometimes it just means urging them to take the questionnaire seriously—to care as I do about the value of the results for making things better for all. In any event, I try to break down the barriers between us.

Time for Reflection

What ways can you think of to develop and use questionnaires in the classroom in a manner that encourages students to become partners in the process and to use results to create a better classroom for all?

Selected Response Formats.   We have at our disposal a variety of response formats to choose from as we design questionnaires. For example, Gable (1986) suggests that we can ask students if they agree with specific statements, how important they regard specific things, how they would judge the quality of an object of interest, or how frequently an event occurs. The examples listed below demonstrate possible response options for these kinds of scales. Note that each scale represents both direction and intensity of feelings. Let's see how they apply to our defined kinds of affect.

We might wish to assess student attitudes toward a specific instructional strategy. One way to do this is to assert a positive statement:

Do you agree or disagree with this statement as regards your own learning? The group project we did in class yesterday helped me learn more about my leadership skills.

    a. Strongly agree
    b. Agree
    c. Undecided
    d. Disagree
    e. Strongly disagree

Or, we might assess student interest in participating in certain activities:

> Would you like to do more collaborative group projects in the future? How important are such projects to you?
>
> a. Very important
> b. Important
> c. Undecided
> d. Unimportant
> e. Very unimportant

Other such selected response scales tap the perceived quality of some object:

> How well do you think you performed in preparing your term paper?
>
> a. Excellent
> b. Good
> c. Fair
> d. Poor
> e. Very poor

Some may determine perceived frequency of occurrence of some particular event:

> How frequently do you feel you understand and can do the homework assignment you receive?
>
> a. Always
> b. Frequently
> c. Occasionally
> d. Rarely
> e. Never

One of the most common forms of selected response questionnaire items is the question that asks the student to choose between or among some forced choices. The following examples are designed to help us understand a student's locus of control:

> If I do well on a test, it is typically because
>
> a. my teacher taught me well.
> b. I was lucky.
> c. I studied hard.

or

> I failed to master that particular skill because
>
> a. I didn't try hard enough.
> b. my teacher didn't show me how.

Yet another kind of selected response format, one that I use extensively, is a scale anchored at each end by polar adjectives and offering direction and intensity options in between. Here's an example focused on student interest and motivation:

Use the scales provided below to describe your feelings about participating in the school subjects listed:

Math
very interested __ __ __ __ __ completely disinterested
very motivated __ __ __ __ __ completely unmotivated
Science
very interested __ __ __ __ __ completely disinterested
very motivated __ __ __ __ __ completely unmotivated

Time for Reflection

Let's say you want to tap the attitudes of your students about the textbook you are using. Create five to ten bipolar scales like those above that reflect key elements of a textbook. Plan to gather information about the direction and intensity of their most important feelings about this book. Once gathered, how might such information be used to advantage?

An easy adaptation of the selected response format can provide a means of tapping the attitudes of very young students. Rather than using words to describe feeling states, we can use simple pictures:

Given an object about which to express their feelings, such as free reading time, for example, the student is instructed to circle the face that tells how they feel about that object.

Time for Reflection

If you teach or plan to teach primary grades, think of additional kinds of affective outcomes you might like to assess using the face scale illustrated. Generate some ideas for how you might use the results of such assessments to advantage in your classroom.

If you focus these kinds of response scales on specific school-related objects, students can have a relatively easy time revealing their attitudes, interests, school-related values, preferences, academic self-concept, and the like. Further, it is usually easy to summarize results across respondents. The pattern of response and therefore the feelings of a group of students is easily seen by tallying the number and percent of students who select each response option—a straightforward data analysis task.

Written Response.   Another kind of question we can pose on a questionnaire is the essay, in which the respondents are free to write in their response. If we ask specific questions eliciting direction and intensity of feelings about specific school-related issues, even responses to unstructured questions can be easily interpreted:

> Write a brief paragraph describing how you feel about our guest speaker today. Please comment on your level of interest in the presentation, how well informed you thought the speaker was, and how provocative you found the message to be. Also, express any other feelings you might have had during the presentation. As you write, be sure to tell me how strong your positive or negative feelings are. I will use your reactions to plan for guest speakers for the future.

We may combine some assessment of affect with some practice in evaluative thinking:

> As you think about the readings we did this month, which three did you find most worthwhile? For each, specify why you found it worthwhile.

A thoughtful reading of the responses to these kinds of questions will reveal the consensus of or differences in opinion that can be useful in planning for future instruction.

Additional Thoughts about Questionnaires.   Very often, questionnaire developers will combine selected response and open-ended formats. However, it is usually very clear on these questionnaires which set of questions received the most attention. Crisp, clean, straightforward queries and associated rating scales will appear on them, affording the respondent an excellent opportunity to express clear opinions. And then, very often, these will be followed by the world's most unfocused invitation: "Comment" or "Please comment" or "Any further comments?" These fishing expeditions are usually a waste of time for all involved. If you seek focused commentary on some issue, ask for it—in clear specific terms. On the other hand, if the nature of your question is unclear to you, don't ask it.

   This leads us to another general guideline regarding questionnaire development that will maximize the efficiency and value of the results obtained: Always connect your questions to direct action. By this, I mean ask only those questions that will provide you with the specific and significant information you need to make your decisions. For each question you pose, you should be able to anticipate the course of action you will take given each possible response: "If my students respond this way, I will do. . . . If they respond the other way, the results will mean that I should instead do. . . ." Discard any query that leaves you wondering exactly why you're asking it.

I have one more critical piece of advice: If you promise respondents that the information will be gathered anonymously, stick with that promise under *all* circumstances. Never try to subvert such a promise with invisible coding or other identification systems. Students need only be caught in that trap once to come to believe that neither teachers nor administrators can be trusted. We face a hard enough challenge establishing open channels of communication without having to overcome this kind of obstacle, too.

Time for Reflection

Have you ever been promised anonymity and then had that trust violated? If so, what was that experience like for you? What impact did it have? If you have not had this experience, ask around and find someone who has. Ask them to describe their experience, and listen to their affect!

And remember, if you plan your selected response questionnaire carefully and coordinate the response modes with a mark-sensing optical-scan response sheet, you can use scanning technology to save time and effort in summarizing the questionnaire results for you. Very often, these machines can produce frequency of response tallies in record time, making your job much easier. If there is one mistake I see inexperienced questionnaire designers make, it is failing to comprehend what it will take to process and summarize the results. Use available technology if you can.

Performance Assessments of Affect

In one sense, using observations and judgments as the basis for evaluating affect is a practice that is as old as mankind. In another sense, it is an idea that has barely been tried.

The sense in which performance assessment has been a standard indicator of affect has to do with the inferences we tend to draw when we see students doing certain things. Adhering to classroom rules, for example, is often cited as evidence of a "positive attitude." Or, tardiness is seen as evidence of a lack of value for school or as evidence of irresponsibility. Sometimes we observe and reflect upon our interactions with students, such as when they appear not to be trying or not seeming to care, and we infer that they are "unmotivated and have a poor academic self-concept."

While in some sense, these inferences may be correct, they also can be dangerous. What if our casual observations and intuitive conclusions are wrong? What if adhering to the rules reflects a low willingness to take risks, tardiness is due to some factor beyond the student's control, or the apparent lack of motivation is not a result of low self-esteem, but rather an indication that we were not clear in helping that student understand the task to be completed? If our inferences are wrong, we may well plan and carry out responses that completely miss the point.

A Very Important Note of Caution.   My point is that the cavalier manner in which we have observed and drawn inferences about student attitudes, values, interests, and the like, very often reflects our own lack of regard for the basic principles of sound assessment. The rules of evidence for observing and judging don't change just because the nature of the outcome changes. Vague targets, inappropriately cast into the wrong methods, that fail to sample or control for bias lead to incorrect assessments of affect just like they lead to incorrect inferences about achievement. The rules of evidence for sound assessment are *never* negotiable.

For this reason, developing performance assessments of affect requires that we follow exactly the same basic design sequence used for performance assessment of achievement. We must specify the performance to be evaluated, select a context and method within which to observe, and devise a method to record and store results.

This does not mean spontaneous observations and judgments about affect are unacceptable. But assessors must remain vigilant, for many things can go wrong with such on-the-spot assessments. That awareness can serve to make us appropriately cautious when making snap judgments.

Time for Reflection

Have you ever been the victim of a performance assessment in which a teacher's observation and judgment of your actions led to an incorrect inference about your affect? What were the circumstances? What impact did this mismeasurement have on you?

As developers of affective performance assessments, we face the same design decisions that were spelled out in detail in Chapters 8 and 10. They are translated into design questions for the assessment of affect in Figure 12–3.

I know this list of design questions looks imposing in this context. You might read it and ask, Why be so formal? It's not like we're conducting an assessment for a final grade or something! In fact, many regard it as instinctive for teachers to observe some behavior and infer almost intuitively about student attitudes, values, and so on.

But this is exactly my point. We often think that, just because this is "only affect," we can disregard all of the requirements of sound assessment. I promise you, if you disregard the rules of evidence in conducting assessments based on observation and judgment—whether assessing attitude or writing proficiency—your assessment will almost always produce incorrect results. For this reason, it is *always* important to strive for quality assessment.

A Classroom Application.   Here is an example of a productive affective performance assessment in the classroom: Let's say we want to assess students' motivational predisposition to apply their best critical thinking skills when they are needed. Remember when we spoke of the concept of the "critical spirit" defined by Norris and Ennis (1989) in Chapter 10? Let's plan to assess the direction and intensity of this affective characteristic.

To conduct this assessment, we plan to focus on individual student performance in a team problem-solving context. To make the assessment as efficient as possible, we randomly select a few students to observe each day.

1. How shall we define the affective characteristic to be assessed?
   What shall we focus on to evaluate student feelings?

   - A behavior exhibited by the student?
   - A product created by the student?

   Who will our assessment focus on?

   - Individual students?
   - Students in groups?

   What specific performance criteria will guide our observations and inferences about student affect?

2. How shall we elicit performance to be evaluated in terms of the affect it reflects?
   Which format will we use?

   - Structured exercises?
   - Observe students during naturally occurring classroom events?

   How many instances of performance will we need to observe to make confident generalizations about student feelings?
   If we use structured exercises, what will we tell students to do under what conditions, according to what standards of performance?

3. What method will we use to record results of our observations?
   Which do we wish to obtain?

   - A single overall judgment about student affect?
   - Are there specific aspects of their feelings we wish to tap?

   What record will we create of student affect?

   - Checklist?
   - Rating scale?
   - Anecdotal record?

   Who will make the judgment regarding the level of affect demonstrated?

   - The teacher?
   - Students themselves?

Figure 12-3
Designing Performance Assessments of Affect

Further, let's say that we know from prior assessments that the students have mastered critical thinking skills and we have verified that they know how and when to bring these skills into play in group work contexts. So the essential procedural knowledge is in place. Now the question is, Will they use appropriate skills when indicated?

Our primary source of evidence will be student interaction behaviors. That is, when working in a group under conditions of normal motivation, if they exhibit proper critical thinking skills at appropriate times, we will infer from this that they are, in fact, predisposed to display a "critical spirit."

Our performance criteria, therefore, will be the list of group interaction skills indicative of those who reason critically. We will look for their application during teamwork time. And so, in this case—just as with performance assessment of achievement—we must know in advance how a high-level performer differs from a low-level performer. If we cannot specify that difference, we cannot dependably assess.

Because we want to observe performance under conditions of normal motivation, we will conduct our assessment unobtrusively by watching and evaluating interaction skills during our regularly scheduled team work time in class. Thus, we will rely on naturally occurring events to trigger performance.

Our record-keeping method will be a simple checklist of attributes of those with a critical spirit. A sample of such a list is shown in Figure 12–4. We will randomly select a student and watch that student's interactions. Every time an instance comes up in which a certain skill should have come into play, we check that skill. If the student comes through and delivers as needed, we check that, too. The question is, What proportion of invitations to exhibit specific critical thinking skills actually elicits the required skill? The higher the proportion, the stronger the "critical spirit."

The key point of this example is that the use of performance assessment as the basis for the evaluation of affect requires that we observe behaviors or study products and draw inferences about attitudes, values, interests, and so on. This means we must conduct the kind of analysis of performance required to specify how a student with one direction and intensity of attitude (or interest or values or self-

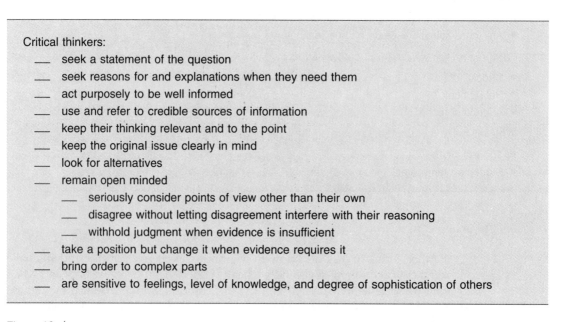

Critical thinkers:
___ seek a statement of the question
___ seek reasons for and explanations when they need them
___ act purposely to be well informed
___ use and refer to credible sources of information
___ keep their thinking relevant and to the point
___ keep the original issue clearly in mind
___ look for alternatives
___ remain open minded
   ___ seriously consider points of view other than their own
   ___ disagree without letting disagreement interfere with their reasoning
   ___ withhold judgment when evidence is insufficient
___ take a position but change it when evidence requires it
___ bring order to complex parts
___ are sensitive to feelings, level of knowledge, and degree of sophistication of others

Figure 12-4
Checklist for Evaluating Critical Spirit (Adapted from *Evaluating Critical Thinking* (Chapter 1) by S. Norris and R. Ennis, 1989, Pacific Grove, CA: Midwest Publications. Copyright 1989 by Midwest Publications. Adapted by permission of the publisher.)

concept, etc.) differs from a student with another. If we cannot differentiate in this way, we have no basis for drawing inferences about affective characteristics from behaviors or products.

In that sense, this is an indirect assessment method. We rely on external indicators to infer about internal states of mind. When we use questionnaires or interviews, we ask students direct questions about their feelings. This typically is not the case with performance assessment. That means we could draw incorrect inferences if we have not planned carefully and carried out a thoughtful assessment, according to the rules of performance assessment evidence.

Personal Communication as a Window to Student Feelings

Most would regard this as an excellent path to student feelings about school-related topics. We can interview students individually or in groups, conduct discussions with them, or even rely on casual discussion to gain insight as to their attitudes, values, preferences, and the like.

This method offers much. Unlike questionnaires, we can establish personal contact with the respondent, and can ask followup questions. This allows us to more completely understand student feelings. Unlike performance assessment, we can gather our information directly, avoiding the danger of drawing incorrect inferences. This assures a higher level of accuracy and confidence in our assessment results.

Keys to Success.   Of course, one key to success in tapping into true student feelings is *trust.* I cannot overemphasize the critical importance of trust. The respondent must be comfortable expressing the direction and intensity of his or her feelings honestly. Respondents who lack trust will either tell us what they think we want to hear (i.e., give the socially desirable response) or they will shut us out altogether. For many students, it is difficult to communicate honest feelings in an interview setting with the real power sitting on the other side of the table, because all hope of anonymity evaporates. This can seem risky to them.

Another key to success is to have the luxury of time to plan and conduct high-quality assessments. This is a labor-intensive means of soliciting information.

In many ways, the remaining keys to success in an interview setting are the same as those for questionnaires:

- Prepare carefully.
- Ask focused, clear, brief questions that get at the direction and intensity of feelings about specific school-related topics.
- Make sure respondents know why you are gathering this information.
- Act on results in ways that serve students' best interests.

In other ways, this assessment format brings with it some unique challenges. Figure 12–5 offers guidelines to help you meet those challenges.

- *Don't overlook the power of group interview.* Marketing people call these *focus groups.* Sometimes students' feelings come clear to them and to you by bouncing them off or comparing them to others. Besides, there can be a feeling of safety in numbers, allowing respondents to open up a bit more.
- *Rely on students as interviewers or discussion leaders.* Often, they know how to probe the real and important feelings of their classmates. Besides, they have credibility in places where you may not.
- *Become an attentive listener.* Ask focused questions about the direction and intensity of feelings and then listen attentively for evidence of the same. Very often, interviewers come off looking and acting like robots. Sometimes just a bit of interpersonal warmth will open things up.
- *Be prepared to record results in some way.* Often we use tape recorders in interview contexts, but this is certainly not the only way to capture student responses. For example, you could create a written questionnaire form but ask the questions personally and complete the questionnaire as you go. Or, you could just take notes and transcribe them into a more complete record later. In any event, students will appreciate that you asked how they felt, but only if you seem to remember what they said and take it into consideration in your instructional planning.

Figure 12-5
Guidelines for Conducting Interviews to Assess Affect

CHAPTER SUMMARY: ASSESSING AFFECT AS AN OUTCOME AND AS A PATH TO HIGHER ACHIEVEMENT

The fifth and final target in our array of valued educational outcomes is affect: attitudes, interests, motivation, values, preferences, academic self-concept, and locus of control. These forms of affect relate to feelings we all have about certain specific objects and vary both in intensity and direction, ranging from strongly positive to strongly negative. Our assessment challenge is to capture and record both intensity and direction.

There are two basic reasons why it can be important to define and assess affect in the classroom. First, these outcomes are important in themselves. They represent characteristics that we value as a society, such as strong interests, high levels of motivation, and a positive self-concept. It is the American way to want all citizens to feel as though they are in control of their own destiny.

The second reason to care about classroom dimensions of affect is that attitudes, motivation, interests, and preferences are closely related to achievement. While it may be arguable which comes first, achievement or positive affect, we know that they both support each other in important ways.

Time for Reflection

What ways can you think of to involve students in the process of preparing to assess and of assessing affect that will encourage them to have positive feelings and higher achievement?

Our assessment options are the same as those we use to track student achievement: paper and pencil, performance assessment, and personal communication. Paper and pencil alternatives take the form of questionnaires. We reviewed several kinds of item formats for use in these instruments. Performance assessments have us observing student behaviors and/or products and drawing inferences about affective states. Systematic preparation to assess prevents incorrect inferences. Personal communication takes the form of interviews, discussions, and conversations. When used effectively, these can take us inside student feelings to gain the clearest insights.

We began the chapter with three specific ground rules intended to prevent the misassessment of these important student characteristics and to prevent the misuse of the results. They bear repeating as final thoughts on this topic.

- **Ground Rule 1:** Always remain keenly aware of the sensitive interpersonal nature of student feelings and strive to promote positive affect through your assessment of these outcomes.

- **Ground Rule 2:** Know your limits when dealing with affective dimensions of instruction. Assess school-related feelings only, and get help when you need it.

- **Ground Rule 3:** If you care enough to understand affective outcomes and to develop quality assessments of them, then care enough to take the results seriously and change your instruction when needed.

EXERCISES TO ADVANCE YOUR LEARNING

Knowledge Outcomes

1. Identify two specific reasons why all teachers should attend to student feelings in their classrooms.

2. List the key attributes of quality assessments of affect.

3. What are the essential differences between classroom assessments of achievement and assessments of affect?

4. Specify critical ground rules for the productive assessment of student feelings in the classroom, and state why each is important.

5. List and define the seven specific affective targets outlined in this chapter.

6. Create your own version of a chart identifying alternative methods of assessing those targets and detailing strengths, limitations, and keys to effective use of each.

7. For each method, list five practical development and use ideas from material presented in this chapter.

Reasoning Outcomes

1. Return to Table 12–1. For each type of affective outcome listed there, select a focus or object that might be of interest to you and develop two sample probes that you might use either on a questionnaire or in an interview to assess the direction and intensity of the affect of your students.

2. Find a previously developed questionnaire and evaluate it to determine if it meets our standards of quality.

Skill Outcomes

1. Using Figure 12–3 as your model, create a blueprint of a performance assessment of the affect of your students. Be sure to create a complete set of performance criteria reflecting the feelings you intend to assess.

2. Devise a brief questionnaire tapping some dimension(s) of school-related affect of interest to you.

Product Outcomes

1. We have spoken repeatedly of the key ingredients of sound performance criteria. Evaluate the product (the performance criteria) you developed above for skill exercise number one in terms of those standards. Did you do a good job?

2. Evaluate the questionnaire you developed in response to skill exercise number two in terms of the attributes of a sound assessment.

Affective Outcomes

1. Write about the direction and intensity of your feelings about the value of affect (a) as an outcome of classroom instruction, and (b) as one key contributor to high levels of student achievement.

2. Describe the direction and intensity of your feelings about the need for high-quality assessment of affective outcomes if and when such outcomes are assessed.

CHAPTER 13

Classroom Perspectives on Standardized Testing

Chapter Objectives

As a result of studying the material presented in Chapter 13, reflecting on that material, and completing the learning exercises presented at the end of the chapter, you will:

1. Master content knowledge:
   a. Know the various purposes for standardized testing.
   b. State the various levels at which standardized tests are administered.
   c. Specify how the four basic forms of assessment come into play in the standardized testing context.
   d. List the steps in the standardized test development sequence.
   e. Understand the meaning and proper interpretation of the commonly used test scores.
   f. Know the basic standardized testing responsibilities of the classroom teacher.

2. Be able to use that knowledge to reason as follows:
   a. Understand the contradictions and misconceptions that permeate the realm of standardized testing.
   b. Evaluate the match between local curriculum and standardized test coverage of content, reasoning, and other skills.
   c. Interpret standardized test scores correctly.
   d. Determine whether standardized test results are likely to provide information relevant to a particular decision.

3. Become proficient at the following skills:
   a. Participate productively in the selection of standardized tests for local use.

4. Attain the following affective outcomes:
    a. Value a balanced perspective in the use of standardized tests:
        —in terms of their impact on student well-being relative to classroom assessment.
        —with respect to the various outcomes to be assessed and assessment methods to be used.
    b. Value an assessment-literate school culture and community that understands standardized tests.
    c. See a clear sense of purpose as central to effective use of standardized tests.
    d. Value high-quality assessment in the standardized test context.

Note: The objectives of this chapter do not include the creation of any products.

The American educational system has included a strong standardized test tradition for decades. You may recall that Chapter 2 detailed the various strata of that tradition. Standardized testing programs use their resources to develop and implement assessments in which large numbers of students respond to the same or similar sets of exercises under approximately the same conditions. Thus, it is test exercises, conditions of test administration, scoring procedures, and test score interpretation that are "standardized" across all examinees. As a result, the scores can be interpreted to mean the same for all examinees, and thus can be compared across students and classrooms.

Often, school districts participate in layer upon layer of standardized testing, from districtwide to statewide to national and sometimes even international programs. Some districts may administer a dozen or more different standardized testing programs involving different students for different purposes in a given year. Some districts test every pupil at every grade, while others sample students or grade levels.

Some tests are *norm-referenced;* they permit us to interpret student performance in terms of how it compares with that of others who took the same test under like conditions. Others are *criterion-referenced;* they permit us to compare a student's performance with a preset standard of acceptable performance—no reference is made as to how other students compared to that standard. These tests cover many different school subjects and involve the use of all four of our basic forms of assessment, although nearly all rely on selected response formats.

The purpose of this chapter is to provide you with enough background information about large-scale standardized assessment to permit you to understand how such assessments fit into the classroom and into the larger world of educational assessment in general. It is also intended to help you comprehend your own professional responsibilities with respect to these testing programs.

CHAPTER ROADMAP

During this phase of our journey through the realm of assessment, we will analyze and discuss the following:

- standardized test purposes, making it clear why standardized tests have so much less impact on student learning than do classroom assessments, even though they remain in the spotlight in other decision-making and public-relations contexts

- the complex array of assessment forms that appear at all of these testing levels, providing examples of both norm-referenced and criterion-referenced tests, and revealing how and why all four of the common assessment methods (selected response, essay, performance assessment, and personal communication) are used at this level of assessment

- the standardized test development process, revealing techniques test developers use to attain quality in their assessments

- practical guidelines for interpreting commonly used standardized test scores

- the specific list of responsibilities to be fulfilled by teachers and administrators who administer, interpret, and use standardized testing

In this last section, we address the classroom teacher's primary standardized testing issue: What should the conscientious teacher do in response to unrelenting pres-

	SELECTED RESPONSE	ESSAY	PERFORMANCE ASSESSMENT	PERSONAL COMMUNICATION
Know				
Reason				
Skill			(Some Experimentation)	
Product				
Affect				

FIGURE 13-1

Aligning Achievement Targets and Assessment Methods

sure to "raise those test scores"? The darkened cells in Figure 13–1 indicate that portion of the comprehensive assessment picture discussed in this chapter.

But, before we begin our discussion, we need to set the stage by exploring the current context of standardized testing.

TROUBLING CONTRADICTIONS

Standardized testing is troubled with apparent contradictions these days. The conflicting perspectives usually arise out of a general lack of assessment literacy—a lack of understanding of these tests—within and around our school culture. Let me illustrate.

As a society, we continue to ascribe great value to standardized tests. We assign great political visibility and power to the results they produce at local, state, and national levels. The paradox is that, as a society (both within and outside schools), we seem to have been operating on blind faith that these are sound tests used appropriately by educators. As a society, almost to a person, we actually know very little about standardized tests or the scores they produce. This blind faith has prevented us from understanding some very important limitations of standardized tests. As a result, the discrepancy is immense between what most educators and the public think these tests can do and what they actually are capable of delivering.

We have tended to ascribe a level of precision to test scores that belies the underlying reality. Many believe we can use standardized test scores to track student acquisition of new knowledge and skills so precisely as to detect deviations from month-to-month norms; so precisely that we can use them to predict success at the next grade level or success in college or life after school. But, as you shall see later in the chapter, standardized tests typically are not the precision tools or accurate predictors most think they are. They do not produce high-resolution portraits of student achievement. Rather, they are designed to produce broad general indicators of that achievement.

In addition, because we grant power to these tests and assign great precision to the scores they produce, we are relentless in our attempts to make them powerful instructional tools that are relevant in the classroom. The problem is that they provide little information of value for day-to-day instruction. There are two reasons for this. First, the tests often are so broad in their coverage that they are too imprecise for teacher use. Second, tests are administered only once a year, while teachers must continually make decisions. For these reasons, standardized tests typically are of little value at the instructional level. But, of course, that does not preclude their use at other important levels of decision making.

From a different but equally contradictory perspective, some have noticed these problems and concluded that we should do away with such tests. And so they have attacked standardized tests as being of poor quality. But, standardized tests generally do a good job of assessing the characteristics they are intended to measure. These tests are designed to sample student achievement in broad classifications of content and to tap specific kinds of reasoning and problem solving. Typically, a careful analysis by an assessment literate educator will reveal that a good one does that very well.

These societal habits of assigning great power to standardized tests, ascribing unwarranted precision to the scores they produce, striving against all odds to make them instructionally relevant, and generally misunderstanding them even while attacking them have conspired to create a major dilemma in education today: We have permitted these tests to form the basis of a school accountability system that is incapable of contributing to much-needed school improvement efforts. Sadly, our general lack of understanding of these tests from classroom to boardroom to legislative chamber has prevented us from achieving the *real* accountability that we all desire.

Addressing the Contradictions

To achieve the goal of real school accountability for student learning, we need to untwist the seemingly paradoxical circumstances in which we find ourselves.

First, we must acknowledge that standardized tests as we have defined them in the past really only cover a small fraction of our most valued outcomes. They have tended to assess mastery of broad domains of content knowledge, and of some kinds of reasoning. They cover these critical outcomes very well. But by the same token, they have tended not to assess complex multistep reasoning and problem solving. They have failed to assess student mastery of achievement-related skills or the ability to create complex achievement-related products—all critical outcomes in this day and age. As a result, we must acknowledge that the scope of coverage of most standardized tests is insufficient to warrant dependable inferences as to the overall effectiveness of our teachers or schools.

Second, we must continue our emerging attempts to discover better ways to assess a broader array of valued outcomes. We must invest the resources needed to experiment with and devise assessments and record-keeping systems that permit us to produce high-quality multidimensional portraits of student achievement, as that achievement grows over the long haul. These will require the commonsense application of all four assessment methods developed and used by an education community schooled in the basic principles of sound assessment.

And that leads directly to our third course of action: We must strive to create a society (both within and outside of schools) that understands the differences between sound and unsound assessment. Whether we are advocates or opponents of large-scale standardized assessment, we can only hope for a positive result of our national testing debate if we argue from an informed perspective. Comprehensive professional development in assessment is a must for all educators, and in-depth dialogue with our communities about the basic principles of sound assessment is equally important.

If we fail to take these steps, we will continue to rely on misplaced blind faith. With them, we begin to clarify outcomes, select proper assessment methods, sample appropriately, and control for extraneous interference—all keys to sound assessment. To apply these approaches consistently and appropriately, we must think and act within the framework of a usable, fair, and self-consistent philosophy or set of principles. Below, I state what I believe to be such a productive standardized testing philosophy.

A GUIDING PHILOSOPHY

Our challenge as a school culture and as a larger society is to keep these standardized tests in perspective in terms of their impact on student learning. Large-scale assessment results do not have as big an impact on student learning as do classroom assessments. Yet our allocation of assessment resources, media attention to test results, and political emphasis on such assessments would lead one to believe that they represent the only assessments worth caring about. In this regard, our assessment priorities have been out of balance.

If we are to establish a more balanced set of assessment priorities, therefore, we must give far greater attention to assuring the quality of classroom assessments. Having said this, let me hasten to add that a balanced perspective encourages the effective use of *all* of the assessment tools we have at our disposal. This includes standardized tests. In the hands of informed users who know and understand both the strengths and limitations of these tests, they can contribute useful information to educational decision making. Besides, they are so deeply ingrained in our educational fabric that our communities have come to expect to see scores from these tests periodically.

For these reasons, I believe that districts that abandon this kind of testing altogether, as some are doing, make a strategic mistake. The reason is that the vast majority of districts are unable to develop and implement the kinds of sound assessment alternatives needed to provide quality information for policy-level decision making. And similarly, most districts lack the expertise needed to develop assessments in which their communities are likely to have confidence.

Therefore, I think sound practice is conveyed through behavior such as that displayed in the opening vignette of Chapter 1. Remember how the members of that district school system did three things:

- They left their traditional standardized testing program in place.
- They changed from testing every pupil to sampling methods that reduced the number of students tested, and thus reduced testing costs.
- They used the savings to begin the kind of professional development needed to begin to deliver alternative assessments that can illuminate those aspects of student achievement not currently measured.

This is the kind of plan that can permit us to introduce the full array of assessments needed to profile the full set of achievement targets we expect of students. But, we need to complete several years of solid professional development and serious local assessment development to achieve this goal. So, as a nation, we had better get started. In the meantime, most of our communities will demand that we continue with some form of standardized testing.

This leads me to the following philosophy: We should continue the limited use of standardized tests where relevant to inform instructional support and policy decisions, but at the same time make absolutely certain each and every user of the assessment results (from the classroom to the living room to the board room to the legislature) is thoroughly schooled in the meaning and limitations of the scores that result. Ill-prepared users misunderstand, misinterpret, and misuse test results. From the perspectives of student well-being, sound public policy, and effective instructional practice, this is completely unacceptable.

If, as educators, parents, and policy makers, we presume to make decisions that impact student well-being based on scores on these tests, we absolutely must know what we are doing. This means that all involved must be schooled in basic assessment literacy by an educational community conversant with those principles as they apply to standardized tests.

Your preparation to provide leadership in this effort begins here and now.

LARGE-SCALE ASSESSMENT PURPOSES

Standardized testing, as noted in Chapter 2, arose in the 1930s and 1940s from a desire to assist schools in their social function of sorting along a continuum of achievement. Tests designed to serve these sorting functions highlighted achievement differences between and among students to produce a dependable rank order of achievers from lowest to highest. Such tests refer each individual student's performance back to a norm group for interpretation—how that student compared to other examinees who took the same test under the same conditions. This is called *norm-referenced* test interpretation.

Time for Reflection

What are some instructional support and policy decisions we make that necessitate ranking students (individually or in groups) so as to compare them?

Beginning with the accountability movement of the 1960s, however, the function of assessment started to shift from sorting to verifying student attainment of specific educational outcomes. As this shift in our large-scale assessment purpose has unfolded through the 1970s, 1980s, and 1990s, we have seen steady emergence of a different way of interpreting student performance.

Rather than referring scores back to a norm group for comparative interpretation, each student's score is compared with a preset standard of acceptable performance, or a criterion. Assessments interpreted in this way are said to be *criterion-referenced*.

Time for Reflection

What are some of the kinds of decisions that require a criterion-referenced interpretation of test results?

Neither norm-referenced nor criterion-referenced score interpretation is inherently superior or more appropriate. Each fits into certain assessment contexts. Therefore, issues of large-scale standardized test quality must be discussed first and foremost in terms of purpose.

Revisiting Users and Uses

In Chapter 3, we analyzed the users and uses of assessment at three levels: instruction, instructional leadership, and policy. We revisit those here, to establish a context for this chapter.

The prime assessment users at the instructional level are students, teachers, and parents. Nearly all of the key questions they face require the continuous collection of fairly precise individual student achievement information. Of the fifteen instructional uses of assessment listed in Table 3–2 for students, teachers, and parents, only two called for the kind of periodic assessment typically provided by standardized testing. At this level of assessment, the need for comparable test scores is not nearly as strong as the need for precise detail on specific student attainments.

However, you may recall that those in instructional support positions, including building principals, curriculum personnel, counselors, support teachers, and the like, need general achievement information that is comparable across all students in their context, so scores can be summarized as needed to inform key decisions (see Table 3–3). Periodic assessments of group achievement of the kind provided by standardized testing programs administered about once a year often can provide sufficient detail regarding achievement for these users.

Depending on the particular decision to be made, some users at the instructional support level may require norm-referenced (comparative) information. For instance, selecting students for special remedial or gifted programs often requires comparative scores. But most require criterion-referenced results reflecting student attainment of outcomes included in the school, district, or state curriculum.

Finally, think about the policy level of assessment use, involving superintendents, school board members, state department of education personnel, legislators, and citizens. Their decision-making frameworks are spelled out in Table 3–4. Here again, we find strong need for general information on group achievement—comparable scores gathered periodically and aggregated at various levels, such as school, district, and state. As at other levels, we find a prominent place for criterion-referenced information among those concerned with student attainment of specific state, district, or building outcomes.

Consider the key differences among assessment users in information needs as depicted in Tables 3–2, 3–3, and 3–4. Clearly, large-scale standardized tests are tools for instructional support and policy, where decisions require information summarized over large numbers of students. They do not serve classroom-level decision makers well, because of their relative infrequency and the low-resolution picture of student achievement they convey.

THE MANY FORMS OF LARGE-SCALE ASSESSMENT

Large-scale standardized testing programs come from many sources and take different forms. In fact, they can be developed by a department- or grade-level team within an individual school building, by district or state assessment personnel, or by test publishers for general sales and distribution or under contract for a particular client. To use these various forms of assessment well, we must understand them and how they differ.

Local Assessment Programs

Locally developed districtwide tests typically are designed to reflect valued outcomes within that district. As such, they most often take the form of criterion-referenced tests. An excellent example of such a program is the Portland Levels Test designed, developed, and managed by the Portland, Oregon, Public Schools. Mathematics, reading, and English usage tests have been developed using selected response exercises, and a direct writing assessment has been added using performance assessment methodology. All assessments are specifically designed to reflect valued district outcomes. Further, each selected response test item is placed on a numerical scale in terms of content and degree of difficulty to permit results to track student development continuously across grade levels.

Portland also has added an innovative and sophisticated "computer adaptive" option for test administration. In this case, the respondent is presented with test items of known difficulty one at a time on a computer screen. Based on the respondent's performance on these, the computer selects subsequent items that are progressively easier or more difficult, until it locates the approximate level of proficiency for that student. This form of standardized testing can estimate student achievement using a fraction of the test items required on traditional test forms.

This is just one example of many such assessments developed at the local level. These kinds of assessments typically are developed by larger districts, which have the resources needed to support the technical staff required to build such a program.

It is not uncommon for districts to conduct their local standardized testing programs in two parts. They might administer both a norm-referenced standardized achievement test battery districtwide and locally developed criterion-referenced tests reflecting some priority outcomes in their particular community. A variation on this theme that is growing in popularity is to administer the norm-referenced test battery to a random sample of students—because this can produce the group achievement data needed for policy level decisions at greatly reduced cost—and use the cost savings for local criterion-referenced assessment at the instructional level.

It has been my experience that those who know the basic principles of sound test development can meet the challenge of local criterion-referenced test development very well. However, those who attempt local development of standardized tests without expertise have great difficulty developing sound assessments.

Published Achievement Tests

The most commonly used form of assessment in districtwide programs is the commercially published, norm-referenced standardized achievement test battery. These tests are designed, developed, and distributed by test publishers for purchase by local users. Each battery covers a variety of school subjects, offering several test forms tailored for use at different grade levels. Users purchase test booklets, answer sheets, and test administration materials, as well as scoring and reporting services. It is not uncommon these days for districts with their own response sheet scanning technology to also purchase test scoring software from the test publisher to analyze their own test results.

The unique feature of these tests is the fact that they are *normed* to facilitate test score interpretation. This simply means that the tests are administered to large numbers of students before they are made available for general purchase by users. Test results from this preliminary administration are used as a basis for comparing each subsequent examinee's score. The resulting scores are given percentile rank, grade equivalent, normal curve equivalent, and other labels. In a later section of this chapter, we will see exactly how these scores and labels are interpreted.

In addition, most test publishers now report at least some criterion-referenced information on score reports. Items in the test battery that test the same skill or objective are collected into a small test within a test, allowing the publisher to generate a score for that specific objective. The publisher typically sets a cutoff score of, say, 80 percent correct to conclude if that objective has been mastered by the student. Results are reported in terms of whether or not the objective has been mastered. Typically, results are reported for several such objectives.

Such information summarized across students can help districts identify skills or objectives in need of more attention within the curriculum. Another way districts analyze student performance that helps to identify student needs is by requesting item analysis data as part of their score reporting service. Given information on how students tended to perform on items in specific performance categories, instructional leaders can zero in on needed adjustments in instructional priorities.

Table 13–1 lists some of the currently available multisubject norm-referenced standardized achievement test batteries. Also, test publishers develop and distribute a variety of single-subject tests designed for use at various grade levels. Publishers provide catalogues of their products on request.

The key issue faced by consumers of these products is, Which test battery should we buy and use? To answer this question, a district must compare coverage of the various tests available with its local curriculum priorities at the grade level(s) where the test is to be used. The user's guide for each test will present tables of test specifications, like the ones we studied in Chapter 6, representing the content and reasoning coverage of every test in the battery. That coverage will vary greatly for the same grade levels across test batteries. Since there is no universally accepted national curriculum in the United States, test publishers test different content under the same subject label aimed at the same grade levels. Each district must compare and decide which test battery most closely aligns with their curriculum. Only this kind of analysis can assure sound sampling of student achievement. We will discuss this further below.

TABLE 13-1
Partial List of Published Multisubject Standardized Test Batteries

Test	Most Recent Publication	Tests for Grades Ranging	Publisher
California Achievement Test (CAT-5) Forms E & F	1992	K–12.9	CTB Macmillan/McGraw-Hill Del Monte Research Park 2500 Garden Road Monterey, CA 93940
Comprehensive Tests of Basic Skills (CTBS/4) Forms A & B	1989	K–12.9	CTB Macmillan/McGraw-Hill Del Monte Research Park 2500 Garden Road Monterey, CA 93940
Iowa Tests of Basic Skills (ITBS)	1989	K–12	Riverside Publishing Co. 8420 Bryn Mawr Ave. Chicago, IL 60631
Metropolitan Achievement Tests Survey (MAT-7)	1992	K–12	Psychological Corporation 555 Academic Court San Antonio, TX 78204
National Test of Basic Skills (NTBS)	1985	Pre-K–12.9	American Testronics Suite 910-North 8600 W. Bryn Mawr Ave. Chicago, IL 60631
SRA Achievement Series (SRA ACH) Forms 1 & 2	1985	K.5–12.9	CTB Macmillan/McGraw-Hill Del Monte Research Park 2500 Garden Road Monterey, CA 93940
Stanford Achievement Tests (SAT 8) Forms J & K	1989	K–12.9	Psychological Corporation 555 Academic Court San Antonio, TX 78204

State Assessments

The development of state assessments over the past twenty years has paralleled the emergence of concern over the effectiveness of schools, both in its timing and in the nature of the assessments that have emerged. As the accountability movement gained momentum in the late 1960s and early 1970s, statewide assessments began to appear with increasing frequency. Beginning with just a handful of assessments, by 1993, forty-six states had their own assessment programs.

Because these tests were created to see if students were meeting state standards of educational attainment, many statewide tests include criterion-referenced components. Norm referencing, however, remains prominent.

In the beginning, most relied on selected response formats because of the large numbers of students being tested. Machine scoring made the job easier and relatively inexpensive. Recently, however, state assessments have been experimenting with large-scale applications of performance assessment methodology, as they strive for more accurate representations of the complex outcomes articulated during the 1980s. Clearly, the most popular applications of performance assessment have been in writing assessment, where writing prompts are standardized for administration across the state, scoring criteria have been devised, and raters trained to evaluate performance. States also are experimenting with large-scale performance assessment in math, science, social studies, the arts, and other performance arenas.

Figure 13–2 gives a brief status report on state assessment programs.

National Assessment

Yet another level of large-scale assessment that reflects growing concern over school quality during the past two decades is the National Assessment of Educational Progress (NAEP). This federally funded testing program samples student achievement across the nation over time to track the pulse of changing achievement patterns. Results are intended for use by policy makers to inform decisions about national educational priorities. Since its first test administration in 1969, NAEP conducted criterion-referenced assessments of valued outcomes in the areas of reading, writing, math, science, citizenship, literature, social studies, career development, art, music, history, geography, computers, life skills, health, and energy. All four assessment methods have been used in the NAEP information gathering procedures, with selected response methods dominating.

These biannual assessments gauge the performance of national samples of 9-, 13-, and 17-year-olds, as well as young adults, reporting results by geographic region, gender, and racial and ethnic background. In recent years, the U.S. Congress has authorized NAEP to experiment with a voluntary state-level sampling plan permitting a state-by-state comparison of achievement results.

College Admissions Testing

Yet another form of standardized testing is the college admissions test—norm-referenced assessments of student achievement conducted near the end of high school for purposes of selection into college, placement in college courses, and awarding of scholarships. Two such admission tests are currently in use in the United States: the ACT Assessment Program, conducted by the American College Testing Program of Iowa City, Iowa, and the Scholastic Aptitude Test (SAT), conducted by the College Board.

While these tests are often cited as classic examples of norm-referenced tests, most don't realize that they have a strong basis in mastery of content and reasoning skills, too. The ACT Assessment, for example, includes four separate selected response tests, each of which yields several scores reflecting content mastery as well as reasoning skills. The scores reported include English (usage and rhetoric), Mathematics (pre and elementary algebra, intermediate algebra/geometry, plane geometry/trigonometry), Reading (social studies/science, arts/literature), and Science (reasoning). This strong content-based coverage allows the scores to serve educational and vocational planning, as well as course placement purposes.

The Scholastic Aptitude Test, developed by Educational Testing Service for the College Board, defines scores in a different manner, starting with two general ex-

	Number of States
Total Number of States Testing	46
Subjects Tested	
Reading, Writing, Math, Science, Social Studies	20
Writing, Reading, Math	35
Reading, Math	44
Writing	36
Science	33
Social Studies	28
Language Arts	23
Health & PE	4
Vocational Subjects	4
Art & Music	2
Grades Tested	Usually 3 to 6 grades per state; Most common: 3, 4, 5, 6, 8, 9, 10, 11
Tests Used	
Origin	
Commercially developed (off the shelf)	24
Modified published	8
Custom tests developed under contract	7
State-developed	36
Form of interpretation	
Norm-referenced components	34
Criterion-referenced components	33
Writing assessment	
Samples of student writing in response to prompt	41
Multiple-choice usage test	15
Assessment of existing work samples or portfolios	5
Using or experimenting with performance assessment	18
Purpose Cited for Assessment	
Accountability	41
Improve instruction	39
Program evaluation	31
Student diagnosis	23
High school graduation	18
School accreditation	10
Student promotion	9
Student recognition	7
School recognition	6
Kindergarten readiness	4

FIGURE 13-2

1993 Summary of State Testing Programs (Adapted from *State Student Assessment Program Database, 1992–1993* (n.p.) by L. Bond and E. Roeber, 1993, Oakbrook, IL: North Central Regional Educational Laboratory. Copyright 1993 by North Central Regional Educational Laboratory. Adapted by permission of the publisher.)

aminations that result in Verbal and Math scores and then adding a variety of advance placement examinations in many subjects.

Scores on these tests serve college admissions, as well as guidance and placement purposes. Examinees direct that their scores be sent to the colleges of their choice. Admissions officers use these data, along with high school grade-point average and a variety of other information about students, to select their freshman class. Scores also are passed along to course placement personnel for assigning students to the level of instruction that will best meet their needs. Performance on the College Boards and the ACT Assessment also feed into various local, state, and national scholarship award programs, including the National Merit Scholar program.

Summary of the Forms of Standardized Testing

Clearly, large-scale standardized tests come in many shapes and sizes. They can be developed at building, district, state, national, and even international levels to inform a variety of decisions. Many are intended for purposes of comparing students and for use at district, state, and national levels of decision making. However, as schools become performance-driven institutions, criterion-referenced interpretations are becoming prominent.

We next explore how our four basic methods of assessment are used in this context.

MATCHING METHOD TO TARGET IN STANDARDIZED TESTING

Across these many applications, all four of the commonly used forms of assessment—selected response, essay, performance assessment, and personal communication—have their roles.

Selected Response

The most popular form is and always has been the selected response format. It is relatively easy to develop, administer, and score in large numbers. When the achievement targets are content mastery and/or certain kinds of thinking and problem solving, its great efficiency makes this the method of choice by large-scale test developers. Its major drawback, as we have discussed, is the limited range of outcomes that can be translated into this format.

Essay

The essay format, a dominant form of assessment in European testing tradition, is rarely used in the United States. The one exception has been its recent popularity in writing assessments. But this application, where it is the form of communication and not the content mastery or reasoning that counts, is really an example of product-based performance assessment. However, it may be that the future may hold a larger role for traditional essay tests in large-scale assessment contexts, as the high costs of full-blown performance assessments become clear. Time will tell.

Performance Assessment

This option is the focus of much current discussion and experimentation in large-scale assessment. The assessment research and development community is exploring applications in writing, mathematics problem solving, science, reading, foreign language, interdisciplinary programs, and other performance areas. The great strength of this methodology is its ability to capture useful information about student performance on complex outcomes. Its limitations are the complexity of sampling and costs of the scoring process.

Sampling can be a problem because of uncertainty regarding the number of instances of student performance needed to lead to confident generalizations about mastery. This problem is exacerbated by the amount of time respondents must take to respond to each contributing exercise.

For example, if we wish to assess writing proficiency, how many samples of student writing do we need to draw confident generalizations about student achievement in this complex area? The answer depends on how broadly or narrowly we define the target. Broad definitions will require sampling student performance across many forms of writing (narrative, persuasive, expository, etc.). If each writing sample requires an hour or two for the student to generate, the cumulative cost of test administration can be high. When these costs are added to the costs of labor-intensive performance assessment scoring, the overall price tag can become frightening.

The two most attractive solutions to this problem from a cost-cutting perspective (always an issue in these contexts) both can have decidedly negative affects on the interpretability of the resulting scores. One is to sample broad targets with very few exercises, yielding results that do not systematically reflect the real domain of interest. The other is to define targets very narrowly, thus failing to reflect real-world complexity in the assessment and its results.

In these times of limited assessment resources and increasing demand for the higher-fidelity results of performance assessments, assessment experts continue to experiment with new and better ways to solve these problems. This experimentation is likely to continue, as we seek more efficient means of using this uniquely adaptable methodology in large-scale assessment.

Time for Reflection

Why do you think this experimentation is continuing in the face of the huge cost of performance assessment?

Personal Communication

The role of personal communication in large-scale assessment is beginning to change too, as researchers begin to discover the strengths of interviews as a method of data collection. By having students "think aloud" about what they have read, reading specialists gain insight into student comprehension (Wade, 1990). Math and science assessments also can take advantage of this idea. By having students reason out loud as they solve complex problems and respond to carefully crafted questions, assessors can gain insight into the reasoning processes of respondents and into their ability to communicate effectively. Of course, the drawback of this labor-intensive assessment method is the time required to interview large numbers of students. For this reason this method will be most attractive in contexts where relatively small samples of students are to be assessed. But it is an idea with great potential.

TEST DEVELOPMENT

While standardized tests may differ in coverage to meet the requirements of particular users, most test developers rely on the same underlying test development process. If we understand that process, we gain an appreciation of how much work must be done, and how dedicated local, state, and national large-scale test developers are to quality.

Clarifying Targets

Typically, standardized test developers begin with the thoughtful study of valued achievement targets in the context in which the test is to be used. Since most published norm-referenced tests still rely on selected response exercises, the targets of interest include student mastery of content knowledge and the ability to use that knowledge to solve specified kinds of problems. In the context of state and local assessments, targets also may include skills and products. In any event, comprehensive studies of opinions of instructional leaders are conducted to identify valued outcomes. Curriculum materials and commonly used textbooks also are tapped for information as to what should be tested. Most test developers place a priority on involving practicing teachers in their planning process, in order to be sure the resulting assessments connect with the appropriate outcomes.

The objective of these studies is to plan or blueprint the assessments to be developed. In those cases where selected response exercises are to be used, a table of specifications like those presented in Chapter 6 are created for each test. When performance assessments are to be developed, skills and products are outlined as a starting point.

In terms of our five attributes of sound assessment, therefore these tests typically arise from very clear targets. But most users don't realize that these targets usually are very broad in scope, often including several grades' worth of content in a single forty-item test. That means the coverage of any single topic may be very shallow, including no more than a few items to cover a year's worth of material. Indeed, given this constraint, you can see why the vast majority of material covered in any textbook or local curriculum will not be tested. But these tests cannot be made too long, or they will take up too much instructional time.

Time for Reflection

In what way could this limited content coverage become a problem for the test publisher? On the surface, it appears to be the user's problem, demanding cautious interpretation. From what perspective(s) is it more than that?

Translating Target to Method

Developers of large-scale standardized tests typically know how to match their target with a proper assessment method. In the past, they have relied on selected response formats because these formats have allowed them to tap the valued targets. Now, however, these same test publishers are beginning to turn to performance assessment for more complex skill and product targets.

When assessment plans are ready, test construction begins. Some developers use their own in-house staff of item writers; others involve qualified practicing teachers to create exercises. In either case, item writers are trained in the basic principles of sound item construction. Further, in most cases, those who are trained must still demonstrate an appropriate level of proficiency on a screening test before being asked to contribute to test development.

Attention to Sound Sampling and Control of Interference

Typically, far more test exercises are written than will be used on the final test. A careful screening process is used to select the best of these. Great care is taken to sample performance with enough exercises to represent the test plan or blueprint fairly and completely.

Once selected, the exercises are reviewed by qualified test development experts, content area experts, and members of appropriate minority groups for accuracy, appropriateness, and bias. Poor-quality or biased exercises are replaced. Through this process, extraneous sources of interference are minimized.

To uncover and eliminate other potential problems, the next step in test development is to pretest or pilot-test the items; developers recruit classrooms, schools, or districts to administer the exercises under conditions as similar as possible to those in which the final test will be used. The objectives are to find out if respondents interpret exercises as the authors intended and to see how well the exercises "functioned." Test developers want to know how difficult the items are and how well they differentiate between those who know and did not know the material. All of this helps them retain only the most appropriate exercises for the final test.

When items have been selected to match the content, thinking, and other outcomes of the test, yet another external review takes place. Item-development specialists, content-area experts, and appropriate minorities examine the final collection of test items again to assure quality and appropriateness.

Test Norming

The result is a polished new test. But the work doesn't stop there. Many test development plans call for the administration of the final test as a whole for further quality control analysis and, in the case of norm-referenced tests, to establish norms for score interpretation.

As soon as a test is completed, the publisher launches a national campaign to recruit school districts to be part of the norming sample. The aim is to involve large and small, urban and rural districts in all geographic regions, striving to balance gender and ethnicity—in short, to generate a cross section of the American student population.

Even though thousands of students may be involved, understand that these norm groups are voluntary participants. For this reason, they *cannot* be regarded as systematically representative of the national student population. Thus, when we compare a student's score to national norms, we are not comparing them with the national student population, but to the norm group recruited by that test publisher for that particular test.

Because of the voluntary nature of norm group selection, test publishers end up recruiting different districts to serve in the norming process for their particular test. Because none is randomly equivalent to the national student population nor to any norm group used by another publisher, norm-referenced scores attained on different test batteries cannot be meaningfully compared to one another.

Norm-referenced standardized tests are revised and renormed every few years to keep them up to date in terms of content priorities, and to adjust the score scale. This is necessary because, as the test remains on the market, districts align their curricula to the material covered. This is how they meet the accountability challenge of producing high scores. Over time, however, more and more students will score higher on the test. This makes it difficult for the test to differentiate among top-end students, so publishers renorm periodically to adjust the difficulty of the test. Users are advised to keep track of the occurrence of such "restandardizations," as they can affect the interpretation of test scores. Ask your test publisher about this.

Summary of Test Development

Clearly, standardized tests are products of hard work and careful attention to detail on the part of professional assessment and subject matter experts. As traditionally conceived, these tests have limitations. Paramount among those limitations has been their heavy reliance on selected response formats and the narrowness of the definition of academic success this engenders. But one thing that is typically not a limitation is test quality. These tests are carefully developed.

INTERPRETATION OF COMMONLY USED TEST SCORES

Standardized tests that rely on selected response items can report any of a variety of kinds of scores. We will review the five most common of these in this section by explaining how each score is derived and suggesting how each score can be used to understand and interpret test performance. We will study raw scores, percent correct, percentile ranks, stanines, and grade equivalents.

While these do not represent the only scores you will confront as a test user, they are the ones you are most likely to use and have to interpret for others. You must be conversant with these scores to interpret and use them appropriately.

Raw Score

When students take a test, the number of items they answer right is called a *raw score*. In the standardized test context, this forms the basis of all the other scores. Without knowing the raw score—the number of items answered correctly by the respondent—we cannot interpret test performance.

This score is important for two reasons. First, as you shall see, all other scores are derived from it. Second, it should be the starting point in the interpretation of standardized test score reports, because the raw score tells the interpreter whether other scores reported can be meaningfully interpreted and used.

To illustrate, if the items on a multiple-choice test offer four response options, a student who simply guesses will answer about a quarter of the items right. Thus, the guesser will attain a raw score very close to a quarter of the highest possible raw score.

This means that every selected response test has a "chance" or guessing score that can be calculated in advance. Take the number of items on the test and multiply it by the proportion of items a blind guesser could be expected to get right. For a four-choice multiple choice test that figure is .25. For a five-choice format, it is .20. So for a forty-item test with four choices per item, a person who was guessing would receive a score of about 10.

Time for Reflection

What is the chance score for a true/false test? Given this, what is the effective range of the test in terms of possible scores, calculated in terms of percent correct?

If you know that chance score for your standardized test, you can scan the score report for raw scores within a point or two of that chance score and identify students who either may have guessed or whose academic development may be far below that assessed by the test you used. For those students, followup testing at a lower level may be needed to obtain accurate information on their true level of achievement. Only a careful analysis of student scores close to the chance score can lead you to these students.

Percent Correct

This score is as familiar and easy to understand as the raw score. *Percent correct* reflects the percent of test items answered correctly by the examinee: raw score divided by total items on the test. This is the kind of score we use in the classroom to promote a common understanding and interpretation of performance on classroom tests. As the total number of items changes from test to test, we can always convert raw scores to percent correct and obtain a relatively standard index of performance.

There are two reasons why this kind of score is important in the context of standardized tests. First, this is the kind of score large-scale test developers use to determine mastery of objectives for a criterion-referenced score report. Examinees are judged to have mastered the objective if they answer correctly a certain percentage of the items covering that objective. The exact cutoff varies at around 70 to 80 percent correct across standardized tests.

The second reason for addressing this kind of score is to differentiate it from percentile. Very often, test users confuse percent correct with percentile scores or percentile rank. They are fundamentally different kinds of scores bringing completely different interpretations to the meaning of test performance. To understand the differences, we must first understand each.

Percentile Rank

For me, this represents the prototypical norm-referenced test score. The reason we compare student performance on standardized tests to that of other students (i.e., in the norm group) is to see how that student's score ranked among others who have taken the same test under the same conditions. Does the student score higher than most? Lower? Somewhere in the middle? This is the question addressed by this score.

Specifically, the *percentile rank* tells us what percent of the norm group a student with any given raw score *outscored*. A student with a percentile of 85 outscored 85 percent of the examinees on whom the test was normed.

Our objective in the following analysis is to create a conversion table that will allow us to convert every possible raw score on a test to a percentile, thus depicting what percent of the norm group scored below that particular raw score. This will permit us simply to check an examinee's raw score and know instantly what percent of the norm group that examinee outscored.

Table 13–2 provides the information we need to understand how a student's raw score can be converted to a percentile score. It describes the performance of our norm group on a new test. We will study this table column by column to describe this conversion process.

Column one tells us we will be analyzing student performance on a thirty-item test. Let's say it's a four-choice multiple-choice test. Possible raw scores range from 0 to 30, although the principle of chance suggests that a score of 7 or 8 represents the functional floor of the performance continuum.

Column two tells us how many students in our 1,500-person norm group actually attained each raw score. For instance, twenty students scored 25 on the test, seventy scored 13, and so on.

Column three presents a simple conversion of column two; it simply presents the percentage of students who attained each raw score. Look at raw score 20. One hundred and fifty students actually achieved this score, which represents 10 percent of the total of 1,500 examinees in the norm group.

Column four is where it begins to get tricky. This column presents the percentage of students attaining each raw score or any raw score below that score. Start at the bottom of the column. What percent of students attained a raw score of 7? One

TABLE 13-2
Understanding Percentile Scores

(1) Raw score	(2) Number of students	(3) Percent of students	(4) Cumulative percent	(5) Percentile
30	10	0.5	99.5	99
29	10	0.5	99.0	98
28	20	1.5	98.5	97
27	20	1.5	97.0	96
26	30	2.0	95.5	94
25	20	1.5	93.5	92
24	40	2.5	92.0	90
23	60	4.0	89.5	86
22	80	5.5	85.5	80
21	120	8.0	80.0	72
20	150	10.0	72.0	62
19	180	12.0	62.0	50
18	170	11.5	50.0	39
17	130	8.5	38.5	30
16	120	8.0	30.0	22
15	90	6.0	22.0	16
14	80	5.5	16.0	11
13	70	4.5	10.5	6
12	40	2.5	6.0	4
11	20	1.5	3.5	2
10	10	0.5	2.0	2
9	10	0.5	1.5	1
8	10	0.5	1.0	1
7(Chance)	10	0.5	0.5	0
6				
5				
4				
3				
2				
1				
TOTAL	1,500	100		

half of one percent. Move up the column. What percent of students attained a raw score of 17 or lower? 38.5 percent. So, a student who attains a raw score of 17 scored equal to or higher than 38.5 percent of those in the norm group.

But remember, that's *not* our definition of percentile score. For each raw score, we need to know what percentage of those who took the test were outscored by those attaining each raw score. Look at raw score 26. These students outscored everyone with scores of 25 or lower. We see that 93.5 percent of examinees attained a score of 25 or lower. If we round to whole numbers, then the percentile score for a raw score of 26 is 94. Anyone attaining that score outscored 94 percent of those in the norm group. These percentiles appear in column five.

So, in effect, we can create the conversion table we need for comparing raw scores of all future examinees who take the same test under the same conditions with the performance of the norm group—that is, for ranking students in terms of performance—simply by matching the raw score to the percent from column five, and reading it into the computer to make all future conversions for us. This is exactly what test publishers do. A raw score of 29 reflects a level of achievement on this test that is higher than 98 percent of the examinees in the norm group. This will remain true until the test is renormed.

Time for Reflection

Let's say a test is renormed every seven years. That means the conversion table will remain unchanged over those years. While the test is on the market and in use in a school culture that values high scores, teachers will naturally strive to learn about and cover what it tested. Over the long haul, what effect is this likely to have on average raw scores? On average percentile scores? Fill in the blank: These tests need to be renormed _____.

When test publishers norm a test, they create conversion tables for their national norm group, and typically also offer percentile conversions based on geographic region, gender, race/ethnicity, and local performance only. This means that exactly the same kind of conversion table is generated for students who are like one another in these particular ways.

You can see why I refer to percentile as the prototypical norm-referenced score. It provides a straightforward comparison of student performance as the basis for score interpretation.

It also should be clear how percent correct and percentile differ. The former refers scores back to the number of items on the test for interpretation, while the latter compares the score to those of other examinees for interpretation. Their points of reference are fundamentally different.

Stanine

This score represents a basic reduction of the broad conversion of the scores given in Table 13–2, as depicted in Table 13–3, from twenty-four points (raw scores 7 to 30) down to nine score points, thus the name *stanine,* short for *standard nine.* This conversion is done by dividing the percentile column into nine parts and assigning a numerical score to each part. Thus a student is assigned a stanine based on percentile rank. It simply represents a less-precise score scale, each point of which can be interpreted quite easily. When interpreted in terms of the general descriptors listed in the righthand column on the table, this score is easy to understand. A student

TABLE 13-3
Understanding Stanines

Stanine	Percent of scores	Percentile range	Descriptor
9	4	96–99	well above average
8	7	89–95	
7	12	77–88	above average
6	17	60–76	
5	20	40–59	average
4	17	23–39	
3	12	11–22	below average
2	7	4–10	
1	4	1–3	well below average

who attains a stanine of 3 on a test is interpreted to have scored below average in terms of the performance of the norm group.

Grade Equivalent Scores

This score scale represents yet another way to describe the performance of a student in relation to that of other students. The basis of the comparison in this case is students in the norm group at specified grade levels.

For instance, an examinee with a raw score of 20 on a test might have achieved the same raw score as students in the norm group who were just beginning fourth grade. This examinee would be assigned a *grade equivalent score* of 4.1: "fourth grade, first month." These scores are said to place students on the performance continuum in terms of a grade and month during the school year. But how does the publisher go about creating a conversion table for such scores?

Let's say the publisher is norming a newly developed forty-item test of fifth- and sixth-grade math. They administer their test to large numbers of students in those two grades at the very beginning of the school year. Each student receives a raw score ranging from 10 to 40. On further analysis of test results, let's say that the average score for fifth graders is 23, while sixth graders score an average of 28 correct. With this information, as represented graphically in Figure 13-3, Graph A, we can begin to create our conversion table. The first two conversions from raw to grade equivalent scores are those for the average raw scores. Because 23 was the average score for fifth graders, we assign that raw score a grade equivalent of 5.0. Because 28 was the average raw score of sixth graders when we administered our test, it is assigned a grade equivalent of 6.0. That accounts for two of the thirty raw score points to be converted. What about the rest?

Under ideal circumstances, the best way to convert the rest would be to administer our new test to students each month, so we could compute averages for them

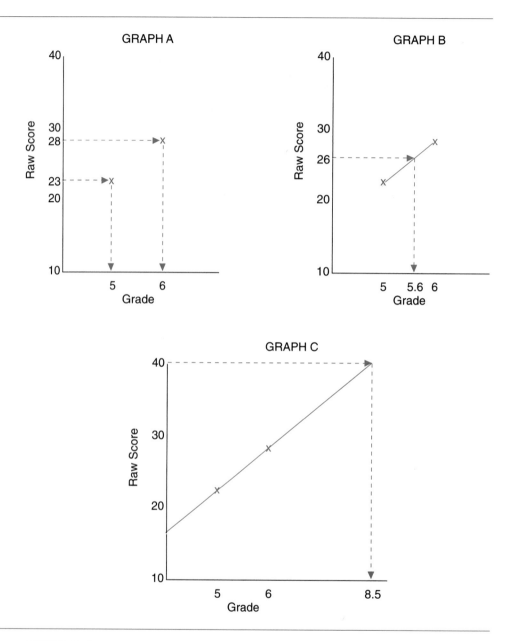

FIGURE 13-3
The Derivation of Grade Equivalents

and complete more of our conversion table. Unfortunately, resources are limited and few schools would put up with that much test administration.

So as an alternative, we can simply make the assumption that students grow academically at a predictable rate and we interpolate. By connecting the two averages, we create a mathematical equation that allows us to convert the scores between 23 and 28 to grade equivalents, as in Figure 13–3, Graph B. By projecting each raw score point over to the linear function on the graph and then down to the corresponding point on the grade scale, we find the grade equivalent to assign to each raw score.

But what about scores above and below this range? How shall we convert these? We have two choices: (a) administer the new test to students at higher and lower grade levels, compute averages, and complete the table, or (b) rely on our assumption that students grow at a predictable rate and simply extend our mathematical function down from 23 and up from 28. Option (b) is depicted in Figure 13–3, Graph C. This provides a means for completing the raw score conversions.

Once the conversion table is completed and read into the computer, henceforth, any student who attains a given raw score will be assigned the corresponding grade equivalent. Thus, the grade equivalent score reflects the approximate grade level of students in the norm group who attained that raw score.

The strength of this kind of score is its apparent ease of interpretation. But this very strength also turns out to be its major flaw. Grade equivalent scores are easily misinterpreted. Here is an example of what can go wrong:

Let's say a very capable student scores a perfect raw score of 40 on our new math test. As you can see from Figure 13–3, graph C, this will convert to a very high grade equivalent score. For the sake of this illustration, say that score is 8.5. An uninformed parent is going to see that and say "We must start my fifth grader using the eighth-grade math book at once!"

Time for Reflection

Based on the foregoing discussion, you may be able to see the two critical fallacies in this parent's reasoning. Before you read on, see if you can identify them.

First of all, no information was gathered whatever about this student's ability to do seventh- or eighth-grade math. All that was tested was fifth- and sixth-grade math. No inference can be made about the student's proficiency at higher levels. Second, eighth graders have probably never taken the test. The score represents an extrapolation on the part of the test score analyst as to how eighth graders would be likely to score if they took a test of fifth- and sixth-grade math. Thus, again no conclusion can be drawn about any connections to eighth-grade math.

The bottom line is that grade equivalent scores are *not* criterion-referenced scores. There is no sense in which the grade equivalent score is anchored in any body of defined content knowledge or skill mastery. It is only a comparative score referring a student's performance back to the typical performance of students at particular grade levels in the norm group.

IMPLICATIONS FOR TEACHERS AND INSTRUCTIONAL SUPPORT PERSONNEL

So what does all of this mean for those concerned primarily with classroom assessment? For educators, it means understanding that you have some large-scale assessment responsibilities that revolve around the need to use these tests appropriately. In that regard, you have a simple, yet demanding, three-part responsibility.

Responsibility 1: Student Well-being

Your first and foremost responsibility is to see to the well-being of your students—to keep them from being harmed. That means you must do everything you can to be sure all students come out of large-scale assessment experiences with their academic self-concepts intact. You can do several specific things to fulfill this professional obligation:

- *Be constantly mindful of when standardized tests are likely to contribute useful information and when they are not.* You can do this only if you understand the meaning of test results and how that meaning relates to the reasons for testing. In my opinion, we have entirely too much standardized testing being conducted merely as a matter of tradition and with no sense of purpose. Always insist on attention to purpose: What are the specific decisions to be made by whom and what kind(s) of information do they need?

- *Participate in the standardized test selection process within your district whenever possible.* And be sure to bring your knowledge of the attributes of sound assessments to the process. You know the standards of quality. Table 13–4 translates those standards into critical consumer questions you can ask. Demand quality.

- *Be sure your instructional program sets students up for maximum achievement.* Make sure the curricula to be tested are covered. But keep this in perspective. If the standardized tests you are using only represent a fraction of your total curriculum, allocate your instructional time accordingly. To do otherwise is to permit the test to inappropriately narrow your instructional program. Make sure everyone knows what proportion of your curriculum is covered so they can keep these tests in perspective!

- *Prepare your students to participate productively and as comfortably as possible in large-scale testing programs.* Take time to be sure they understand why they are taking these tests and how the results are to be used. Be sure they know going into the testing situation what the scores mean and do not mean. Provide practice with the kinds of test items they will confront, so they know how to deal with those formats. Communicate with parents about the importance of a settled home environment during the times of standardized testing. Be sure they, too, are advised on how to keep these tests in perspective. And above all, be positive and encouraging to all before, during, and after these assessments. All of these steps promote students who are "testwise."

TABLE 13-4
Key Questions to Ask in Standardized Test Selection

Standard of Quality	Critical Questions
Tests arise from clear and appropriate achievement targets	Which of the tests under consideration most closely approximates local curriculum priorities? What percent of the items to be used at a given grade level actually test material our district teaches at that level?
Assessments serve clear and appropriate purposes	What are our specific purposes for standardized testing—who are the users and what information do they need? Which of the tests under consideration is most capable of providing the needed information, in understandable terms and in a timely manner?
Method accurately reflects the valued outcomes	What are all of our valued school and/or district outcomes? Which of these outcomes require the use of which methods of assessment? Which of the standardized tests under consideration rely on proper methods for our outcomes?
Assessments sample achievement appropriately	How does each test under consideration sample student achievement and how does that plan relate to our local outcomes? Which test samples our curriculum most completely?
Assessments control for extraneous interference	What sources of interference present potential problems, given our standardized testing context? Which of the tests under consideration allow us to control for the most sources of potential problems?

- *When asked to participate in administering standardized tests, take the responsibility seriously and follow the prescribed instructions.* Standards of ethical practice must be followed. Anything you may do to cause students to misrepresent their real levels of achievement has the potential of doing harm to them, to you as a professional, and to the integrity of the educational community as a whole. If you are opposed to a particular set of standardized testing practices, bring all of your assessment literacy tools to bear during the debate. That is your right and your responsibility. But when assessment begins, adhere to prescribed procedures so results can be accurately interpreted.

- *Whenever standardized test results are being reviewed, discussed, or used in a decision-making context, be a voice for complete understanding and proper interpretation and use of those results.* If you determine that users do not understand the meaning and/or limitations of the particular scores in question, strive to explain them, or, if necessary, urge that users seek professional assessment expertise. Be diplomatic in this effort, but assertive. Do not permit misinterpretation. The well-being of your students hangs in the balance.

If you are a teacher or support person who is not in charge of planning or carrying out the standardized program, obviously you cannot dictate your district's course of action. But you can always be a voice for reasoned use of these tests. The higher your level of assessment literacy, the more persuasive you can be.

Responsibility 2: Community Awareness

Promote understanding within your community of the role of standardized testing and the meaning of test results. Members of the school board, parents, citizens, and members of the news media may need basic assessment literacy training to participate productively in the proper use of results. Only when they, too, understand the meaning of sound assessment will they be in a position to promote the wise use of these tests. Here are suggestions:

- *Encourage those responsible for district staffing to create a position for an assessment specialist* (if there is no such person now). This position will provide a focal point for leadership and services in this arena. Experience dictates that such staff members will be kept very busy—with both professional development activities and public relations!
- *Ask those test publishers who provide you with standardized testing services to assist you in your efforts to promote more complete community understanding of both the strengths and limitations of standardized tests.* This should be regarded as a legitimate part of their professional responsibility.
- *Seek out and take advantage of agencies who provide assessment training services.* These may include assessment service units of state departments of education, professional development units within intermediate educational service districts, staff developers from regional laboratories, other local private or public service agencies, and nearby colleges and universities.

Responsibility 3: Maintaining Perspective

We must all constantly urge those who support, design, and conduct standardized testing programs to keep these tests in perspective in terms of their relative importance in the larger world of educational assessment. We must constantly remind ourselves and others that these tests represent but a tiny fraction of the assessments in which students participate and that they have little influence on day to day instruction. While standardized tests should continue to command resources, we must begin to move rapidly toward a more balanced expenditure of those very limited resources so as to support quality classroom assessment, too.

This chapter appears in this book on student-centered classroom assessment to provide you with the motivation, understanding, and tools you need to follow these simple guidelines. I urge you to be a critical consumer of standardized tests and the scores they produce and to encourage others to do likewise.

CHAPTER SUMMARY: NEGOTIATING THE
CHALLENGES OF STANDARDIZED TESTING

Our purpose in this chapter has been to understand and learn to negotiate the challenges presented to teachers and those in positions of instructional support by standardized testing. Throughout our discussion, we spoke of the need for a balanced perspective on all fronts: leave traditional tests in place; economize whenever possible; use the cost savings to develop greater local assessment capacity; and experiment with innovative new assessment methodologies, but always with a sense of the need to meet standards of quality (clear targets, clear purpose, proper methods, proper samples, and interference controlled).

We reviewed the array of assessment purposes introduced in Chapter 3, emphasizing again the place of standardized testing in the larger context of educational assessment. These tests serve both policy and instructional support functions. They tend to be of little specific value to teachers, because the assessment demands of the classroom require greater frequency of assessment and higher resolution pictures of student achievement than can be generated with the typical standardized test.

We studied the various levels of standardized testing, from local to state to national to college admission testing, pointing out that all four assessment methods are used at some level. And we discussed their development.

Next, our attention turned to understanding and interpreting commonly used standardized test scores: raw scores, percent correct, percentile, stanine, and grade equivalent. These and other such scores are safe and easy to use when the user understands them. But, by the same token, they can be easily distorted by the uninformed. Your challenge is to become informed.

This led to a quick summary of our professional responsibilities. We emphasized that our concern first and foremost should be for the well-being of the students. Under all circumstances, we must demand quality assessment of our local curriculum. Each of us should strive to be an activist with a voice of reason in this arena. Only then will we be able to keep this form of assessment in proper perspective.

EXERCISES TO ADVANCE YOUR LEARNING

Knowledge Outcomes

1.   Based on your review of material presented in Chapter 3 and reexamined in this chapter, list the decisions informed by standardized test results and identify the various decision makers who use these results.

2.   Identify the various forms of large-scale standardized tests.

3.   List the various steps in the standardized test development process, explaining how test publishers attend to issues of test quality at each step.

4. Identify and define the kinds of standardized test scores discussed in this chapter.

5. List the basic standardized testing responsibilities of the classroom teacher.

6. Explain how *percent correct* and *percentile* are different.

Reasoning Outcomes

1. Turn to the section in this chapter, "Troubling Contradictions." List each of the contradictions identified and explain why it represents a potential problem in our effective use of standardized tests in schools.

2. Assume that your careful analysis of commercially available standardized tests reveals that no more than half of the items in any of those tests covers material specified in your curriculum for particular subjects at specified grade levels. That is, the best overlap you can get between what you want to test and any available test is 50 percent. This means half of the material tested will not have been taught during the year when it is tested. Yet your school board and administration compel you to choose and administer a test anyway. How should you proceed? What should you do to minimize harm and maximize the value of the assessment?

3. Compare and contrast norm-referenced and criterion-referenced interpretation of test scores. How are they alike and different?

4. Give one example of each type of score and explain how it should be interpreted.

5. Assume a student attains a raw score at the chance level on a particular test. The computer converts that score to a grade equivalent score that turns out to be three grades below the student's current assigned grade. The next year that same student scores at the chance level again. Again the conversion reveals the student still to be three years behind. The student's teacher the second year notes that the two grade equivalent scores reveal the student (a) remains three years behind, but (b) showed one year of growth over the past year. Upon reflection, this second teacher concludes that "this student is three years behind but growing." Is this a proper conclusion? Why?

Skill Outcomes

1. Your supervisor has asked you to take charge of and prepare the agenda for the first meeting of a committee to select the standardized test battery to be used in your districtwide testing program. The committee will consist of a member of your school board, a parent, a principal, and three teachers (elementary, middle school, and high school). What specific topics would you include in your first meeting agenda? Why? What important issues do you think this committee should address in fulfilling its responsibilities?

Affective Outcomes

1. List the advantages and drawbacks of developing an assessment-literate school culture and community. Do you believe assessment literacy to be important? Why?

2. Very often, large-scale standardized tests and their results are used uncritically by consumers. Why do you think this occurs? Why have we been so generally uncritical of these assessments, as a society? Does this represent sound public policy and practice, in your opinion? Why?

PART FOUR

Communicating About Student Achievement

Vague and insignificant forms of speech, and abuse of language, have long passed for mysteries of science; and hard or misapplied words with little or no meaning have, by prescription, such a right to be taken as deep learning . . . that it will not be easy to persuade either those who speak or those who hear them, that they are but the covers of ignorance . . .

John Locke (1632–1704)

CHAPTER 14

Communicating with Report Card Grades

Chapter Objectives

As a result of studying the material presented in Chapter 14, reflecting on that material, and completing the learning exercises presented at the end of the chapter, you will:

1. Master content knowledge:
   a. Know the principles of effective communication about student achievement.
   b. Specify the reasons why we need to reevaluate our communication systems for the future.
   c. State arguments for and against factoring achievement, aptitude, effort, and attitude into report card grades.
   d. List the steps in the report card grading process and the specific activities that make up each step.
   e. State practical strategies for avoiding common grading problems.
2. Be able to use that knowledge to reason as follows:
   a. Differentiate between achievement communications that do and do not satisfy the principles of effective communication.
   b. Compare grading based on rank order (on a curve) with grading in terms of student competence (with preset standards).
   c. Evaluate arguments for and against factoring various student characteristics into the report card grade.
3. Become proficient at the following skills:
   a. Be able to carry out the steps in effective report card grading, avoiding common problems.

4. Attain the following affective outcomes:
    a. See the need for more than the appearance of accountability for student learning in our grading systems.
    b. Value more effective communication about achievement in the future than we have attained in the past.
    c. See the need to define the meaning of academic success for each student within a given classroom.
    d. Value accurate description of student achievement in report card grades.

Note: The objectives of this chapter do not include the creation of any products.

With this chapter, we begin that part of our journey that deals with communication about student achievement. We will address the transformation of assessment results into information for students, parents, teachers, and others. As we proceed, it will become clear that we have many communication options at our disposal, from traditional report cards, to checklists of achievements, narrative reports, conferences, and collections of actual samples of student work. We will explore all of these. And as we do, bear in mind that we live in the information age. We have at our disposal a wondrous array of sophisticated ways to collect, summarize, interpret, and deliver information about student achievement—information processing technologies undreamed of just a decade ago. Our mission in this final part of our journey is to come to understand some of those communication options.

We will divide this facet of our work into three parts. First, in this chapter, we will address the most common and traditional of all communication options, report card grades. How can we use this familiar method to send clear messages about student achievement? In Chapter 15, we will examine options that enable us to deliver more specific information about student achievement by means of detailed written reports, conferences with and about students, and portfolios. What roles can these alternative modes of communication play in our future? And then in Chapter 16, the final stage of our journey, we will discuss again those principles that will allow us to define clear outcomes and transform them into solid assessments so we have quality information to integrate into instruction. With meaningful things to communicate, as we send out our messages about student achievement, can we assemble all of the pieces of the classroom assessment puzzle to create a positive, constructive assessment environment.

CHAPTER ROADMAP

As a teacher, until recently, I spent a great deal of time and energy wondering if I was grading "the right way." I asked myself the following questions:

• Exactly what distribution of grades was I to assign—how many As, Bs, and so on?

- Should I grade on a curve or use preset standards?

- Should my grades reflect absolute achievement at one point in time or improvement over time?

- What should I do with students who already knew all the material at the beginning of the term?

- Should I grade just on achievement, or also consider effort and attitude?

- How am I supposed to gather information on all these student characteristics?

- What should I do if my tests are too hard and everyone fails?

- Are my grades supposed to mean the same thing as those of other professors who teach the same course?

- If we all reflect different expectations and standards in our grades, how can anyone interpret grades accurately?

My list of questions, uncertainties, and concerns seemed endless.

If we are to use grades as an effective means of communication, each of us must come to terms with these issues. For this reason, we will devote this chapter to considering them in detail.

Two cautions before we proceed. First, as it turns out, there is no "right way" to manage report cards and grades. Rather, we can choose from several procedural options. Which we choose is a function of what we value about grading practices and student learning. Therefore, each of us faces the challenge of understanding and analyzing our own values in the grading context. We may not all agree with each other. But we each must be able to defend our practices in terms of our understanding of the assessment and evaluation process and our philosophy of student learning. This chapter is intended to assist you in this.

Second, much of the material covered in this chapter on grades and grading may sound like it is written for upper elementary, middle school, and high school teachers. Early elementary teachers have often said to me, "We don't use grades in our school. We use check, check plus, and check minus." Or, "We use O for outstanding, S for satisfactory, and U for unsatisfactory. So we don't have to worry about grades." The material covered in this chapter applies in these contexts, also. Grading is the process of abstracting a great deal of information into a single symbol for ease of communication. The only things that change in the instances cited above are the symbols used. The underlying issues remain the same.

As a general framework within which to examine and evaluate our grading and reporting options, we need to keep in mind some specific standards of communication quality. Before we start our journey through this chapter, we will take a moment and look at those guidelines.

Our communication goal in schools is to provide quality information about student achievement to users in a form they understand and in time to use it effectively. If we are to achieve these goals, we must start with the following:

- *A clear and appropriate definition of the achievement target(s) about which we intend to communicate.* We can only devise effective communication systems when we know what we want to communicate about.

- *Quality information about student proficiency with respect to the valued outcomes.* The quality of our communication is only as good as the quality of the achievement information we have gathered—that is, the quality of our assessments.

- *A clear reason to communicate.* We can only prepare and deliver effective communication in a context where we understand why we are communicating—how the information conveyed is to be used, by whom, for what purpose. That purpose must be clear for both message sender and receiver.

- *A shared language for message sender and receiver to use in passing information.* Effective communication requires that all participants in the communication link understand the meanings of all words, pictures, scores, or other symbols used.

- *An opportunity to share information.* There must be a time, place, and set of circumstances when message sender and receiver can attend to the information being shared.

As we discuss report cards and grades, we will need to remain constantly aware of these standards.

Time for Reflection

What are your feelings about report cards and grades? List as many things as you can that are good about them. Then list as many negatives as you can. Be specific.

THE NEED FOR CLOSER SCRUTINY

As a society, we have tended to place implicit faith in grades as accurate reflections of actual student achievement. Further, we have operated on the belief that grades are productive motivators for students. In fact, we may need to be more cautious in making such assumptions.

When schools serve the social purpose of sorting students along an achievement continuum, it matters little how teachers grade students. Even if the achievement targets are vague, the underlying assessments of poor quality, and the underlying true meaning of the grade unclear, we can still collect many grades over time, average them, and achieve at least the appearance of a dependable rank order of students. And from a motivational point of view, we have assumed that we could elicit sufficient seriousness of purpose from enough students to justify report card grading simply by demanding that students strive to win the competitive race.

In short, few educators, parents, or communities ever questioned our system of report cards and grades because they seemed to have been working.

But has our faith been justified? Have our grading procedures really been working as a communication system, when two teachers teaching the same subject in the same school to the same types of students at the same time very often hold fundamentally different expectations, assess in fundamentally different ways, and produce grades that appear identical on the transcript but have vastly different underlying meaning? Can we really trust a communication system in which those charged with assessment and grading sometimes lack sufficient understanding of the valued outcomes to assess them well, one in which few teachers have been provided with the assessment training needed to gather accurate information on student achievement? Our faith can only be justified if we act purposefully to overcome these kinds of problems.

Time for Reflection

Can you think of any conditions under which a student who had learned very little might receive a very high report card grade, or a student who learned a great deal receive a very low grade? What might make such miscommunication possible?

Schools are rapidly becoming institutions where high achievement is the expectation for all students, not just a few. We face this different mission with different communication needs. Rather than striving to sort, we strive for competence. School effectiveness is defined in terms of the proportion of students who hit the key targets.

Rather than serving as the means of ranking, assessments are seen as an integral part of the learning process as they verify the attainment of specified outcomes. Assessment quality is defined in terms of its accuracy in reflecting valued outcomes.

And so it is that the role of grades must change, too. Rather than representing uncertain reflections of uncertain achievement targets, report card grades must become sharply focused, understandable reflections of student attainment of those specified outcomes. Rather than rewarding and motivating only those who place high in the rank order, grades must bring the promise of success for all students who care, try, and achieve.

In addition, grading practices of the future, or whatever alternative communication systems we develop, must account for these emerging realities:

- Our achievement targets—those aspects of student achievement about which we must communicate—are becoming more numerous, presenting the need to communicate more information.

- Our targets are becoming more complex, making it necessary to communicate a higher level of detail about student achievement than ever before.

- Teachers will need to be able to share specific information with each other as they help students progress along the many alternative routes to competence.

- Achievement targets are becoming more individualized, as students within the same classroom aim for and achieve different outcomes at different rates.

For all of these reasons, as we look to the future, we will need to be sure that whatever communication systems we use, whether they rely on grades or other symbols, permit us to accurately gather, summarize, and share achievement information.

Time for Reflection

What additional reasons can you think of why we might need to be more attentive to the meaning and quality of our communications about student achievement in the future than we have in the past?

The reality we face is that, for the immediate future, teachers are going to assign grades on report cards as the primary means of communicating with students and families about student achievement. So for now, the relevant questions are these:

- How can we devise report card grading systems that help us communicate as effectively as possible?

- How can we devise report card grading methods that promise to motivate all students to strive for excellence?

To reach these goals, each teacher must do the following:

- Begin each grading period with a complete vision of the full set of achievement targets to be hit by students.

- Translate those targets into high-quality assessments, aligning targets to methods in sound and appropriate ways.

- Use those tools to assess student attainment of outcomes, keeping accurate records.

- Combine data collected over time into a high-quality composite index of achievement, assigning grades in a manner assuring accurate interpretation.

My meaning regarding the first two points in this list should be clear to you by now. Put simply, the basis of sound grading is sound assessment. Sound assessments arise from clear targets, fit a specific purpose, use proper methods, sample appropriately and control for extraneous interference. In this chapter on grading, we will address the following three aspects of the issue listed above:

- What targets should we factor into our report card grade?

- How much information must we gather and store to generate a high-quality composite index of achievement?

- How should we compute overall indices of achievement for our students and translate them into grades?

Sound grading, like educational assessment in general, is a challenge in clear thinking and effective communication—it is not just an exercise in quantifying achievement.

SELECTING ACHIEVEMENT TARGETS FOR GRADING PURPOSES

If we are to devise grading schemes that reflect real achievement and that contribute to a supportive, productive, and motivating environment, the first issue we must confront is what it is that we wish to communicate about. We must decide which student characteristics should be used as the basis for report card grades.

Traditionally, we appear to have had many choices. For example, many teachers factor in the following student characteristics:

- *achievement*—those who learn more receive higher grades
- *aptitude*—those who "overachieve" in relation to their ability receive higher grades
- *effort*—those who try harder receive higher grades
- *attitude*—those who demonstrate more positive attitudes receive higher grades

Of course, no two teachers will define these terms the same, or give them the same relative weight in their assessments. It is interesting to speculate just how interpretable a single letter grade would be into which some or all (we don't know which) of these elements have been factored—each bearing unknown definitions assessed with unknown methods and assigned unknown weights in the unknown grade computation equation. If we expect to communicate effectively about student achievement via grades, we must remove *all* of the unknowns from this equation. To do this, we must thoughtfully analyze each characteristic listed above to determine the advisability of factoring it into the grade. What are the arguments for and against each, and which set of arguments should win out, given the stated purpose of wanting to use grades to communicate and to motivate? We analyze each in turn below.

Achievement as a Grading Factor

If we use achievement as one basis for a grade, in effect, our contract with students is that those who master a larger amount of the required material—who attain more of the valued outcomes—will be assigned higher grades than those who attain less. This is a simple agreement to understand. It has long represented the foundation of our grading process.

Arguments For.   One reason this factor has been so prominent in grading is that schools exist to promote student achievement. In that sense, it is the most valued outcome for schools. If students achieve, schools are seen as working effectively. Grades are supposed to reflect a student's level of success in learning the required material.

Besides, students are expected to achieve in life after school. School is an excellent place to learn about this fundamental reward system. And in addition, achievement in most academic disciplines can be clearly defined and translated into sound assessments. So we can build a strong basis for grading achievement in our assessments of that achievement. In short, it can be done well, given currently available technology.

These are all compelling reasons why we traditionally have factored achievement into the report card grade, most often as the most prominent factor. Who would question the wisdom of grading in this way? Are there compelling reasons not to factor in achievement?

Arguments Against.   In fact, there are. For example, what if achievement is defined in complex terms that are very difficult to assess well, and we inadvertently mismeasure it? Or, what if we grade student performance based on a very important term-length homework assignment that the student did not do—a well-meaning parent did, instead? If we factor the results of such assessments into the grade, that grade misrepresents real student achievement. Those who read the grade later would draw incorrect inferences about student achievement and would make inappropriate decisions.

Or, what if the teacher lacks sufficient assessment expertise in the valued outcome to adequately evaluate student achievement of it? Again, mismeasurement is likely and the grade could be misleading with respect to real achievement.

Or, a more serious and more likely dilemma, what if each teacher has a different definition of the meaning of successful achievement, assesses it differently, and assigns it a different weight in the grade computation? Now our attempts to communicate about achievement are full of static, not clear, meaningful signals. When this happens, grades become uninterpretable.

Besides, if we factor achievement in, isn't there a danger that perennial low achievers will never experience success? For them, factoring achievement into the grade simply means more failure.

These seem to represent compelling reasons not to grade on achievement. So, which should win out—arguments for or against?

The Resolution.   The answer lies in our ability to address the arguments against factoring achievement into the grade. Let's explore this further.

Time for Reflection

Before reading on, how do these factors balance out for you? Do we grade on achievement or not? Take a stand, list your reasons, and then continue.

If we can devise and implement practices that overcome *every* argument against factoring achievement into the grade, then the argument must fall in favor of including it. In other words, it is unethical and therefore unacceptable to know that there are compelling reasons not to grade in a certain way and then simply decide to do it anyway.

So, can we address all of the arguments against factoring achievement into the grade and eliminate them?

If there is a danger of mismeasurement due to the complexity of outcomes, we can either simplify outcomes, or we can participate in professional development to help us to (a) refine our vision of the outcome to capture its complexity, and (b) devise more accurate assessments. These actions can prevent inadvertent mismeasurement of achievement.

If the problem is a lack of assessment expertise on the part of teachers responsible for grading, this may be alleviated by providing them with high-quality professional development in assessment so they may attain essential expertise. Or, we can work with qualified colleagues, supervisory staff, or higher-education faculty to devise sound assessments.

If problems arise because some teachers hold different definitions of achievement, we can meet to compare definitions. By airing differences of professional opinion, we can find the common ground on which to build sound grading practices.

If the problem is inevitable failure for the perennial low achiever, we can establish achievement targets that are within the grasp of each student, grading students in terms of standards that hold the promise of success for all and communicating individualized results.

Thus, if we act purposefully to develop and implement practices that remove objections by setting clear and specific targets, that are within the grasp of all students, using sound assessments, we can find ample justification for including achievement in the report card grade.

But remember, it is not enough simply to acknowledge each potential problem—specific calculated action must be taken to eliminate it. Fail to act and the arguments against must win out.

Aptitude as a Grading Factor

Here is this grading issue in a nutshell: Assume two students demonstrate exactly the same level of achievement, and that level happens to be right at the cutoff between two grades. If the teacher judges one of the students to be an overachiever in relation to expectations based on ability, aptitude, or intelligence, and judges the other to be an underachiever, is it appropriate for the teacher to assign them different grades? In other words, is it appropriate to factor a judgment about a student's aptitude into the grading equation?

Arguments For.   If we consider aptitude, or ability, in the equation, it provides us with an opportunity to individually tailor achievement targets to the talents of our students, thus increasing the chances of student success. In doing so, we hold out the promise of success for every student—a positive motivator.

And as students gain a sense of their own efficacy, teachers also will gain a source of motivation. What teacher is not energized by the promise of individualized achievement targets set so as to match the capabilities of each individual student, thus assuring each student at least the chance of academic success?

Besides, if we can identify those underachievers, we can plan the special motivational activities they need to begin to work up to their fullest potential. And we do so with no grading penalty to the perennial low achiever. This is a win-win proposition!

These are compelling arguments indeed. Factoring aptitude or ability into the grading process makes perfect sense. Who could argue against it?

Arguments Against.   Once again, there are some important counterarguments. For example, the definition of this thing called *aptitude,* or sometimes *intelligence,* is far from clear. Scholars who have devoted their careers to the study of this construct and its relationship to achievement do not agree among themselves as to whether each of us has one of these or many. They disagree on whether this is a stable or volatile human characteristic, and disagree as to whether this characteristic is stable at some points in our lives and unstable at others. They disagree about how this attribute (or these attributes) should be assessed (Sternberg, 1986).

Given this uncertainty among experts, how can we who have no background presume to know any student's aptitude or intelligence? That is not to say that all students come to school with the same intellectual tools—we know they do not. But it is one thing to sense this to be true and quite another matter to assume that we possess enough refined wisdom about intelligence to be able to capture it in a single index and then manipulate that index to factor it into such an important decision as a report card grade. We do not have sufficient knowledge or assessment expertise in hand yet to justify such practices.

But even if this problem of definition were to be resolved, we would face a serious assessment dilemma. Given the absence of training in aptitude assessment, even teachers with a dependable definition would face severe difficulty generating the classroom-level data needed to classify students according to their aptitude. Remember the key attributes of a sound assessment? Each would have to be met—for an attribute called *aptitude*—independent of achievement!

Then, each teacher would have to address the dilemma of defining the over- and underachiever. Specifically, each teacher would need a formula for deciding precisely how many units of achievement are needed per unit of aptitude to be labeled an over- or underachiever—and that formula would have to treat each and every student in exactly the same manner to assure fairness. We do not know how to do this.

Besides, what if we made the mistake of mislabeling a student as an underachiever? The student may be misclassified for years and suffer the consequences.

Even if the label were correct, is there not a danger of backlash from the student labeled as being a bright high achiever? At some point, might this student ask, How come I always have to strive for a higher standard to get the same grade as others who have to do less?

And finally there is the same "signal-noise" dilemma we faced with achievement. To the extent that different teachers define intelligence or ability or aptitude differently, assess it differently, and factor it into the grade computation equation differently, those who try to interpret the resulting grade later cannot hope to sort out the teacher's intended message. Only noise is added into our communication system.

The Resolution.   There are compelling arguments for and against factoring a traditionally important student characteristic into the report card grade. Which shall win?

Time for Reflection

Again, how do you sort these out? Take a position and state why before continuing.

The requirements for inclusion do not change. To justify incorporating aptitude or intelligence into the report card grade, all compelling objections must be addressed and removed through specific action by the grader. Can we devise a definition of aptitude that translates into sound assessment, that promises to treat each student in an equitable manner? Perhaps someday, but not today. There is no place for aptitude, ability, or intelligence in the report card grading equation. For now, the definition and assessment problems are insurmountable.

But, you might ask, what about all of those compelling arguments in favor of this practice? What about our desire to individualize so as to motivate student and teacher with the promise of success? What about the hope this practice could offer to the perennial low achiever? Must we simply abandon these hopes and desires?

The answer is a clear and definite No! But we must individualize on the basis of a student characteristic that we can define clearly, assess dependably, and link effectively to the learning process. I submit that a far better candidate—a candidate that meets all requirements while not falling prey to the problems we experience in struggling with aptitude or intelligence—is *prior achievement*. If we know where a student stands along a path to ultimate competence, we can tailor instruction to help that student take the next step.

If teachers set achievement targets based accurately on student entry characteristics, share that expectation with the student, and grade on mastery of knowledge, demonstrated problem-solving proficiency, performance of required skills, and/or creation of required products, then we can conceive of a continuous progress assessment and communication system based entirely on achievement. Think of it as a contract between teacher and student set at the outset and monitored for success.

Effort as a Grading Factor

Again, the issue is easily framed: Assume two students demonstrate exactly the same level of achievement, and that level happens to be right on the borderline between two grades. If one student obviously tried harder to learn, demonstrated more seriousness of purpose, or exhibited a higher level of motivation than did the other, is it appropriate for the teacher to assign them different grades? Does level of effort have a place in the report card grading equation?

Arguments For.   Many teachers include effort in their grading process for a variety of apparently sound reasons. We see effort as being related to achievement: those who try harder learn more. So by rewarding effort with higher grades and punishing lack of effort with lower grades, we strive to promote achievement.

As a society, we value effort. Those who strive harder contribute more to our collective well-being. School seems an excellent place to begin teaching what is, after all, one of life's important lessons.

A subtle but related, and important, reason for factoring effort into the grade is that it appears to encourage risk taking—another characteristic we value in our society. A creative and energetic try to reach for something new and better should be rewarded, even if ultimate success falls short. And so, some think, it should be with risky attempts at achievement in school.

This may be especially important for perennial low achievers, who may not possess all of the intellectual tools and therefore may not have mastered all of the prerequisite knowledge needed to achieve. But the one thing that is within their control is how hard they try. So even if students are trapped in a tangle of inevitable failure because of their intellectual and academic history, at least they can derive some rewards for trying.

Thus, there are compelling reasons, indeed, for using effort as one basis of the grade. Could anyone argue against such a practice?

Arguments Against.   In fact, we can argue against it for many good reasons. A primary reason is that definitions of what it means to try hard vary greatly from teacher to teacher. Some definitions are relatively easy to translate into sound assessments: *those who complete all homework put forth effort.* But other definitions are not: *trying hard means making positive contributions to the quality of the learning environment in our classroom.* To the extent that teachers differ in their definition, assessment, and manner of integrating information about effort into the grading equation, we add noise—unclear, meaningless signals—into the grade interpretation process.

Besides, we may say we want students to participate in class as a sign of their level of effort, but who most often controls who gets to contribute in class? The teacher. How, then, do we justify holding students accountable for participating when they don't control this factor?

Further, *apparent* level of effort is manipulable by students. If I know you grade in part on the basis of my level of effort and I care what grade I receive, you can bet that I may *act* in such a way as to make you think I am trying hard, whether I am or not. How can you know if I'm being honest?

From a different perspective, effort often translates into assertiveness in the learning environment. Those who assertively seek teacher attention and participate aggressively in learning activities are judged to be motivated. But what of naturally quieter students? Effort is less likely to be visible in their behavior regardless of its level. And this may carry with it gender and/or racial-ethnic differences, yielding the potential of systematic bias in grades as a function of factors unrelated to achievement. Members of some groups are enculturated to avoid competition. Gender, ethnicity, and personality traits have no place in the grading equation.

And finally, factoring effort into the grade may send the wrong message to students. In real life, just trying hard to do a good job is virtually never enough. If we don't deliver relevant, practical outcomes, we will not be deemed successful, regardless of how hard we try.

Besides, from the perspective of basic school philosophy, what is it we really value, achieving the desired outcomes or achieving the desired outcomes and knowing how to make it look like we tried hard? What if it was easy?!

The Resolution.   The balance scale tips in favor of including effort only if arguments against doing so can be eliminated.

Time for Reflection

How do you come down on this one? How does the scale tip and why?

First, we must face the issue of what we value as the outcomes of school. If we value learning, then we must define it and build our reporting systems around it. If we value effort too, then again we must arrive at a mutually acceptable definition of it and its assessment. If we value both, why must we combine them into the same grading equation? We know how to devise reporting systems that present information on each—separately.

If the objection is the lack of consistency in the underlying definition, then we must come together to agree on clear and appropriate definitions—*and* this definition must account for students who need little effort to learn. There can be no penalty for them.

If the problem is poor-quality assessment, we must understand and adhere to all appropriate rules: sound assessment of effort must arise from a clear target, have a clear purpose, rely on a proper method of assessment, sample effort in a systematically representative manner, and control for all relevant sources of extraneous interference. But again, if we go to all this work to create rigorous assessments, why bury the results in the far reaches of some complex grade computation equation? Why not report the achievement and effort results separately?

When students set out purposely to mislead us with respect to their real level of effort, they can seriously bias our assessment. This may be impossible to eliminate as a problem. If we address 30 students per day all day for a year and some are misleading us about their real level of effort, we may well see through it. But as the number approaches and exceeds 150 students for one hour a day and sometimes only for a few months, as it does for most middle and high school teachers, there is no way to confidently, dependably determine how hard each student is trying.

Moreover, if effort influences the grades of some, equity demands that it have the same influence on all. The assessment and record-keeping challenges required to meet this standard are immense, to say the least.

But a more serious challenge again arises from the personality issue. Less aggressive people are not necessarily trying less hard. Quiet effort can be very diligent and very productive. As teachers, we really do have difficulty knowing how much effort most students are putting forth. And we have few ways of overcoming this problem—especially when most of the effort is expended outside the classroom.

If you can define effort clearly, treat all students consistently, and meet the standards of sound assessment, then gather your data and draw your inferences about each student's level of effort. Just be *very* careful how you use those results at report card grading time. This is a mine field that becomes even more dangerous when effort and achievement data are combined in the same grade. I urge you to report them separately, if you report effort outcomes at all.

Finding Better Ways to Motivate.   We grade on effort to motivate students to try hard. We feel that if they try hard, they will learn more. And for those students who care about their grades, it may work. But if we are to understand other ways to motivate, we must also consider those cases in which our leverage has lost its power. How shall we motivate those students who could not care less what grade we assign them—those who have given up and who are just biding their time until they can get out? For them, grades have lost all motivational value. If you think they are going to respond to our admonitions that they try harder so they can raise their grade, you are being naive.

The general issue is this: What would you do to encourage students to come to school and participate with you in the learning experiences you had designed for them if you could no longer use grades and report cards as a source of reward and punishment to control students?

Consider these options: You might strive to sense students' needs and interests and align instruction to those. You might work with students to establish clear and specific targets so they would know that they were succeeding. In short, you could try to take the mystery out of succeeding in school.

You would be sure instructional activities were interesting and provocative—keeping the action moving, always bearing agreed-upon targets in mind. You would share the decision-making power so as to bring them into the learning process as full partners, teaching them how to gauge their own success. In short, you would strive to establish in your students an internal sense of control over their own academic well-being. If they participate, they benefit—and they know this going in.

This is just a beginning list of ideas. You can probably think of more. These ideas will work better as motivators than saying to students, "If you don't look like you're making an effort, I will lower your final grade."

Attitudes as a Grading Factor

You can probably frame this problem by yourself: Two students attain exactly the same level of achievement. Their semester academic average is on the cutoff between two grades. One has constantly exhibited a very positive attitude, while the other has been consistently negative. Is it justified to assign them different grades?

Arguments For.   A positive attitude is a valued outcome of school, too, so anything we can do to promote it is an effective practice. People with positive attitudes tend to secure more of life's rewards. School is an excellent place to begin to teach this lesson.

Besides, this just may be the most effective classroom management tool we teachers have at our disposal. If we define positive attitude as treating others well, following classroom rules, listening to the teacher, getting work in on time, and the like, then we can use the controlling leverage of the grade to maintain a quiet, compliant learning environment.

And, once again, this represents a way for us to channel at least some classroom rewards to the perennial low achiever. As with effort, attitude is within the control of students. If they're "good," they can experience some success. Sounds good—let's make it part of the grading equation!

Arguments Against.   It is seldom clear exactly which attitudes are supposed to be positive. Are students supposed to be positive about fellow students, the teacher, school subjects, school in general, or some combination of these? Must all or just some be positive? What combinations are acceptable?

How shall we define a positive attitude? Is it positive to accept an injustice in the classroom compliantly, or is it positive to stand up for what you think is right, causing a disruption? Is it positive to act as if you like story problems in math, when in fact you're frustrated because you don't understand them? The definition of positive is not always clear.

Further, if apparent effort can be manipulated, so can apparent attitude. Regardless of my real feelings, if I think you want me to be positive to get a better grade and if I care about that grade, you can bet that I will exhibit whatever behavior you wish. Is honesty not also a valued outcome of education?

Assessment also can be a source of difficulty. It takes a special understanding of paper and pencil assessment methodology, performance assessment methods, and personal communication to evaluate affective outcomes such as attitudes. The rules of evidence for quality assessment are challenging, as you will recall from Chapter 13. So mismeasurement is a very real danger.

Oh, and as usual, to the extent that different teachers hold different values about which attitudes are supposed to be positive, devise different definitions of *positive,* assess attitudes more or less well, and assign them different weights in the grading equation, we factor even more noise into our communication system.

Some tough problems . . .

Time for Reflection

Once again, are you for or against? Make your stand and then read on.

The Resolution.   To decide which side of the balance sheet wins out here, we must determine which use of attitude information produces the greatest good for students. Let's say we get an inkling of an extremely negative attitude on the part of one student about a particular school subject. Which use serves that student better: Citing your evidence of the attitude problem (gathered through a good performance assessment) and telling that student they had better turn it around before the end of the grading period or their grade will be lowered? Or, accepting the attitude as real and talking with the student honestly and openly about the attitude and its origins (using good-quality assessment through personal communication) in an honest attempt to separate it from achievement and deal with it in an informed manner?

The power of attitude data lies not in its potential to help us control behavior but in our ability to promote a more positive learner, and learning environment. If we go to the difficulty of (a) defining the attitudes we want to be positive (and this can be done), (b) devising systematic, high-quality assessments of those attitudes (which can be done, too), and (c) collecting representative samples of student attitudes (an eminently achievable goal), and then fail to use the results to inform instructional design—choosing only to factor the results into grades—we have wasted an immense opportunity to help students.

And if we enlist students as partners in this process, they are likely to be even more honest with us about how they feel about their learning environment, thus providing us with even more ammunition for improving instruction. But if you think for one moment students are likely to be honest with us in communicating attitudes if they think the results might be used against them at grading time, you are again being naive.

Although we probably can overcome all of the difficulties associated with defining attitudes for grading purposes and overcome the assessment difficulties attendant to these kinds of outcomes, I personally think it is bad practice to factor attitudes into report card grades.

Summary of Grading Factors

If report card grades are to serve us at all in our transition into the era of achievement-driven schools, they *must* reflect our valued educational outcomes. For this reason, grading systems must include indicators of student achievement unencumbered with indicators of other student characteristics, such as aptitude, effort, or attitude. That is not to say that information might not be reported on effort or attitude, if definition and assessment difficulties can be overcome, which is no small challenge. Under any circumstances, aptitude or intelligence or ability have no place in the grade reporting process.

Grades can reflect valued outcomes—meaning *achievement*—only if those outcomes are clearly defined in each grading context for a given grading period, sound assessments are developed for those outcomes, and careful records kept of student attainment of the outcomes over the grading period. In the next section, we explore these ideas in detail.

GATHERING ACHIEVEMENT INFORMATION FOR GRADING PURPOSES

If report card grades are to inform students, parents, other teachers, administrators, and others about student achievement, then the actual achievement underpinning each grade must have been clearly and completely articulated and assessed. To be done effectively, the valued outcomes must be spelled out *before* the grading period begins. Further, an assessment plan must be laid out in advance to systematically sample those outcomes. While it sounds like a great deal of preparation to complete before teaching begins, it is not. And further, it saves a great deal of assessment work during instruction.

Besides, remember the great benefits of being clear about achievement targets:

- It sets limits on teacher accountability—you know the limits of your teaching responsibility. When the target is clear and appropriate and all of your students can hit it, you are successful as a teacher.

- It sets limits on student accountability—they know the limits of their learning responsibility. When they can hit the valued target, they are successful as students. And the less mysterious that target is, the more serious they will be about striving to hit it.

- Students can share a great deal of the assessment work, thus turning assessment time into valuable teaching and learning time.

1. Begin with a comprehensive view of expected outcomes.
2. Turn that big picture into a specific assessment plan.
3. Turn the plan into assessments.
4. Turn assessments into information about achievement.
5. Summarize the information into individual achievement composites for each student.
6. Convert each composite into a grade.

FIGURE 14-1
Steps in the Report Card Grading Process

Let's look at a six-step plan for gathering sound and appropriate achievement information for grading purposes. This is not the only way to grade, but it is one that can be effective and efficient. Figure 14–1 lists the six key steps.

Step 1: Spelling Out the Big Achievement Picture

To draw a complete picture of the valued achievement targets for a given subject over a grading period, gather together all relevant curricular and text materials and ask four questions (they will sound very familiar—we have seen examples of these in each chapter of this book):

- What is the subject matter knowledge that students are to master?
- What, if any, reasoning and problem-solving proficiencies are they to demonstrate?
- What, if any, skills are to be mastered—things students need to be able to do?
- What, if any, products are they to create?

Generate brief descriptions of your answers to these four questions for each unit to be covered during the grading period. A short outline or a few brief sentences will suffice. Further, if you have a sense of the relative importance of the various targets, state them, too.

By the way, affective outcomes are not listed above, not because they are unimportant, but because, as discussed above, they do not play a role in the report card grading decision.

Later, as you actually prepare to present each unit, you will need to fill in the specific detail:

- the actual propositions that capture the important knowledge outcomes of that unit, noting their order of importance
- the specific kinds of reasoning to be demonstrated, again, noting priorities as appropriate
- key elements in successful skill performance

- the nature of the products to be created and the key elements of a high-quality product

These will form the basis of your assessments. For now, simply create a general outline of the important elements of the big picture—spelled out in your own words. In short, immerse yourself in this big picture and force limits onto it.

As you do this, if any part of this picture remains unclear, you have several places to turn for help: state or local curriculum goals and objectives, your text and its support materials, your principal, department chair, or colleagues, and your professional library.

Here is another productive way to think about this planning process (we have discussed this idea before): States or districts that adopt an outcomes-based philosophy for their schools typically begin by working with their communities to agree upon a set of ultimate outcomes for students in their educational system. You and your colleagues may divide each of these outcomes into enabling outcomes that represent paths to ultimate competence. Those paths can then be subdivided again into their constituent parts. At some appropriate level of specificity, you may then integrate these enabling components into the curriculum, level by level, so as to create progressive frameworks of outcomes to lead your students to ultimate success. In this way, you may come together and plan to share responsibility for helping students to grow academically.

For grading purposes, the comprehensive question you must answer is this: Which of those knowledge, reasoning, skill, and product outcomes that constitute attainment of ultimate district or state outcomes are my responsibility? This question is answered most productively when an entire faculty, from kindergarten through twelfth grade, answers it together or at least in collaboration with one another. Only then can the progression of student growth be coordinated over the years of schooling.

Step 2: Turning the Big Picture into an Assessment Plan

Once your big picture is clear, your report card grading challenge is clearly drawn. The next question is, How shall you assess student attainment of your classroom outcomes so you may state with confidence what proportion of the total array of outcomes each student has mastered? In other words, how shall you relate information from selected response, essay, performance, and personal communication assessments, as appropriate, to give you an accurate sense of how much of the required material each student has mastered? You need an assessment plan.

You don't need the assessments themselves—not yet. Those come later, as each unit of instruction unfolds. But you do need to know how you will take each student down the assessment road, from "Here are my expectations" to "Here is your grade." This assessment plan needs to satisfy certain conditions:

- It must include listings for each grade-related assessment event during the grading period:
  1. the achievement focus of the assessment
  2. when the assessment is to take place
  3. the assessment method to be used

- Each assessment listed in the plan needs to supply an important piece of the puzzle with respect to the priority outcomes of the unit and grading period within which it occurs.

- Each assessment must accurately represent the particular outcome(s) it is supposed to depict (i.e., each must be a sound assessment according to our quality criteria).

- The full array of assessments conducted over the entire grading period needs to accurately represent student mastery of the big picture.

- And, most importantly, the entire assessment plan must involve a reasonable assessment workload for the teacher and students.

A Reality Check.   This last condition may be easier to meet than you think. The report card grading challenge is to gather just enough information to make confident grading decisions and no more. Ask yourself: How can I gather the fewest possible assessments for grading purposes and still generate an accurate estimate of term-length performance? Most teachers spend entirely too much time gathering and grading too many assessments for *grading* purposes. Some feel they must grade virtually everything students do and enter each piece of work into the gradebook record to assign accurate report card grades. Not true. With planned, strategic assessments, you can generate accurate estimates of performance very economically.

I see many teachers operating on the shotgun principle of grading: Just gather a huge array of graded student work over the course of the grading period, and somewhere, somehow, some of it is sure to reflect valuable outcomes. While this may be true to some unknown extent, as an approach, it is at best inefficient. Why not plan ahead and minimize your assessment work?

If you can zero in on the key outcomes and draw dependable inferences about student mastery of big picture outcomes with a few unit assessments and a final exam or project assignment, that's all you need for report card grading purposes.

Assessments for Learning But Not for a Grade.   Let's be sure to remember that grading is not the only reason for classroom assessment. We established that fact very early. We also can use assessments for diagnosing student needs, providing students with practice performing or evaluating performance, and tracking student growth during instruction.

For example, I give my students assignments every class and inform them that practice is important for performing well on the final essay exam. Our agreement is that if they wish to hand in assignments for feedback, I'll be pleased to provide it. Some take advantage of this opportunity. Some do not. But there is no grade involved in this "homework for practice" process.

Performance on assessments used for purposes other than grading need not be factored into the report card grading process. Self-assessment is for diagnosing needs. We don't grade students when they are evaluating their own needs. Practice assessments are for polishing skills, overcoming problems, fine-tuning performance. We don't (or shouldn't) grade students when they are trying to learn from their mistakes.

Experienced teachers who read this might say, "If I don't assign a grade and have it count toward the report card grade, the students won't take it seriously—they won't do it!" That depends. Once they come to understand that practice helps, but performance is what counts, I think they will learn to practice and they will perform. While it might take some time to break old habits, once they come to understand that good grades are not the rewards for doing work but rather are the rewards for learning, I think they will practice—especially if that practice can take place in a supportive, success-oriented classroom.

Time for Reflection

Whose responsibility is it if students don't take ungraded work seriously and don't practice? Whose responsibility should it be? With whom should the consequences reside if learning fails to occur? Think about this before continuing.

Success requires a collaborative partnership—with both partners fulfilling their part of the bargain. Has that occurred? As a teacher, you can provide the supportive environment, opportunity, and means to learn. But you cannot do the learning for your students. As a teacher, you must set limits on your contribution. All you can do is be sure your students see the relationship between practice and successful performance on the periodic assessments that contribute to their grades.

But, let's say a student fails to practice on interim assessments and performs poorly on the assessment that counts for the grade. As a teacher, how do you respond? One option is to say, "I told you so," and let it go. Another response is, "I guess you found out how important practice is, didn't you? Nevertheless, I value your learning whenever it occurs. Do you want to practice now and redo the assessment? If you do, I will reevaluate your performance—no penalties. But I will have to fit that reevaluation within my schedule."

Time for Reflection

Have you ever had the opportunity to retake an exam? Did your performance change? What was the effect on your mastery of the material?

Incidentally, you can prepare for such retest eventualities by developing more than one form of your grading assessments. That may mean creating more than one set of items reflecting your tables of test specifications or more than one sample of exercises for your performance assessments. Just be sure these alternate forms are parallel, that they sample the same outcomes.

Your job as a teacher is to set appropriate targets that reflect your share of the building blocks to competence and that your students can achieve, and then agree with your students and your supervisor that you will do everything ethical within your power to ensure student success.

That means there is no artificial scarcity of high grades—only 7 percent can get As—to limit the number of students who succeed. If everyone succeeds, everyone receives a high grade. The more students know and believe this, the more seriously they will practice in preparation for the assessments that contribute to the grade. You need conduct only enough assessments during a grading period to identify when that has happened.

Step 3: From Plan to Assessments

So, we begin the grading period with our strategic assessment plan in hand. What next? We need to devise or select the actual assessments as each unit unfolds, being sure to follow the assessment development guidelines specified in Chapters 6 through 9. Each assessment will need to be created and conducted, and results evaluated and recorded.

In each case where there are knowledge and problem-solving targets to be assessed via selected response or essay assessments, we need categories of knowledge, kinds of reasoning, tables of specification, propositions, and finally test exercises themselves, assembled into assignments, quizzes, and tests that fill in those parts of the big picture.

When there are skill and product outcomes to be assessed, we need detailed descriptions, performance criteria, exercises to elicit performance, and rating scales or checklists assembled into performance assessments that supply those pieces of the puzzle.

All assessments should align exactly with our vision of student competence. Some might be developed in advance, to save time later. Others might be developed during instruction—with students involved in the process.

This may sound like a great deal of work, but remember five important facts:

- This method is not nearly as much work as the shotgun approach.
- It affords the conscientious teacher a great deal more peace of mind. When your students succeed, so do you, and you will know that you have been successful.
- Students can play key roles in specific ways spelled out earlier, thus turning nearly all of this assessment time and energy into productive learning time and energy.
- Student motivation to learn is likely to increase.
- The results of your hard work remain intact for you to use or adapt next time, and the time after that. Thus, the cost of development is amortized over the useful life of your plan and its associated assessments.

Step 4: From Assessments to Information

Obviously, the next step is to carry out your plan, administering your assessments when appropriate as the grading period progresses. As the achievement information begins to come in, what should be recorded? A few guidelines follow:

- Maintain written records. Remember the fallibility of the human mind—no mental record keeping.

- Maintain as much detail in the accumulated records as you can. If numerical data results, record it as is. Don't convert it to a grade and record the grade, thus unnecessarily sacrificing information that could be useful later. Or, if a profile of performance data results, such as when you use a performance assessment with several rating scales, record the profile. Again, don't covert to a grade and lose valuable detail. Record percent correct or actual profile ratings.

- If scores are to be weighted differently later to compute a composite index of achievement (i.e.,you regard some as more important, or some cover more material than others and will be given more weight at grading time), store those scores in the same units, such as percent of total available points. This is illustrated below.

Time for Reflection

Many teachers have discovered that grading records can be easily stored, retrieved, summarized, and converted to actual grades using their personal computers. Software packages are available that can serve as your gradebook and much more. How might you find out more about these options?

When the assessment plan has been carried out and the records collected, the time has come to generate a composite index of achievement for conversion to a grade.

Step 5: Summarizing the Resulting Information

At the end of the grading period, the recording process should result in a range of information indicating student performance on each of the components in your strategic assessment plan. This constitutes a portrait of how well each student mastered the outcomes that made up your big picture. The question is, how do you get a grade out of all of this information?

I urge that you rely on a computational sequence that treats all students the same and that can be reproduced later, should you need to explain it or revise a grade. Such a sequence helps to control for biases in the grader that can cause an inappropriate inflation or deflation of a grade for reasons unrelated to actual achievement.

Please note that I am not opposing a role for professional judgment in grading. As we established in earlier chapters, that role comes in the design and administration of the assessments used to gather information about student achievement. We need to minimize subjectivity when combining indicators of achievement for grading purposes.

Combining Achievement Information.   To derive a meaningful grade from several existing records of achievement, again, each piece of information gathered should indicate the proportion of its related outcomes each student has mastered. So, if we combine them all, we should obtain an estimate of the proportion mastered for the total grading period. That is our goal. Two ways to achieve it are the percent method and the total points method.

Percent Method.   One simple way to accomplish this is to be sure each assessment is providing a representative sample of its target. Then convert each student's performance into the percent of total available points earned. For instance, if a selected response test has forty items, and a student scores thirty correct, we enter 75 percent in the record. Or if a student scores all fours on six five-point performance assessment rating scales, that totals twenty-four of thirty possible points, or 80 percent.

Time for Reflection

Think about the assumption being made here. The forty items on the test are a representative sample of a larger domain of all possible test items that could have been asked. So 75 percent on the test leads to an inference that 75 percent of the domain has been mastered. Under what specific conditions is this a dependable inference? What could cause the inference to be wrong?

If the individual assessment results recorded as percentages are averaged across all assessments for a total grading period, then the result will equal that proportion of the total array of outcomes for that grading period that each student has mastered. In effect, translating each indicator to percentages places all on the same scale for averaging purposes and permits them to be combined in an interpretable manner—in terms of intended outcomes.

With this procedure, if you wish to assign more weight to some assessment results than others, you can accomplish this by multiplying the percentage for those particular assessments by their weight before adding them into the overall computation of the average. For instance, if some are to count twice as much as others, simply multiply their percentages by two before summing to average.

Time for Reflection

Under what conditions might some assessment results be assigned a higher weight than others in the grading process?

Total Points Method.   Another way to combine information is to define the total target for a grading period in terms of a total number of points. Students who earn all or most of the points demonstrate mastery of all or most of the valued outcomes, and earn a high grade.

In this case, each individual assessment contributes a certain number of points to the total. If this is carefully planned so the points earned on each assessment reflect their fair share of the big picture, then at the end of the grading period we can simply add up each student's points, and can determine what percentage of the total each student earned. That percentage of total points, then, represents the proportion of valued outcomes attained.

Differential weighting is possible here, too. Assign a large number of points to those assessments that cover the largest proportions of the valued outcomes (such as final exams or large projects) and few points to the assessments that are narrower in focus (such as daily assignments).

Either of these options can provide an acceptable basis for clear communication about student achievement through report card grades. But be careful, difficulties can arise! Some of these difficulties, and ways to handle them, are discussed below.

Some Practical Advice.   Depending on how the assessments are defined and averaged, the result may be misleading with respect to the proportion of the total picture mastered. The following discussion will illustrate.

The Most Current Information.   Let's say your strategic assessment plan includes five unit assessments and a comprehensive final exam covering the entire set of targets for the grading period. And, say a particular student starts slowly, scoring very low on the first two unit assessments, but gaining momentum to attain a perfect score on the comprehensive final exam—revealing, in effect, subsequent mastery of the material covered in those first two unit assessments.

The key grading question is this: Which piece of information provides the most accurate depiction of the student's real achievement at the end of the grading period, the final exam score or that score averaged with all five unit tests? If the final is truly comprehensive, averaging it with those first two unit assessments will result in misleading information.

If a student demonstrates achievement at any time that, in effect, renders past assessment information inaccurate as a representation of his actual achievement, then the former assessment must be dropped from the record and replaced by the new. To do otherwise is to miscommunicate about that achievement.

Grading on Status versus Improvement.   A corollary issue is whether a grade should reflect a student's achievement status at the end of the grading period or register improvement over time. The resolution of this issue lies in understanding the immense difficulties we face in dealing with the concept of improvement.

If *improvement* means greater gain gets higher grades, those who happen to arrive knowing less have an advantage. Is that fair to those who arrive knowing more? Besides, under any circumstances, to grade on improvement, we would need to establish a baseline by conducting a comprehensive preassessment of all relevant outcomes for that grading period. We are seldom able to preassess in this manner. And even if we did, we would face challenging statistical problems in dealing effectively with undependable "gain scores" that would result.

For all of these reasons, grades should reflect student status in attaining the specified outcomes for that classroom during a particular grading period.

About Borderline Cases.   Another common problem arises when a particular student's academic average is literally right on the borderline between two grades and you just don't know which way to go. Some teachers allow nonachievement factors to push the grade one way or the other. We addressed the unacceptability of that approach above. A better way to determine such grades is to, during the grading period, collect one or two significant pieces of achievement data that overlap with other assessments, thus double checking previous information about achievement. Hold these assessments in reserve—don't factor them into the grade. Then, if you need "swing votes," use them to help you decide which grade should be assigned. This keeps unrelated factors out of the grading decision and out of the communication system.

Dealing with Cheating.   Here's another kind of grading problem: A student cheats on a test and, as punishment, is given a zero in the gradebook to be averaged with other assessments to determine the semester grade.

Time for Reflection

Before you read on, reflect on this practice. In your opinion, is this an appropriate course of action? Why? Be specific.

The problem here is that the zero may systematically misrepresent that student's real achievement. This is not acceptable under any circumstances. The grade and the discipline for cheating *must* be separated from one another. The student should be retested to determine real levels of achievement and that retest score should be entered into the grade book. Cheating must be punished in some other way.

Policies that Interfere.   Sometimes, district policy can cause serious grading problems. For instance, some districts link grades to attendance. A policy might hold that more than five unexcused absences in a given grading period must result in an F for the student, regardless of actual achievement. In the case in which a student has mastered enough of the material to receive a higher grade, this policy leads to the purposeful misrepresentation of actual student achievement. For this reason, such policies are unacceptable. Administrative policies unrelated to academic achievement and the report card grading process must be kept separate from one another if we are to communicate accurately about student attainment of outcomes.

Advance Notice.   Another critically important guideline to follow is to be sure all students know and understand in advance the procedures that are to be used to compute their grade. What assessments will be conducted when, and how will each be factored into the process? What are students' timelines, deadlines, and important responsibilities? If they know their responsibilities in the partnership we establish with them, students have a good chance of succeeding.

Heterogeneous Grouping.   There is just one more potential problem to address for which we simply must find an acceptable solution. How do we grade different students in the same classroom who are striving to attain vastly and fundamentally different outcomes? This has become a critical issue as we make efforts to mainstream special needs students and students from diverse cultural and linguistic backgrounds.

In a classroom of mixed ability, for instance, one student might be working on basic math concepts, while another is moving toward pre-algebra. If both hit their respective targets, each deserves an A. But those As mean fundamentally different things. How is someone reading the report cards of these two students to be made aware of this critical difference?

In my opinion, this single issue renders simple letter grades out of date and insufficient as a means of communicating about student achievement. The only solution I can find for this problem is to add more information to the reporting system, so as to at least identify the targets covered by the grade reported. Without that detail, we cannot communicate individual differences in the meaning of grades assigned to different students in the same classroom.

The Bottom Line.   In developing grading practices, sound practice dictates that we start with a clear vision of outcomes, translate it into quality assessments, and always remain mindful of that big achievement picture for a given grading period. Then we must follow this simple rule, another part of the art of classroom assessment: Grade students in such a manner as to convey as accurate a picture of real achievement as possible. Any occurrence that has the effect of misrepresenting that real achievement is unacceptable. The guidelines for avoiding the problems discussed above are presented in summary in Figure 14–2.

Step 6: Converting an Achievement Composite to a Grade

Once we have attained an average or total set of points or some other overall index of student achievement for a given grading period, we face the final and in some ways most difficult decision in the grading process: What specifically do we report?

Over the years, some districts and schools have opted simply to report that final achievement average in the form of a percent score. This has the benefit of permitting the record to retain and convey the maximum amount of available information

---

- Grade on achievement of prespecified outcomes only, not intelligence, effort, attitude, or personality.
- Always rely on the most current information available about student achievement.
- Devise grades that reflect achievement status with respect to preset outcomes rather than improvement.
- Decide borderline cases with additional information on achievement.
- Keep grading procedures separate from punishment.
- Change all policies that lead to miscommunication about achievement.
- Advise students of grading practices in advance.
- Add further detail to grade report when needed.

FIGURE 14-2
Practical Guidelines for Avoiding Common Grading Problems

about student achievement. No useful information is sacrificed by converting to other scales.

But most districts require teachers to convert the academic achievement average or point total to a letter or number grade for storage, from A to F or from 4.0 to 0. This has the effect of sacrificing available information in the sense that a range of percent scores (say 100% to 90%) converts to just one point on the grade scale.

Time for Reflection

Under what conditions might a student be harmed as a result of the sacrifice of the more precise percent score? Here's a hint: How do we select a valedictorian?

But the key question is, How do we convert a composite index of student achievement into a report card grade? Traditionally, we have conceived of two ways to accomplish this:

- grading in terms of preset standards of performance
- assigning grades in terms of the student's place in the rank order of all class members

In an era of achievement or performance-driven education, only the first option makes sense. Let's explore each and see why.

Grading with Preset Standards.   Grading in terms of preset standards says, Here are the assessments that represent the achievement targets—score at this level on them and this is the grade you will receive. A set of percentage cutoff scores is set and all who score within certain ranges receive that designated grade.

If two important conditions are met, this method maximizes the probability of success for students. Those conditions are that (a) students possess the prerequisites to master the required outcomes, and (b) sound assessments are used to accurately represent the outcomes upon which the grade is to be based.

One advantage of this system is that the meaning of the grade is clearly couched in the attainment of intended outcomes. Another is that it is computationally simple— one need only know how to compute percentages and averages. Still another strength is that curriculum can be integrated across years, as students' grades reflect attainment of prerequisites for later, more advanced achievement. A fourth advantage is that grading in terms of preset standards increases the possibility that all students can succeed. And finally, from your perspective, if you as a teacher become more effective over time, more students will succeed and will be rewarded with high grades.

However, grading in terms of predetermined percentage cutoff scores is not without its limitations. For instance, the cutoff scores themselves are arbitrary. There is no substantive or scientific reason why 90 to 100 percent should be considered an A. This cutoff, and those used to assign other grades, represent social conventions adopted over decades. As a result, cutoffs vary from district to district, school to school, and even teacher to teacher. The range for an A in some places may be 94 to 100 percent, for example. These differences cannot be eliminated. We can but acknowledge them.

Further, we must recognize that assessments testing attainment of the same valued targets can vary greatly in difficulty. For example, two tests can be devised to cover the same material and, depending on the particular propositions selected and depending on how the items are written, one test could be much harder than the other. As a result, the same student might score differently on the two tests. So assessment difficulty, not just target mastery, can influence the percentage correct and therefore the grade attained by the student.

One way some teachers counter this problem is by arbitrarily labeling the highest student score actually received on an excessively difficult test (i.e., the highest raw score or number correct attained) as a score of 100 percent. The rest of the students' percentages are then based on that new maximum number correct. This practice might have been acceptable under circumstances in which all we wanted the grade to do was sort students. But in times when we care more about absolute achievement—in an era of performance-based education—this practice of shaving off the top of the scale can lead to a systematic misrepresentation of real mastery, because it creates the illusion that students mastered more of the material than they actually did. If the assessment in fact reflects truly important outcomes—key building blocks to later learning—then this misrepresentation can be harmful to that later learning.

A more acceptable way to deal with this problem is for all teachers to learn to translate clearly articulated outcomes into assessments that are of appropriate difficulty for their students. That is, the developers of assessments to be used for report card grading must remain cognizant of the expected outcomes and ability levels of the students to be assessed.

Grading on a Curve.   The tactic of assigning grades based on a student's place in the rank order of achievement scores within a class is commonly referred to as "grading on a curve." In its classic application, the teacher uses the composite index of achievement for each student to rank students from the highest to the lowest score. Then, counting from the top, the teacher counts off 7 percent of the students on the list. These students receive As. Then the next 24 percent receive Bs, and so on down to the bottom 7 percent of students, who are assigned Fs.

A common variation on this method is to rank students in terms of their composite score and then examine the distribution of scores to find natural gaps between groups of scores that appear to permit division into groups of students who can be assigned different grades.

These ranking methods have the strength of yielding a grade that is interpreted in terms of group performance. They also have the effect of promoting competition among students: students will know that their challenge is to outscore the others.

But in a context in which high achievement is the goal, the limitations of such a system become far more prominent than its strengths. The percentage of students receiving each grade is not a matter of science. Again, the cutoffs are arbitrary, and once grades are assigned and recorded on the transcript, no user of that grade information will necessarily know or understand the system of cutoffs used by the grader.

Besides, it's not clear what group should be rank-ordered for grading purposes. Is it all students in the same class at the same time? In the same school? District? In the same semester? Year? Over the years? The answers to these questions can have major implications for the grade a student receives. For instance, if a student happens to fall into an extremely capable cohort, the results might be vastly different than if that same student just happens to be part of a generally lower-achieving group. So issues of fairness come into play.

Further, this system produces grades that are unrelated to absolute achievement. A class could learn very little in fact and the grade distribution would still convey the appearance that all had performed as expected. In other words, in a high-achieving group, some who learned a great deal in an absolute sense would still be doomed to receive a low grade.

And again, from your point of view as a teacher, even if you improve markedly over the years, helping more and more students master the important material, the distribution of grades will appear unchanged. That would frustrate anyone!

Teachers who work in success-oriented partnerships with students have no use for grading on a curve. They know they are not the best teacher they can be until every student attains an A—demonstrating the highest possible achievement on rigorous high-quality assessments.

A Simple Illustration

To tie all of these procedures together, let's work through a hypothetical example of a fifth-grade teacher developing grading procedures in science. The context is a self-contained classroom of thirty-two students.

Step 1.   This teacher's comprehensive picture for this particular ten-week grading period includes knowledge, reasoning, skill, and product outcomes for three three-week units of instruction:

- an ecology unit on wetlands
- a biology unit on amphibians
- a chemistry unit on biodegradable substances

Our teacher lists the priority outcomes for each unit.

Step 2.   The instructor decides to sample student mastery of content and most reasoning outcomes with three weekly quizzes in each unit and a culminating unit test, each combining selected response and essay formats.

In addition, each student will participate in a combined performance assessment for the ecology and amphibian units, in order to tap scientific process outcomes. Each student will produce a brief research report. The combination of nine quizzes corroborated with three unit tests and the report, our teacher reasons, will provide an excellent portrait of student achievement for end-of-term report card grading.

Step 3.   Content and reasoning outcomes are translated into tables of specifications for the short quizzes and the unit tests, the teacher making sure each relevant content category is included, both on a quiz and on a subsequent unit test. Our teacher drafts lists of propositions reflecting important content to be tested, assures their importance, and then writes the required test items. As ungraded exercises, the teacher spends instructional time having students write some practice test questions to ask each other.

Students also prepare for the performance assessment, studying samples of previously written reports that vary in quality and trying to figure out what makes a really good report. With the teacher's guidance, they devise a solid set of performance criteria. The teacher develops the written exercise that spells out each student's research reporting responsibilities.

Step 4.   As the grading period unfolds, the various assessments are administered. Some of the tests and quizzes are open book, some closed. Some are administered in class, others the students take home to work on.

The performance assessment takes place as planned, with the exercise being distributed, performance criteria being developed in class, and students drafting their reports and sharing them with classmates in collaborative teams, for feedback in terms of the agreed-upon criteria before completing the final product.

As each assessment is completed, the teacher enters information into the gradebook (installed on a personal computer), reflecting students' performance in terms of the percentage of total possible points on each test and quiz.

Students who score low have two days to study and take advantage of the regular "after-school retake," another version of the test or quiz covering the required material with different exercises. If they score higher, the new score replaces the old one in the gradebook. If they score lower, student and teacher meet to discuss why and plan further assessment together. Students who miss a test or quiz use the after-school option to make it up.

The research reports are evaluated by three previously trained raters: the teacher, a high school student who has volunteered to help the fifth graders study the wetlands located behind the nearby high school, and a member of the school's community advisory committee who works in the area of environmental science. Each applies the five agreed-upon five-point rating scales.

Time for Reflection

How might the teacher, high school student, and community representative prepare themselves to apply the score scales dependably? How might they check to see if their scores are indeed consistent with one another? If the scores are not, what should they do?

Students receive detailed feedback in the form of profiles of ratings on each criterion used and written comments about their products. The gradebook gets an entry for each student: the combined total of ratings converted to a percentage of the maximum possible score of 75 points (five scales, five points, three raters). Students disappointed with their ratings have one week to redo the work and resubmit. The teacher will reevaluate the work and enter the new score in the record. Otherwise, the old score stands.

Step 5.   The teacher has devised a specific strategy for combining all of these percentages to a composite that reflects student mastery of all relevant outcomes: each of the nine quizzes receives a weight of one, unit tests two, and the performance assessment counts five times. That means the teacher will average twenty scores: nine quiz scores, six test scores (three test scores each counted twice), and the performance assessment score counted five times. These percentages are added and divided by twenty to determine an overall percentage. Composite scores are generated using the teacher's personal computer. Summaries are printed for each student, who checks the record of scores and the composite for any errors.

Step 6.   Our instructor transforms these composites into grades for the report card.

Time for Reflection

Assume you are the teacher in this illustration. You have set specific percent cutoff scores to be used in grade determination and made them public from the beginning of the grading period. A student who scores 90 to 100 percent receives an A. One of your students ends up with an average of 89.5 percent. What grade do you assign and why?

CHAPTER SUMMARY: MAKING THE GRADE

As in all aspects of assessment addressed in this book, the key to effective report card grading is for the teacher to be a master of the material to be learned. The keys are clear and appropriate targets translated into rigorous, high-quality assessments which, in turn, are converted to information that is combined in clear, reproducible ways into grades.

The reference point for interpreting a grade should always be the specific material to be learned—and nothing else. Students deserve to know in advance how this is to be accomplished in their class, and they need to know the standards they are expected to meet. If characteristics other than achievement are to be assessed, appropriate rules of sound assessment must be followed and results should be reported separately from achievement grades.

Gathering information for report card grades in achievement-driven must be well planned. In times when grades were meant to rank students, it mattered little what grades actually meant. Today, however, we strive to produce meaningful communication about student attainment of specific competencies.

You must start a grading period with a clearly stated set of priority outcomes. These are most productively specified when faculty across grade levels and across classrooms within grade levels collaborate, determining the building blocks of ultimate outcomes and integrating them into their classrooms—sharing responsibility for learning.

You must then take responsibility for assembling a strategic assessment plan for generating the information to determine which students attain the desired outcomes. That plan must then be translated into quality assessments along the way, over the course of the grading period. Students might well serve as valuable allies in developing and using these assessments, turning assessment for grading into assessment for learning, too.

As assessments are conducted and results accumulated, you must take care to record as much detail about student achievement as is available. To be sure, nearly all of this useful detail ultimately will be sacrificed in our obsession to describe the rich complexity of student achievement in the form of a single letter grade. But don't give up the detail until you absolutely must. And when report card grading time arrives, share as much of the detail as you can with your students, so they understand what is behind the single little symbol that appears on the report card. Then boil the richness of your detail away only grudgingly.

Remember two final guidelines: (1) You need not assign a grade to absolutely everything a student produces. It's acceptable sometimes simply to use words and pictures to describe your response. Allow room for practice and growth in between grades. (2) Your challenge is not to rank students in terms of their achievement. It is true that the result of your instructional, assessment, and grading efforts may well be a list of students ranging from the highest to the lowest achiever. Someday, however, when we become the outstanding teachers we all are capable of being, everyone will end up at the very top of the list.

EXERCISES TO ADVANCE YOUR LEARNING

Knowledge Outcomes

1. List five key principles of effective communication about student achievement.
2. Identify at least three reasons why we will need to reevaluate our communication systems for student achievement in the future.
3. Create a four-row by three-column chart listing achievement, aptitude, effort, and attitude in the rows. Review the material presented in this chapter and summarize in brief phrases the arguments for and against factoring each into report card grades. Leave column three blank for now.
4. List the six steps in the report card grading process described in this chapter and identify the specific activities that make up each step.
5. Compile a two-part list of practical strategies for avoiding common grading problems. First, identify a potential problem, and then, specify a remedy.

Reasoning Outcomes

1. Three forms of achievement communication are listed below. Which is most likely to reflect the principles of effective communication? Why? Which is next most likely to form the basis of sound communication? Which is least likely to meet standards of communication quality? Why?
   A letter grade on a report card
   An anecdotal record of student achievement
   A portfolio of student work

2. In column three of the chart you created for knowledge exercise three above, for each factor, stipulate whether you believe that the arguments for or against should win out, and briefly state why.

3. Analyze the options of grading based on rank order (i.e., on a curve) and grading in terms of student competence (i.e., preset standards) in terms of underlying assumptions about the mission of schools and the nature of student learning, as well as the specific procedures involved in each. Identify similarities and differences between these two procedures for transforming achievement information into letter grades.

4. Report card grades permit the user to create the appearance of accountability—the appearance that students have learned the required material, whether or not they have in fact achieved. What, if anything, can we do to encourage teachers to commit to more than just the appearance of success?

Skill Outcomes

1. Identify a semester- or quarter-length college or university course you have recently completed, or one school subject you taught recently for a full grading period. Choose a fairly recent educational experience so your recollections are fresh and/or you have access to notes or other instructional materials. Follow the basic steps in effective grading by completing the exercises that follow. You may delve as deeply into these exercises as you wish. If you focus on a program of study you plan to teach in the future, you could use these exercises to devise your complete grading plan.
   1. List the major units of instruction that comprised this program of study—outline the course or subject matter coverage. Review two of these units and specify important knowledge, reasoning, skill, and product outcomes, as appropriate.
   2. Using these two units as examples, and your list of the material comprising the overall coverage of this program, outline the major elements of an assessment plan that you think might sample student performance for grading. What assessments would you use when sampling what kinds of outcomes?
   3. Create blueprints for at least two of the assessments you would use to sample student achievement.

4. Explain in writing how you would compile information over the course of study of this material that would permit computing a composite index of achievement for a final grade.

5. Specify how you would convert your summary of student achievement into a report card grade.

Affective Outcomes

1. Throughout this chapter, I have argued that it is becoming important for us to be able to communicate more accurately about student achievement in the near future than has ever been possible with report card grades. Do you agree? Why?

2. I also have argued that it is important to devise report card systems capable of conveying information about the student's grade and a detailed note about the particular achievement target reflected in that grade. Do you agree? Why?

3. Many continue to feel that students will not complete class work without the motivation of a grade attached. Do you agree? Do you feel that there are no other ways to motivate?

4. Some contend that report cards and grades as we know them will remain in place in schools for a long time into the future, because parents will not accept alternative communication systems. Do you agree? Why?

CHAPTER 15

Innovative Communication Using Reports, Conferences, and Portfolios

---

Chapter Objectives

As a result of studying the material presented in Chapter 15, reflecting on that material, and completing the learning exercises presented at the end of the chapter, you will:

1. Master content knowledge:
   a. Specify key differences between traditional and student-centered systems of communication about achievement.
   b. Describe reports, conferences, and portfolios as communication options, including procedures, advantages, and limitations of each.
   c. State practicalities of implementing alternative communication methods.
2. Be able to use that knowledge to reason as follows:
   a. Evaluate communication systems using as criteria key attributes of effective communication.
   b. Infer solutions to problems that may inhibit effective communication about achievement.
3. Become proficient at the following skills:
   a. Complete the steps required to devise an effective communication system.
4. Attain the following affective outcomes:
   a. Value student-centered communication options as viable alternatives to or supplements for traditional grades and report cards.
   b. See effective communication about achievement as an integral part of a productive community of learners.

Note: The objectives of this chapter do not include the creation of any products.

While report cards and grades represent our most customary and familiar means of communication about student achievement, in this information age, they certainly do not represent our only option. As our desire to communicate more effectively about specific outcomes grows and as the complexity of those outcomes increases, many educators are experimenting with both alternative assessment methods and alternative means of communicating assessment results. In this chapter, we examine some of the new communication ideas being tried by specifying the essential ingredients in effective communication and exploring different means for meeting those standards of quality.

CHAPTER ROADMAP

We begin our travels by contrasting traditional ways of communicating about student achievement with student-centered communication systems.

We then explore a number of examples of alternative communication ideas being developed and used by teachers in the United States and beyond, including innovative new formats for written reports of achievement, new strategies for conferences about achievement, and new ways of collecting samples of student work using portfolios. Each example is described in terms of its procedures, strengths, and limitations.

The objectives are to make you aware of these options and to put you in touch with a few key references so you can pursue them on your own. Thus, you will be able to select applications relevant to your educational setting.

As we discuss these innovative communication alternatives, remember that our communication goal in schools is to provide quality information about student achievement to users in a form they understand and in time for them to use it as they intend. To reach these goals, we must start with the following:

- *A clear and appropriate definition of the achievement target(s) about which we intend to communicate.* We can only devise effective communication systems when we know what we want to communicate about.

- *Quality information about student proficiency with respect to the valued outcomes.* The quality of our communication is only as good as the quality of the achievement information we have gathered.

- *A clear reason to communicate.* The purpose is a function of who is to receive the information about achievement and how they intend to use that information. As reason varies, so does the definition of effective communication. So, the purpose must be clear for both message sender and message receiver.

- *A common language to use in passing information from sender to receiver.* Effective communication requires that all parties in the communication link mutually understand the words, pictures, scores, or other symbols used.

- *An opportunity to share information.* There must be a time, place, and set of circumstances when the message sender and receiver can attend to the information being shared.

The first three of these have been addressed in sufficient depth in previous chapters. We will concentrate on the fourth and fifth entries here.

Our common language can take many forms. For instance, in the past, we have used report cards and grades as though everyone understood those symbols to mean the same thing, even though they rarely did. In Chapter 14, we addressed strategies for finding greater commonalty in the meaning of grades.

Luckily, however, we have at our disposal many other symbols to which we give shared meaning, such as test scores, ratings, checklists, written and oral commentary in various forms, and actual samples of work. We can use these to convey achievement information if we are careful, and make sure that all involved in the communication agree on what our symbols mean.

Further, our opportunities to communicate go far beyond report cards. Other possibilities include written reports of achievement, personal conferences, and portfolios of student work. These vehicles can provide very effective communication—if we use them thoughtfully, relying on agreed-upon language to convey useful information.

When we take advantage of the full array of ways of conveying information and all of the opportunities to communicate, we begin to develop more student-centered communication systems that support the teaching and learning process. This then, is the focus of this portion of our journey together.

THE CHALLENGES OF STUDENT-CENTERED COMMUNICATION

Communicating effectively about student achievement requires the development of new information gathering, management, and delivery systems. The difference between our traditional modes of communication about student achievement and these student-centered systems of communication are detailed in this section and summarized in Table 15–1. After examining the differences, we will see some innovative communication ideas in action.

One difference between traditional and student-centered systems is the manner in which achievement targets are defined in the communication process. It has been our tradition to define our achievement targets very simply. Report cards and test score reports often label achievement categories with a word or two, providing little description of the underlying meaning. They list "Reading," "Mathematics," "Science," "Social Studies," and so on. Our traditions simply have assumed that the message sender and receiver understand the labels, grades, and scores to mean the same thing.

Time for Reflection

Go into your own academic files and retrieve your high school transcript. Study the courses listed there. If a person who knew nothing about high school were to read those labels, would they know what was covered? Look at the grades listed. Would a naive reviewer have any sense of how much you learned?

TABLE 15-1

Traditional and Student-centered Communication Compared

Facet of Communication	Traditional	Student-centered
Definition of targets	Simple labels for grades, subject names	Detail regarding components of academic success
Manager of communication	Teacher	Teacher, student, or parent; varies with context
Keeper of the vision	Teacher	All parties share
Assessor/interpreter of results	Teacher	All parties share
Direction of communication	One-way	Bidirectional for all parties
Primary language used	Grades, test scores	Scores, ratings, examples; oral and written reports
Communication methods	Report cards; conferences	Narrative reports; conferences; portfolios

In student-centered communication, "Reading" is described in richer detail, so as to share more precise information about the key ingredients in the reading process: Are readers able to use context to determine word meaning? Comprehend and monitor their own understanding? Alter reading strategies as needed to fit the material? Achievement is then described either in terms of answers to such questions or as narrative descriptions of the extent to which students demonstrated the component proficiencies. Such focused communication takes the issue of shared meaning far more seriously.

Please realize, therefore, that student-centered communication options like those described in this chapter place a high premium on being absolutely clear about the meaning of academic success. Those who are not masters of the achievement targets in their discipline(s) are far more likely to have their judgments of student achievement challenged with student-centered systems than with report card grades. The entire assessment and communication process in student-centered approaches is far more descriptive. As a result, these systems bring with them a stronger sense of accountability for student learning.

Traditional and student-centered communication systems also differ in terms of the person in charge of communication. Our traditions have made teachers directors of the process, with all information emanating from them and going to students and parents. In student-centered systems, teachers, students, and parents trade off responsibility for preparing and delivering information. Sometimes students take charge, sending information to teacher and parent. Sometimes parents deliver information to student and teacher. At other times, teachers run the system. Circumstances may even arise when two of the three key players (say, teacher and student) team up to inform the third (parents). In short, information about achievement passes in all directions in a student-centered communication system.

Further, our traditions have assigned teachers the role of "keeper of the vision," placing them in charge of defining the meaning of academic success. In the student-centered system, teachers still set targets, but all parties—students, teachers, and (to the extent possible) parents—share an understanding of the formula for success. Only when all individuals actually share a vision of success can they communicate about its attainment.

The assessor differs, too. In the traditional communication system, the teacher has always been the assessor. In a student-centered system, all share responsibility for assessing and interpreting results, but clearly under the teacher's leadership. All three key players in the classroom assessment process understand the meaning of academic success, the standards to be met, and the meaning of results.

As suggested above, the direction of communication changes as we move from traditional systems to student-centered systems. Traditionally, we have relied on a one-way route. I (the teacher) know how you (the student) did on the assessment, and I tell you. In a student-centered communication system, information goes in all directions as student, teacher, and parent share. For instance, students who have internalized performance expectations and have reflected on their own and each other's work, might meet with their teachers to convey the results of their self-assessments so teacher and students can plan together what to do next.

Our primary communication symbols traditionally have been grades and test scores. Student-centered communication might rely on grades and scores, but in a context of deeper understanding and shared meaning. More importantly, other forms of communication are used, too, such as words and examples as conveyed in narratives, portfolios, lists of goals attained, and so on.

And finally, our tradition of relying on report cards as our primary vehicles expands in student-centered systems to include more complete written reports, more multidimensional conferences, and portfolios as treasure troves of information about and reflections on student achievement.

We discuss below examples of emerging student-centered communication systems to illustrate real-world applications of these attributes.

COMMUNICATION ALTERNATIVES

The examples that follow illustrate the experimentation underway to find ways to provide a more complete and detailed picture of student achievement. Six alternative communication ideas are presented. Three are applications of detailed written reports of student achievement, two represent examples of useful conference strategies, and one discusses portfolios as a means of communicating.

Bear in mind that, although these innovative communication alternatives are in use, in many cases, their developers are still refining them and evaluating their success.

Also, understand that these alternatives do not represent panaceas for all of our communication problems. They require every bit as much work as do report cards and grades, can be time consuming to design and use and, like any innovation, can

NAME _____ TEACHER _____ SCHOOL _____

Key

NY	Not Yet
Dev	Developing
Ach	Achieving
NA	Not Applicable at this time

	Fall				Winter				Spring		
	NY	Dev	Ach	NA	NY	Dev	Ach	NA	NY	Dev	Ach
1. Responsible for Own Learning											
2. Positive Self-esteem											
3. Response to Teacher-Directed Activities											
4. Self-control											
5. Social Interaction											
6. Responds to Oral Language											
7. Concepts of Print											
8. Concepts of Books: How They Work											
9. Concepts of Story: How a Story Works											
10. Positive Attitude Toward Own Reading											
11. Positive Attitude Toward Own Writing											
12. Recognizes Words/Logos-Environmental Print											
13. Communicates Through Speaking											
14. Recognizes Most Letters of the Alphabet											

15. Reproduces (by Copying) Most Letters of the Alphabet											
16. Reproduces First Name by Memory and Last Name by Copying											
17. Names Eight Colors											
18. Identifies Four Shapes											
19. Counts to 20 or Above											
20. Numeral Recognition											
21. Number Families/4											
22. Counts Aloud a Set of 12 Objects											
23. Instant Number Recognition											
24. Sorts and Classifies Objects: Two Attributes											
25. Measurement: a. Estimates Length											
b. Measures Length											
26. Graphing a. Creates a Graph											
b. Interprets a Graph											
27. Patterns a. Extends Patterns											
b. Creates Patterns											

FIGURE 15–1

Ann Arbor Public Schools' Kindergarten Report to Parents (Reprinted from "Success for All Kindergarten Students" (n.p.) by Department of Research, Ann Arbor Public Schools, 1993, Ann Arbor, MI: Author. Reprinted by permission of the publisher.)

elicit resistance from some parents and students. Be aware of these potential problems.

And finally, never lose sight of the fact that these communication systems, just like report card grades, require the use of high-quality assessments as the basis for gathering information. Without sound information there will not be accurate communication. We have yet to invent a communication system that can fix flaws in underlying assessment.

More Complete Report Cards

Kindergarten Communication.   In Ann Arbor, Michigan, the public schools' "Success for All Kindergarten Students" initiative, kindergarten faculty developed the twenty-seven outcomes spelled out in Figure 15–1, a report to parents. This form provides the basis for periodic communication about student achievement during the school year, and reflects the outcomes forming the basis of a much more complete assessment and communication system. While space limits will not permit the presentation of the whole package, Figure 15–2 provides insight into the level of information provided to parents to help them understand the ratings they receive in the report.

To produce these reports, teachers are trained to apply a much more complete set of performance criteria, such as those shown in Figure 15–3. These outcomes and criteria provide an excellent basis for communicating about student development at any point, or in terms of student growth over time. Both teachers and parents report more complete and satisfying conferences because they share this common frame of reference and thus have more specific material to discuss.

Time for Reflection

Based on what you have seen of this communication system, what do you anticipate would be its biggest limitations? Can you see any way(s) around the potential problems you identify?

Facing the Practicalities.   As you consider this option, remember that Ann Arbor is succeeding with this project because the entire kindergarten team of teachers collaborated in developing the achievement targets, creating the performance rating system, and implementing the communication system. It represents the collective wisdom and teamwork of many experienced professionals. This kind of backing and commitment is required to make such a system work.

Another important key to successfully using this kind of communication system is that teachers *must* be trained to make dependable ratings of student performance. That training takes time and effort. Resources must be allocated to make it possible.

ATTENDANCE Fall Winter Spring

Name _____

Teacher _____

School _____

Half Days Absent ___ ___ ___

Times Tardy ___ ___ ___

	Not Yet 1	Developing 3	Achieving 5
1. Responsibility for Own Learning	Rarely attends to lessons taught. Completes task with one-to-one teacher help.	Inconsistent attention to lessons taught. Needs occasional help in order to complete task.	Shows interest in and is involved in classroom activities. Completes tasks independently, seeking help only when necessary.
2. Positive Self Esteem	Often demonstrates a negative attitude toward self and others.	Needs continued support to develop positive relationships with self and others.	Communicates a positive attitude toward self and others.
3. Response to Teacher-directed Activities	Cannot follow most directions. Needs one-to-one help in most areas to complete work.	Sometimes needs extra reinforcement to follow directions and/or complete work.	Follows directions and is able to work independently in most areas.
4. Self-control	Demonstrates inappropriate behavior in the classroom and on the playground.	Needs frequent reminders to follow school and classroom rules.	Independently follows school and classroom rules.

FIGURE 15–2

Detailed Performance Criteria for Parents (Reprinted from "Success for All Kindergarten Students" (n.p.) by Department of Research, Ann Arbor Public Schools, 1993, Ann Arbor, MI: Author. Reprinted by permission of the publisher.)   *(continued)*

	Not Yet 1	Developing 3	Achieving 5
5. Social Interaction	Cannot solve social problems with peers without adult help.	Is developing more positive responses to peers.	Solves social problems with peers independently.
6. Responds to Oral Language	Unaware of what speaker is saying in a group setting. Responds to a word or two from the speaker but does not relate to general topic. Needs teacher assistance with 2-step directions.	Sometimes loses track of what is being said. Responds to speaker in a limited manner. Uses help in responding to 2-step directions.	Listens well in a group setting. Responds to speaker indicating understanding of topic. Understands and follows 2-step directions.
7. Concept of Print	*Such as:* Does not know what a letter or word or number is. Unaware that words convey the meaning. Cannot recognize own name.	*Such as:* Sometimes unclear about differences among letters, words, and numbers. Inconsistently tracks left to right.	Knows what letters, words, and numbers are. Knows that words convey the meaning. Tracks from left to right. Recognizes own name.
8. Concepts of Books and How They Work	*Such as:* Incorrectly uses book. Cannot locate words. Does not know where book begins or ends.	*Such as:* Shows inconsistent knowledge of how a book works.	*Such as:* Turns pages front to back. "Reads" from left to right, top to bottom. Can point to title and text.

FIGURE 15–2, *continued*

FIGURE 15-3

Detailed Performance Criteria for Teachers (Reprinted from "Success for All Kindergarten Students" (n.p.) by Department of Research, Ann Arbor Public Schools, 1993, Ann Arbor, MI: Author. Reprinted by permission of the publisher.

(continued)

1. Responsibility for Own Learning.

Not Yet	Developing	Achieving
Such as: Shows little interest in classroom activities. Cannot complete task without one-to-one assistance.	*Such as:* Participates with teacher motivation and/or direction. Needs occasional help or reinforcement in order to complete task.	*Such as:* Shows interest in and is involved in classroom activities. Completes task independently, seeking help only when necessary.

2. Positive Self-esteem.

Not Yet	Developing	Achieving
Such as: Demonstrates a negative attitude/behavior toward self and others: • makes such statements as: *"Nobody likes me," "I can't do this."* • uses put-downs, • is aggressive. May appear to • resist new things, • be withdrawn, • have poor eye contact, • have unexpressive facial expression, • be unresponsive.	*Such as:* Needs continued support to develop positive relationships with self and others. Occasionally uses negative language and behavior. Increasing willingness to try new things. Is learning to accept mistakes as part of the learning process.	*Such as:* Communicates a positive attitude toward self and others. Is proud of own accomplishments, (e.g., *"I can do this," "I like this"*). Willing to try new things. Accepts mistakes as part of the learning process rather than blaming self for the problem. Shows confidence in self when approaching hard tasks.

3. Response to Teacher-directed Activities.

Not Yet	Developing	Achieving
Such as:	*Such as:*	*Such as:*
Complains during teacher-directed activity.	Needs extra support to follow directions and/or complete work.	Willingly participates in teacher-directed activities.
Ignores teacher.	Responds reluctantly when given instructions.	Pays attention during class discussions.
Is easily distracted.	Occasionally pays attention.	Makes connections with concepts being taught.
Is often not on task during learning activity times.	Often needs reminders.	Attends to tasks independently.
Has trouble going from one activity to another.	Moves from one activity to another with teacher giving advanced warning.	Completes learning activities.
		Asks and answers questions.
		Follows directions; moves easily from one activity to another.

4. Self-control

Not Yet	Developing	Achieving
Such as:	*Such as:*	*Such as:*
Does not follow school and classroom rules.	Needs to be reminded to follow school and classroom rules.	Independently follows school/classroom rules.
Inappropriate use of materials and equipment.	Frequent reminders to use equipment and materials appropriately.	Uses equipment and materials appropriately.
Does not clean up after self.	Often reminded to clean up after self.	Assists others with correct use of materials and equipment.
Has tantrums, cries easily, strikes out at others when frustrated.	Beginning to deal with frustrations.	Independently cleans up after self.
Demonstrates inappropriate behavior during "circle" time:	Occasionally demonstrates inappropriate behavior during "circle" time.	Deals with frustrations in appropriate ways:
● talking,	Needs several reminders to change inappropriate behavior.	● uses language,
● playing with objects,		● seeks help when needed,
● daydreaming,		● sets reasonable limits for self.
● constant movement.		Listens attentively during "circle" time.
Needs many reminders to change inappropriate behavior.		Responds positively when reminded of inappropriate behavior.

FIGURE 15-3, *continued*

This system provides a high level of detail about student achievement. Although users report that the performance criteria become second nature and easy to rate with practice and experience, we would be naive to think such records are easy to create and deliver at conference time. Because the report is detailed, communicating results can be time consuming.

Elementary Communication.   Another way to forge a stronger communication link between school and home is to use narrative descriptions of student learning. Rather than grades, to convey meaning, Catlin Gabel School in Portland, Oregon uses this method in its elementary and middle school. The philosophy that guides the evaluation system is effectively summarized in this policy statement:

> We maintain that the student is the unit of consideration, and that our commitment is to create conditions within our school that serve to develop each student's fullest powers as an individual and as a group member. Further, we hold that any system of evaluation ought to:
>
> 1.   enhance intrinsic motivation for learning.
>
> 2.   help students take increasing responsibility for their own learning and be active partners in the learning process through continual self-evaluation.
>
> 3.   serve as a means for direct, sensitive communication between the teacher and student and the teacher and family.
>
> 4.   focus on the specific strengths and weaknesses of individual students and provide prescriptive as well as descriptive information. (Catlin Gabel School, p. 18)

This philosophy, as the following illustrates, is intrinsic to the way Catlin Gabel staff communicate about student achievement with parents:

> The Lower School chooses to write narrative reports rather than issue letter grades because it enables faculty to convey specific information about a child's strengths, weaknesses, progress and problems, as well as suggest strategies for improvement and enhancement. In addition, it provides a vehicle to impart information about a child's motivation, attitudes toward learning, special interests, socialization skills, and emotional tone. The written evaluation also allows the teacher to describe facets of an individual's intellectual and emotional development and compare children to themselves rather than to their peers. Finally, it provides content for conferences, which promotes dialogue between home and school and contributes to the sense of partnership that we seek to develop between student and teacher. (p. 28)

The nature and quality of the communication that results is clearly seen in the sample Catlin Gabel narrative report presented in Figure 15–4, a description of a hypothetical fourth-grade student.

This carefully crafted description reflects a clear vision of achievement, clear criteria and standards, and a vivid sense of how this student relates to those expectations. This report demonstrates how we can use written descriptions and samples of student work, in addition to grades and scores, to communicate about student achievement.

ABC Lower School
June, 1990
Fourth Grade
Teacher's Name

Joan Student

Joan is determination and strength presented in a lively package. This strong-willed student has contributed much to her peers in her fourth-grade year. From her they have learned the importance of fighting for one's point of view. Joan is never wanting for an opinion on any subject. It is easy for her to express her viewpoint. On occasion she takes the opposite point of view solely for the pleasure of differing from the group consensus. Where she has made considerable growth this year is in her willingness to consider the ideas of others. She has learned to back away from a stance when she sees that it is unreasonable or in error. This has helped Joan progress academically because she has become more open to the learning process—the give and take of ideas. Joan is a motivated and independent student who cares deeply that the work she pursues is meaningful. She has grown in her ability to engage fully in an assignment, and has learned that revising an idea only enhances its content.

"I am the Emperor's garden/ With a plum tree by my side/ The blossoms bloom in the sunlight/ while the fragrance is carried by a gentle breeze . . ." Joan has the soul of a poet. She creates strong, vivid images of lovers willing to die for their love, souls tortured by war or gentle gardens peaceful in the sunlight. She allows whole worlds to come alive with her writing. As the year has progressed she has learned how to return to her writing and flesh out her images to make them even more dramatic. Joan has shown great tenaciousness in her willingness to revise a piece, searching for the exact words to make the images strong. She is developing the writer's gift of seeing detail, recognizing its significance, and then understanding how to weave all that she envisions into a finely crafted piece of writing.

Joan has broadened her vocabulary and added many new concepts and words to her knowledge base. This has helped her comprehension improve as the year has progressed. She has taken on increasingly difficult books and relishes the specific details. Joan prefers to read books that are challenging in their content and posses valuable issues with which to grapple. However, she still struggles with jumping to conclusions on first glance of a passage. It is the subtler levels of comprehension that still present her with a challenge. If her interpretation of the information is incorrect, as it sometimes is, she finds it difficult to backtrack and clarify her ideas. The format of read-

FIGURE 15–4
Sample Student Report (Reprinted from "Sample Student Report" (n.p.) by Catlin Gabel School, 1990, Portland, OR: Author. Copyright 1990 by Catlin Gabel School. Reprinted by permission.)

Time for Reflection

What are some of the potential limitations of written narrative description? As you identify problems, see if you can identify possible remedies.

Facing the Practicalities.   The major drawback of these kinds of reports, obviously, is the time required to prepare them. High student-teacher ratios may render this option impractical for many teachers.

In addition, the use of narrative reporting does not absolve the user from beginning with the big achievement picture comprised of all relevant achievement taring group, where the content of a book is carefully analyzed, has helped her to see when she needs to readjust her ideas. There were many incidents where Joan discovered that what she thought was occurring was in error. The growth has occurred in her willingness to accept this and go back to the book to discover where she made the misinterpretation. She needs continued encouragement to ask herself if what she is interpreting from the reading makes sense with what she knows of the details of the book. It would help her to continue reading over the summer with the opportunity to discuss with an adult the content of the books. It would be helpful if she could even take a reading course over the summer.

It was a challenge for Joan to work cooperatively on the Japanese research. Being paired with another strong-willed student gave her both frustration and rewards. Together they explored the topic of Kabuki theater, and they designed a well organized presentation that thoroughly covered the topic. Joan was a very captivated audience during our Japanese unit. She found every experience fascinating and worked hard to glean as much from the study as she could. She was very observant during the Seattle trip, making connections whenever possible. Her determination and passion for knowledge brought her many insights into the culture of the Japanese.

Joan has a solid understanding of the whole-number operations, has mastered multidigit multiplication and long division with remainders. She has secured most of her multiplication tables and she has become quick and proficient at solving mental math problems. As she has grown in her ability to sustain academic effort, Joan has brought perseverance to story problems. She is more likely to struggle with a problem, try a variety of strategies and adjust until she finds the tactic that works. She has added many problem solving techniques to her repertoire. Joan has a good conceptual understanding of fractions and decimals. She has built for herself a fine foundation from which to learn and grow mathematically.

Joan has many successes to celebrate this year. Not all have come easily but her willingness to grow has brought her great satisfaction as a learner. She is a serious student who cares about the quality of her work. She is conscientious about deadlines. Not only has her academic understanding broadened but her social world has expanded. No longer is she on the fringes trying to find an entry into the group. She is a fully vested member of a wide social network with many friends from which to choose. She has come a long way in her fourth-grade year.

Joan, we will miss your determination and voice next year. We hope you have an adventure-filled summer that includes special times with family and friends. Please come next door and check in often so we can keep track of your continued progress.

gets, transforming those targets into rigorous assessments, and writing about the results of those focused assessments. In other words, we must maintain a clear focus on achievement. To use this option productively, users must regard these reports as far more than "free writing time," when they can say whatever comes to mind about the student. The issue in narrative reports is, What does it mean to be academically successful, and how did this student do in relation to those expectations?

Finally, narrative reporting places a premium on being able to write well. Teachers who have difficulty communicating in writing will find a narrative system frustrating to use, and will not use it well.

Continuous Progress Reporting.   Teachers in Victoria, Australia have devised yet another kind of reporting scheme that develops a continuous record of student progress through a series of specifically defined and progressively linked outcomes

(Ministry of Education and Training, 1991). They call these records *profiles* and describe them as follows:

> Profiles are a means of reporting on a student's progress and achievement in key areas of learning. Profiles consist of a series of short descriptive statements, called indicators, arranged in nine levels of achievement called bands. These describe, in order of difficulty, significant skills and knowledge that students must learn to become proficient. A student's progress can be charted over these bands. English Profiles show student progress and achievement in the key areas of reading, writing and spoken language. (p. 7)

The spoken language bands are identified in Figure 15–5, from A at the beginning to I on the high-performance end. In addition, Figure 15–6 illustrates one kind of parental reporting form used, focusing on spoken language band C. Note that it highlights the band the student is working on at the time of reporting, and includes prior and following proficiencies for context. Teachers enter brief comments for the record regarding student progress and achievement.

Time for Reflection

What seem to you to be the strengths of this system compared to the two preceding ones? What apparent limitations do you identify? Can you suggest specific remedies for potential problems?

Facing the Practicalities.   This kind of reporting overcomes some, but not all, of the shortcomings of the systems described previously. First, it minimizes the amount of narrative the teacher must enter. This saves time. Second, it reduces the range of outcomes over which the teacher must comment, focusing on the particular outcomes on which the student is working. This, too, saves time. Third, a concrete record of progress is generated, with cumulative reports of bands of achievement. This helps with interpretation. Fourth, this is quite a comprehensive and carefully articulated communication system, with the span of achievement covered ranging from elementary levels through high school. This makes the system valuable in contexts where students are expected to make continuous progress in acquiring an interlaced series of outcomes across grade levels.

But there remains the challenge of learning about and being able to dependably assess the various levels of achievement reflected in the bands. This will take considerable time. And there always remains the difficulty of trying to keep accurate records for large numbers of students. This, too, takes time.

Communicating in Conferences

Recent developments in our understanding of student, parent, and teacher conferences have markedly increased the potential for effective dialogue about student achievement. In this section, we examine two promising examples.

In the first, teacher and student share both a common vision and definition of academic success that allows them to discuss the student's progress with each other.

Some teachers are using these strategies to transform their classrooms into workshop settings. We describe a writing workshop to illustrate this communication option.

The second example involves student-led parent-teacher conferences. In this approach, the primary responsibility for communicating about expectations and

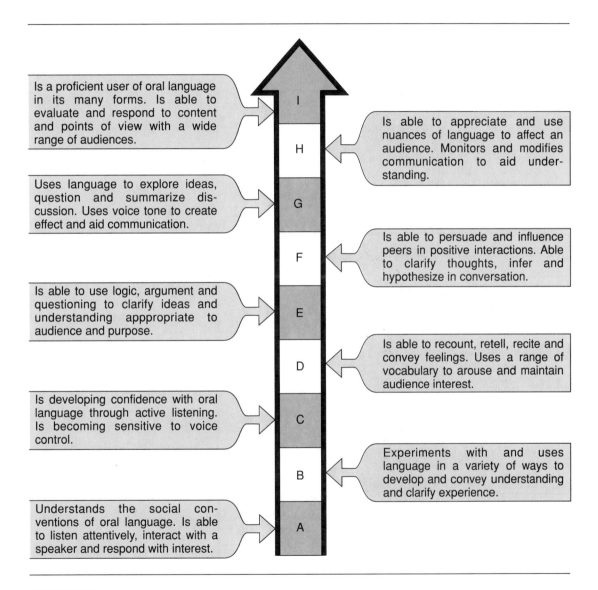

Is a proficient user of oral language in its many forms. Is able to evaluate and respond to content and points of view with a wide range of audiences.

I

H

Is able to appreciate and use nuances of language to affect an audience. Monitors and modifies communication to aid understanding.

Uses language to explore ideas, question and summarize discussion. Uses voice tone to create effect and aid communication.

G

F

Is able to persuade and influence peers in positive interactions. Able to clarify thoughts, infer and hypothesize in conversation.

Is able to use logic, argument and questioning to clarify ideas and understanding apppropriate to audience and purpose.

E

D

Is able to recount, retell, recite and convey feelings. Uses a range of vocabulary to arouse and maintain audience interest.

Is developing confidence with oral language through active listening. Is becoming sensitive to voice control.

C

B

Experiments with and uses language in a variety of ways to develop and convey understanding and clarify experience.

Understands the social conventions of oral language. Is able to listen attentively, interact with a speaker and respond with interest.

A

FIGURE 15–5
The Spoken Language Bands (Reprinted from *English Profiles Handbook* (n.p.) by the Schools Program Division, Ministry of Education and Training, Victoria, Australia, 1991. Reprinted by permission of the publisher.)

ENGLISH PROFILE—SPOKEN LANGUAGE

SCHOOL _____ CLASS _____

NAME _____

LANGUAGE SPOKEN AT HOME _____

TEACHER'S ASSESSMENT
CONTEXTS AND COMMENTS   DATE

SPOKEN LANGUAGE BAND B

Use of Oral Language
Makes short announcements clearly. Tells personal anecdotes in discussion. Retells a story heard in class, preserving the sequence of events. Accurately conveys a verbal message to another person. Responds with facial expressions. Responds with talk when others initiate conversation. Initiates conversation with peers. Holds conversation with familiar adults. Asks what unfamiliar words mean. Uses talk to clarify ideas or experience.

Features of Oral Language
Reacts (smiles, laughs etc.) to absurd word substitutions. Demonstrates an appreciation of wit. Reacts (smiles, laughs) to unusual features of language (such as rhythm, alliteration or onomatopoeia).

SPOKEN LANGUAGE BAND C

Use of Oral Language
Makes verbal commentary during play or other activities with concrete objects.

Speaks confidently in formal situations (e.g., assembly, report to the class).

Explains ideas clearly in discussion.

Discusses information heard (e.g., dialogue, news item, report).

Based on consideration of what has already been said, offers personal opinions.

Asks for repetition, restatement or general explanation to clarify meaning.

Features of Oral Language
Sequences a presentation in a logical order.

Gives instructions in a concise and understandable manner.

Reads aloud with expression, showing awareness of rhythm and tone.

Modulates voice for effect.

Nods, looks at speaker when others initiate talk.

FIGURE 15–6
English Profile—Spoken Language (Reprinted from *English Profiles Handbook* (n.p.) by the School Program Division, Ministry of Education and Training, Victoria, Australia, 1991. Reprinted by permission of the publisher.)   *(continued)*

SPOKEN LANGUAGE BAND D

Use of Oral Language
Tells personal anecdote, illustrating in a relevant way the issue being discussed. Recounts a story or repeats a song spontaneously. Retells scenes from film or drama. Offers predictions about what will come next. Recites poems. Asks questions in conversation. Has a second try at something to make it more precise. Arouses and maintains audience interest during formal presentations (e.g., report to class, announcements).

Features of Oral Language
Uses range of vocabulary related to a particular topic. Maintains receptive body stance in conversation. Speaks in a way that conveys feelings (while keeping emotions under control).

OTHER INDICATORS

progress shifts from teacher to student. I will offer guidelines for using this option, review benefits to students and parents, and share some reactions from users.

Student-Teacher Conferences.   A classroom learning environment turns into a workshop when the teacher shares the vision of achievement with students and then sets them to work individually or in groups in pursuit of the designated target. In this setting, the teacher becomes a consultant or coach, working one-on-one or in groups to improve students' performance. Much of the communication between teacher and student occurs in conferences—one-on-one conversation between teacher and student.

According to experienced writing instructor Vickie Spandel, who uses this idea in writing instruction, a conference is both an excellent means of communicating achievement information to students and an effective teaching device (Spandel & Stiggins, 1990). Conferences give students personal attention. Besides, the students who are reticent to speak out in class often will come forth in conference. As a result, that two-way communication so essential to effective instruction can take place. And finally, according to Spandel, the conference provides an excellent context in which to provide specific feedback. Teachers can provide commentary on student performance and students can describe what is and is not working for them.

To understand the kind of dialogue that can emerge from this idea, read the example provided in Figure 15–7. It depicts a conference between teacher and student focusing on a particular piece of student writing. Ed, the teacher, has been holding conferences with his students since the beginning of the school year. It is now January. He tries to confer with each student every two to three weeks, and, though it takes a fair amount of time, he feels that the payoff is worth it.

The dynamics of the conferences are changing a bit. In the beginning, the teacher had to ask lots of questions. Now, students usually come to a conference with things to say.

Jill, the student, has never been an exceptional writer. Until recently, she didn't like to write and wrote only when forced. She didn't like talking about her writing, and her most frequent comment was, "I can't write."

At first, she didn't want to speak about her writing. The last two conferences, however, have been somewhat different. Jill is beginning to open up. She is writing more on her own. She keeps a journal. She is still, however, reluctant to voice opinions about her own writing; she looks to her teacher for a lead. In the dialogue shown in Figure 15–7, they are talking together about a paper Jill wrote about her dog, Rafe.

Time for Reflection

In your opinion, what are the keys to making conferences like this work? What are some of the barriers to effective conferences? How might the barriers be removed?

Facing the Practicalities.   Those who have turned classrooms into workshops tell us that conferences need not be long. A great deal of information can be communicated in just a few minutes. However, thoughtful preparation is essential. Teachers must examine student work beforehand with performance criteria in mind and prepare focused commentary. And students need to do the same.

Good listening is essential. If you prepare a few thoughtful questions in advance, you can draw insight out of students, triggering their own self-reflection. Effective conferences don't rely on the traditional one-way mode of communication. Rather, they work best when teachers share both the control of the meeting and the responsibility for directing the communication.

Over time, and with experience in conferences, it will become easier to open the dialogue because both you and your students will become more at ease with each other. Hopefully, over time students also will become more familiar with your expectations and they will develop both the conceptual frameworks and vocabulary needed to communicate efficiently with you about their progress. So begin with modest expectations and let the process grow.

The conference focuses on this sample of Jill's writing:

My Dog

Everyone has something important in their lives and the most important thing to me, up to now, has been my dog. His name was Rafe. My brother found him in an old barn where we were camping in a field near my grandpa's house. Somebody had left him there and he was very weak and close to being dead. But we nursed him back to health and my mom said we could keep him, at least for a while. That turned out to be for ten years.

Rafe was black and brown and had a long tail, floppy ears, and a short, fat face. He wasn't any special breed of dog. Most people probably wouldn't of thought he was that good looking but to us he was very special.

Rafe kept us amused a lot with funny tricks. He would hide in the shadows and try to spook the chickens but they figured out he was just bluffing so he had to give up on that one. When Rafe got hit by a truck I thought I would never stop crying. My brother misses him too, and my mom, but no one could miss him as much as I do.

FIGURE 15-7

A Student-Teacher Writing Workshop Conference (Adapted from *Creating Writers: Linking Assessment and Writing Instruction* (n.p.) by V. Spandel and R. J. Stiggins, 1990, White Plains, NY: Longman. Copyright 1992 by Longman Publishing Group. Adapted by permission.)   *(continued)*

And now their conversation:
   "Pretty terrible, huh?" she asks him.
   "What do you think of it?" he asks, tossing the question back to her. She doesn't answer right away, but Ed doesn't break the silence. The seconds tick by. Ed waits.
   "I don't like the ending," Jill volunteers at last.
   "Tell me why."
   "Well, it just stops. The whole thing just doesn't tell how I really feel."
   "How do you feel?"
   She thinks for a minute. "Oh, it isn't like I miss him all the time. Some days I don't think about him at all. But then—well, it's like I'll see him at the door, or I'll see this shadow dashing around the side of the barn. Sometimes when we cook out, I think about him because he used to steal hotdogs off the grill, and one time my dad yelled at him when he did that and he slipped and burned one of his feet real bad."
   "Now there's the real Jill and Rafe story beginning to come out! You're telling me about Rafe in your real personal *voice* and I sense some of your feelings. When you wrote about Rafe, did you speak like that? Let's read part of your writing again."
   After doing so, Jill comments, "Pretty blah, not much me!"
   "If you did write like you were speaking, how do you think it might read?"
   "Like a story, I guess."
   "Try it and let's see what happens. Talk to me about Rafe in your own personal voice Besides, stealing hotdogs off the grill conjures up a funny picture—doesn't it? Those are the kinds of mental pictures great stories tell. When I can picture what you're saying, that's *ideas.* You're giving the story some imagery and focus that I like very much. What kind of imagery do you see in this writing?"
   "They scan the piece again. Jill says in a low voice, "No images here—just facts."
   "How about if you think up and write about some of those personal things you remember about Rafe?"
   "Do you think I should?"
   "Well, when you were talking, I had a much better sense of *you* in the story—of how much you missed your dog and how you thought about him."
   "I think I could write about some of those things."
   "How about if you give it a try, and we'll talk again in about a week?"
   "How about the spelling, punctuation, and sentences? Were those okay?" Jill asks.
   "Let's leave that 'til later. Think about the *ideas*, the *organization*, the *voice*. We'll come back to the other."
   "I don't want any mistakes, though," she confesses.
   "But is this the right time to worry about that?"
   "I don't know; I just don't want to get a bad grade."
   "Okay," Ed nods. "Suppose we agree that for now, we'll just assess the three traits I mentioned: ideas, organization, and voice."
   "That's all?"
   Ed nods again. "And if you decide you want to publish this paper in the school magazine . . ."
   "We can fix the other stuff, right?"
   "You will have time to fix it, yes."

Student-led Parent-Teacher Conferences.   This is an easy concept to understand. However, it can be a bit complex in operation. For those who have tried it, though, the results have been startlingly positive.
   Little (1988), Guyton and Fielstein (1989), and Davies, Cameron, Politano, and Gregory (1992) provide excellent guidance for making this idea work. They list three benefits of putting students in charge at conference time:

- It fosters a sense of accountability within the student for academic progress.
- It encourages students to take pride in their work.
- It encourages student-parent communication about school performance.

The Procedures.   Here's how Guyton and Fielstein use student-led conferences: They begin preparing students by explaining and discussing the report card and grading process in their classroom, interpreting test scores, displaying examples of daily work, communicating effectively in the conference situation, and leading a meeting. In short, they cover with students the nature of the information to be shared in the meeting and they provide practice in coordinating the process. They even role play to prepare for the real conference. The very process of preparing for the conference provides outstanding learning experiences that focus on important life skills.

As conference time approaches, students draft a letter to parents inviting them to the conference. As soon as parents accept the invitation and a meeting time is set, students draft and deliver a letter of confirmation. As meeting time approaches, student and teacher collaborate in fine tuning the information to be shared, and prepare to co-lead the conference discussion.

Guyton and Fielstein typically have students plan for thirty-minute conferences. This is much longer than normal. This additional time demand is balanced by being able to conduct several conferences simultaneously in the same classroom. This, however, is possible only when the teacher plays the role of coach and advisor to well-prepared student communicators. In addition, parents or the teacher also can request a followup meeting alone on another day if needed—just in case some sensitive information needs to be communicated.

The Results.   Based on their experience, these teachers report impressive results. For instance, followup evaluations revealed that virtually every parent reported that the conference did, in fact, increase student accountability, help students take pride in their work, and promote greater student-parent communication about school performance. But even more importantly, they report 100 percent parent participation in conferences! Further, students like being given the adult responsibility of initiating, planning, and conducting such a conference.

As of the time of this writing, virtually every teacher I have spoken with who has tried this idea has found it to be a compellingly positive experience. Figure 15–8 shares the thoughts of two sixth-grade teachers (Arnold & Stricklin, 1993, personal communication) on their experiences with student-led conferences.

Facing the Practicalities.   Great care must be taken to conduct student-led conferences well, however. At least six conditions must be satisfied for these conferences to work:

- Students need to be willing to evaluate their own learning with their parents.
- The teacher must have sufficient confidence that students can take charge to be able to step aside and serve as a backup resource for the student.
- All achievement targets discussed in the conference must be clearly and completely defined.

- Both teacher and student must share a common language for talking about attainment of each important target.
- Students must have time to prepare for and practice their leadership roles.

When these conditions are satisfied and students take the lead in evaluating their learning, many good things occur. For example, because student and teacher must work closely together to prepare for the conference, it builds a greater amount of individual attention into the instructional process. This gives students a greater sense of their own importance in the classroom. But the cost to the teachers is, of course, that it takes careful management to coordinate a large number of individual preparations and presentations.

A second benefit is that time spent planning and preparing for student-led conferences becomes high-quality teaching and learning time. Students work to understand the vision of success, master the language needed to communicate about it, and learn to describe their achievements. Is this not the essence of a productive learning environment? Besides, as they prepare for the meeting, students might prepare demonstrations, set up exhibitions, and/or develop other documentary evidence of success. It is difficult to envision more engaging student learning experiences.

Nevertheless, this kind of preparation requires some maturity on the part of the student. In all probability, the lower age limit for student-led conferences would be

---

With a combined 31 years of teaching experience, we have rarely found a more valuable educational process than student-led conferences. During preparation the students experienced goal setting, reflected upon their own learning, and created a showcase portfolio.

Once underway, the conferences seem to have a life of their own. We, the teachers, gave up control and became observers, an experience that was gratifying and revealing. It validated our growing belief that students have the ability to direct their own learning and are able to take responsibility for self-evaluation. For many of our students, we gained insights into individual qualities previously hidden from us in the day to day classroom routine.

Students blossomed under the direct and focused attention of their parents. In this intimate spotlight, where there was not competition except that which they placed on themselves, they stepped for a moment into the adult world where they took command of their own conference as well as their own development. Parents were surprised and delighted at the level of sophistication and competence their children revealed while sharing personal accomplishments.

In order to refine and improve this process, we surveyed both students and parents. Parents were emphatic in their positive response to student-led conferences, with most requesting that we provide this type of conference more often. Students, even those at risk and with behavior problems, overwhelmingly responded with, "We needed more time; a half an hour was not enough."

FIGURE 15-8

Teacher Commentary on Experience with Student-Led Conferences (By Harriet Arnold and Patricia Stricklin, 1993, Central Kitsap School District, Washington. Reprinted by permission of the authors.)

fourth or fifth grade. But students may still be part of and contribute to the conference in lower grades.

A third benefit is that a great deal of positive motivation can result, for all conference participants. As students and teachers prepare, the meaning of success becomes clear. Clearly defined goals are easier to attain. As evidence of success is compiled, a sense of being in control can emerge for students, spurring them to greater heights—especially in the hope that they might be able to achieve those last-minute gains that will impress their parents even more. Parents acquire new understanding of their children, and of the teacher. In short, the stakes change for students, and so does their opportunity to succeed.

A fourth benefit is that conference preparation and practice affords yet another opportunity for students to help each other succeed. Cooperative conference planning teams might be used to help each team member compile evidence for presentation, prepare effective presentation aids, and practice and refine their conference presentation.

Fifth, this offers another excellent place for students to practice productive performance assessment, by participating in the development of performance criteria and applying those criteria to their own and each other's conference presentations. This is also a productive way to integrate assessment with instruction.

Sixth, parents typically are far more willing to participate in conferences when their children play a key role in the meeting. Parents seem to sense that this kind of conference will mean more to them and to their children than traditional parent-teacher conferences. Further, those who have experimented with this communication option find parents responding positively to the level of detail about achievement they receive and the level of commitment they see in their children to succeed in the classroom.

But, this idea has a potential downside, too. What about the student who prepares carefully, only to have parents miss the meeting? Or what if parents are unavailable, or unwilling to participate from the outset?

Time for Reflection

How might parental concern and attendance problems be avoided in the planning stages of the conference? If parents or other invited guests fail to arrive for the conference, how might this be handled in a manner that keeps the student's ego intact?

Communicating with Portfolios

In 1990, Lewis & Clark College in Portland, Oregon, initiated a new admissions policy in which academically talented students had the opportunity to submit portfolios of their academic work instead of SAT scores and the standard admissions essay. The college explained this new portfolio policy as follows:

> If you select the Portfolio Path, we ask that you submit materials which demonstrate that you meet Lewis & Clark's criteria for admission. You might, for example, include

samples of papers and exams from a variety of courses over a period of years or from a particular course through a term. In either case, we suggest you choose 3-5 papers which show intellectual growth and an ability to write clearly and think critically. You might also include in your portfolio science projects, complicated mathematical proofs or computer programs of your own devising, sample work from advanced placement or honors courses, programs from musical or theatrical events in which you have participated (and audio or video tapes if you have them) or photographs of artistic work. Your portfolio should contain an official high school transcript, a letter from your college counselor or principal certifying that the work submitted is your own, and at least three letters in sealed envelopes from recent teachers assessing your academic abilities. We also ask that you fill out the first page of the regular application materials. Standardized test scores, additional recommendations from teachers and others, a statement describing your academic goals and interests, and an admissions essay are optional. (Lewis and Clark College, 1990)

This is only one illustration of the fact that portfolios have become the focus of many local initiatives and statewide mandates across all levels of education. While most applications are occurring in language arts contexts, such as writing portfolios, other uses are emerging in math, science, and arts education. Some districts and state licensing boards are even beginning to conceive of portfolios as the basis for teacher and principal evaluation.

Defining a Portfolio.   A *portfolio* is a collection of student work assembled to demonstrate student achievement or improvement. The material to be collected and the story to be told can vary greatly as a function of the assessment context. The context determines the following:

- *Purpose*—As the reason for assessment varies, so will the story to be told and the audience. For example, a portfolio intended to document a student's improvement over a semester for motivational purposes will contain different ingredients from a portfolio to be evaluated for high school graduation.
- *Nature of the outcome(s)*—The knowledge, reasoning, skills, products, and/or affect to be described in the portfolio will dictate the student work samples to be collected.
- *Focus of the evidence*—The portfolio can either show change in student performance over time or status at one point in time. This factor is an issue in grading as well as in designing portfolios.
- *Time span*—If student improvement is the focus, over what time period—a month, a term—should work be collected?
- *Nature of the evidence*—What kind of evidence will be used to show student proficiency—tests, work samples, observations?

These context factors can come together in many combinations. For instance, a foreign language teacher might use an audio portfolio to help students see and be motivated by their improvement in speaking proficiency. A continuous series of recordings of speaking samples made during the term might do the trick. A writing teacher might diagnose student needs by having students collect papers written in other courses over a short time span. A drama teacher might help students refine upcoming performances by recording rehearsals on videotape. A vocational or technical teacher might ask students to collect samples of projects completed during the year for presentation to potential employers as evidence of certain kinds of proficiency.

The Basic Ingredients.   Although possible uses for portfolios are nearly infinite, some standards of sound portfolio practice, as stated by Arter and Spandel (1992), seem to be consistently emerging among users across the country. These include, first, that guidelines for the selection of material to be included need to be established in advance of assembling the portfolio. This keeps the collection from growing haphazardly.

In addition, students must play a key role in telling at least part of their own story. In terms of specific practice, that means that students select some of the material to be included, to be sure the story depicts them as they see themselves. It also means that the portfolio is to include evidence of student self-reflection about the work included.

Further (you probably saw this one coming!), clear and appropriate criteria must be established for describing and evaluating the quality of the work collected. These criteria can apply to individual samples of work within or to the evaluation of the portfolio as a whole. They serve as the basis of both student and teacher reflection on the work. And to the extent that criteria are cast as rating scales and checklists, we lay the groundwork for being able to aggregate performance across portfolios to describe improvements in the class as a whole. In some settings, these summaries could also be used to advantage in program evaluation.

And finally, most portfolio users are taking advantage of this communication system to put students in touch with the nature and extent of their improvements in performance over time. Written, audio, or video records compared over time are a powerful tool for increasing the learners' sense of control over their own academic success.

Time for Reflection

Portfolios have represented the primary means of communicating competence in the visual arts, both in academia and the workplace, for years. Why do you suppose this has been the case? What did arts educators and professional artists discover long ago that the rest of us are just discovering now?

Facing the Practicalities.   One common area of concern about portfolios deals with the logistics and management of the collection. To whom does the portfolio belong? How is it to be stored? Who has access? How shall portfolios be transmitted from one user to another? The answers to these questions, once again, are a function of the context. Answers are best formulated early in the portfolio planning process to avoid confusion and frustration.

With respect to ownership and access, portfolios are part of the formal school records and therefore subject to the same privacy constraints as those of other personal academic records. They belong to school personnel and the student's family. Access is obtained only by their permission.

However, within the classroom, I think students develop the strongest feeling of pride in their work when they and their teachers become equal partners in the ownership of the portfolios. The collection remains in the hands of the student and ultimately is taken home or shown to the next teacher by the student. But if both students and teachers share responsibility for selecting material to be included, if both reflect on the work periodically and confer on those reflections, and if both share responsibility for communicating about contents and progress with parents, then students maintain the strongest possible sense of themselves as learners.

Imagine a student who enters the year unable to solve complex math story problems, as evidenced in a portfolio by inept solutions to even the simplest problems. Imagine the pride that would emerge later in the year when that same student could compare early performance with sophisticated problems efficiently solved! What if this student were able to creatively discuss the criteria for solving such problems at an end-of-year student-led parent-teacher conference? As teachers, we simply cannot attain that kind of pride and quality of communication with a report card entry that says "Mathematics" followed by a simple letter grade.

Designing Portfolio Systems.   The creation of useful portfolio systems, therefore, requires the developer to answer a number of important design questions. These are listed below. I know the list is long, but the more complete your plan, the easier the implementation of your ideas. Invest thoughtful design time up front and your system will serve you well, according to Arter and Spandel (1992):

- Who will be involved in the portfolio design? These are the people whose communication needs are likely to be met by the portfolio. List all of the possibilities and choose. Include students on the list of possible contributors.

- What will be the purpose of the portfolio: to motivate students, to demonstrate improvement, to assess achievement? List the possible purposes and select those that fit your context.

- What specific outcomes will be reflected in portfolio material? Remember, this does not call for a listing of the *kinds* of evidence that will be compiled, such as papers, tests, or anecdotal comments. Rather, it calls for the refined articulation of the knowledge, reasoning, skill, product, and/or affective targets to be depicted within.

- What kinds of assessment information will be considered appropriate to meet the portfolio's purpose? Here is where you specify the kinds of evidence: work samples, papers, recordings, tests, anecdotal records, and so on.

- What guidelines will govern the selection of material for the portfolio? This is a sampling issue. Remember, the task you share with students is to tell an accurate and dependable story about student performance. So, each sample collected, and the constellation of material assembled, must be sufficient to give you and the student confidence in the conclusions being drawn about performance.

- Who shall make the selections? Share responsibility for this!

- What criteria will be used to evaluate entries in the portfolio? Follow prescribed guidelines for the development of performance criteria.

- How will student self-reflection be worked into the system? Make this a concrete part of the plan. How shall students learn to apply the prescribed performance criteria? Could they be involved in developing those criteria? When and how often will students reflect? How shall they record their reflections? When will you and your students discuss these reflections and compare notes?

- What criteria will be used to evaluate the quality of the self-reflections? Students can help develop these, too. Help them figure out the differences between analytical, probing self-reflections and those that are superficial.

- Will you develop criteria for evaluating the portfolio as a whole? These criteria arise out of the purpose for building portfolios. The standards of portfolio quality are determined by the story to be told and the reason for telling it. How shall you and your students know if an accurate and complete story has been told? What do the terms *accurate* and *complete* description of performance mean in your setting? Answer this question and your criteria will be clear.

- Who owns the portfolio? If your answer is anyone other than "the student," you are missing the point!

- How will portfolios be stored and transmitted to users? Make students responsible for at least some of the work to be done here.

- Who has access to portfolios? Again, portfolios are like any other academic record. Rules of access are the same.

Answering these design questions may not be easy. Both Yancey (1992) and Tierney, Carter, and Desai (1991) offer practical advice that can help. Designing a good portfolio takes time and planning on the part of both developers and users. However, if you assemble the right team and address this list one issue at a time, the results will be worth the effort.

A FINAL THOUGHT ON EFFECTIVE COMMUNICATION

Throughout these two chapters on communicating about student achievement, we have spoken of five standards of effective communication. In fact, however, we may need to consider a sixth key to success in communicating: If we want our students to use feedback on their achievement as the basis for academic improvement, they need to be able to hear and accept the truth about their current achievement. When that truth is positive, this may not be a problem. But when it is negative—particularly when it always seems to have been negative—acceptance of the message can be difficult. We can and often do find ways to brush these messages aside, to rationalize them, to discredit the source, or to find some other way to escape. Some might call this human nature. The problem is, however, that in a learning community, such avoidance is immensely counterproductive.

And so, we must be mindful of conditions that may need to be satisfied for students to really listen to and accept negative information about ourselves. For instance, students may need to begin with certain attitudes and perspectives to be able to receive and act upon such messages. They may need to see themselves as key players in the search for information about their own achievement. In addition, students may need assistance in developing a sufficiently strong academic self-concept so they can acknowledge their shortcomings and not feel defeated. Further, the students must see the provider of the feedback as credible, honest, and helpful. And finally, they must come to see the benefits of the message very quickly, so they can muster the resources needed to act purposefully.

From the other point of view, the giver of the feedback must be able to present it constructively, delivering a clear and focused message using understandable language. The provider must be able to communicate acceptance of the students while critiquing their achievement. Even more importantly, the message sender must help the student understand that student and teacher share a common mission: greater achievement for the student.

Clearly, it is no simple task to communicate to students that they have missed the target but still have the hope of success and reason to stay motivated. But as a teacher/communicator, that is exactly what you must do. The suggestions offered in previous chapters for clearly defining the meaning of academic success, assessing it well, and transforming the results into quality information are intended to help you fulfill this most important of your responsibilities.

Time for Reflection

Reflect on the various communication options offered in Chapters 14 and 15, including report card grades, detailed written reports, conferences, and portfolios, and decide which hold the greatest promise of productive communication with the student.

CHAPTER SUMMARY: FINDING EFFECTIVE WAYS TO COMMUNICATE

We have reviewed and discussed six examples of alternatives to report cards and grades for communicating about student achievement. Three of these alternatives rely on greater detail in written reports. One conveys information in the form of checklists or rating scales that describe all of the key elements in successful performance. Another relies on extended narrative description to describe student performance. The third is a hybrid of the first two. Like report cards, these options result in enduring records of performance. These options trade a more labor-intensive recording method for much higher-resolution pictures of achievement than can be obtained with grades on report cards.

We also explored two communication systems that rely on direct contact among students, teachers, and parents in the classroom assessment process. One uses workshop conferences to exchange information between teachers and students. The other places students in charge of parent-teacher conferences. Both of these require that students understand expectations well enough to be able to converse about them. They also permit students the opportunity of gathering and communicating information about their own achievement. Proficient assessors and communicators rapidly become better performers. But the tradeoff is the complexity of coordinating large numbers of such conferences.

Finally, we reviewed some of the basic principles of portfolio development and use. Here again, we find that the great strength of this communication system lies in its potential to put students in touch with their own emerging competence. Given the level of detail, students can see and understand strengths to grow on.

We must continue to explore, develop, and implement these kinds of communication systems as our achievement targets become more numerous, complex, and individualized. Implementation will be made easier as modern information processing technology evolves and we learn new ways to apply it to the art of assessment. In the meantime, for the immediate future, these alternatives will most often be used in conjunction with or parallel to report card grading systems.

Even if our transition from traditional to student-centered communication is a slow one, the methods of conveying information reviewed in this chapter hold the promise of allowing students to tell their own story about their own academic success. That, in and of itself, represents one of the most powerful learning experiences we can offer them.

EXERCISES TO ADVANCE YOUR LEARNING

Knowledge Outcomes

1. In your own words, detail the differences between traditional modes of communication about student achievement and student-centered systems.

2. Create a chart in which you summarize basic procedures, advantages, and limitations of the three kinds of communication options discussed in this chapter: detailed reports, conferences, and portfolios.

3. List the key practical considerations to be accounted for in using each of the communication alternatives discussed.

Reasoning Outcomes

1. Focus on the system of communication used in your school or the college or university in which you study. Evaluate that system in terms of the keys to effective communication. In your opinion, does it represent a sound system? Why?

2. If you are able to identify problems within the system evaluated in exercise one above, how might they be overcome?

3. Some who have experimented with alternative communication systems have met with parental resistance. Parents wanted report cards and grades, like they had received when they were in school. If you developed a sound communication system in your school and were confronted with this kind of resistance, how would you respond? Why?

Skill Outcomes

1. Select a course of study you have taken recently at your college or university or a unit of instruction you recently completed. Devise a sample of a detailed narrative report, checklist, or other detailed written report designed to enhance communication about achievement in that context.

2. Devise a conference plan designed to contribute to the communication process.

3. Outline a portfolio plan designed to serve as a useful means of gathering and sharing information about student achievement.

Affective Outcomes

1. Having studied the options presented in this chapter, which, if any, seem most worthy of further study and experimentation? Why?

2. How do these alternative communication suggestions strike you? Do you like them? Dislike them? Feel uncertain? Why?

CHAPTER 16

Creating a Positive, Constructive Classroom Assessment Environment

---

Chapter Objectives

As a result of studying the material presented in Chapter 16 and reflecting on that material, you will:

1. Master content knowledge:
   a. List five specific parts of an action plan for creating positive, constructive assessment environments.
2. Be able to use that knowledge to reason as follows:
   a. Infer how each teacher can take the lead in developing positive, productive classroom assessments.
3. Attain the following affective outcomes:
   a. Be strongly motivated to develop and use quality assessments.

Note: The objectives of this chapter do not include the mastery of any process skills or the creation of any products.

This concluding chapter summarizes the keys to creating the positive, constructive assessment environment we want and need in our classrooms. In Part 1 of this book, we established the need for a constructive environment to replace the one that brought us to regard assessment only as a negative source of anxiety. In Parts 2 and 3, we established the kinds of assessments and student-centered applications needed to make such an environment possible. In Part 4, we have discussed effective ways to communicate about student achievement—a critical facet of any learning environment. In this chapter, we summarize all of the elements that must come together if we are to establish new assessment environments.

CHAPTER ROADMAP

From the outset of our journey, we have said that the foundation from which to build high-quality student-centered classroom assessment environments is a deep understanding of the meaning of assessment quality and the strongly held value that high-quality assessment is absolutely required throughout our assessment systems, from classroom to boardroom. In addition, however, each of us must develop and carry out specific plans to thoughtfully coordinate five interconnected efforts. These five are all familiar to you by now. They map the route for the final chapter of our journey together.

First, we must continue to articulate ever clearer and more appropriate learning outcomes. The ultimate outcomes of instruction must be specified and those outcomes must be integrated into the curriculum to reflect the various paths learners can take to academic success.

Second, we need comprehensive professional development programs designed to help teachers, administrators, and policy makers face new assessment challenges. Only then will all involved in the educational process be able to share the meaning of success with students and document attainment of valued outcomes.

Third, given success with these efforts, we will be in a position to achieve our goal of high-quality assessment in every classroom. To do so, we must all understand the meaning of quality and put that knowledge to work in gathering sound information about student achievement.

Fourth, we must establish an assessment policy environment that supports positive, constructive assessment. Those policies must require competence at all levels by assuring the presence of assessment-literate, competent staff in schools and districts, promoting staff evaluation and development in assessment, and demanding, from the very highest levels of policy, that all levels of assessment adhere to the highest quality standards.

Fifth, we must conduct a public relations effort to help our communities understand the key role of sound assessment in achieving effective schools. This effort must reveal to the public the increasing complexity of the educational outcomes we seek for students and why we must develop a richer array of assessments if schools and students are to achieve the outcomes we value.

If we are to merge these components into an effective plan for achieving a productive assessment environment, many will need to contribute. We all need to share that responsibility, from legislative chamber to boardroom to classroom to living room. However, because you—the teacher—are the focal point of all classroom assessment and therefore of school effectiveness, you can provide leadership and encouragement.

Time for Reflection

This is the only "Time for Reflection" in this chapter, and there are no end-of-chapter exercises. Your final challenge is this: At the end of each subsection, stop for a moment and write a brief personal plan identifying the role you would like to play, if any, in advancing the state of assessment as detailed in that section. List those things you intend to do to promote sound assessment. Save this plan and use it as your roadmap for your next journey into the world of assessment—which will, I hope, be soon.

ASSEMBLING HIGH-QUALITY ENVIRONMENTS

Let's explore the specific contributions you can make in the processes of articulating outcomes, professional development, attainment of quality assessments, setting policy, and public relations. In each case, you have an assertive role to play.

Defining the Meaning of Academic Excellence

For the past decade, as a society, we have been striving to articulate the meaning of academic success. This work has proceeded on several fronts. We have national educational goals, and most states have identified state goals and objectives. Districts across the country have assembled educational and civic leaders to agree on the meaning of academic excellence in their communities.

But the work has not stopped there. Our major research universities have contributed by conducting the educational research needed to promote clearer understanding of the meaning of academic success. Further, during the past decade, virtually every national professional association of teachers has assembled representatives of its membership to identify valued outcomes in their particular discipline.

As teachers, we have these successes to build on. Now we must move forward on two important fronts. First, we must not assume that the visions of our achievement target that we possess today are final. Like so many aspects of our educational enterprise today, they, too, represent works in progress. We each have a responsibility to stay in touch with developments in the disciplines in which we teach. Further, when the opportunities present themselves, we must involve ourselves in refining these visions of success.

Each of us also must take responsibility for understanding and articulating the knowledge, reasoning, and skill outcomes that drive instruction in our own classrooms. And further, we must frame as best we can the various ways in which these outcomes contribute to learners' attainment of ultimate competence. Only then will we and other contributors to student success know what to teach and assess when and under what conditions. Only then can responsibility for teaching and learning be divided and assigned, to produce a curriculum that is truly integrated across levels. Only then can limits be set on student and teacher accountability in ways that promote success for all.

Attaining Professional Excellence

Effective schools depend on the professional competence of the teachers and administrators who staff them. In this context of quality assessment, two key dimensions of that competence become relevant: the appropriateness and quality of our visions of outcomes (discussed above), and our ability to translate those outcomes into quality assessments.

As we strive for sound visions and quality assessments, again, we have a great deal going for us. As mentioned above, our definitions of academic success are becoming clearer all the time. Further, a decade of classroom assessment research has resulted in a thorough understanding of the meaning of assessment literacy for teachers (see Appendix B) and administrators (see Appendix C). And not only do we know what teachers and administrators need to know, but outstanding training materials are beginning to emerge to help us attain the goal of an assessment-literate school culture.

In this case too, our path is clear. First, teacher and administrator training programs must adjust their curricula where needed to be sure they are producing new faculty and staff well trained in the meaning of academic success and in the basic principles of sound assessment. Second, we must conduct the kind of state and local inservice training programs needed to equip a national faculty with sufficient tools and wisdom to face their new and challenging responsibilities.

As teachers, we bear major responsibility for our own growth and development as assessors. As we become the primary source of information on the meaning of excellence and directors of assessment in our learning environments, it will become increasingly important that we take this responsibility seriously. In this context, you can urge that resources be allocated in your school and district for training and professional development in these arenas, and you can participate in such activities in assessment whenever offered.

Assuring Assessment Quality

We have spent an entire fifteen-chapter journey together coming to understand what *assessment quality* means. Table 16–1 summarizes many of the concepts we have learned along the way. Given the opportunity, resources, and trust to become confident, competent assessors, we can meet these standards of quality in our classrooms.

Each and every teacher must adopt these standards, striving to become as proficient as possible at meeting them and striving to integrate every assessment event

TABLE 16–1
Standards of Assessment Quality

Standard of Quality	Selected Response	Essay	Performance Assessment	Personal Communication
Clear and appropriate target	Table of specs or list of objectives must match instructional priorities	Table of specs or list of objectives must match instructional priorities	Performance criteria must match instructional priorities	Questions asked must match instructional priorities
Assessment serves clear purpose	User's need must be clear Results must serve needs User must understand results	User's need must be clear Results must serve needs User must understand results	User's need must be clear Results must serve needs User must understand results	User's need must be clear Results must serve needs User must understand results
Method matches target	This method can assess: Knowledge Some kinds of reasoning Affect	This method can assess: Large structures of knowledge Complex reasoning Affect	This method can assess: Reasoning Skills Products Affect	This method can assess: Knowledge Reasoning Affect
Sample representative and sufficient	Enough items sample material to be learned	Enough exercises sample material to be learned	Enough exercises sample relevant applications of skills	Enough questions sample material to be learned
Sources of extraneous interference to be controlled	Unclear target Poor items Poor sample Problems within student Problems within the assessment environment	Unclear target Poor exercises Poor sample Lack of criteria Scorer bias Problems within student Problems within the assessment environment	Unclear target Poor exercise Poor sample Lack of criteria Scorer bias Problems within student Problems within the assessment environment	Unclear target Poor sample Lack of criteria Interpreter bias Problems within students Problems within the assessment environment

into the learning process in some meaningful way. Review the summary of standards (in Table 16–1). Keep this summary handy and commit to quality assessment.

Building a Supportive Policy Environment

If educational policy directs our actions, several policy arenas that influence assessment practice need thoughtful reevaluation. As you begin to read this section, you will ask, What can I do about these things? Others set policy, I just follow it. Be advised that, with diplomacy and commitment, you can influence assessment policy and thus enhance assessment practice.

Among the policies in need of revision are those related to teacher licensing and certification. Those who set these standards need to be sure professional competence in assessment is listed among the requirements. Hopefully, this will cause teacher and administrator training programs in higher education to reevaluate their policies with respect to their allocation of credit hours for assessment training. Such training has been missing in the past and that, we have established, is unacceptable.

At the district level, there are several personnel policies that can support sound classroom assessment. For instance, hiring standards for new teachers and administrators can require assessment literacy. Teacher evaluation criteria and professional development processes can be adjusted as needed to reflect competence in classroom assessment practice. And personnel reward and recognition programs can acknowledge outstanding performance in classroom assessment practice.

Also at the district level, assessment, evaluation, and grading policies can be reviewed to be sure they acknowledge the full range of roles of assessment in instruction, the acceptability of many forms of assessment, and a commitment to quality at all levels.

We also can evaluate our local policies with respect to the expenditure of assessment resources to assure a balanced allocation between sound large-scale and classroom assessment.

School district personnel can review both district-level and local assessment policies to determine the level of support they offer to those concerned about quality assessment throughout the system. Figure 16–1 illustrates a supportive district assessment policy. You can be an activist on behalf of such policies.

Finally, all district personnel policies, policies governing higher education curriculum, and licensing and certification standards might be reexamined to be sure the specific competencies listed in Appendices B and C are reflected therein. These appendices spell out agreed-upon national standards of professional competence for teachers and administrators that have been jointly adopted by the American Federation of Teachers, the National Council on Measurement in Education, the National Education Association, and the National Policy Board for School Administration. Acting on your own or through your professional associations of teachers, you can urge that definitions of professional excellence reflect these standards wherever appropriate.

This (sample) school district assessment policy addresses the philosophical base, focus, roles, and responsibilities for all engaged in assessment in this district.

Definitions of Key Terms

In this policy, three key terms are used extensively. They are defined below to promote complete understanding:

- *Assessment* is the process of gathering information that reflects levels of student achievement.
- *Evaluation* is the process of judging achievements (results of assessment) to see if they match desired standards.
- *Communication* is the process of transforming assessment and evaluation results into information for decision making.

District Assessment Philosophy

The development, administration, use, and evaluation of assessments in this district shall be guided by the following basic tenets:

- Sound assessment is an essential ingredient in high-quality instruction. For this reason, it is paramount that assessment and instruction be integrated at all times.
- All assessment users must have the desire (i.e., incentives), opportunity (i.e., responsibility and time), and resources (i.e., training and support) needed to develop and use sound, instructionally relevant assessment.
- All assessments used in this district will meet five standards of quality. They will: (1) arise from and reflect a clear and specific target; (2) serve a clearly articulated purpose; (3) rely on a proper assessment method; (4) sample the target appropriately; and (5) control for extraneous factors that can cause the mismeasurement of achievement. All educators in the district will understand these standards and know how to apply them in their own assessment, evaluation, and communication contexts. All assessments not satisfying these quality criteria will be discarded.
- A variety of assessment forms are acceptable in this district, including paper and pencil tests and quizzes, performance assessments (assessments based on observation and judgment), and assessments based on personal communication with students. All district staff and faculty will understand these formats and know how to use them in their own assessment, evaluation, and communication contexts. Given this understanding, teachers and administrators are encouraged to experiment with innovative applications of these methods.
- Whenever possible, assessment procedures will be integrated and coordinated across levels of decision making (i.e., from individual students, to classroom, to building, to district) so as to promote efficient, cost-effective assessment and consistency in communication.

The Focus of Assessment

The focus of assessment in this district will be student attainment or mastery of those foundational skills, abilities, and dispositions (mastery of content knowledge, use of knowledge to reason and solve problems, demonstration of valued skills, creation of valued products, and development of positive attitudes) needed to satisfy the ultimate student outcomes listed below.
Those successfully completing our programs will be able to do the following, and more: (Note: These listed items are intended only as placeholders. Each district will determine its own ultimate valued goals)

- communicate effectively in school, work-related, and social contexts
- solve problems that arise in everyday school, work, and personal life
- lead safe and healthy school, work, and personal lives
- function effectively as part of a team

FIGURE 16-1
Sample District-Level Assessment Policy

continued

All faculty and staff shall take responsibility for articulating in writing how the knowledge, thinking, behaviors, products, and affective targets they teach and assess contribute to student progress toward these outcomes. All assessments not calculated to contribute in a clear and appropriate manner are regarded as unsound and shall be discarded.

Assessment Roles and Responsibilities

Each participant in the educational process listed below is acknowledged to have the right and responsibility to use assessment results to inform the decisions specified. Each user has the responsibility to understand what constitutes sound assessment, the role of assessment in their context, and how to use the resources at their disposal to assure that assessment plays its intended role.

Decision-Maker	Uses Assessment Results to Define:
School Board Member	Are district resources being allocated so as to promote goal attainment? Is the superintendent setting and implementing policies that promote goal attainment?
Superintendent	Which goals and enabling targets are being attained and which need attention?
Curriculum Director	Which targets need attention? Which instructional programs need attention?
Principal	Which targets need attention in this building? Which programs need attention? Which teachers need help?
Teacher	Which targets need attention? Which students need help? How shall they be helped?
Student	Which targets need attention? What help do I need?
Parent/Community	What does my child need? What other students, teacher, principals, programs, superintendents, and board members need attention?

All district staff and faculty will understand their own uses of assessment, the importance of the uses of others, how their uses relate to the uses of others, and what kind(s) of assessment results are needed to fulfill their responsibilities.

Regulatory Implications

It is the responsibility of the superintendent to assure that the conditions required for all to fulfill their assessment responsibilities are met; that is, all educators in the district have the incentives, opportunity, and resources needed to assess student achievement in a sound and appropriate manner.

Further, it is the responsibility of the superintendent and building administrators to hire faculty and staff who possess all competencies required to fulfill their assessment, evaluation, and grading responsibilities; secure or provide training for those currently employed who lack the necessary assessment competence; and institute ongoing staff evaluation procedures to ensure the ongoing presence of appropriate levels of assessment competence at classroom, building, and district levels. As a corollary, the superintendent shall take responsibility for assuring that all members of the school board receive the training they need to fulfill their roles as users of assessment information.

Finally, it is the responsibility of the superintendent and principals to maintain a professional environment surrounding assessment, evaluation, and grading in which those unable to fulfill their responsibilities are encouraged to admit this need and obtain appropriate assistance.

FIGURE 16–1, *continued*

Including Our Communities as Partners

All involved and invested in the educational process must be advocates of and spokespersons for sound assessment—especially as we communicate with parents and others in the community about quality schools. As teachers, we must provide leadership in this effort.

You can take advantage of every opportunity to open channels of communication. No one is in a better position to do this. You can make positive, assertive statements about the quality of schools by involving everyone, from students leading their parents through a parent-teacher conference to the news reporter writing the story about outstanding student performance on a complex and demanding science project. Use these opportunities to reveal the underlying rigor of classroom assessments and, at the same time, to reveal the immense power of student involvement in the assessment process.

As spokespersons for sound assessment, we must help our communities understand the nature of the changes taking place in the achievement targets being set by society for youth. These outcomes are becoming more numerous, complex, and individualized. As a result, we must help our communities see that we will be using a broader array of assessments in the future than we have in the past—to assess these outcomes accurately.

And, anything we can do to bring students into the assessment process so they also can present and represent examples of academic excellence to their community will be of great benefit.

HIGH-QUALITY CLASSROOM ASSESSMENT: A MATTER OF PRINCIPLE

A few general themes emerge from this analysis of contributors and contributions to creating a new and more positive assessment environment in schools. They relate directly to the seven basic principles of sound classroom assessment with which we began in Chapter 1. They provided the roadmap for our journey through a vast array of philosophical positions, assessment strategies, and examples of assessment at work in the classrooms, and it is appropriate to return to them now to reflect upon and reaffirm their meaning for teachers and students.

Principles of Sound Assessment

Principle 1.   Sound assessment requires clear thinking and effective communication. We must think clearly about many things:

- the appropriateness of our achievement targets

- the clarity of our definitions of these targets

- how best to reflect our targets in sound exercises and performance expectations

- how best to attend to the rules of evidence appropriate for whatever assessment methods we use
- what kinds of feedback are likely to have maximum benefit for students and other users of assessment results

Effective communication is essential also if we are to share targets, assessments, and results with students, parents, and other users. It should be clear now that the quantification of student achievement, while useful in some contexts, is by no means the only way to communicate. We also can and should use words, pictures, and examples to depict student achievement of specified outcomes in rich detail.

Principle 2. *Classroom assessments exert greatest influence on student learning and academic self-concept.* While centralized, standardized, large-scale assessments at the local, state, national, and international levels command all the media coverage, assessment resources, and political spotlight, it is day-to-day classroom assessment that works diligently out of the limelight to power the teaching and learning process.

Nearly all of the assessment events that take place in a student's life happen at the behest of the teacher. They align most closely with day-to-day instruction and are most influential in terms of their contribution to student, teacher, and parent decision making.

While large-scale standardized tests may appear to have great influence at specific times, no assessments imposed from outside the classroom even begin to approach classroom assessments in terms of their impact on student well-being. Without question, teachers are the drivers of the assessment systems that determine the effectiveness of schools.

Principle 3. *Students are the most important users of classroom assessment information.* Students use the results of classroom assessments to decide whether they can succeed in this place called school. Unless students feel able to succeed and make the conscious decision to try in school (i.e., operate with an internal locus of control with respect to their academic well-being), our efforts as teachers cannot work—regardless of the decisions made by other players at other levels in the hierarchy of that system. Our challenge, therefore, is to develop and use high-quality assessments that produce results students understand and can act upon.

Principle 4. *The quality and impact of any assessment turns first and foremost on the clarity and appropriateness of the definition of achievement to be assessed.* We simply cannot assess (or teach) reading, writing, thinking, and so on unless we can clearly define what academic success means in these performance arenas.

We have spoken consistently of five kinds of outcomes or targets:

- mastery of knowledge
- development of reasoning and problem-solving abilities
- demonstration of skills

- creation of products
- attainment of affective states

All are important. Our challenge at national, state, and district levels is to articulate the building blocks of ultimate competence in terms of these five categories. Only then can teachers share responsibility for assessing and teaching the ever-growing and increasingly complex outcomes. Only then can teachers share the vision of success with their students. Only then will schools become productive, achievement-driven institutions.

Principle 5. *All assessments must meet high standards of quality.* As a corollary, all who assess and/or use assessment results must understand the difference between sound and unsound assessment. We have spoken consistently of five standards: First, sound assessments reflect clear and appropriate targets. Second, they are designed with the purposes to which the assessment information is to be put clearly in mind. Third, they depict achievement through the use of a method that is, in fact, capable of reflecting the valued target. Fourth, they sample student achievement appropriately, so as to generate assessment results in which we can have confidence. Fifth, they control for all sources of extraneous interference that can cause us to mismeasure achievement.

I hope these standards have taken on clear meaning for you now, as they apply to each of our four basic assessment methods.

Principle 6. *Assessment is a complex interpersonal activity.* Each assessment event carries with it personal antecedents and personal consequences. For this reason, classroom assessment can be a force for either good or harm. Because assessments link students to their growing and changing academic self-concepts, if we can use assessments to lead them consistently to the conclusion that they can *succeed,* that they can *learn,* then we use them as a force for good. However, if assessments lead them chronically to infer that they will inevitably fail, then our other attempts to motivate them most assuredly will fail. Students must feel some success to embrace learning, to develop an appetite for it, to begin to regard success as being within reach, and to take charge of their own learning.

Our assessment challenge is to help students realize that their efforts and their academic success truly are linked. The best way I know of to do this is to share the vision of success and help students be in charge of accumulating the evidence that their efforts are bringing them closer to that target. I know of no more motivating or empowering moment for a student than to have in hand a concrete example of work from a year ago and work today—and the two show vast improvement and the student knows why. Pride shines through.

Principle 7. *Teaching and assessment can be one in the same.* I hope you understand the many meanings of this principle by now. Under some circumstances, it means that, if we conduct selected response assessments for which students know the target in advance, we can help them interpret test results more completely. Under other circumstances, it means that, if we conduct performance assessments with clear and appropriate criteria, we can provide the kind of focused feedback that will help students improve. And if students help in the development of the criteria, so much the better!

It also means that, if we begin instruction with a clear set of expectations for student performance on a final assessment, we can focus instruction on the true keys to student success. We can bring students into the assessment process as full partners, making teaching and assessment one in the same. Students can contribute to the clarification of targets, the development of assessments, the administration of assessments, and the scoring and interpretation of results. They can help each other to understand the meaning of success and to hit the valued target, if we eliminate the mystery that often shrouds that target and share the power to evaluate success.

THE END OF OUR JOURNEY

Let me conclude our journey together with one final story. Our storyteller is Anthony D. Fredericks, a reading specialist with the Catasauqua Area School District in Pennsylvania.[1]

The Latest Model

It was time once again to assess student performance, so I gathered up my catalogs and headed down to the local showroom of Ernie's Evaluation Emporium and spoke to the manager, Norm Reference.

"I'm in the market for a new assessment tool," I said.

"Have I got a hot little number for you!" He pulled me over to one of the showcases. "This little baby here not only gives you percentiles, grade equivalents, stanines, raw scores, means, medians, Z scores, and instructional reading levels, but plots the market value of the dollar on the Gold Exchange as well as the prime lending rate of 10 major banks for the next 6 months."

"I don't think that's what I had in mind," I replied.

"Well, this model over here not only graphs, calibrates, plots, scores, and interpolates all your students' scores, but also sends a four-color report home to parents every 3 weeks listing the colleges their youngsters will be eligible for after graduation."

"But these are elementary kids we're talking about," I said.

"I know, but there's no time like the present for parents to start saving up for those outlandish tuition bills."

"Perhaps I could look at something else," I said.

"Certainly. This sleek model here provides grade equivalent scores out to 6 decimal places, is renormed every other Tuesday, and the publisher guarantees that every child

[1]Reprinted from "The Latest Model" by A. D. Fredericks, 1987 from *The Reading Teacher, 40*(8), pp. 790–791. Copyright 1987 by *The Reading Teacher.* Reprinted by permission.

scoring over the 90th percentile will receive a simulated gold bracelet with his or her score etched on the back.

"Or how about this flashy number. Not only does it provide an accurate assessment of each child's reading growth, but also charts their height and weight over the next 20 years, their individual horoscope, and their predicted income bracket by age 40.

"And this model here has been used exclusively by a school district in Iowa. Their scores were so high last year that the taxpayers overwhelmingly voted in favor of building a new school, erected a statue of the principal in the town square, and sent the entire student body to Hawaii for 2 weeks."

"All these sound exciting," I said, "but I'm really not quite sure. . . ."

"Well, you do look like the selective type. Perhaps we can fix you up with something from the back room. You realize, of course, that we can only show these models to our most discriminating customers."

I nodded and followed him behind a black curtain in the rear of the store.

"If you're not familiar with this model, you should know that they provide a daily evaluation of student performance, chart growth and progress during the course of the entire school year, make full and complete reports to administrators and parents, structure reading groups according to interest and ability, and guide instruction on an individual basis. In fact, I know of several principals who use these exclusively."

"These do seem interesting, but I wonder how long they'll be effective," I said.

"Several administrators have reported that they last forever and consistently give accurate diagnostic and evaluative information on students. And, believe me, the price is right!"

"Well, I think you've sold me. By the way, what do you call this model?"

He motioned me over and in a low voice he said "Teachers."

Thank you for traveling with me.

APPENDIX A

Additional Readings

Classroom Assessment Methodology

Assessment of Reasoning

Development of Portfolios

Reading Assessment

Mathematics Assessment

Assessment in Science

Assessment in Social Studies

These readings are selected from assessment bibliographies compiled and published by the Test Center, Northwest Regional Educational Laboratory, Portland, Oregon. Reprinted by permission of the publisher.

ADDITIONAL READINGS ON CLASSROOM ASSESSMENT METHODOLOGY

Ebel, R. L. & Frisbie, D. A. *Essentials of Educational Measurement,* 5th edition, 1991. Available from: Prentice Hall, 200 Old Tappan Rd., Old Tappan, NJ 07675.

Gronlund, N. E. & Linn, R. L. *Measurement and Evaluation in Teaching,* 6th edition, 1990. Available from: Macmillan, 100 Front St., Box 500, Riverside, NJ 08075.

Mehrens, W. A. & Lehmann, I. J. *Measurement and Evaluation in Education and Psychology,* 1991. Available from: Holt, Rinehart and Winston, Great West Region, West Coast Office, 577 Airport Blvd., Suite 185, Burlingame, CA 94010.

Oosterhoff, A. *Classroom Applications of Educational Measurement,* 1990. Available from: Macmillan, 100 Front St., Box 500, Riverside, NJ 08075.

Popham, W. J. *Modern Educational Measurement: A Practitioner's Perspective, 2nd Edition,* 1990. Available from: Prentice Hall, 200 Old Tappan Rd., Old Tappan, NJ 07675.

Stiggins, R. J. & Conklin, N. F. *In Teachers' Hands: Investigating the Practices of Classroom Assessment,* 1992. Available from: State University of New York Press, State University Plaza, Albany, NY 12246.

ADDITIONAL READINGS ON ASSESSMENT OF REASONING

Baron, J. & Sternberg, R. *Teaching Thinking: Theory and Practice,* 1987. Available from: W. H. Freeman and Co., 4419 West 1980 South, Salt Lake City, UT 84104.

Bransford, J. D. & Vye, N. J. A Perspective on Cognitive Research and Its Implications for Instruction. Located in: *1989 ASCD Yearbook.* Available from: Association for Supervision and Curriculum Development, 1250 N. Pitt St., Alexandria, VA 22314.

Beyer, B. K. *Developing a Thinking Skills Program,* 1988. Available from Allyn and Bacon, Inc., via

Simon and Schuster, 200 Old Tappan Road, Old Tappan, NJ 07675.

Chi, M. T. H., Glaser, R., & Rees, E. Expertise in Problem Solving. Located in: Robert J. Sternberg (Ed.), *Advances in the Psychology of Human Intelligence, Volume 1,* 1982, pp. 7–75. Available from: Lawrence Erlbaum Associates, Inc., 365 Broadway, Hillsdale, NJ 07642.

Costa, A. L. (Ed.) *Developing Minds: A Resource Book for Teaching Thinking,* 1985. Available from: Association for Supervision and Curriculum Development, 1250 N. Pitt St., Alexandria, VA 22314.

Educational Testing Service. Critical Thinking: Critical Issues. Located in: *FOCUS,* 24, 1990. Available from: FOCUS, Educational Testing Service, Princeton, NJ 08541.

Halpern, D. F. *Thought and Knowledge, An Introduction to Critical Thinking,* 2nd edition, 1989. Available from: Lawrence Erlbaum Associates, Inc., 365 Broadway, Hillsdale, NJ 07642.

Inquiry: Critical Thinking Across the Disciplines. Publication available from: Institute for Critical Thinking, Montclair State College, Upper Montclair, NJ 07043.

Jones, B. F. & Idol, L. (Eds.) *Dimensions of Thinking and Cognitive Instruction,* 1990. Available from: Lawrence Erlbaum Associates, Inc., 365 Broadway, Hillsdale, NJ 07642.

Kearney, C. P. *Assessing Higher Order Thinking Skills,* April 1986. Available from: ERIC Document Reproduction Service, 3900 Wheeler Ave., Alexandria, VA 22304.

Marzano, R. J., Brandt, R. S., & Hughes, C. S. *Dimensions of Thinking: A Framework for Curriculum and Instruction,* 1988. Available from: Association for Supervision and Curriculum Development, 1250 N. Pitt St., Alexandria, VA 22314.

Paul, R. *Critical Thinking: What Every Person Needs to Survive in a Rapidly Changing World,* 2nd edition, 1992. Available from: Foundation for Critical Thinking, 4655 Sonoma Mountain Road, Santa Rosa, CA 95404.

Snow, R. E. & Lohman, D. F. Implications of Cognitive Psychology for Educational Measurement. Located in: Robert Linn (Ed.), *Educational*

Measurement, 3rd edition, 1989, pp. 263–331. Available from: Macmillan, 100 Front St., Box 500, Riverside, NJ 08075.

Swartz, R. J. & Perkins, D. N. *Teaching Thinking: Issues and Approaches,* 1989. Available from: Midwest Publications, PO Box 448, Pacific Grove, CA 93950.

Teaching Thinking and Problem Solving. Publication available from: Lawrence Erlbaum Associates, Inc., 365 Broadway, Hillsdale, NJ 07642, or Research for Better Schools, 444 N. Third St., Philadelphia, PA 19123.

Wolf, D., Bixby, J., Glenn III, J., & Gardner, H. To Use Their Minds Well: Investigating New Forms of Student Assessment. Located in: *Review of Research in Education,* 17, 1991, pp. 31–74. Available from: AERA, 1230 17th St., NW, Washington, DC 20036.

ADDITIONAL READINGS ON DEVELOPMENT OF PORTFOLIOS

Adams, D. & Hamm, M. Portfolio Assessment and Social Studies: Collecting, Selecting, and Reflecting on What Is Significant, 1992. Located in: *Social Education,* February 1992, pp. 103–105.

Archibald, D. & Newmann, F. *Beyond Standardized Testing,* 1988. Available from: National Association of Secondary School Principals, 1904 Association Drive, Reston, VA 22091.

Arter, J., Culham, R., & Spandel, V. *Using Portfolios of Student Work in Assessment and Instruction,* 1992. A video workshop available from: IOX Assessment Associates, 5301 Beethoven St., Suite 109, Los Angeles, CA 90066-7061.

Bird, T. *Notes On An Exploration Of Portfolio Procedures For Evaluating High School Biology Teachers,* 1989. Available from: Teacher Assessment Project, Stanford University, School of Education, CERAS 507, Stanford, California 94395.

Bishop, W. Revising the Technical Writing Class: Peer Critiques, Self-Evaluation, and Portfolio Grading. Located in: *The Technical Writing Teacher,* 16, 1989, pp. 13–25.

Buell, N. *An Overview of Six Portfolio Assessment Projects in the State of Alaska (or "At First They Thought It Was An Animal They Were Going To Feed"),* 1991. Available from: The Alaska State Department of Education, P. O. Box F, Juneau, AK 99811-0500.

Burnham, C. Portfolio Evaluation: Room to Breathe and Grow. Located in: C. Bridges (Ed.), *Training the Teacher,* 1986. Urbana, IL: NCTE, 1111 Kenyon Road, Urbana, IL 61801.

Calkins, A. *Juneau Integrated Language Arts Portfolio for Grade 1,* 1991. Available from: Juneau Borough School District, 10014 Crazy Horse Drive, Juneau, AK 99801.

Camp, R. Thinking Together About Portfolios. Located in: *The Quarterly of the National Writing Project,* 27, Spring 1990, pp. 8–14. Also available from: The Center For The Study of Writing, 5513 Tolman Hall, School of Education, University of California, Berkeley, CA 94720.

Camp, R. & Levine, D. Portfolios Evolving: Background and Variations in Sixth- Through Twelfth-Grade Classrooms. Located in: Pat Belanoff and Marcia Dickson (Eds.), *Portfolio Grading: Process and Product,* 1990, Boynton Cook Publishers, Portsmouth, NH.

Campbell, J. Laser Disk Portfolios: Total Child Assessment. Located in: *Educational Leadership,* 49, 1991, pp. 69–70. Also available from: Conestoga Elementary School, 4901 Sleepy Hollow Blvd., Gillette, WY 82716.

Carr, B. Portfolios: A Mini-Guide. Located in: *School Arts,* 1987, 86, pp. 55–56.

Collins, A. Portfolios for Assessing Student Learning in Science: A New Name for a Familiar Idea? Located in: Champagne, Lovitts, and Calinger (Eds.), *Assessment In The Service of Instruction,* 1990, pp. 157–166. Available from: American Association for the Advancement of Science, 1333 H Street, NW, Washington, D.C. 20005.

Elbow, P. & Belanoff, P. State University of New York, Stony Brook Portfolio Based Evaluation Program. Located in: Connelly and Vilard (Eds.), *New Methods in College Writing Programs,* 1986, pp. 95–104. Available from: Modern Language Association, New York, NY.

EQUALS Project. *Assessment Alternatives in Mathematics,* 1989. Available from: Lawrence Hall of

Science, University of California, Berkeley, CA 94720.

Erickson, M. Developing Student Confidence to Evaluate Writing. Located in: *The Quarterly of the National Writing Project & the Center for the Study of Writing and Literacy,* 14, 1992, pp. 7–9.

Farr, R. & Farr, B. *Integrated Assessment System,* 1990. Available from: Psychological Corporation, 555 Academic Court, San Antonio, TX 78204.

Feeney, T. M. *ROPE: Rite of Passage Experience Handbook,* 1984. Available from: Walden III Alternative High School, 1012 Center St., Racine, WI 53403.

Ferguson, S. Zeroing in on Math Abilities. Located in: *Learning92,* 21, 1992, pp. 38–41.

Flood, J. & Lapp, D. Reporting Reading Progress: A Comparison Portfolio For Parents. Located in: *Reading Teacher,* March 1989, pp. 508–514.

Frazier, D. & Paulson, F. L. *Portfolio Assessment: Students Finding a Voice,* 1991. Available from: Multnomah ESD, 11611 N.E. Ainsworth Circle, Portland, OR 97220.

Gardner, H. & Hatch, T. Multiple-Intelligences Go To School. Located in: *Educational Researcher,* 18, 1989, pp. 4–10.

Gearhart, M., Herman, J., Baker, E., & Whittaker, A. *Writing Portfolios at the Elementary Level: A Study of Methods for Writing Assessment,* 1992. Available from: National Center for Research on Evaluation, Standards, and Student Testing, UCLA Graduate School of Education, University of California, Los Angeles, CA 90024.

Gentile, C. *Exploring New Methods for Collecting Students' School-Based Writing,* 1992. Available from: Education Information Branch, Office of Educational Research and Improvement, U.S. Department of Education, 555 New Jersey Ave., NW, Washington D.C. 20208.

Grady, E. *Grady Profile Portfolio Assessment Product Demo,* 1991. Available from: Aurbach & Associates, Inc., 8233 Tulane Ave., St. Louis, MO 63132.

Graves, D. & Sunstein, B. *Portfolio Portraits,* 1992. Available from: Heinemann Educational Books, Inc., 361 Hanover St., Portsmouth, NH 03801.

Griffin, P., Jones, C., Maher, M., Mount, J., O'Brien, S., Ryan, D., Smith, P., Smyth, A., & Baker, G. *Literacy Profiles Handbook: Assessing and Reporting Literacy Development,* 1990. Available from: School Programs Division, Ministry of Education, Victoria, Australia. Also available from: TASA, Field's Lane, P.O. Box 382, Brewster, NY 10509.

Gursky, D. *Maine's Portfolio-Based Recertification Process Overcomes Administrators' Initial Skepticism,* 1992. Located in: *Education Week,* 11, May 20, 1992.

Hansen, J. Literacy Portfolios: Helping Students Know Themselves. Located in: *Educational Leadership,* 49, 1992, pp. 66–68.

Hawaii Department of Education. *Using Portfolios: A Handbook for the Chapter 1 Teacher,* 1991. Available from: Hawaii Department of Education, Chapter 1 Office, 3430 Leahi Ave., Bldg. D, Honolulu, HI 96815.

Hebert, E. A. Portfolios Invite Reflection—From Students and Staff. Located in: *Educational Leadership,* 49, 1992, pp. 58–61.

Herter, R. Writing Portfolios: Alternatives to Testing. Located in: *English Journal,* January 1991, pp. 90–91.

Hetterscheidt, J., Pott, L., Russell, K., & Tchang, J. Using the Computer as a Reading Portfolio. Located in: *Educational Leadership,* 49, 1992, p. 73.

Howard, K. Making the Writing Portfolio Real. Located in: *The Quarterly of the National Writing Project,* 27, Spring 1990, pp. 4–7. Also available from: The Center For The Study of Writing, 5513 Tolman Hall, School of Education, University of California, Berkeley, CA 94720.

Hunt, D. Preparing a Portfolio. Located in: *The Instrumentalist,* 41, 1986, pp. 30–38.

Ingalls, B. & Jones, J. There's a Lot of Things You Learn in English That You Really Can't See. Located in: *The Quarterly of the National Writing Project & The Center for the Study of Writing and Literacy,* 14, 1992, pp. 1–4.

International Reading Association. Portfolios Illuminate the Path for Dynamic, Interactive Readers. Located in: *Journal of Reading,* May 1990, pp. 644–647.

Jongsma, K. Portfolio Assessment. Located in: *Reading Teacher,* December 1989, pp. 264–265.

Knight, P. How I Use Portfolios in Mathematics. Located in: *Educational Leadership,* 49, 1992, pp. 71–72.

Krest, M. Adapting The Portfolio To Meet Student Needs. Located in: *English Journal,* 79, 1990, pp. 29–34.

LeMahieu, P. *Writing Portfolio: Current Working Model,* 1991. Available from: PROPEL, Pittsburgh Public Schools, Division of Writing & Speaking, 341 S. Bellefield Ave., Pittsburgh, PA 15213.

Levi, R. Assessment and Educational Vision: Engaging Learners and Parents. Located in: *Language Arts,* 67, 1990, pp. 269–273.

Little, N. *Student-Led Teacher Parent Conferences,* 1988. Available from: Lugus Productions Limited, 48 Falcon Street, Toronto, Ontario, Canada M4S 2P5.

MacIntosh, H. *Reviewing Pupil Achievements Through a Portfolio of Evidence,* 1989. Available from: International Association for Educational Assessment, Brook Lawn, Middleton Road, Camberley, Surrey, GU15 3TU, England.

Malarz, L., D'Arcangelo, M., & Kiernan, L. *Redesigning Assessment: Portfolios,* 1992. A video available from: ASCD, 1250 N. Pitt St., Alexandria, VA 22314-1403.

Marienberg, J. *Portfolio Contents,* 1990. Available from: Hillsboro High School District, 3285 SE Rood Bridge Rd., Hillsboro, OR 97123.

Marsh, H. F. & Lasky, P. A. The Professional Portfolio: Documentation of Prior Learning. Located in: *Nursing Outlook,* 32, 1984, pp. 264–267.

Mathews, J. From Computer Management To Portfolio Assessment. Located in: *The Reading Teacher,* February 1990, pp. 420–421.

McLean, L. D. Time to Replace the Classroom Test With Authentic Measurement. Located in: *Alberta Journal of Educational Research,* 36, 1990, pp. 78–84.

Meyer, C., Schuman, S., & Angello, N. *NWEA White Paper On Aggregating Portfolio Data,* 1990. Available from: Northwest Evaluation Association, 5 Centerpointe Dr., Suite 100, Lake Oswego, OR 97035.

Moss, P. Portfolios, Accountability, and an Interpretive Approach to Validity. Located in: *Educational Measurement: Issues and Practice,* 11, 1992, pp. 12–21.

Murdick, W. Portfolios and Patterns of Choice. Located in: *Portfolio News,* 2(2), 1991, p. 2. Available from: Portfolio Assessment Clearinghouse, San Dieguito Union High School District, 710 Encinitas Boulevard, Encinitas, CA 92024.

Murphy, S. & Smith, M. A. Talking About Portfolios. Located in: *The Quarterly of the National Writing Project,* Spring 1990, pp. 1–3, 24–27.

Myers, M. Institutionalizing Inquiry. Located in: *The Quarterly of the National Writing Project & The Center for the Study of Writing,* 9, July 1987, pp. 1–4.

National Center for Research on Evaluation, Standards, and Student Testing (CRESST). *Portfolio Assessment and High Technology,* 1992. Available from: CRESST, 405 Hilgard Ave., Los Angeles, CA 90024-1522.

Paris, S. G. Portfolio Assessment: Reflections on Learning. Located in: Robert Smith and Deanna Birdyshaw (Eds.), *Perspectives on Assessment, Volume 1,* 1992, pp. 209–219. Available from: Michigan Reading Association, P.O. Box 7509, Grand Rapids, MI 49510.

Paulson, L. *Portfolio Guidelines in Primary Math,* 1992. Available from: Multnomah Education Service District, P.O. Box 301039, Portland, OR 97220.

Paulson, L., Paulson, P., & Meyer, C. What Makes A Portfolio A Portfolio? Located in: *Educational Leadership,* February 1991, pp. 60–63.

Raju, N. *Integrated Literature and Language Arts Portfolio Program,* 1991. Available from: Riverside Publishing Company, 8420 Bryn Mawr Avenue, Chicago, IL 60631.

Rief, L. Finding the Value in Evaluation: Self-Assessment in a Middle School Classroom. Located in: *Educational Leadership,* March 1990, pp. 24–29.

Rousculp, E. E. & Maring, G. H. Portfolios for a Community of Learners. Located in: *Journal of Reading,* 35, 1992, pp. 378–385.

Sack, M. *Portfolio Assessment,* 1991. Available from: Urban Corps Expansion Project, Public/Private

Ventures, 399 Market Street, Philadelphia, PA 19106.

Schwartz, J. Let Them Assess Their Own Learning. Located in: *English Journal,* February 1991, pp. 67–73.

Simmons, J. Portfolios For Large-Scale Assessment. Located in: Donald Graves and Connie Sunstein (Eds.), *Portfolio Portraits,* 1992. Available from: Heinemann Educational Books, 361 Hanover St., Portsmouth, NH 03801.

Stenmark, J. *Mathematics Assessment: Myths, Models, Good Questions, and Practical Suggestions,* 1991. Available from: National Council of Teachers of Mathematics, 1906 Association Drive, Reston, VA 22091.

Sugarman, J. Teacher Portfolios Inform Assessment. Located in: *The American Educator,* May 1989, pp. 5–6.

Teacher Assessment Project. *Portfolio Development Handbook for Teachers of Elementary Literacy,* 1988. Available from: Stanford University, School of Education, CERAS 507, Stanford, CA 94395.

Tierney, R. J., Carter, M. A., & Desai, L. E. *Portfolio Assessment in the Reading-Writing Classroom,* 1991. Available from: Christopher Gordon, Publishers, Norwood, MA.

Valencia, S. A Portfolio Approach To Classroom Reading Assessment: The Whys, Whats and Hows. Located in: *The Reading Teacher,* January 1990, pp. 338–340.

Valencia, S. Portfolios: Panacea or Pandora's Box? Located in: Fredrick Finch (Ed.), *Educational Performance Assessment,* 1991, pp. 33–46.

Valencia, S. W. & Calfee, R. The Development and Use of Literacy Portfolios for Students, Classes, and Teachers. Located in: *Applied Measurement in Education,* 4, 1991, pp. 333–345.

Valeri-Gold, Olson, M., Olson, J., & Deming, M. Portfolios: Collaborative Authentic Assessment Opportunities for College Developmental Learners. Located in: *Journal of Reading,* 35, pp. 298–305.

Vavrus, L. Put Portfolios To the Test. Located in: *Instructor,* August 1990, pp. 48–53.

Wilson, J. The Role of Metacognition in English Education. Located in: *English Education,* 17, December 1985, pp. 212–220.

Wolf, D. P. Portfolio Assessment: Sampling Student Work. Located in: *Educational Leadership,* April 1989, pp. 35–39.

Yancey, K. *Portfolios in the Writing Classroom,* 1992. Available from: National Council of Teachers of English, 1111 Kenyon Road, Urbana, IL 61801.

ADDITIONAL READINGS ON READING ASSESSMENT

Bailey, J., et al. Problem Solving Our Way to Alternative Evaluation Procedures. Located in: *Language Arts,* 65, April 1988, pp. 364–373.

Barrs, M., Ellis, S., Hester, H., & Thomas, A. *The Primary Language Record Handbook for Teachers,* 1988. Available from: Heinemann Educational Books, 361 Hanover St., Portsmouth, NH 03801.

Baskwell, J. & Whitman, P. *Evaluation: Whole Language, Whole Child,* 1988. Available from: Scholastic, Inc., 730 Broadway, New York, NY 10003.

Bean, T. Organizing and Retaining Information by Thinking Like an Author. Located in: Susan Glazer, Lyndon Searfoss, and Lance Gentile (Eds.), *Reexamining Reading Diagnosis, New Trends and Procedures,* 1988, pp. 103–127. Available from: International Reading Association, 800 Barksdale Rd., P.O. Box 8139, Newark, DE 19714.

Brown, C. & Lytle, S. Merging Assessment and Instruction: Protocols in the Classroom. Located in: Susan Glazer, Lyndon Searfoss, and Lance Gentile (Eds.), *Reexamining Reading Diagnosis, New Trends and Procedures,* 1988, pp. 94–102. Available from: International Reading Association, 800 Barksdale Rd., P.O. Box 8139, Newark, DE 19714.

Calfee, R. & Hiebert, E. The Teacher's Role in Using Assessment to Improve Learning. Located in: *Assessment in the Service of Learning, Invitational Conference Proceedings,* 1988, pp. 45–61. Available from: Educational Testing Service, Princeton, NJ 08541.

Clark, C. H. Assessing Free Recall (Analytical Reading Inventory). Located in: *The Reading Teacher,* 35, January 1982, pp. 434–439.

Clay, M. Concepts About Print. Located in: *The Early Detection of Reading Difficulties,* 1985. Available from: Heinemann Educational Books, 361 Hanover St., Portsmouth, NH 03801.

Costella, L. *(Fredrick County Alternative Assessment Project) Essential Curriculum: Learning and Assessment in Frederick County Public Schools; An Overview of Assessment that Promotes Learning,* 1991. Available from: Frederick County Public School System, 115 E. Church St., Frederick, MD 21701.

Degrees of Reading Power, 1986. Available from: Touchstone Applied Science Associates, Fields Lane, P.O. Box 382, Brewster, NY 10509.

Dole, J., Duffy, G., Roeher, L., & Pearson, D. Moving From the Old to the New: Research on Reading Comprehension Instruction. Located in: *Review of Educational Research,* 61, Summer 1991, pp. 239–264.

Eeds, M. Holistic Assessment of Coding Ability. Located in: Susan Glazer, Lyndon Searfoss, and Lance Gentile (Eds.), *Reexamining Reading Diagnosis: New Trends and Procedures,* 1988, pp. 48–66. Available from: International Reading Association, 800 Barksdale Rd., P.O. Box 8139, Newark, DE 19714.

Eggleton, J. *Whole Language Evaluation: Reading, Writing and Spelling,* 1990. Available from: The Wright Group, 18916 North Creek Parkway, Bothell, WA 98011.

Fagan, W. T., Jensen, J. M., & Cooper, C. R. *Measures for Research and Evaluation in the English Language Arts,* Vol. 2, 1985. Available from: National Council of Teachers of English, 1111 Kenyon Road, Urbana, IL 61801.

Farr, R. & Carey, R. F. *Reading: What Can Be Measured?,* 1986. Available from: International Reading Association, 800 Barksdale Rd., P.O. Box 8139, Newark, DE 19714.

Farr, R., Lewis, M., Faszhoz, J., Pinsky, E., Towe, S., Lipschutz, J., & Faulds, B. Writing in Response To Reading. Located in: *Educational Leadership,* 47, March 1990, pp. 66–69. Also available from: River Forest School District Administration Building, 7776 Lake St., River Forest, IL 60305.

Fisher, B. Assessing Emergent and Initial Readers. Located in: *Teaching K–8,* Nov./Dec. 1989, pp. 56–58.

Flood, J. & Lapp, D. Reporting Reading Progress: A Comparison Portfolio for Parents. Located in: *The Reading Teacher,* March 1989, pp. 508–514.

Fredericks, A. & Rasinski, T. Involving Parents in the Assessment Process. Located in: *The Reading Teacher,* 44, 1990, pp. 346–349.

Gillet, J. & Temple, C. *Understanding Reading Problems: Assessment and Instruction,* 3rd edition, 1990. Available from: Harper Collins, 1000 Keystone Industrial Park, Scranton, PA 18512.

Glaser, S. M., Searfoss, L. W., & Gentile, L. M. *Reexamining Reading Diagnosis, New Trends and Procedures,* 1988. Available from: International Reading Association, 800 Barksdale Rd., P.O. Box 8139, Newark, DE 19714.

Goodman, K., Bird, L. B., & Goodman, Y. *The Whole Language Catalog Supplement on Authentic Assessment,* 1992. Available from: American School Publishers, 1221 Farmers Lane, Suite C, Santa Rosa, CA 95405.

Grant, A. Towards a Transactive Theory of the Reading Process and Research in Evaluation. Located in: Sue Legg and James Algina (Eds.), *Cognitive Assessment of Language and Math Outcomes,* 1990, pp. 192–240. Available from: Ablex Publishing Corp., 355 Chestnut St., Norwood, NJ 07648.

Griffin, P., Jones, C., Maher, M., Mount, J., O'Brien, S., Ryan, D., Smith, P., Smyth, A., & Baker, G. *Literacy Profiles Handbook: Assessing and Reporting Literacy Development,* 1990. Available from: School Programs Division, Ministry of Education, Victoria, Australia. Also available from: TASA, Field's Lane, P.O. Box 382, Brewster, NY 10509.

Hansen, J. Literacy Portfolios: Helping Students Know Themselves. Located in: *Educational Leadership,* 49, 1992, pp. 66–68. Also available from: University of New Hampshire, Morrill Hall, Curham, NH 03825.

Hetterscheidt, J., Pott, L., Russell, K., & Tchang, J. Using the Computer as a Reading Portfolio. Located in: *Educational Leadership,* 49, 1992, p.

73. Also available from: Bellerive School, 666 Rue De Fleur, Creve Coeur, MO 63141.

International Reading Association. Portfolios Illuminate the Path for Dynamic, Interactive Readers. Located in: *Journal of Reading,* May 1990, pp. 644–647.

Johnston, P. Steps Toward a More Naturalistic Approach to the Assessment of the Reading Process. Located in: Sue Legg and James Algina (Eds.), *Cognitive Assessment of Language and Math Outcomes,* 1990. Available from: Ablex Publishing Corp., 355 Chestnut St., Norwood, NJ 07648.

Kay, G. A Thinking Twist On the Multiple-Choice Question. Located in: *Journal of Reading,* 36, 1992, pp. 56–57.

Kinney, M. & Harry, A. An Informal Inventory for Adolescents That Assesses the Reader, the Text, and the Task. Located in: *Journal of Reading,* 34, 1991, pp. 643–647.

Knight, J. Coding Journal Entries. Located in: *Journal of Reading,* 34, 1990, pp. 42–47.

Lock, L., Miler, L., & Masters, J. *A Preliminary Evaluation of Pennsylvania's 1990 Wholistic Model Reading Tests,* 1991. Available from: Pennsylvania Department of Education, Division of Educational Testing and Evaluation (12th Floor), 333 Market St., P.O. Box 911, Harrisburg, PA 17126.

Mathews, J. From Computer Management To Portfolio Assessment. Located in: *The Reading Teacher,* February 1990, pp. 420–421.

McCormick, S., Cooter, R., & McEneaney, J. Assessment of Disabled Readers: A Survey of Current Teacher Beliefs and Practices. Located in: *Journal of Reading,* 35, 1992, pp. 597–599.

McEneaney, J. Computer-Assisted Diagnosis in Reading: An Expert Systems Approach. Located in: *Journal of Reading,* 36, 1992, pp. 36–47.

McKenna, M. & Kear, D. Measuring Attitude Toward Reading: A New Tool for Teachers. Located in: *The Reading Teacher,* 43, 1990, pp. 626–639.

McTighe, J. *Maryland School Performance Assessment Program—Reading, Writing, Language Arts,* 1991. Available from: Maryland Department of Education, 200 W. Baltimore St., Baltimore, MD 21201.

Morrow, L. Retelling Stories as a Diagnostic Tool.

Located in: Susan Glazer, Lyndon Searfoss, and Lance Gentile (Eds.), *Reexamining Reading Diagnosis: New Trends and Procedures,* 1988, pp. 128–149. Available from: International Reading Association, 800 Barksdale Rd., P.O. Box 8139, Newark, DE 19714.

Paratore, J. R. & Indrisano, R. Intervention Assessment of Reading Comprehension. Located in: *The Reading Teacher,* April 1987, pp. 778–783.

Paris, S., Wasik, B., & Van der Westhuizen, G. Meta-Metacognition: A Review of Research on Metacognition and Reading. Located in: John Readence, Scott Baldwin, John Konopak, and Patricia O'Keefe (Eds.), *Dialogues in Literacy Research,* 1988. Available from: National Reading Conference, Inc., 11 East Hubbard, Suite 200, Chicago, IL 60622.

Phillips-Riggs, L. Categories of Inferencing Strategies, 1981. Located in: W. T. Fagan, J. M. Jensen, and C. R. Cooper (Eds.), *Measures for Research and Evaluation in the English Language Arts, Vol. 2,* 1985. Available from: NCTE, 1111 Kenyon Rd., Urbana, IL 61801.

Pikulski, J. The Assessment of Reading: A Time For Change? Located in: *The Reading Teacher,* October 1989, pp. 80–81.

Pikulski, J. Informal Reading Inventories. Located in: *The Reading Teacher,* March 1990, pp. 514–516.

Pumphrey, P. D. *Reading: Tests and Assessment Techniques,* 2nd edition, 1985. Available from: Hodder and Stoughton Ltd., Mill Road, Dunton Green, Sevenoaks, Kent, England, UK. Also available from: International Reading Association, 800 Barksdale Rd., P.O. Box 8139, Newark, DE 19714.

Rea, D. W. & Thompson, D. K. Designing Transformative Tests for Secondary Literature Students. Located in: *Journal of Reading,* 34(1), 1990, pp. 6–11.

Royer, J. The Sentence Verification Technique: A New Direction in the Assessment of Reading Comprehension. Located in: Sue Legg and James Algina (Eds.), *Cognitive Assessment of Language and Math Outcomes,* 1990, pp. 144–181. Available from: Ablex Publishing, 355 Chestnut St., Norwood, NJ 07648.

Schmitt, M. C. Metacomprehension Strategies Indexes, A Questionnaire to Measure Children's Awareness of Strategic Reading Processes. Located in: *The Reading Teacher,* March 1990, pp. 454–461.

Shannon, A. Using the Microcomputer Environment for Reading Diagnosis. Located in: Susan Glazer, Lyndon Searfoss, and Lance Gentile (Eds.), *Reexamining Reading Diagnosis: New Trends and Procedures,* 1988, pp. 150–168. Available from: International Reading Association, 800 Barksdale Rd., P.O. Box 8139, Newark, DE 19714.

Sharp, Q. Q. *Evaluation: Whole Language Checklists For Evaluating Your Children,* 1989. Available from: Scholastic, Inc., 730 Broadway, New York, NY 10003.

Stayter, F. & Johnston, P. Evaluating the Teaching and Learning of Literacy. Located in: Timothy Shanahan (Ed.), *Reading and Writing Together: New Perspectives for the Classroom,* 1990. Available from: Christopher-Gordon Publishers, 480 Washington St., Norwood, MA 02062.

Stiggins, R. J. *Assessing Reading Proficiency,* 1991. A video workshop available from: IOX Assessment Associates, 5301 Beethoven St., Suite 109, Los Angeles, CA 90066-7061.

Taylor, D. Teaching Without Testing: Assessing the Complexity of Children's Literacy Learning. Located in: *English Education,* 22, 1990, pp. 4–74.

Thistlethwaite, L. L. Critical Reading For At-Risk Students (Critical Reading Checklists). Located in: *Journal of Reading,* May 1990, pp. 586–593.

Tierney, R., Carter, M., & Desai, L. *Portfolio Assessment in the Reading-Writing Classroom,* 1991. Available from: Christopher Gordon Publishers, Inc., 480 Washington St., Norwood, MA 02062.

Valencia, S. A Portfolio Approach to Classroom Reading Assessment: The Whys, Whats and Hows. Located in: *The Reading Teacher,* January 1990, pp. 338–340.

Valencia, S., McGinley, W., & Pearson, D. Assessing Reading and Writing: Building A More Complete Picture. Located in: G. Duffey (Ed.), *Reading in the Middle School,* 1989. Available from: International Reading Association, 800 Barksdale Rd., P.O. Box 8139, Newark, DE 19714.

Valencia, S., Pearson, D., Peters, C., & Wixson, K. Theory and Practice in Statewide Reading Assessment: Closing the Gap. Located in: *Educational Leadership,* April 1989, pp. 57–63.

Wade, S. E. Reading Comprehension Using Think Alouds. Located in: *The Reading Teacher,* March 1990, pp. 442–451.

White, J. Taxonomy of Reading Behaviors. Located in: W. T. Fagan, J. M. Jensen, and C. R. Cooper (Eds.), *Measures for Research and Evaluation in the English Language Arts, Vol. 2,* 1985, pp. 120–124. Available from: NCTE, 1111 Kenyon Rd., Urbana IL 61801.

Winograd, P., Paris, S., & Bridge, C. Improving the Assessment of Literacy. Located in: *The Reading Teacher,* 45, 1991, pp. 108–116.

Wixson, K. K., Bosky, A. B., Yochum, N., & Alvermann, D. E. An Interview For Assessing Students' Perceptions of Classroom Reading Tasks. Located in: *The Reading Teacher,* January 1984, pp. 347–353.

ADDITIONAL READINGS ON MATHEMATICS ASSESSMENT

Algina, J. & Legg, S. (Eds.). Special Issue: The National Assessment of Educational Progress. Located in: *Journal of Educational Measurement,* 29, Summer 1992.

Bagley, T. & Gallenberger, C. Assessing Students' Dispositions: Using Journals to Improve Students' Performance. Located in: *The Mathematics Teacher,* 85, November 1992, pp. 660–663.

Baxter, G. P., Shavelson, R. J., Herman, S. J., Brown, K. A., & Valadez, J. R. Mathematics Performance Assessment: Technical Quality & Diverse Student Impact. Located in: *Journal for Research in Mathematics Education,* 24, 1993, pp. 90–216.

Braswell, J. *Overview of Changes in the SAT Mathematics Test in 1994. SAT Mathematics—Student Produced Responses,* 1991. Available from: Educational Testing Service, Princeton, NJ 08541.

California State Department of Education. *A Ques-*

tion of Thinking: A First Look at Students' Performance on Open-Ended Questions in Mathematics, 1989. Available from: California State Department of Education, PO Box 944272, Sacramento, CA 94244-2720.

Center for Innovation in Education. *Math Their Way,* 1990. Available from: Center for Innovation in Education, 20665 4th Street, Saratoga, CA 95070.

Charles, R., Lester, F., & O'Daffer, P. *How to Evaluate Progress in Problem Solving,* 1987. Available from: National Council of Teachers of Mathematics, 1906 Association Drive, Reston, VA 22091.

Collis, K. & Romberg, T. A. *Assessment of Mathematical Performance: An Analysis of Open-ended Test Items,* 1989. Available from: National Center for Research in Mathematical Sciences Education, Wisconsin Center for Education Research, University of Wisconsin, School of Education, 1025 W. Johnson St., Madison, WI 53706.

Commission on Standards for School Mathematics. *Curriculum and Evaluation Standards for School Mathematics,* 1989. Available from: National Council of Teachers of Mathematics, 1906 Association Drive, Reston, VA 22091.

Csongor, J. E. Mirror, Mirror On The Wall . . . Teaching Self-Assessment To Students. Located in: *The Mathematics Teacher,* 85, November 1992, pp. 636–637.

EQUALS. *Assessment Alternatives in Mathematics,* 1989. Available from: University of California, Lawrence Hall of Science, Berkeley, CA 94720.

Fraser, B. J., Malone, J. A., & Neale, J. M. Assessing and Improving the Psychosocial Environment of Mathematics Classrooms. Located in: *Journal for Research in Mathematics Education,* 20 (2), 1989, pp. 191–201.

Hall, G. *Alberta Grade 9 Performance-Based Assessment—Math,* 1992. Available from: Greg Hall, Student Evaluation Branch, Alberta Education, Box 43, 11160 Jasper Ave., Edmonton, AB T5K 0L2, CANADA.

Halpern, D. (Ed.) *Enhancing Thinking Skills in the Sciences and in Mathematics,* 1992. Available from: Lawrence Erlbaum Associates, 365 Broadway, Hillsdale, NJ 07642.

Higgins, K. *Assessing Mathematical Power,* 1992. A video workshop available from: IOX Assessment Associates, 5301 Beethoven St., Suite 109, Los Angeles, CA 90066-7061.

Knight, P. How I Use Portfolios in Mathematics. Located in: *Educational Leadership,* 49, 1992, pp. 71–72.

Kulm, G. (Ed.) *Assessing Higher Order Thinking in Mathematics,* 1990. Available from: American Association for the Advancement of Science, 1333 H Street, NW, Washington, DC 20005.

Leach, E. L. An Alternative Form of Evaluation That Complies with NCTM's Standards. Located in: *The Mathematics Teacher,* 85, November 1992, pp. 628–632.

Legg, S. & Algina J. (Eds) *Cognitive Assessment of Language and Mathematics Outcomes,* 1990. Available from: Ablex, 355 Chestnut St., Norwood, NJ 07648.

Lehman, M. *Assessing Assessment: Investigating a Mathematics Performance Assessment,* 1992. Available from: The National Center for Research on Teacher Learning, 116 Erickson Hall, Michigan State University, East Lansing, MI 48824-1034.

Massachusetts Educational Assessment Program. *On Their Own: Student Response to Open-Ended Tests in Mathematics, (Math Open-Ended and Performance Tasks),* 1991. Available from: Commonwealth of Massachusetts, Department of Education, 1385 Hancock St., Quincy, MA 02169.

Medrich, E. A. & Griffith, J. E. *International Mathematics and Science Assessments: What Have We Learned?,* 1992. Available from: National Technical Information Service, Springfield, VA 22161.

Mumme, J. *Portfolio Assessment in Mathematics,* 1990. Available from: California Mathematics Project, University of California, 522 University Rd., Santa Barbara, CA 93106.

National Science Foundation. *Educating Americans for the 21st Century: A Plan of Action for Improving Mathematics, Science and Technology Education,* 1983. Available from: National Science Board Commission on Precollege Education in Mathematics, Science and Technology, Forms & Publications Unit, 1800 G St., NW, Room 232, Washington, DC 20050.

Pandey, T. Power Items and the Alignment of Curriculum and Assessment. Located in: Gerald Kulm (Ed.), *Assessing Higher Order Thinking in Mathematics,* 1990. Available from: American Association for the Advancement of Science, 1333 H Street, NW, Washington, DC 20005.

Romberg, T. A. *Mathematics Assessment and Evaluation: Imperatives for Mathematics Educators,* 1992. Available from: State University of New York Press, State University Plaza, Albany, NY 12246.

Romberg, T. A. & Wilson, L. D. Alignment of Tests with the Standards. Located in: *Arithmetic Teacher,* September 1992, pp. 18–22.

Schoenfeld, A. H. Teaching Mathematical Thinking and Problem Solving. Located in: Loren B. Resnick and Leopold E. Klopfer (Eds.), *Toward The Thinking Curriculum: Current Cognitive Research,* 1989. Available from: Association for Supervision and Curriculum Development, 1250 N. Pitt St., Alexandria, VA 22314-1403.

Silver, E. A., & Kilpatrick, J. Testing Mathematical Problem Solving. Located in: Charles Randall and Edward Silver (Eds.), *The Teaching and Assessing of Mathematical Problem Solving,* 1988. Available from: National Council of Teachers of Mathematics, Inc., 1906 Association Drive, Reston, VA 22091.

Stenmark, J. K. *Mathematics Assessment: Myths, Models, Good Questions, and Practical Suggestions,* 1991. Available from: National Council of Teachers of Mathematics, 1906 Association Drive, Reston, VA 22091.

Szetela, W. & Nicol, C. Evaluating Problem Solving in Mathematics. Located in: *Educational Leadership,* May 1992, pp. 42–45.

Webb, N. *Alternative Strategies for Measuring Higher Order Skills in Mathematics: The Role of Symbol Systems,* 1991. Available from: CRESST, University of California, Los Angeles, 145 Moore Hall, Los Angeles, CA 90024.

Wells, B. G. Journal Writing in the Mathematics Classroom. Located in: *Communicator,* 15 (1), 1990, pp. 30–31. Available from: California Mathematics Council, Ruth Hadley, 1414 South Wallis, Santa Maria, CA 93454.

ADDITIONAL READINGS ON ASSESSMENT IN SCIENCE

Abraham, M. R., Grzybowski, E. B., Renner, J. W., & Marek, E. A. Understandings and Misunderstandings of Eighth Graders of Five Chemistry Concepts Found in Textbooks. Located in: *Journal of Research in Science Teaching,* 29, 1992, pp. 105–120.

Ault, C. R., Jr. *Assessment in the Science Classroom,* 1992. A video workshop available from: IOX Assessment Associates, 5301 Beethoven St., Suite 109, Los Angeles, CA 90066-7061.

Barnes, L. W. & Barnes, M. B. Assessment, Practically Speaking. Located in: *Science and Children,* March 1991, pp. 14–15.

Bennett, D. *Assessment & Technology Videotape.* Available from: The Center for Technology in Education, Bank Street College of Education, 610 W. 112th St., New York, NY 10025.

California Assessment Program (CAP). *New Directions in CAP Science Assessment,* 1990. Available from: California Department of Education, PO Box 944272, Sacramento, CA 94244.

Champagne, A., Lovitts, B., & Calinger, B. *Assessment in the Service of Instruction,* 1990. Available from: American Association for the Advancement of Science, 1333 H St., NW, Washington, DC 20005.

Chi, M. T., Feltovich, P. J., & Glaser, R. Categorization and Representation of Physics Problems by Experts and Novices. Located in: *Cognitive Science,* 5, 1981, pp. 121–152.

Collins, A. Portfolios: Questions for Design. Located in: *Science Scope,* 15, March 1992, pp. 25–27.

Collins, A. Portfolios for Science Education: Issues in Purpose, Structure, and Authenticity. Located in: *Science Education,* 76, 1992, pp. 451–463.

Collins, A., Hawkins, J., & Frederiksen, J. R. *Three Different Views of Students: The Role of Technology in Assessing Student Performance, Technical Report No. 12,* April 1991. Available from: Center for Technology in Education, Bank Street College of Education, 610 W. 112th St., New York, NY 10025.

Doran, R. *Performance Assessment in Science at the 12th Grade Level,* 1991. Available from: Graduate School of Education, University of New York at Buffalo, Buffalo, NY 14260.

Gong, B., Venezky, R., & Mioduser, D. Instructional Assessments: Lever for Systemic Change in Science Education Classrooms. Located in: *Journal of Science Education and Technology,* n.p. 1 (3), 1992.

Halpern, D. (Ed.). *Enhancing Thinking Skills in the Sciences and in Mathematics,* 1992. Available from: Lawrence Erlbaum Associates, 365 Broadway, Hillsdale, NJ 07642.

Kanis, I. B. Ninth Grade Lab Skills. Located in: *The Science Teacher,* January 1991, pp. 29–33.

Koballa, T. R. Goals of Science Education. Located in: D. Holdzkom and P. Lutz (Eds.), *Research Within Reach: Science Education,* 1989, pp. 25–40. Available from: National Science Teachers Association, Special Publications Department, 1742 Connecticut Ave., NW, Washington, DC 20009.

Kulm, G. & Malcom, S. M. *Science Assessment in the Service of Reform,* 1991. Available from: American Association for the Advancement of Science, 1333 H St., NW, Washington, DC 20005.

Laboratory Leadership Group. *Laboratory Assessment Builds Success,* 1990. Available from: Institute for Chemical Education, University of Wisconsin-Madison, Department of Chemistry, 1101 University Ave., Madison, WI 53706.

Liftig, I. F., Liftig, B., & Eaker, K. Making Assessment Work: What Teachers Should Know Before They Try It. Located In: *Science Scope,* 15, March 1992, pp. 4–8.

Lock, R. Gender and Practical Skill Performance in Science. Located in: *Journal of Research in Science Teaching,* 29, 1992, pp. 227–241.

Lunetta, V. N., Hofstein, A., & Giddings, G. Evaluating Science Laboratory Skills. Located in: *The Science Teacher,* January 1981, pp. 22–25.

Marshall, G. Evaluation of Student Progress. Located in: D. Holdzkom and P. Lutz (Eds.), *Research Within Reach: Science Education,* 1989, pp. 59–78. Available from: National Science Teachers Association, Special Publications Department, 1742 Connecticut Ave., NW, Washington, DC 20009.

Massachusetts Department of Education. *Massachusetts Educational Assessment Program. Open-ended and performance tasks in science,* 1989–91. Available from: The Commonwealth of Massachusetts, Department of Education, 1385 Hancock St., Quincy, MA 02169.

Medrich, E. A. & Griffith, J. E. *International Mathematics and Science Assessments: What Have We Learned?,* 1992. Available from: National Technical Information Service, Springfield, VA 22161.

National Assessment of Educational Progress. *Learning by Doing: A Manual for Teaching and Assessing Higher-Order Thinking in Science and Mathematics. Report No. 17-HOS-80,* 1987. Available from: Educational Testing Service, CN 6710, Princeton, NJ 08541.

New York State Elementary Science Program Evaluation Test (ESPET), 1989. General information available from: Bureau of Science Education, Office of General and Occupational Education, Division of Arts and Sciences Instruction, The State Education Department, The University of the State of New York, Albany, NY 12234.

Pine, J., Baxter, G., & Shavelson, R. J. *Assessments for Hands-On Elementary Science Curricula,* 1991. Available from: Physics Department, California Institute of Technology, Pasadena, CA 91125.

Psychological Corporation. *Integrated Assessment System—Science Performance Assessment,* 1992. Available from: Psychological Corporation, Order Service Center, PO Box 839954, San Antonio, TX 78283-3954.

Psychological Corporation. *GOALS: A Performance-Based Measure of Achievement—Science,* 1992. Available from: Psychological Corporation, Order Service Center, PO Box 839954, San Antonio, TX 78283-3954.

Raizen, S. A. & Kaser, J. Assessing Science Learning in Elementary School: Why, What, and How? Located in: *Phi Delta Kappan,* May 1989, pp. 718–722.

Raizen, S. A., Baron, J. B., Champagne, A. B., Haertel, E., Mullis, I. V. S., & Oakes, J. *Assessment in Elementary School Science Education,* 1989. Available from: The National Center for Improving Science Education, 2000 L St., NW, Suite 602, Washington, DC 20036.

Roth, K. Three Alternatives for Elementary Science.

Located in: *The IRT Communication Quarterly,* 2(3), 1990, pp. 2–4, published by the Institute for Research on Teaching, Michigan State University, East Lansing, MI 48823.

Roth, Wolff-Michael. Dynamic Evaluation. Located in: *Science Scope,* 15, March 1992, pp. 37–40.

Semple, B. M. *Performance Assessment: An International Experiment,* 1992. Available from: ETS, Scottish Office, Education Department, Rosedale Rd., Princeton, NJ 08541.

Shavelson, R. J., Carey, N. B, & Webb, N. M. Indicators of Science Achievement: Options for a Powerful Policy Instrument. Located in: *Phi Delta Kappan,* May 1990, pp. 692–697.

Shavelson, R. J., Baxter, G. P., Pine, J., & Yure, J. *New Technologies for Large-Scale Science Assessments: Instruments of Educational Reform,* 1991. Available from: University of California, 552 University Rd., Santa Barbara, CA 93106.

Small, L. & Petrek, J. Teamwork Testing. Located in: *Science Scope,* 15, March 1992, pp. 29–30.

Vargas, E. M. & Alvarez, H. J. Mapping Out Students' Abilities. Located in: *Science Scope,* 15, March 1992, pp. 41–43.

Yager, R. E. & McCormack, A. J. Assessing Teaching/Learning Successes in Multiple Domains of Science and Science Education. Located in: *Science Education,* 73, 1989, pp. 45–58.

ADDITIONAL READINGS ON ASSESSMENT IN SOCIAL STUDIES

Adams, D. & Hamm, M. Portfolio Assessment and Social Studies: Collecting, Selecting, and Reflecting on What Is Significant. Located in: *Social Education,* 56, 1992, pp. 103–105.

Kon, J. & Martin-Kniep, G. Students' Geographic Knowledge and Skills in Different Kinds of Tests: Multiple-Choice versus Performance Assessment. Located in: *Social Education,* 56, February 1992, pp. 95–98.

Littleton Public Schools. *Using Alternative Assessments to Measure Progress Toward School and District Outcomes (Littleton Alternative Assessment Project),* 1991. Available from: Littleton Public Schools, 5776 S. Crocker St., Littleton, CO 80120.

Mosenthal, P. & Kirsch, I. Using Knowledge Modeling as a Basis for Assessing Students' Knowledge (Learning from Exposition). Located in: *Journal of Reading,* 35, May 1992, pp. 668–678.

National Council for the Social Studies (NCSS). *Testing and Evaluation of Social Studies Students,* 1991. Available from: NCSS, 3501 Newark St., NW, Washington, DC 20016. Also located in: *Social Education,* September 1991, pp. 284–286.

Neveh-Benjamin, M., McKeachie, W., Lin, Y., & Tucker, D. G. Inferring Students' Cognitive Structures and Their Development Using the "Ordered Tree Technique." Located in: *Journal of Educational Psychology,* 78, 1986, pp. 130–140.

Palmquist, K. Involving Teachers in Elementary History and Social Science Test Development: The California Experience. Located in: *Social Education,* 56, 1992, pp. 99–101.

Zola, J. Scored Discussions. Located in: *Social Education,* 56, February 1992, pp. 121–125. Also available from: NCSS, 3501 Newark St., NW, Washington, DC 20016.

APPENDIX B

Standards for Teacher Competence in Educational Assessment of Students

Standards for Teacher Competence in Educational Assessment of Students by American Federation of Teachers, National Council on Measurement in Education, & National Education Association (AFT/NCME/NEA), 1990, Washington, DC: Author.

STANDARDS

1. *Teachers should be skilled in* choosing *assessment methods appropriate for instructional decision.*

Skills in choosing appropriate, useful, administratively convenient, technically adequate, and fair assessment methods are prerequisite to good use of information to support instructional decisions. Teachers need to be well acquainted with the kinds of information provided by a broad range of assessment alternatives and their strengths and weaknesses. In particular, they should be familiar with criteria for evaluating and selecting assessment methods in light of instructional plans.

Teachers who meet this standard will have the conceptual and application skills that follow. They will be able to use the concepts of assessment error and validity when developing or selecting their approaches to classroom assessment of students. They will understand how valid assessment data can support instructional activities such as providing appropriate feedback to students, diagnosing group and individual learning needs, planning for individualized educational programs, motivating students, and evaluating instructional procedures. They will understand how invalid information can affect instructional decisions about students. They will also be able to use and evaluate assessment options available to them, considering among other things, the cultural, social, economic, and language background of students. They will be aware that different assessment approaches can be incompatible with certain instructional goals and may impact quite differently on their teaching.

Teachers will know, for each assessment approach they use, its appropriateness for making decisions about their pupils. Moreover, teachers will know where to find information about and/or reviews of various assessment methods. Assessment options are diverse and include text- and curriculum-embedded questions and tests, standardized criterion-referenced and norm-referenced tests, oral questioning, spontaneous and structured performance assessments, portfolios, exhibitions, demonstrations, rating scales, writing samples, paper-and-pencil tests, seatwork and homework, peer- and self-assessments, student records, observations, questionnaires, interviews, projects, products, and others' opinions.

2. *Teachers should be skilled in developing assessment methods appropriate for instructional decisions.*

While teachers often use published or other external assessment tools, the bulk of the assessment information they use for decision making comes from approaches they create and implement. Indeed, the assessment demands of the classroom go well beyond readily available instruments.

Teachers who meet this standard will have the conceptual and application skills that follow. Teachers will be skilled in planning the collection of information that facilitates the decisions they will make. They will know and follow appropriate principles for developing and using assessment methods in their teaching, avoiding common pitfalls in student assessment. Such techniques may include several of the options listed at the end of the first standard. The teacher will select the techniques which are appropriate to the intent of the teacher's instruction.

Teachers meeting this standard will also be skilled in using student data to analyze the quality of each assessment technique they use. Since most teachers do not have access to assessment specialists, they must be prepared to do these analyses themselves.

3. *The teacher should be skilled in administering, scoring and interpreting the results of both externally produced and teacher-produced assessment methods.*

It is not enough that teachers are able to select and develop good assessment methods; they must also be able to apply them properly. Teachers should be skilled in administering, scoring, and interpreting results from diverse assessment methods.

Teachers who meet this standard will have the conceptual and application skills that follow. They will be skilled in interpreting informal and formal teacher-produced assessment results, including pupils' performances in class and on homework assignments. Teachers will be able to use guides for scoring essay questions and projects, stencils for scoring response-choice questions, and scales for rating performance assessments. They will be able to use these in ways that produce consistent results.

Teachers will be able to administer standardized achievement tests and be able to interpret the commonly reported scores: percentile ranks, percentile band scores, standard scores, and grade equivalents. They will have a conceptual understanding of the summary indexes commonly reported with assessment results: measures of central tendency, dispersion, relationships, reliability, and errors of measurement.

Teachers will be able to apply these concepts of score and summary indices in ways that enhance their use of the assessments that they develop. They will be able to analyze assessment results to identify pupils' strengths and errors. If they get inconsistent results, they will seek other explanations for the discrepancy or other data to attempt to resolve the uncertainty before arriving at a decision. They will be able to use assessment methods in ways that encourage students' educational development and that do not inappropriately increase students' anxiety levels.

4. *Teachers should be skilled in using assessment results when making decisions about individual students, planning teaching, developing curriculum, and school improvement.*

Assessment results are used to make educational decisions at several levels: in the classroom about students, in the community about a school and a school district, and in society, generally, about the purposes and outcomes of the educational enterprise. Teachers play a vital role when participating in decision making at each of these levels and must be able to use assessment results effectively.

Teachers who meet this standard will have the conceptual and application skills that follow. They will be able to use accumulated assessment information to organize a sound instructional plan for fa-

cilitating students' educational development. When using assessment results to plan and/or evaluate instruction and curriculum, teachers will interpret the results correctly and avoid common misinterpretations, such as basing decisions on scores that lack curriculum validity. They will be informed about the results of local, regional, state, and national assessments and about their appropriate use for pupil, classroom, school, district, state, and national educational improvement.

5. *Teachers should be skilled in developing valid pupil grading procedures which use pupil assessments.*

Grading students is an important part of professional practice for teachers. Grading is defined as indicating both a student's level of performance and a teacher's valuing of that performance. The principles for using assessments to obtain valid grades are known and teachers should employ them.

Teachers who meet this standard will have the conceptual and application skills that follow. They will be able to devise, implement, and explain a procedure for developing grades composed of marks from various assignments, projects, in-class activities, quizzes, tests, and/or other assessments that they may use. Teachers will understand and be able to articulate why the grades they assign are rational, justified, and fair, acknowledging that such grades reflect their preferences and judgments. Teachers will be able to recognize and to avoid faulty grading procedures such as using grades as punishment. They will be able to evaluate and to modify their grading procedures in order to improve the validity of the interpretations made from them about students' attainments.

6. *Teachers should be skilled in communicating assessment results to students, parents, other lay audiences, and other educators.*

Teachers must routinely report assessment results to students and to parents or guardians. In addition, they are frequently asked to report or to discuss assessment results with other educators and with diverse lay audiences. If the results are not communicated effectively, they may be misused or not used. To communicate effectively with others on matters of student assessment, teachers must be able to use assessment terminology appropriately and must be able to articulate the meaning, limitations, and implications of assessment results. Furthermore, teachers will sometimes be in a position that will require them to defend their own assessment procedures and their interpretations of them. At other times, teachers may need to help the public to interpret assessment results appropriately.

Teachers who meet this standard will have the conceptual and application skills that follow. Teachers will understand and be able to give appropriate explanations of how the interpretation of student assessments must be moderated by the student's socioeconomic, cultural, language, and other background factors. Teachers will be able to explain that assessment results do not imply that such background factors limit a student's ultimate educational development. They will be able to communicate to students and to their parents or guardians how they may assess the student's educational progress. Teachers will understand and be able to explain the importance of taking measurement errors into account when using assessments to make decisions about individual students. Teachers will be able to explain the limitations of different informal and formal assessment methods. They will be able to explain printed reports of the results of pupil assessments at the classroom, school district, state, and national levels.

7. *Teachers should be skilled in recognizing unethical, illegal, and otherwise inappropriate assessment methods and uses of assessment information.*

Fairness, the rights of all concerned, and professional ethical behavior must undergird all student assessment activities, from the initial planning for and gathering of information to the interpretation, use, and communication of the results. Teachers must be well versed in their own ethical and legal responsibilities in assessment. In addition, they should also attempt to have the inappropriate assessment practices of others discontinued whenever they are encountered. Teachers should also participate with the wider educational community in defining the limits of appropriate professional behavior in assessment.

Teachers who meet this standard will have the conceptual and application skills that follow. They will know those laws and case decisions which affect their classroom, school district, and state assessment practices. Teachers will be aware that various assessment procedures can be misused or overused resulting in harmful consequences such as embarrassing students, violating a student's right to confidentiality, and inappropriately using students' standardized achievement test scores to measure teaching effectiveness.

APPENDIX C

Standards for Principals in Educational Assessment

Adapted from *Principals for Changing Schools: Knowledge and Skill Base* (Measurement and Evaluation, Domain 12) edited by Scott Thomson, 1993, Fairfax, VA: National Policy Board for Educational Administration. Copyright 1993 by NPBEA. Adapted by permission.

DEFINITION

Measurement and evaluation represent important components in an effectively functioning educational system. For this reason the principal must be able to act to assure sound practice in this performance domain.

Measurement is the process of gathering information about student traits, attributes, or characteristics. Educators use a wide variety of tools and methods to carry out this assessment process, such as paper and pencil instruments, performance assessments, and direct personal communications with students. Once the status of a particular student characteristic is assessed (such as achievement, for example), then evaluation is required. Evaluation requires that educators compare student performance to a particular standard to determine how the student measures up. Depending on the result, decisions are made regarding how or whether to strive to improve student performance.

Because different kinds of decisions are informed by measurement and evaluation results, different kinds of standards are needed. Some decisions require the comparison of student performance to that of other students, so as to permit the ranking of students. Educational and vocational placement and guidance decisions often use this kind of information to advantage.

On the other hand, some decisions require the comparison of student performance to a preset standard of performance. Comparison to other students make no sense in some contexts. When educators seek to diagnose student needs, for example, preset standards are required to define need.

This is familiar ground to the competent principal. They understand the need to define outcomes to be assessed, gather sound information about the outcomes and use the assessment results appropriately, so all fall within the limits of this domain. Those concerned with sound measurement and evaluation practices must know how sound practice differs from unsound practice. Principals clearly are among those who must know and act upon their knowledge of this difference.

ASSESSMENT KNOWLEDGE AND SKILLS

We propose a framework of assessment competencies for principals which reflects current thinking both about the leadership role of the principal in the building, and about what constitutes sound assessment.

We propose three fundamental roles for the principal with respect to the use of assessment in their schools: The roles of *Instructional Leader, Instructional Manager,* and *Communication Facilitator.* As an *Instructional Leader,* the principal has prime responsibility for developing and operationalizing a vision of assessment as an integral part of instruction in *every* classroom. As an *Instructional Manager,* the principal has responsibility to be an informed user of assessment in his or her own management of the decision-making process. And as *Communication Facilitator,* the principal has responsibility for ensuring the timely and accurate delivery of sound assessment information to those who make decisions both within and beyond the school building (i.e., at the district level, to the community, and so on). Clearly these are not mutually exclusive roles. They overlap in various ways. Those overlaps are depicted in Figure C–1 and through the descriptions of competencies that follow. While it is clear that principals are not the only educational leaders who fulfill these roles, the competencies outlined below frame the knowledge and skill requirements of the principal only. Variations on these themes as they relate to superintendents, associate superintendents, curriculum directors, etc., are not addressed.

This set of competencies attempts to answer the question: "What do principals need to *know* and what do they need to be *able to do* in order to ensure the development and use of instructionally-relevant assessments in their schools?" Because the list is limited to competencies only, it should be regarded as addressing only one of the *necessary* conditions for ensuring sound assessment in schools. Competence alone is not *sufficient* for achieving this goal. Other conditions that must be satisfied are (a) the development of assessment *policies* at district and building levels that enable the use of sound assessment, and (b) specific assertive *action* on the part of the competent principal to put their knowledge and ability to work in the school building.

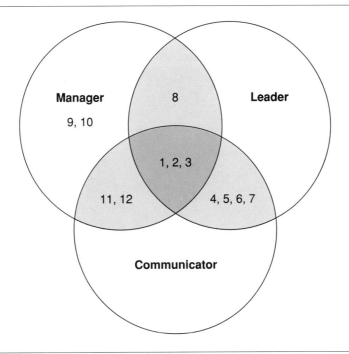

FIGURE C-1
Overlap Among Competencies Across Roles

In other words, these competencies form the basis of an evaluation of a principal's preparation to do the job, but would be considered insufficient as a basis for an evaluation of their actual on-the-job performance. As such, these competencies can provide a basis for the design of training programs that will prepare principals with the knowledge and skills required to do the assessment part of their job.

The assessment competencies are broken into four categories: those that cross the three roles and those unique to each of the three roles. We have listed each competency under the role to which it is *most* essential. After each competency statement, we provide brief explanatory notes. Since some competencies can be important for more than one role, we include the list of competencies with the overlapping roles in the figure shown above.

The list of competencies was developed through a process of reviewing the literature for cur-

rent lists of competencies, and expert review by several groups of principals.

Assessment Competencies Needed for All Three Roles

1. *The principal knows the attributes of sound student assessment and how to apply them to the assessments used in the school building.*

This competency underlies all the rest. If the principal cannot differentiate between sound and unsound assessments, then he or she will not be able to plan and carry out quality assessment, nor adequately interpret and use the results of such assessment. The competent principal:

- Can describe curriculum goals valued at the building level, and explain why each target is important
- Can link valued achievement targets to proper assessment formats—paper and

pencil, performance, and/or personal communication-based methods

- Knows and understands how to control for sources of extraneous interference that can cause the mismeasurement of student achievement
- Understands and can apply methods of sampling that can assure the fair and complete, yet efficient assessment of student achievement
- Can train others to apply the attributes to their assessments

2. *The principal knows the attributes of a sound assessment system and how to integrate them into an assessment system.*

While competency number one refers to knowledge concerning the design of individual assessments, competency number two refers to knowledge about how all the assessments in a building should fit together. The competent principal can:

- Ensure that a range of achievement targets are assessed, and this range represents what the local educational community feels are the important educational outcomes for students
- Describe all of the uses of or purposes for assessment for each decision maker in the building, including students, teachers, parents, guidance counselors, and other support staff
- Describe why classroom, building-level and district-level assessment all are important, and the difference that sound assessment at all levels can make for instruction
- Describe how assessment can be integrated with instruction in the classroom
- Describe the process for aligning assessment, curriculum, and instruction, and
- Describe how the various types and levels of assessment should fit together

3. *The principal knows the issues surrounding unethical and inappropriate use of assessment information and knows how to protect students and staff from such misuses.*

The competent principal can:

- Describe procedures for the maintenance of test security when this is necessary

- Describe procedures for ensuring that assessment results of individual students are kept confidential
- Describe potential sources of bias in assessment and how to minimize them, and
- Articulate equity issues with respect to assessment

Competencies Needed for the Instructional Leader Role

4. *The principal knows the importance and features of assessment policies and regulations that contribute to the development and use of sound assessments at all levels of use.*

The competent principal can:

- Describe the contexts where building policies are required
- Describe and explain district, state, and national assessment policies and their potential effects on building practice
- Involve staff in devising appropriate building policies that are sensitive to both the needs of the building and to the larger policy context of district, state, and national assessment
- Advocate for district, state, and national policies that support sound assessment at the building level

5. *The principal knows the importance of and can work with staff to set specific goals for the integration of assessment into instruction, and can assist teachers in reaching those goals.*

The competent principal can:

- Cite specific strategies to engage staff in the process of goal setting to promote the sound development and use of assessment in the classroom, and
- Describe ways teachers can integrate assessment into the teaching/learning process, such as teaching students to be self-assessors, and using critiques based on clear criteria for success

6. *The principal knows the importance of and can evaluate teachers' classroom assessment competencies and build such evaluations into the supervision process.*

The competent principal can:
- Describe essential assessment competencies for teachers
- Set performance criteria for each teacher
- Gather sound information from the classroom regarding actual teacher performance with respect to those criteria, and
- Provide meaningful feedback to the teacher on performance

7. *The principal knows the importance of and can plan and present or secure the presentation of staff development experiences for staff that contribute to the development and use of sound assessment at all levels of decision making.*

The competent principal can describe staff development priorities in assessment and the action needed to meet those staff needs.

8. *The principal knows the importance of and how to use assessment results for instructional improvement at the building level.*

The competent principal:
- Knows the importance of a written plan for the process by which assessment information will be used for program improvement
- Can cite ways to combine information across classroom assessments to reflect building-level improvement priorities
- Can involve teachers in this process, and
- Can devise processes of tracking the impact that such improvement efforts have on student achievement

Competencies needed for the Instructional Manager Role

9. *The principal knows how to accurately analyze and interpret building-level assessment information.*

The competent principal can:
- Explain the issues related to aggregation and disaggregation of assessment information and when it is appropriate to disaggregate information

- Appropriately analyze and interpret multiple sources of information even when they conflict
- Use knowledge of the error of measurement and statistical significance to interpret assessment results appropriately, and
- Appropriately determine the extent to which learner outcomes meet or exceed previously defined standards

10. *The principal acts upon assessment information.*

The competent principal can:
- Describe how available assessment information is best used to inform instructional decisions at the building-level, and
- Describe how building, district, state, and national results relate to each other, and their implications for instruction in the building

Competencies Needed for the Communicator Role

11. *The principal knows and can create the conditions necessary for the appropriate use of achievement information.*

The competent principal:
- Knows that essential conditions include: a principal who is seen by staff and others as valuing the use of assessment results and as one who can help solve assessment problems; teachers who have clear indicators of degrees of success with assessment; members of advisory boards who understand the principles of sound assessment; assessment information that is part of the regular discourse of school life; and accurate assessment results that are available to those who need them and are inaccessible to those who have no right to them
- Can describe strategies for meeting these conditions in their building

12. *The principal can communicate effectively with all interested members of the school com-*

munity about assessment results and their relationship to instruction.

The competent principal:

- Understands and can explain the meaning and significance of relevant assessment information to all who need to understand it

- Knows how to use assessment information in the political arena to support quality education

References

American Council of Teachers of Foreign Language. (1989). *Oral Proficiency Interview: Tester Training Manual.* Yonkers, NY: Author.

American Federation of Teachers, National Council on Measurement in Education, & National Education Association (AFT/NCME/NEA). (1990). *Standards for teacher competence in educational assessment of students.* Washington, DC: Author.

American Psychological Association. (1985). *Standards for educational and psychological testing.* Washington, DC: Author.

Anderson, L. W. (1981). *Assessing affective characteristics in the schools.* Needham, MA: Allyn and Bacon.

Ann Arbor Public Schools. (1993). Success for all first grade students. Ann Arbor, MI: A report of the Department of Research Services.

Ann Arbor Public Schools. (1993). Success for all kindergarten students. Ann Arbor, MI: A report of the Department of Research Services.

Arnold, H. & Stricklin, P. (1993). *Teacher Commentary on Experience with Student-Led Conferences.* Silverdale, WA: Central Kitsap School District.

Arter, J. & Spandel, V. (1992). Using portfolios of student work in instruction and assessment. *Educational Measurement: Issues and Practice,* 11(1), 36–44.

Baron, J. B. (1991). Strategies for the development of effective performance exercises. *Applied Measurement in Education,* 4(4), 305–318.

Berk, R. A. (Ed.). (1986). *Performance assessment: Methods and applications.* Baltimore, MD: Johns Hopkins University Press.

Bloom, B. S., Englehart, M. D., Furst, E. J., Hill, W. H., & Krathwohl, D. R. (Eds.). (1956). *Taxonomy of educational objectives: Handbook 1, Cognitive domain.* New York: McKay.

Bloom, B. S., Hastings, J. T., & Madaus, G. F. (1971). *Handbook on formative and summative evaluation of student learning.* New York: McGraw-Hill.

Bond, L. & Roeber, E. (1993). *State student assessment program database, 1992–1993.* Oakbrook, IL: North Central Regional Educational Laboratory and Washington, DC: Council of Chief State School Officers.

California Department of Education. (1991). *History-social science group assessment in California, California assessment program.* Sacramento, CA: author.

Catlin Gabel School. (n.d.). *Student evaluation criteria policy manual.* Portland, OR: Author.

Catlin Gabel School. (1990). Sample student report. Portland, OR: Author.

Davidson, L., Myford, C., Plasket, D., Scripp, L., Swinton, S., Torff, B., & Waanders, J. (1992). *Arts propel: A handbook for music.* Princeton, NJ: Educational Testing Service.

Davies, A., Cameron, C., Politano, C., & Gregory, K. (1992). *Together is better: Collaborative assessment, evaluation and reporting.* Winnipeg, MB Canada: Peguis.

Dunbar, S. B., Koretz, D. M., & Hoover, H. D. (1991). Quality control in the development and use of performance assessments. *Applied Measurement in Education, 4*(4), 289–304.

Fredericks, A. E. (1987). The Latest Model. *The Reading Teacher, 40*(8) 790–791.

Gable, R. (1986). *Instrument development in the affective domain.* Boston, MA: Kluwer-Nijhoff.

Graves, D. H. (1986). *In Breaking ground: Teachers relate reading and writing in the elementary school.* Portsmouth, NH: Heinemann Educational.

Gray, P. A. (1991). Speak up Illinois! Speech assessment guidelines for the English teacher. *Illinois English Bulletin,* n.p.

Gronlund, N. E. & Linn, R. L. (1990). *Measurement and evaluation in teaching,* (6th ed.). New York: Macmillan.

Guyton, J. M. & Fielstein, L. L. (1989). Student-led parent conferences: A model for teaching responsibility. *Elementary School Guidance and Counseling, 24*(2), 169–172.

Haertel, E., Farrara, S., Korpi, M., & Prescott, B. (1984). Testing in secondary schools: Student perspectives. Paper presented at the annual meeting of the American Educational Research Association, New Orleans.

Hillocks, G., Jr. (1986). *Research on written composition: New directions for teaching.* Urbana, IL: ERIC Clearinghouse on Reading and Communications Skills.

Hoskyn, J. & Quellmalz, E. (1993). *Multicultural reading and thinking program resource notebook.* Little Rock, AR: Arkansas Department of Education.

Koretz, D., Klein, S., McCaffrey, D., & Stecher, B. (1993) *Interim Report: The Reliability of Vermont Portfolio Scores in the 1992–'93 School Year.* Los Angeles, CA: RAND Institute on Education and Training, National Center for Research on Evaluation, Standards, and Student Testing.

Koretz, D., McCaffrey, D., Klein, S., Bell, R., & Stecher, B. (1992). *The reliability of scores from the 1992 Vermont portfolio assessment program.* Los Angeles, CA: RAND Institute on Education and Training, National Center for Research on Evaluation, Standards, and Student Testing.

Lane, S. (1993). The conceptual framework for the development of a mathematics performance assessment instrument. *Educational Measurement: Issues and Practices, 12*(2), 16–23.

Legg, S. M. & Buhr, D. C. (1992). Computerized adaptive testing with different groups. *Educational Measurement: Issues and Practice, 11*(2), 23–27.

Lewis & Clark College. (1990). Press release on new admissions initiatives. Portland, OR: Author.

Linder, T. W. (1990). *Transdisciplinary play-based assessment.* Baltimore, MD: Paul H. Brookes.

Lindquist, E. F. (1951). Preliminary considerations in objective test construction. In E. F. Lindquist (Ed.), *Educational Measurement* (pp. 4–22). Washington, DC: American Council on Education.

Little, N. (1988). *Student-led teacher-parent conferences.* Toronto, Ontario: Lugus.

Marzano, R. J. (1991). *Cultivating thinking in English and the language arts.* Urbana, IL: National Council of Teachers of English.

Marzano, R. J. (1992). *A different kind of classroom.* Alexandria, VA: Association for Supervision and Curriculum Development.

Marzano, R. J., Pickering, D. J., & McTighe, J. (1993). *Performance Assessment Using the Dimensions of Learning.* Aurora, CO: Mid-continent Regional Educational Laboratory.

Messick, S. (1989). Validity. In R. L. Linn (Ed.), *Educational measurement* (3rd ed.) (n.p.) New York, NY: Macmillan.

Ministry of Education and Training, Victoria. (1991). *English profiles handbook: Assessing and reporting students' progress in English.* Melbourne, Australia: Ministry of Education and Training, Victoria, School Programs Division.

National Council of Teachers of Mathematics (1989). *Curriculum and evaluation standards for school mathematics.* Reston, VA: Author.

National Science Foundation. (1962). *Scientific Manpower Bulletin No. 17.* Washington, DC: Author.

Neill, D. M. & Medina, N. J. (1991). Standardized testing: Harmful to educational health. *Phi Delta Kappan, 73,* 688–697.

Norris, R. J. (1991). *A different kind of classroom: Teaching with dimensions of learning.* Alexandria, VA: Association for Supervision and Curriculum Development.

Norris, S. P. & Ennis, R. H. (1989). *Evaluating critical thinking.* Pacific Grove, CA: Midwest.

Novak, J. D. & Gowin, D. B. (1984). *Learning how to learn.* New York, NY: Cambridge University Press.

Oregon Department of Education. (1992). Final Draft from State Certificate of Initial Mastery Taskforce. Salem, OR: Author.

Oregon Department of Education. (1993). Dimensions of Mathematiccs Scoring Guide. Salem, OR: Author.

Quellmalz, E. (1987). Developing reasoning skills. In J. B. Baron and R. J. Sternberg (Eds.), *Teaching thinking skills: Theory and practice.* New York, NY: W. H. Freeman.

Quellmalz, E. (1991). Developing criteria for performance assessments: The missing link. *Applied Measurement in Education, 4*(4), 319–332.

Quellmalz, E. & Hoskyn, J. (1988). Making a difference in Arkansas: The multicultural reading and thinking project. *Educational Leadership, 45,* 51–55.

Rowe, M. B. (1978). Specific ways to develop better communications. In R. Sund and A. Carin (Eds.), *Creative Questioning and Sensitivity: Listening Techniques* (2nd ed.) (n.p.). New York: Merrill/Macmillan.

Scates, D. E. (1943). Differences between measurement criteria of pure scientists and of classroom teachers. *Journal of Educational Research, 37,* 1–13.

Schafer, W. D. & Lissitz, R. W. (1987). Measurement training for school personnel: Recommendations and reality. *Journal of Teacher Education, 38*(3), 57–63.

Shavelson, R. J. & Stern, P. (1981). Research on teachers' pedagogical thoughts, judgments, decisions, and behavior. *Review of Educational Research, 41*(4), 455–498.

Shavelson, R. J., Baxter, G. P., & Pine, J. (1991). Performance assessment in science. *Applied Measurement in Education, 4*(4), 347–362.

Silver, E. A. (1991). *Quantitative understanding: Amplifying student achievement and understanding.* Pittsburgh, PA: University of Pittsburgh, Learning Research and Development Center.

Smith, M. L. & Rottenberg, C. (1991). Unintended consequences of external testing in elementary schools. *Educational Measurement: Issues and Practice, 10*(4), 7–11.

Spandel, V. & Stiggins, R. J. (1990). *Creating writers: Linking assessment and writing instruction.* White Plains, NY: Longman.

Sternberg, R. J. (1986). The future of intelligence testing. *Educational Measurement: Issues and Practice, 5*(3), 19–22.

Stiggins, R. J. & Conklin, N. F. (1992). *In Teachers' Hands: Investigating the Practices of Classroom Assessment.* Albany, NY: State University of New York Press.

Swartz, M. & O'Connor, J. R. (1986). *Exploring American History.* Englewood Cliffs, NJ: Globe.

Thomson, S. (Ed.). (1993). Measurement and Evaluation, Domain 12. *Principals for changing schools: Knowledge and skill base.* Fairfax, VA: National Policy Board for Educational Administration.

Tierney, R. J., Carter, M. A., & Desai, L. E. (1991). *Portfolio assessment in the reading-writing classroom.* Norwood, MA: Christopher Gordon.

Township High School. (n.d.). District 214's Speech Assessment Rating Guide. Arlington Heights, IL: Author.

U.S. Congress, Office of Technology Assessment. (1992). *Testing in American schools: Asking the right questions.* Washington, DC: U.S. Government Printing Office.

Valencia, S. W. & Pearson, P. D. (1987). Reading assessment: Time for a change. *The Reading Teacher, 40*(8), 726–32.

Vermont Department of Education. (1990). Looking beyond "The Answers": The report of Vermont's mathematics portfolio assessment program. Montpelier, VT: Author.

Wade, S. E. (1990). Reading comprehension using thinkalouds. *Reading Teacher, 43*(7), 442–451.

Ward, A. W. (1991). *Item banking and item banks.* Daytona Beach, FL: The Techné Group.

Wiggins, G. (1989). A true test: Toward more authentic and equitable assessment. *Phi Delta Kappan,* 703–713.

Yancey, K. (Ed.). (1992). *Portfolios in the writing classroom.* Urbana, IL: National Council of Teachers of English.

Zola, J. (1992). Middle and high school scored discussions. *Social Education, 56*(2), 121–125.

Index

About the Author

Richard J. Stiggins, B.S., M.A., Ph.D., is presently director of the Assessment Training Institute, Portland, Oregon. He received his bachelor's degree in psychology from the State University of New York at Plattsburgh, master's degree in industrial psychology from Springfield (MA) College, and doctoral degree in education measurement from Michigan State University. Dr. Stiggins began his assessment work on the faculty of Michigan State before becoming director of research and evaluation for the Edina, Minnesota, Public Schools and a member of the faculty of educational foundations at the University of Minnesota. In addition, he has served as director of test development for the American College Testing Program, Iowa City, Iowa, and as director of the Centers for Classroom Assessment and Performance Assessment at the Northwest Regional Educational Laboratory, Portland, Oregon, and has been invited to Stanford University as a visiting scholar.

Dr. Stiggins has devoted his career to the study of the task demands of classroom assessment and to supporting teachers in their preparation to meet those demands. He recently coauthored *In Teachers' Hands: Investigating the Practice of Classroom Assessment* (Albany, NY: SUNY Press, 1992), summarizing a decade of his classroom assessment research. As a part of this research and development effort, Dr. Stiggins directed the development of a 14-workshop video-based classroom assessment training program for teachers, as well as a wide variety of training guides and manuals designed to demystify the assessment process for teachers and help them integrate it into the teaching and learning process.

ISBN 0-02-417350-9

90000>